THE ROVERS RETURN
PUB QUIZ BOOK

Coronation Street is a Granada Television Production
based on an idea by Tony Warren

First published in Great Britain in 2001
by Granada Media, an imprint of
Andre Deutsch Ltd
20 Mortimer Street
London
W1T 3JW

0-233-99955-8

THE ROVERS RETURN
PUB QUIZ BOOK

GRANADA

Contents

Introduction

For the last forty years viewers have become hooked on the comings and goings of the residents of Coronation Street. The landmark of the Street is, of course, the Rovers Return, that hotbed of drinking and gossip which has bought the street's residents and the nation's viewers together time after time.

So what better way to bring together two passions than the *Rovers Return Pub Quiz Book*! You can now enjoy Coronation Street whilst at the pub, and a pub quiz book whilst at home! And it's so easy: All you need to do is whip up some enthusiasm amongst a group of fellow beer/Corrie fanatics (you'd be surprised how many there are out there. Or maybe you wouldn't...) and wrack your brains in a state of gentle inebriation until you are forced to admit defeat when you can't answer questions like: 'Who was the first recorded holder of the pub's licence in Daran Little's novelisation of World War One on the Street'? or 'When did Newton & Ridley celebrate their bi-centenary?'

Of course, these are just scary questions from the hard round, so don't worry, if you have trouble recalling who Jack Duckworth's wife is, there may still be hope for you on the section titled 'Easy'. What's more, the *Rovers Return Pub Quiz Book* isn't just a quiz about a pub in Weatherfield, it's also brimful of general knowledge questions, from twentieth century who's who to soccer, the Royals and blockbuster films.

The main aim of the *Rovers Return Pub Quiz Book* is to entertain, so it is important that you retain a good sense of humour, or try to get one if needs be, before you embark on your new career as pub quiz foreman at your local boozer.

Don't be surprised at the high jinx and high spirits that ensue – pub quizzes are not to be taken lightly – so stick to the three Cs: Cool, Calm and Collected, and, if that fails and the locals get testy, your best bet is to head for the door, while tossing Prawn Cocktail crisps into the air to throw your by now rabid competitors off your scent. Hopefully it won't come to this, so pretend you're tucking into your favourite pint of ale from Newton & Ridley and settle down to waking up your grey matter, with brainteasers from the world of Corrie and beyond...

How To Use This Book

It couldn't be easier. *The Rovers Return Pub Quiz Book* is divided into three sections: Easy, Medium and Hard, which are then subdivided by specialist and pot-luck rounds, including the Coronation Street sections. Answers are provided at the bottom of each page.

The Easy Questions

If you think that Louis Armstrong was the first man on the moon or that Uri Geller was the first man in space then you will no doubt struggle through the next few questions terribly. For the rest of us though these are the EASY questions, so called because if the quizzee falters on these they are either three sheets to the wind or far too young to be in the pub – either state rendering them toddling buffoons whose social graces will equal their breadth of knowledge. So beware their flailing arms as you attempt to collect the answers.

These questions are perfect when used in the first round of an open entry quiz as they lull everyone into a false sense of security although you must make sure that contestants don't shout answers out which creates a problematic precedent for the later, harder questions. Another way of placing these questions is to dot them about throughout the quiz thus making sure that on every team everyone should know the answer to at least one question despite their age.

If you are running a league quiz then some of your team members may heap derision on such obvious questions but don't worry even the cleverest quiz team member can come a cropper, as was noted in a championship final. When a contestant was asked to name the continents he deliberated before eventually beaming out the answer, "A, E, I, O, U!".

Quiz 1 20th C Who's Who

Level 1

1 Who thought that everyone would be famous for 15 minutes?
2 Who led Iraq into the 90s Gulf War?
3 Which former cabinet minister was jailed for 18 months in 1999?
4 Who was manager of The Beatles?
5 Which Russian introduced policies of glasnost?
6 Who became the first woman to lead a British political party?
7 Whose dresses raised £2 million for charity in a June 97 auction?
8 Which British monarch died in 1901?
9 Which 60s model was known as 'The Shrimp'?
10 Who became king of Spain in the 70s following General Franco's death?
11 Which G B wrote the play *Pygmalion* that was adapted into *My Fair Lady*?
12 Whose ancient tomb was discovered in Egypt in 1922?
13 Who was the ex-peanut farmer who became US President?
14 Who delivered Labour's first budget of the 90s?
15 Who was awarded a Nobel Peace Prize for her work with the poor in India?
16 Which Ken was leader of the GLC?
17 Who was the man who created The Muppets?
18 Who promised he would bring 'really sexy football' to Newcastle?
19 Which Screaming Lord stood unsuccessfully in many parliamentary elections?
20 Which pop star married Linda Eastman in the 60s?
21 Who declared he had 'a dream' where all Americans would live as equals?
22 Who teamed up with Benny, Bjorn and Anni-Frid to form Abba?
23 Which Christian unveiled the New Look of the late 40s?
24 Mahatma Gandhi led the non-violent struggle for which country to break free from Britain?
25 Who formulated the theory of relativity early in the century?

Answers

20th C Who's Who

1 Andy Warhol. **2** Saddam Hussein. **3** Jonathan Aitken. **4** Brian Epstein. **5** Gorbachev. **6** Margaret Thatcher. **7** Princess Diana. **8** Victoria. **9** Jean Shrimpton. **10** Juan Carlos. **11** Shaw. **12** Tutankhamun. **13** Jimmy Carter. **14** Gordon Brown. **15** Mother Theresa. **16** Livingstone. **17** Jim Henson. **18** Ruud Gullit. **19** Sutch. **20** Paul McCartney. **21** Martin Luther King. **22** Agnetha. **23** Dior. **24** India. **25** Albert Einstein.

Quiz 2

CORONATION ST.

Level 1

The Barlows

1 Ken proposed to Deirdre in February 2001 and she refused. Why?
2 Ken and Mike Baldwin still hate each other but they did have a brief reconciliation at the end of 2000. What brought them together?
3 Which school did Ken used to teach at?
4 Who did Ken tutor to help her with her exams?
5 Who does Deirdre work for?
6 Which accessory is Deirdre famous for?
7 Ken recently wrote a book. What was it about?
8 Why did Deirdre lose her job at Sunliners?
9 Deirdre was once a local councillor: True or false?
10 Who donated a kidney to Tracy Barlow in 1995?
11 Who was Deirdre's best friend before she left the Street?
12 Who stopped Ken from commiting suicide in 1990?
13 What house number do Ken and Deirdre live at?
14 What is Ken's current job?
15 Who plays Deirdre's mum, Blanche Hunt?
16 Which of these ladies has Ken not had an affair with: Alma, Bet, or Rita?
17 Jon Lindsay pretended to be an airline pilot to impress Deirdre. What was his real job?
18 Is Ken a university graduate?
19 In what year did the famous Ken/Mike/Deirdre love triangle happen?
20 Which actress plays Deirdre?
21 Who was Deirdre's cellmate in prison?
22 Who funded her appeal?
23 What was the name of Ken's first wife?
24 Which actress, recently seen in *Dinnerladies*, played her?
25 And how did she die?

Answers

Coronation Street – The Barlows
1 He only wanted to get custody of Adam **2** The Freshco seige. **3** Bessie Street and Weatherfield Comprehensive. **4** Toyah Battersby. **5** Dev Alahan. **6** Glasses. **7** Weatherfield's history. **8** She was accused of fraud. **9** True. **10** Samir Rachid. **11** Liz McDonald. **12** Bet Gilroy. **13** Number 1. **14** Trolley pusher at Freshco. **15** Maggie Jones. **16** Bet. **17** Tie salesman. **18** Yes. **19** 1983. **20** Anne Kirkbride. **21** Jackie Dobbs. **22** Mike Baldwin. **23** Valerie. **24** Anne Reid. **25** Electrocuted by a hairdryer and then died in the fire.

Quiz 3 Celebs

Level 1

1 Which Patsy married Liam Gallagher?
2 Jerry Hall hails from which oil state?
3 Where does Dame Edna Everage hail from?
4 Who accompanied Hugh Grant to the premiere of *Four Weddings and a Funeral* in a dress held together with safety pins?
5 Which blonde Ms Jonsson advertised crisps with Gary Lineker?
6 Which celebrity chef had a TV series called *Rhodes Around Britain*?
7 Twiggy was the most famous model of which decade?
8 Jane Asher is also famous for baking and selling what?
9 Which Richard did Elizabeth Taylor marry twice?
10 Which Italian actress launched her own perfume, Sophia?
11 Which quintet switched on the Oxford Street Christmas lights in 1996?
12 Who was Julia Carling's first husband?
13 Which Prime Minister's son did Emma Noble marry in 1999?
14 Which Spice Girl was the first to marry?
15 Michael Jackson's first wife was the daughter of which 'King'?
16 Which Rolling Stone did Jerry Hall marry?
17 Which supermodel Naomi wrote a novel called *Swan*?
18 Which Bob who founded Band Aid received an honorary knighthood in 1986?
19 Giorgio Armani is famous in which field?
20 Fashion designer Donatella, sister of the murdered Gianni, has what surname?
21 What does the R-J part of the PR agency R-JH stand for?
22 Model Rachel Hunter was married to which veteran rock star?
23 Ivanka Trump has a similar name to her mother; what is it?
24 Brigitte Bardot was awarded the freedom of her capital city; what is it?
25 Which 1980s US president survived an assassination attempt?

Answers

Celebs
1 Kensit. **2** Texas. **3** Australia. **4** Elizabeth Hurley. **5** Ulrika. **6** Gary Rhodes. **7** 60s. **8** Cakes. **9** Burton. **10** Sophia Loren. **11** The Spice Girls. **12** Will. **13** John Major's. **14** Mel B. **15** Elvis Presley. **16** Mick Jagger. **17** Campbell. **18** Geldof. **19** Fashion design. **20** Versace. **21** Rhys-Jones. **22** Rod Stewart. **23** Ivana Trump. **24** Paris. **25** Ronald Reagan.

Quiz 4 Pot Luck

Level 1

1 What is Cherie Booth's married name?
2 What animal name was given to the terrorist Carlos who was tried in 1997?
3 In what month did Prince Edward get married?
4 Which MP Mrs Currie landed in hot water about eggs?
5 Who is Griff Rhys Jones' comic TV partner?
6 With which sport is Charles Barkley associated?
7 Which Ford first mass produced the car?
8 Which annual sporting event was hit by sit-downs and go-slows in 1998?
9 Which song took Rolf Harris back to the charts in the 90s?
10 Which Michael revived his TV chat show of the 70s in the late 90s?
11 In ASCII what does the letter C stand for ?
12 Guides wear what colour of uniform?
13 Who was the first of the Queen's children to marry?
14 Truro is the administrative centre of which English county?
15 Clare Short has represented which party in parliament?
16 What kind of Girls featured in Anna Friel's film set in the Second World War?
17 In banking what does T stand for in TSB?
18 Which comedy show, broadcast around the time of the evening news, launched the career of Rowan Atkinson?
19 Django Reinhardt was associated with which musical instrument?
20 Whose first European ad campaign was for Max Factor in 1999?
21 What did Ceylon change its name to in 1970?
22 Chris Woods represented England at which sport?
23 In which country was comedian Dave Allen born?
24 What colour did the Redcoats adopt at Butlins after a 90s revamp?
25 The deepwater port of Malmo was developed in which country?

Answers

Pot Luck

1 Blair. **2** The Jackal. **3** June. **4** Edwina. **5** Mel Smith. **6** Basketball. **7** Henry. **8** Tour de France. **9** Stairway To Heaven. **10** Parkinson. **11** Code. **12** Blue. **13** Anne. **14** Cornwall. **15** Labour. **16** Land. **17** Trustee. **18** Not the Nine O'Clock News. **19** Guitar. **20** Madonna. **21** Sri Lanka. **22** Soccer. **23** Ireland. **24** Red. **25** Sweden.

Quiz 5 TV - On the Box

Level 1

1 What does E stand for in the medical drama ER?
2 In which series did Dr Frasier Crane first appear?
3 In which country was *Ballykissangel* set?
4 Which children's show was introduced with, and named after, a native North American greeting?
5 Which Colin created Inspector Morse and appeared as an extra in every episode of the series?
6 What type of animal was Basil Brush?
7 Dogtanian and the Three Muskehounds was based on which classic book?
8 In which US TV series did Pamela Anderson shoot to fame?
9 Which long running comedy series about three OAPs was filmed in Holmfirth?
10 Which Sci-Fi freedom fighters were led by a man called Roj Blake?
11 In which show might you see Charlie and Duffy in A & E?
12 In which part of Eastern Britain was Lovejoy set?
Which Andrew wrote the book on which the Sky mini series *Diana: Her True Story* was based?
13 Who was Tony's flatmate in *Men Behaving Badly*?
14 On whose show were Gotcha Oscars presented?
15 *Oh Doctor Beeching* was a sitcom about the closure of what?
16 Which sport was the subject of the sitcom *Outside Edge*?
17 Which drama series told of a Practice called The Beeches in Derbyshire?
18 Rab C. Nesbitt was a native of which Scottish city?
19 80s drama *St Elsewhere* was set in what type of institution?
20 What was the surname of cartoon characters Homer, Marge and Bart?
21 In which army series did Robson and Jerome find fame?
22 *South Park* is situated in which US state famous for its ski resorts?
23 What relation was Harold to Albert Steptoe?
24 Which series about twentysomething lawyers starred Daniela Nardini and Jack Davenport?

Answers

TV – On the Box

1 Emergency. **2** Cheers. **3** Ireland. **4** How. **5** Dexter. **6** Fox. **7** The Three Musketeers. **8** Baywatch. **9** Last of the Summer Wine. **10** Blake's 7. **11** Casualty. **12** East Anglia. **13** Morton. **14** Gary. **15** Noel Edmonds. **16** Railways. **17** Cricket. **18** Peak Practice. **19** Glasgow. **20** Hospital. **21** Simpson. **22** Soldier Soldier. **23** Colorado. **24** Son. **25** This Life.

Quiz 6 CORONATION ST. Level 1

Pub Questions

1 Who were the first landlord and landlady of the Rovers Return?
2 What dish is pub cook Betty famous for?
3 Which three Weatherfield businessmen once jointly owned the Rovers?
4 What is the name of the brewery that supplies the Rovers with beer?
5 Who was the first Rovers barmaid?
6 What is Mike Baldwin's favourite tipple?
7 Which business is currently situated opposite the Rovers?
8 Name the previous owner of the Rovers Return who left the Street on New Year's Eve 2000.
9 What was the name of the pub that Liz and Jim McDonald used to run?
10 What fabric was Bet Gilroy (née Lynch) famous for wearing?
11 Which of these ladies has not worked as a Rovers barmaid: Raquel Watts, Rita Sullivan or Sally Webster.
12 Which barmaid did actress Michelle Holmes play in the 1980s?
13 What colour are the seats in the Rovers Return?
14 Which character currently lives in the flat above the pub?
15 Name the portly pot man played by Fred Feast in the 1970s and 1980s.
16 Which three ladies used to sit in the 'Snug' in the 1960s?
17 Which event in 1986 resulted in the pub having to be refurbished?
18 Name the club that Alec Gilroy used to run in the 1980s before marrying Bet and taking over the Rovers.
19 Who has worked as both cellar man and landlord of the Rovers?
20 What was Ena Sharples' favourite tipple?
21 What headgear was pub cleaner Hilda Ogden rarely seen without?
22 Eva Pope played which scheming barmaid from 1993–4?
23 Who worked as both barmaid and landlady of the Rovers Return?
24 Where did the Duckworths find the money to buy the Rovers in 1995?
25 What colour are the beer mats in the Rovers Return?

Answers

Coronation Street – Pub Questions

1 Annie and Jack Walker. **2** Hot Pot. **3** Mike Baldwin, Fred Elliott, Duggie Ferguson. **4** Newton & Ridley. **5** Concepta Riley. **6** Scotch. **7** Audrey's Hair Salon. **8** Natalie Barnes. **9** The Queens. **10** Leopardskin. **11** Rita Sullivan. **12** Tina Fowler. **13** Red. **14** Duggie Ferguson. **15** Fred Gee. **16** Ena Sharples, Minnie Caldwell, Martha Longhurst. **17** A fire. **18** The Graffiti Club. **19** Jack Duckworth. **20** Milk Stout. **21** Headscarf and curlers. **22** Tanya Pooley. **23** Bet Gilroy. **24** Insurance money from Jack's brother's death. **25** Green.

Quiz 7 Soccer

Level 1

1 Alex Ferguson joined Man Utd after managing which club?
2 Who had the last kick in England's 1998 World Cup campaign?
3 What nickname was Italian superstar Roberto Baggio given?
4 Which country does world record transfer man Christian Vieri play for?
5 Which soccer team moved to the Reebok Stadium in the 90s?
6 Who hit Man Utd's winner in the 1999 European Champions' Cup Final?
7 Who was Blackburn's manager when they won the Premier League?
8 In 1999 Ron Atkinson announced his retirement as a soccer boss while with which club?
9 John Gregory took over from Brian Little as boss of which club?
10 Which Arsenal player was sent to jail for a drink-driving offence in 1990?
11 Carlos Alberto was a World Cup winning skipper of which country?
12 Jonathan Woodgate was with which club when he first played for England?
13 Which 90s star is known as 'The Iceman'?
14 Ronald Coeman was a star international with which country?
15 Alan Shearer and Matt Le Tissier have both been at which club?
16 Manager Jim Smith is known as the Bald what?
17 Which soccer ground did Sunderland leave in 1997?
18 At which soccer club did David O' Leary establish an appearance record?
19 England players Shearer, Sherwood, Sutton have all played for which soccer club?
20 Which British manager put Barcelona back on winning ways in the 1980s?
21 Which English keeper made the save of the century against Brazil in a 1970 World Cup game?
22 With which club did John Barnes begin his league soccer career?
23 Which keeper of the 80s and 90s glories in the nickname 'Lurch'?
24 At which British soccer club did an Italian take over from a Dutchman?
25 Dwight Yorke joined Man Utd from which club?

Answers

Soccer
1 Aberdeen. **2** David Batty. **3** The Divine Ponytail. **4** Italy. **5** Bolton. **6** Solskjaer. **7** Kenny Dalglish. **8** Nottm Forest. **9** Aston Villa. **10** Tony Adams. **11** Brazil. **12** Leeds. **13** Dennis Bergkamp. **14** Holland. **15** Southampton. **16** Eagle. **17** Roker Park. **18** Arsenal. **19** Blackburn. **20** Terry Venables. **21** Gordon Banks. **22** Watford. **23** Dave Beasant. **24** Chelsea. **25** Aston Villa.

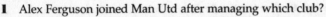

Quiz 8 Pot Luck

Level 1

1 Who set up the Virgin group?
2 Most people know this, but what is Michael Caine's real first name?
3 Who did Ffion Jenkins marry?
4 With which sport is Oliver Bierhoff associated?
5 Which word went with Britannia to describe the supposedly vibrant late 90s?
6 According to the TV theme song what do neighbours become?
7 Which country did Greta Garbo come from?
8 Robbie Coltrane and Whoopi Goldberg have played in films where their characters disguise themselves as what?
9 Which cash-making event was cancelled after revelations about Will Carling's private life in 1998?
10 Which three letters came to describe a farm shop where the buyer gathers in the goods?
11 In which country did Ho Chi Minh come to power?
12 Entertainer Michael Parker changed his last name to what?
13 Which area of West London established a summer holiday carnival?
14 Which Man From Auntie, Ben, replaced Terry Wogan temporarily on *Wogan* while the Irishman went on holiday?
15 The village at Bourneville near Birmingham was set up for workers of which chocolate factory?
16 Which musical instrument did Pablo Casals play?
17 Which English nurse Edith was executed by the Germans in WWI?
18 Catherine and William Booth were founders of which Army?
19 Which country has A as its international vehicle registration letter?
20 Which Kate became the face of L'Oreal in 1998?
21 In 1999, which BBC 1 show was dropped after a rumpus over fake guests?
22 Which Welsh politician Aneurin oversaw the formation of the welfare state?
23 What was the first name of Laurie in *A Bit of Fry & Laurie* on TV?
24 Everything Changes was a 90s No 1 for which group?
25 What did the U stand for in USSR?

Answers

Pot Luck

1 Richard Branson. **2** Maurice. **3** William Hague. **4** Soccer. **5** Cool. **6** Good friends. **7** Sweden. **8** Nuns. **9** His testimonial. **10** PYO. **11** Vietnam. **12** Barrymore. **13** Notting Hill. **14** Elton. **15** Cadbury's. **16** Cello. **17** Cavell. **18** Salvation Army. **19** Austria. **20** Moss. **21** The Vanessa Show. **22** Bevan. **23** Hugh. **24** Take That. **25** Union.

Quiz 9 Blockbusters

Level 1

1 Who played Jack in *Titanic*?
2 Which 1996 musical had Madonna making 85 costume changes?
3 Which Kevin starred in the spectacularly money-losing *Waterworld*?
4 Which Buzz from *Toy Story* caused a Christmas buying frenzy in 1996?
5 Which Landings were the subject of *Saving Private Ryan*?
6 Which British actor/director Richard was Dr Hammond in *Jurassic Park*?
7 Who sang I Will Always Love You in her film, *The Bodyguard*?
8 In which Disney classic was Robin Williams first the voice of the Genie?
9 Whose name appears with Dracula in the title of the 1992 movie?
10 In which 80s film did Meryl Streep play a Polish holocaust survivor?
11 Up Where We Belong was the theme music to which 80s film with Richard Gere and Debra Winger?
12 Which 1982 Spielberg classic was about a little boy and his pet alien?
13 Which actor Ben played the title role in *Gandhi*, and also played Ron Jenkins in *Coronation Street*?
14 In which 70s film did 'Love means never having to say you're sorry.'?
15 Which fruit is named in the title of the controversial Clockwork film directed by Stanley Kubrick?
16 Which film, the first of a series with Sigourney Weaver, had the line 'In Space no one can hear you scream' on the cinema poster?
17 Which wartime classic, named after a port of North Africa, starred Humphrey Bogart and Ingrid Bergman?
18 In which blockbuster did Anthony Perkins first appear as Norman Bates?
19 In *Some Like It Hot*, which gangster city are Jack Lemmon and Tony Curtis forced to leave after witnessing the St Valentine's Day massacre?
20 In which country did *The Sound of Music* take place?
21 Which film about a gorilla was a massive success for RKO in 1933 and has had a cult following ever since?
22 What was the first full length colour animated film?
23 If Billy Crystal was Harry who was Meg Ryan?
24 In which 90s film did Jeremy Irons speak the voice of wicked feline Scar?
25 Which 30s film about the American Civil War is 'the first blockbuster'?

Answers

Blockbusters

1 Leonardo DiCaprio. **2** Evita. **3** Costner. **4** Lightyear. **5** D Day. **6** Attenborough. **7** Whitney Houston. **8** Aladdin. **9** Bram Stoker's. **10** Sophie's Choice. **11** An Officer and a Gentleman. **12** E.T. **13** Kingsley. **14** Love Story. **15** Orange. **16** Alien. **17** Casablanca. **18** Psycho. **19** Chicago. **20** Austria. **21** King Kong. **22** Snow White and the Seven Dwarfs. **23** Sally. **24** The Lion King. **25** Gone With the Wind.

Quiz 10 CORONATION ST.

Level 1

Love Is In The Air

1 In which country did Nick and Leanne Tilsley get married?
2 Which dithering couple stood each other up at the altar before finally tying the knot in 1988?
3 In which unusual venue did Hayley and Roy get married?
4 Name the toyboy that Deirdre married in 1994.
5 Who was the truck driver who had an affair with Bet Gilroy but ended up leaving the Street with Tanya Pooley?
6 Who ran away to Germany with Bill Webster?
7 Name the Irish nanny who became obsessed with Martin Platt in 1993.
8 Name Percy Sugden's blue-haired admirer.
9 Who did Kevin Webster have an affair with while still married to Sally?
10 Name Toyah Battersby's eco-warrior ex-boyfriend.
11 What was the name of Des Barnes' first wife?
12 How many times was Elsie Tanner married?
13 Who married Steve McDonald in the Caribbean, only to find out he was only interested in her money?
14 What was the name of Betty Williams' first husband?
15 Who was Raquel in love with before marrying Curly?
16 How did Curly get back together with Kimberly?
17 Which couple had an unfortunate incident with a burst water bed in the flat above the Corner Shop?
18 Which blonde bride punched her husband-to-be at the altar after finding out he was having an affair with Natalie Barnes?
19 Who goes out with Bobbi Lewis?
20 Who was dating Dev Alahan?
21 Which father and son were both in love with Fiona Middleton?
22 Who recently bought his wife a new kitchen and a cruise with the proceeds of a big win at the bookies?
23 Who found happiness with redhead Paula Shipley after his wife died?
24 Who was Gail Platt's first husband?
25 How many times has Ken been married?

Answers

Coronation Street – Love Is In The Air

1 Scotland. **2** Mavis and Derek Wilton. **3** In Roy's Rolls. **4** Samir Rachid. **5** Charlie Whelan. **6** Maureen Elliot. **7** Carmel Finnan. **8** Phyllis Pearce. **9** Natalie Horrocks. **10** Spider Nugent, **11** Steph, **12** Three. **13** Vicky Arden. **14** Cyril Turpin. **15** Des Barnes. **16** They were paired up through a dating agency. **17** Maureen and Reg. 18 Sharon Gaskell. **19** Vik Desai. **20** Geena Gregory. **21** Jim and Steve McDonald. **22** Jack Duckworth. **23** Gary Mallett. **24** Brian Tilsley. **25** Three.

Quiz 11 Around The UK

Level 1

1 The A2 ends up at which Channel port?
2 What colour are road signs which lead to heritage sites and places of interest?
3 What type of Show is held regularly at Farnborough?
4 In 1988 which Norfolk waterways were designated a national park?
5 Aston University was founded in 1966 in which city?
6 What is Britain's second largest airport after Heathrow?
7 On which Devon Moor is there a famous prison?
8 London's Carnaby Street shot to fame in the 60s for what type of shops?
9 In which London Lane is the Dorchester Hotel?
10 In which Scottish city is an annual festival of music and drama held?
11 What sort of thoroughfare is the Grand Union?
12 The Fastnet Race is over what type of surface?
13 In which Yorkshire city is the National Railway Museum?
14 Aintree racecourse is near which UK city?
15 Which industry famously moved to Wapping from Central London in the 1980s?
16 Which leisure park is near Stoke on Trent in Staffordshire?
17 Where in Wales is the Driver and Vehicle Licensing Centre?
18 Which cultural centre, the London base of the RSC, was opened in 1982?
19 In which area of London is the All England Tennis Club?
20 The first Borstal opened in which SE England county in 1902?
21 What type of products does Fortnum & Mason sell?
22 Glamis Castle near Dundee was the home of which royal before her marriage?
23 If you caught the train called The Clansman you would travel from London to which part of the UK?
24 Which Birmingham shopping centre was opened in 1960 on the site of a former cattle market?
25 Holyhead is on which island off Wales?

Answers

Around the UK

1 Dover. **2** Brown. **3** Air. **4** Broads. **5** Birmingham. **6** Gatwick. **7** Dartmoor. **8** Boutiques. **9** Park Lane. **10** Edinburgh. **11** Canal. **12** Water. **13** York. **14** Liverpool. **15** Newspaper. **16** Alton Towers. **17** Swansea. **18** Barbican. **19** Wimbledon. **20** Kent. **21** Food. **22** The Queen Mother. **23** Scotland. **24** Bull Ring. **25** Anglesey.

Quiz 12 Pot Luck

Level 1

1 The 90s Good Friday agreement sought peace in which country?
2 Elton John was born with which surname?
3 Which Frank formed a comedy writing team with Denis Norden?
4 In which decade did Channel 5 begin broadcasting?
5 Until 1998 what had been banned for 200 years by the MCC?
6 Which actor starred in the TV comedy *Father Ted*?
7 Who was the outgoing president when Bill Clinton took office?
8 Maurice Cole found fame as which Kenny?
9 The first modern cassette was produced in which decade?
10 Which Justin set the 98 Open alight as an amateur?
11 Which impressionist had a TV series called *Who Else?*
12 What did politician Richard Crossman leave behind that was published in the 70s after his death?
13 What does the letter C stand for in RSPCA?
14 Who had a 90s hit with The Shoop Shoop Song?
15 Which Harold wrote the play *The Caretaker*?
16 What was the setting for the TV sitcom *The Brittas Empire*?
17 Which chemist Marie became the first woman to win a Nobel prize?
18 With which sport is Herbie Hide associated?
19 In which city was Charles de Gaulle airport built?
20 Norman Fowler has represented which party in parliament?
21 In 1930 which comic duo made the film *Another Fine Mess*?
22 PW Botha was Prime Minister of which country?
23 Which Lily was the mistress of Edward VII?
24 What was the occupation of Jacko in TV's *Brush Strokes*?
25 Andy Gregory represented England at which sport?

Answers

Pot Luck

1 N Ireland. **2** Dwight. **3** Muir. **4** 90s. **5** Women. **6** Dermot Morgan. **7** George Bush. **8** Everett. **9** 40s. **10** Rose. **11** Rory Bremner. **12** Diaries. **13** Cruelty. **14** Cher. **15** Pinter. **16** Leisure centre. **17** Curie. **18** Boxing. **19** Paris. **20** Conservative. **21** Laurel & Hardy. **22** South Africa. **23** Langtry. **24** House painter. **25** Rugby League.

Quiz 13 Karaoke

Level 1

1 Which song starts, 'It's a little bit funny, This feeling inside'?
2 Which Shania Twain song includes, 'Okay, so you're Brad Pitt'?
3 What is the first word of She?
4 In Gina G's Eurovision song what follows 'Ooh ahh just a little...'?
5 Which Cliff Richard hit starts, 'Used to think that life was sweet, Used to think we were so complete'?
6 Which Dire Straits song starts, 'These mist covered mountains...'?
7 Which Swedish Eurovision winner's song said 'Take me to your heaven..'?
8 Which chilly Madonna song begins 'You only see what your eyes want to see'?
9 Which organ of the body is mentioned in the theme song to *Titanic*?
10 Judy Garland sang about going somewhere over the what?
11 Who Get Going When The Going Gets Tough?
12 Which Queen classic starts, 'Is this the real life...'?
13 In Candle in the Wind 1997 what did Elton John sing instead of 'Goodbye Norma Jean'?
14 In 1996 which band sang 'It's only words and words are all I have.....' as The Bee Gees had done in 1968?
15 What number was Perfect according to The Beautiful South in 1998?
16 In the Bowie song who was Ground Control trying to make contact with?
17 How many times did the Spice Girls sing 'really' in the first two lines of Wannabe?
18 What's the response to, 'See you later, alligator'?
19 Which song starts, 'Sometimes it's hard to be a woman'?
20 Which group thought, 'It's fun to stay at the YMCA'?
21 Which Elton John song has the colour yellow in the title?
22 Which words of encouragement did S Club 7 sing after 'Don't stop..' in Bring It All Back?
23 Who was 'the fastest milkman in the West'?
24 Who made Little Richard sing Good Golly?
25 Which song begins 'I feel it in my fingers'?

Answers

Karaoke

1 Your Song. **2** That Don't Impress Me Much. **3** She. **4** Bit. **5** We Don't Talk Anymore. **6** Brothers In Arms. **7** Charlotte Nilsson. **8** Frozen. **9** Heart. **10** Rainbow. **11** The Tough. **12** Bohemian Rhapsody. **13** England's rose. **14** Boyzone. **15** 10. **16** Major Tom. **17** 4. **18** In a while, crocodile. **19** Stand By Your Man. **20** Village People. **21** Goodbye Yellow Brick Road. **22** Never give up. **23** Ernie. **24** Miss Molly. **25** Love Is All Around.

Quiz 14 CORONATION ST. Level 1

Family Ties

1 What is the shared surname of Liz, Andy, Steve and Jim?
2 Name Alec Gilroy's granddaughter.
3 What were the names of Tricia Armstrong's two sons?
4 Who was the mother of Tommy Duckworth?
5 What was the name of Ken's uncle, played by Jack Howarth?
6 What was the name of Annie and Jack Walker's son?
7 What is the shared surname of Judy, Gary, Billy and Becky?
8 Who is the mother of Ken Barlow's son, Daniel?
9 What is the relationship between Rita Sullivan and Sharon Gaskell?
10 What is the name of Vikram Desai's sister?
11 Who is Leanne and Toyah Battersby's half-brother?
12 What is Blanche Hunt's relationship to Deirdre Rachid?
13 How many grandsons do Jack and Vera have?
14 What was the name of Fiona Middleton's son?
15 Who was Gail Platt's first mother-in-law?
16 Name Audrey's son who lives in Canada.
17 What are Sally and Kevin's daughters called?
18 What is the real relationship between Ashley Peacock and 'Uncle' Fred Elliot?
19 Who is related to both Mike Baldwin and Ken Barlow and how?
20 What was Sally Webster's maiden name?
21 Which famous family does Vera believe she is related to?
22 What was the name of Ken Barlow's brother?
23 What is the relationship between Vikram Desai and Dev Alahan?
24 What are the names of Eileen Grimshaw's two sons?
25 What is the name of Deirdre's daughter?

Answers

Coronation Street – Family Ties

1 McDonald. **2** Vicky Arden. **3** Jamie and Brad. **4** Lisa Duckworth. **5** Uncle Albert Tatlock. **6** Billy. **7** Mallett. **8** Denise Osbourne. **9** Foster mother and daughter. **10** Nita Desai. **11** Greg Kelly. **12** Mother. **13** Three. **14** Morgan. **15** Ivy Tilsley. **16** Stephen Reid. **17** Rosie and Sophie. **18** Father and son. **19** Adam, Mike's son by Susan Barlow, and Ken's grandson. **20** Seddon. **21** The Royal family. **22** David. **23** Cousins. **24** Jason and Todd. **25** Tracy.

Quiz 15 60s Newsround

Level 1

1 Which Harold became leader of a British political party in the 60s?
2 Who managed England to World Cup triumph?
3 Which Basil was involved in the cancelling of an English tour to South Africa?
4 Mrs Gandhi became Prime Minister in which country?
5 Donald Campbell was killed trying to break which speed record?
6 Which literary Lady had a Lover that resulted in an Old Bailey obscenity trial?
7 Dubcek's reforms were crushed by Soviet tanks in which country?
8 Maria Bueno was a 60s champion in which sport?
9 Which city became Brazil's new capital in 1960?
10 The World Wildlife Fund was set up with which animal as its logo?
11 The LSE, the scene of student unrest, was the London School of what?
12 Which Italian city hosted the 1960 Olympics?
13 Where in America was the world's biggest rock festival staged?
14 Pierre Trudeau became Prime Minister of which country?
15 Who was the only British winner of the British Open in the 60s?
16 Mia Farrow's controversial film concerned whose baby?
17 What type of vehicle was involved in the fatal accident at Chappaquiddick?
18 Which pop star married a Cynthia and later a Yoko?
19 What was Vidal Sassoon creating?
20 What was the name of call girl Miss Keeler involved in a ministerial sex scandal?
21 Which road was linked with the murder trial involving James Hanratty?
22 What type of creature was headline-making Goldie who escaped in London?
23 Who was 'the Louisville Lip'?
24 Who was Lee Harvey Oswald charged with murdering?
25 Which Francis completed his solo round the world yacht journey?

Answers

60s Newsround

1 Wilson. **2** Alf Ramsey. **3** D'Oliveira. **4** India. **5** Water. **6** Lady Chatterley. **7** Czechoslovakia. **8** Tennis. **9** Brasilia. **10** Panda. **11** Economics. **12** Rome. **13** Woodstock. **14** Canada. **15** Tony Jacklin. **16** Rosemary's. **17** Car. **18** John Lennon. **19** Hairstyles. **20** Christine. **21** A6. **22** Eagle. **23** Cassius Clay. **24** President Kennedy. **25** Chichester.

Quiz 16 Pot Luck

Level 1

1 What was Eileen Drewery's role in England's 1998 World Cup preparations?
2 Which quizmaster said, 'I've started so I'll finish'?
3 Who created the three-dimensional cube in the 70s and 80s craze?
4 Whose son was called Prince Michael Jr?
5 Which European country was divided into East and West in 1949?
6 Which Spice Girls hit starts, 'I'll tell you what I want'?
7 Which government minister took his dog to work?
8 Which country does Ray Reardon come from?
9 Sophia Scicoloni became famous as which actress?
10 What are the first two words of the much recorded song I Believe?
11 Which Julian once called himself The Joan Collins Fan Club?
12 What does the letter B stand for in RSPB?
13 Chester is the administrative centre of which English county?
14 Who played James Bond in Doctor No?
15 The legendary cricketer Learie Constantine played for which country?
16 Who did Doctor Crippen poison?
17 What name is given to the charity which was set up by comedians to raise money for those in need?
18 Which high office has been held by Dr George Carey?
19 What was the first name of *Rebecca* writer du Maurier?
20 If the K stands for Kosovo what do L and A stand for in the KLA?
21 What colour is Mickey Mouse's nose?
22 Which *EastEnders* landlord found fame as himself on *The Comedians*?
23 What was The Simpsons' 90s No 1 hit?
24 With which sport is Thomas Hearns associated?
25 Madhur Jaffrey chiefly writes about cookery from which country of the world?

Answers

Pot Luck

1 Faith healer. **2** Magnus Magnusson. **3** Rubik. **4** Michael Jackson's. **5** Germany. **6** Wannabe. **7** David Blunkett. **8** Wales. **9** Sophia Loren. **10** I Believe. **11** Clary. **12** Birds. **13** Cheshire. **14** Sean Connery. **15** W Indies. **16** His wife. **17** Comic Relief. **18** Archbishop of Canterbury. **19** Daphne. **20** Liberation Army. **21** Black. **22** Frank Butcher. **23** Do The Bartman. **24** Boxing. **25** India.

Quiz 17 Famous Names

Level 1

1 What is novelist Lord Archer's first name?
2 By what first name is Jeremy John Durham Ashdown best known ?
3 What is Zoe Ball's dad called?
4 What is the name of Margaret Thatcher's husband?
5 Which part of him did Ken Dodd insure for £4 million?
6 Betty Boothroyd became the first female Speaker where?
7 How was Elaine Bickerstaff better known on the West End stage?
8 Which chain of environmentally friendly shops did Anita Roddick found?
9 What did Nigel Kennedy change his name to professionally in the late 90s?
10 Which Gordon was Tony Blair's first Chancellor of the Exchequer?
11 Which musical instrument is Dudley Moore famous for playing?
12 How is Paul O'Grady better known in high heels, blonde wig and Liverpool accent?
13 Martina Navratilova changed nationality from Czech to what?
14 Why would you consult Nicky Clarke professionally?
15 What two initials is crime novelist Baroness James known by?
16 Henry Cecil is a famous name in which sport?
17 Which Nigel found fame as a writer of a newspaper Diary about celebs?
18 In 1999 Sean Connery campaigned on behalf of which political party?
19 Eddie George became Governor of what in 1993?
20 What is Ffion Jenkins' married surname?
21 Michael Flatley was dubbed Lord of the what?
22 Which Spice nickname did Geri Halliwell have?
23 Which actor Stephen walked out of the West End play *Cell Mates* in 1995?
24 Michael Heseltine's nickname was that of which film hero?
25 Opera star Lesley Garrett hails from which county?

Answers

Famous Names

1 Jeffrey. **2** Paddy. **3** Johnny. **4** Denis. **5** Teeth. **6** House of Commons. **7** Elaine Paige. **8** Body Shop. **9** Kennedy. **10** Brown. **11** Piano. **12** Lily Savage. **13** American. **14** To do your hair. **15** P D. **16** Horse racing. **17** Dempster. **18** Scots Nationalist. **19** Bank of England. **20** Hague. **21** Dance. **22** Ginger. **23** Fry. **24** Tarzan. **25** Yorkshire.

Quiz 18 CORONATION ST. Level 1

Pot Luck

1 What number Coronation Street did the Ogdens live at?
2 Which writer created *Coronation Street*?
3 How did Ernie Bishop die in the 1970s?
4 In which year did Ken and Deirdre marry?
5 Who did Gail Potter and Suzie Birchall lodge with in the 1970s?
6 Who was the Ogdens' lodger in the 1970s and 1980s?
7 Who was Victor Pendlebury in love with for many years?
8 Which actor from *Dad's Army* was once a *Coronation Street* actor?
9 What was the name of Elsie Tanner's son?
10 Who worked at the Mission of Glad Tidings in the 1960s?
11 Which outrageous items of jewellery was Bet Lynch most famous for?
12 How did evil Alan Bradley die?
13 Which *Coronation Street* baby was born in the back of Don Brennan's taxi on Christmas Eve, 1990?
14 Who did Alf Roberts make his mayoress after wife Audrey failed to take the job seriously?
15 What was the name of the supermarket where Curly Watts and Reg Holdsworth first worked together?
16 What is the name of Mike Baldwin's garment factory?
17 Which *Coronation Street* character has been in the programme since the first episode?
18 How did Derek Wilton die?
19 Who tried to kill Alma by driving his car into Weatherfield Quays?
20 Who was the secretary that Ken Barlow had an affair with, resulting in the end of his marriage to Deirdre?
21 Where did Ivy move to when she left Coronation Street?
22 What is Roy's cafe called?
23 Who plays Maria Sutherland?
24 Who became obsessed with Curly Watts, but met a grizzly end in one of Freshco's Freezers?
25 Which actress played Elsie Tanner?

Answers

Coronation Street – Pot Luck

1 Thirteen. **2** Tony Warren. **3** He was shot in a wages snatch at the factory. **4** 1981. **5** Elsie Tanner. **6** Eddie Yeats. **7** Mavis Riley. **8** Arthur Lowe. **9** Dennis. **10** Ena Sharples. **11** Earrings. **12** He was run over by a Blackpool tram. **13** Rosie Webster. **14** Betty Williams. **15** Bettabuys. **16** Underworld. **17** Ken Barlow. **18** He had a heart attack in his car. **19** Don Brennan. **20** Wendy Crozier. **21** A convent. **22** Roy's Rolls. **23** Samia Ghadie. **24** Anne Malone. **25** Pat Phoenix.

Quiz 19 TV Classics

Level 1

1 Which drama series was based on the books of vet James Herriot?
2 *Going Straight* was the follow-up to which classic prison sitcom?
3 In 70s/80s TV how was The Hulk described?
4 Which Croft & Perry sitcom was set in holiday camp?
5 *Auf Wiedersehen Pet* was chiefly set on a building site where?
6 Which classic game show with a crossbow was called *Der Goldener Schuss* in Germany?
7 Which show spawned the catchphrase 'Here's one I made earlier'?
8 How were Terry Collier and Bob Ferris known collectively?
9 Which children's TV classic asked 'Who was that masked man?'?
10 Which satirical series lampooned politicians through latex puppets?
11 Which Citizen's catchphrase was 'Power to the People'?
12 What was Dr Who's Time Machine called?
13 *Elizabeth R*, with Glenda Jackson, was based on the life of whom?
14 The Fall and Rise of which Reginald starred Leonard Rossiter?
15 What was the female follow-up to *The Man from U.N.C.L.E* called?
16 Which green vegetable was the booby prize on Crackerjack?
17 In which comedy classic did John Cleese announce 'And now for something completely different'?
18 In Morecambe & Wise shows, Eric's comment 'you can't see the join' referred to what?
19 In *The Muppet Show* what sort of creature was Kermit?
20 Which character's catchphrase was 'I don't believe it'?
21 What were Cassandra and Raquel's surnames after they married Del and Rodney?
22 *Open All Hours* was set in what type of establishment?
23 Which children's character had a famous black and white cat?
24 What was Frank Spencer's wife called in *Some Mothers Do 'Ave 'Em*?
25 Which silent puppet had friends called Sweep and Soo?

Answers

TV Classics

1 All Creatures Great and Small. **2** Porridge. **3** Incredible. **4** Hi-De-Hi!. **5** Germany. **6** The Golden Shot. **7** Blue Peter. **8** The Likely Lads. **9** The Lone Ranger. **10** Spitting Image. **11** Smith. **12** Tardis. **13** Elizabeth I. **14** Perrin. **15** The Girl from U.N.C.L.E.. **16** Cabbage. **17** Monty Python's Flying Circus. **18** Ernie's wig. **19** Frog. **20** Victor Meldrew. **21** Trotter. **22** Shop. **23** Postman Pat. **24** Betty. **25** Sooty.

Quiz 20 Pot Luck

Level 1

1 Which Lara featured in computer game Tomb Raider II?
2 In what decade did *The Sun* newspaper launch in Britain?
3 Which Christine featured in a 60s sex scandal involving a cabinet minister?
4 What was Elvis Presley's middle name?
5 Which country has M as its international vehicle registration letter?
6 In Bryan Adams' mega hit, which three words come before, 'I do it for you'?
7 What were the last names of movie duo Fred and Ginger?
8 In which city was the Three Tenors 1998 World Cup concert?
9 What is the first name of The Queen Mother?
10 Which actor appeared in drag in the movie *Tootsie*?
11 What does the C stand for in BBC?
12 Jim Moir is better known as which comedian?
13 With which sport is Walter Swinburn associated?
14 George W. Bush took over from which US President?
15 Who had a 90s No 1 with Ice Ice Baby?
16 Which group of workers staged a year-long strike in the 80s over closures?
17 Hull is the administrative centre of which English county?
18 What does P stand for in NSPCC?
19 Which comedian Steve created Portuguese superstar Tony Ferrino?
20 Which Bessie was known as Empress of the Blues?
21 Carlsberg was advertised as 'probably the best lager' where?
22 Jim Watt was a world champion in which sport?
23 On TV, what type of goods did Lovejoy deal in?
24 Which classic sitcom was set at Walmington on Sea?
25 On a computer keyboard, what letter is far left on the lowest row of letters?

Answers

Pot Luck

1 Croft. **2** 60s. **3** Keeler. **4** Aaron. **5** Malta. **6** Everything I do. **7** Astaire & Rogers. **8** Paris. **9** Elizabeth. **10** Dustin Hoffman. **11** Corporation. **12** Vic Reeves. **13** Horse racing. **14** Bill Clinton. **15** Vanilla Ice. **16** Miners. **17** Humberside. **18** Prevention. **19** Coogan. **20** Smith. **21** In the world. **22** Boxing. **23** Antiques. **24** Dad's Army. **25** Z.

Quiz 21 Sport: 90s Action Replay

Level 1

1 How many goals were scored in the 1998 World Cup Final?
2 Rugby's man mountain Jonah Lomu plays for which country?
3 Which country hosted the 1998 Winter Olympics?
4 Who did Man Utd defeat in the 1999 European Champions' Cup Final?
5 In 1998 England won a Test series against which country?
6 Which racing team dropped Damon Hill the season he became world champion?
7 Albertville and Lillehammer were the two 90s venues for which event?
8 Which was the first team not called United to win the Premiership?
9 Which best-on-the-planet trophy did Francois Pienaar collect in 1995?
10 Which team inflicted W Indies' first home Test series defeat in over 20 years?
11 Which team were FA Cup beaten finalists in two consecutive seasons?
12 Where do the Super Bowl winning Cowboys come from?
13 Which England skipper resigned after allegations about taking cocaine?
14 Which man managed victory in all the tennis Grand Slam titles?
15 Teddy Sheringham joined Man Utd from which club?
16 Who does Michael Schumacher drive for?
17 Who advertised Adidas and Brylcreem?
18 What did Miguel Indurain win each year from 1991 to 1995?
19 Which Liverpool star was charged with match fixing?
20 Jonathan Edwards was a world champion in 1995 in which athletic event?
21 Ganguly and Tendulkar have played cricket for which country?
22 Which team bought out the Stewart motor racing team?
23 Defeat by which country prompted the Graham Taylor turnip jibes?
24 Which Rugby League team became known as Rhinos?
25 Which England cricketer was accused of ball tampering in a Test?

Answers

Sport: 90s Action Replay

1 Three. **2** New Zealand. **3** Japan. **4** Bayern Munich. **5** South Africa. **6** Williams. **7** Winter Olympics. **8** Blackburn Rovers. **9** Rugby World Cup. **10** Australia. **11** Newcastle. **12** Dallas. **13** Lawrence Dallaglio. **14** Andre Agassi. **15** Spurs. **16** Ferrari. **17** David Beckham. **18** Tour de France. **19** Bruce Grobbelaar. **20** Triple Jump. **21** India. **22** Ford. **23** Sweden. **24** Leeds. **25** Mike Atherton.

Quiz 22 CORONATION ST.

Level 1

Pot Luck

1 Which actress played Raquel Watts?
2 What does Janice Battersby do for a living?
3 Who had a brief fling with Des Barnes' brother Colin?
4 How did Tracy Barlow nearly die in 1995?
5 Who lives at Number 9 Coronation Street?
6 In which year was *Coronation Street* first shown on television?
7 Who runs the Corner Shop?
8 What is Fred Elliot's profession?
9 Who is Tyrone Dobbs' girlfriend?
10 Which actor plays Mike Baldwin?
11 Who was born on Christmas Day, 1990?
12 Who is Spider Nugent's aunt?
13 What was Curly Watts' first job on *Coronation Street*?
14 What item of clothing was Ena Sharples famous for?
15 Who kept pigeons in a loft in the back yard for many years?
16 Actor Bernard Youens played which loveable layabout?
17 Who wrote the famous *Coronation Street* theme tune?
18 Which character used to be a nightclub singer known as 'The Weatherfield Nightingale'?
19 What was the name of Kevin Webster's second wife?
20 How did Alf Roberts die?
21 Which actor plays Ken Barlow?
22 Weatherfield is a fictional suburb of which city?
23 What was Len Fairclough's trade?
24 Who played Ivy Tilsley?
25 Where does part-time stripper Sam Kingston work during the day?

Answers

Coronation Street – Pot Luck

1 Sarah Lancashire. **2** Factory machinist. **3** Liz McDonald. **4** She took an ecstasy tablet. **5** Jack and Vera Duckworth and Tyrone Dobbs. **6** 1960. **7** Dev Alahan. **8** Butcher. **9** Maria Sutherland. **10** Johnny Briggs. **11** David Platt. **12** Emily Bishop. **13** Bin man. **14** Hairnet. **15** Jack Duckworth. **16** Stan Ogden. **17** Eric Spear. **18** Rita. **19** Alison Wakefield. **20** He had a heart attack on New Years' Day, 1999. **21** William Roache. **22** Manchester. **23** Builder. **24** Lynne Perrie. **25** The garage.

Quiz 23 Movies - Who's Who? Level 1

1 Where was Leonardo DiCaprio born?
2 In which 1998 film did Anderson & Duchovny reprise their TV roles of Mulder & Scully?
3 Who or what is Gromit?
4 Who replaced Timothy Dalton as James Bond?
5 Which star of *Home Alone* was the highest paid child movie star of the 20th century?
6 Which star of *Grease* had a career revival with *Pulp Fiction*?
7 Which Tom married Nicole Kidman?
8 Who met husband Richard Burton on the set of *Cleopatra*?
9 Which drummer/singer Phil played the title role in *Buster*?
10 Who went to No 1 with Night Fever after writing the music for *Saturday Night Fever*?
11 Which film director was involved in a long-running custody battle for his children with Mia Farrow?
12 Which ex-Funny Girl starred with Nick Nolte in *The Prince of Tides*?
13 Who was the *Pretty Woman* in the 1990 film with Richard Gere?
14 Which director of *Schindler's List* and *E.T.* was the most commercially successful cinema director of the century?
15 By which first name is Andrew Blyth Barrymore known in *E.T.*?
16 What relation is Jeff to Beau Bridges?
17 Which star of Rocky said 'I built my body to carry my brain around'?
18 Which ex-*Brookside* actress played Nick Leeson's wife in the film *Rogue Trader* about the fall of Barings Bank?
19 Which talk show hostess appeared in *The Color Purple*?
20 Which controversial 80s/90s singer/actress married Sean Penn in 1985?
21 In which country was Arnold Schwarzenegger born?
22 Which pop star's first film was *Purple Rain*?
23 Which Scottish comedian played John Brown in *Mrs Brown*?
24 Cate Blanchett won a BAFTA playing which Queen?
25 Which girl band announced they would make their screen debut in *Honest*?

Answers

Movies – Who's Who?
1 Hollywood. **2** The X Files. **3** Dog. **4** Pierce Brosnan. **5** Macaulay Culkin. **6** John Travolta. **7** Cruise. **8** Elizabeth Taylor. **9** Collins. **10** The Bee Gees. **11** Woody Allen. **12** Barbra Streisand. **13** Julia Roberts. **14** Steven Spielberg. **15** Drew. **16** Brother. **17** Sylvester Stallone. **18** Anna Friel. **19** Oprah Winfrey. **20** Madonna. **21** Austria. **22** Prince. **23** Billy Connolly. **24** Elizabeth. **25** All Saints.

Quiz 24 Pot Luck

Level 1

1 In the 60s what was the name of US President Kennedy's wife?
2 With which sport is Michael Jordan associated?
3 What was George that left a trail of destruction in Florida in 1998?
4 Which Ted was a 90s Poet Laureate?
5 Which world heavyweight boxing champion was jailed in the 90s?
6 Way Down was a hit for which singer after his death?
7 Which country's royal family was virtually wiped out in 2001?
8 In which city were the Shankly Gates built?
9 Under what canine name does rapper Calvin Broadus operate?
10 Sean Fitzpatrick represented New Zealand at which sport?
11 What does the N stand for in NATO?
12 Who was comedian Jack in *Jack & Jeremy's Real Lives*?
13 Which poet Rupert died on his way to action in World War I?
14 Which royal residence does the Queen use in Norfolk?
15 George Eastman invented what type of equipment?
16 Firestarter was a 90s No 1 for which group?
17 Dick Francis' novels revolve around which sport?
18 What's the first name of Frank Sinatra's elder daughter?
19 Which comedian/singer/TV presenter was always the butt of Morecambe & Wise's jokes?
20 Chet Atkins is associated with which musical instrument?
21 Which British city was the Cultural Capital of Europe in 1990?
22 Which Safari Park was set up near to Liverpool?
23 Geoffrey Howe was deputy to which Prime Minister?
24 Which 50s music craze featured a washboard?
25 Which Ken is famous for his vocabulary which includes 'plumpshiousness' and 'tattifilarious'?

Answers

Pot Luck

1 Jackie. **2** Basketball. **3** Hurricane. **4** Hughes. **5** Mike Tyson. **6** Elvis Presley. **7** Nepal's. **8** Liverpool. **9** Snoopy Doggy Dogg. **10** Rugby Union. **11** North. **12** Dee. **13** Brooke. **14** Sandringham. **15** Photographic. **16** Prodigy. **17** Horse racing. **18** Nancy. **19** Des O'Connor. **20** Guitar. **21** Glasgow. **22** Knowsley. **23** Margaret Thatcher. **24** Skiffle. **25** Dodd.

Quiz 25 Euro Tour

Level 1

1 Which southern French town holds an annual international Film Festival?
2 How was Eurotunnel known before its name change in 1998?
3 La Scala is the world's most famous what?
4 Andorra is at the foot of which mountains?
5 Which Arctic country's Finnish name is Lapin Li?
6 Which country is known locally as Osterreich?
7 The Left Bank generally refers to the Left Bank of the Seine in which city?
8 Which Mediterranean island's capital is Valletta?
9 Which country was divided into East and West between the 1940s and 1990s?
10 The Strait of Gibraltar connects the Atlantic Ocean with which Sea?
11 The airline Danair is based where?
12 Which mountainous European country is divided into cantons?
13 Flemish is an official language of which kingdom?
14 Which English location would the French call Douvres?
15 In Greenland a native of the country might be called Inuit or what?
16 Which country is also called the Hellenic Republic?
17 In Norway, a fjord is made up largely of what?
18 Majorca is part of which group of islands?
19 Which German city is known locally as Koln?
20 Tuscany is part of which country?
21 What is Europe's most mountainous country?
22 The province of Calabria is at the southernmost tip of which country?
23 The island of Rhodes belongs to which Mediterranean country?
24 Alsace is a province of which country?
25 What is the currency of Spain?

Answers

Euro Tour

1 Cannes. **2** Le Shuttle. **3** Opera house. **4** Pyrenees. **5** Lapland. **6** Austria. **7** Paris. **8** Malta. **9** Germany. **10** Mediterranean. **11** Denmark. **12** Switzerland. **13** Belgium. **14** Dover. **15** Eskimo. **16** Greece. **17** Water. **18** Balearics. **19** Cologne. **20** Italy. **21** Switzerland. **22** Italy. **23** Greece. **24** France. **25** Peseta.

Quiz 26 CORONATION ST.

Level 1

Pot Luck

1 Jaqueline Pirie (who plays Linda Baldwin) has also appeared in *Emmerdale*. What was the name of her character?
2 Who bought the Duckworths' house in 1995?
3 What was the name of the religious cult which Zoe Tattersall joined?
4 Who is the current producer of *Coronation Street*?
5 Who is Tracy Barlow's real father?
6 What is Steve McDonald's twin brother called?
7 How many times has Mavis Wilton been married?
8 What was Stan Ogden's job?
9 What number Coronation Street does Emily Bishop live at?
10 Which actress plays Maxine Peacock?
11 Linda Baldwin's brother was killed in an armed seige at Frescho. Who fired the shot?
12 Name Natalie Barnes' son
13 To whom did Ken Barlow try to teach conversational French?
14 What was the name of Minnie Caldwell's cat?
15 Who was Martin Platt's girlfriend, who now lives in Dubai?
16 Who gave birth to her son on the floor of the Rovers living room on Valentine's Day 1997?
17 Where does Norris Cole work?
18 Who is Sarah Platt's best friend?
19 How many times did Gail marry Brian Tilsley?
20 Which actress plays Toyah Battersby?
21 Kenneth Cope (who played Jed Stone) became famous for his role in which comedy detective series?
22 Thelma Barlow (who played Mavis Wilton) went on to star with Victoria Wood in which popular comedy?
23 What is Tyrone's dog called?
24 What colour is the stone cladding on the Duckworth's house?
25 What business was Derek Wilton in?

Answers

Coronation Street – Pot Luck

1 Tina Dingle. **2** Judy and Gary Mallett. **3** The Cult of Nirab. **4** Jane Macnaught. **5** Ray Langton. **6** Andy. **7** Once. **8** Window Cleaner. **9** Three. **10** Tracy Shaw. **11** 1 Emma Taylor (now Watts). **12** Tony Horrocks. **13** Raquel. **14** Bobby. **15** Rebecca Hopkins. **16** Tricia Armstrong gave birth to Brad. **17** The Kabin. **18** Candice Stowe. **19** Twice. **20** Georgia Taylor. **21** *Randall & Hopkirk (Deceased)*. **22** *Dinnerladies*. **23** Monica. **24** Blue and yellow. **25** Stationery.

Quiz 27 Pop Charts

Level 1

1 What was Billie's first No 1?
2 Which port provided a hit for The Beautiful South?
3 What's the only battle to have been the one-word title of a No 1?
4 What colour was UB40's Wine?
5 Which Bob Dylan song was used as the song for Dunblane?
6 Which magazine shares its name with a Madonna No 1?
7 What went with Tonic for Spacedust?
8 Who had her first No 1 as Mrs Sonny Bono?
9 Which seabird took Fleetwood Mac to No 1?
10 Which chart smashing group featured Adams, Brown and Chisholm?
11 50+ Deborah Harry returned to the 99 charts with which group?
12 Which Dad's Army actor had a surprise No 1 with Grandad?
13 Which country does Britney Spears come from?
14 Who did Faith Evans team up with for I'll Be Missing You?
15 Which Starsky and Hutch actor topped the charts?
16 Bitter Sweet Symphony was the first top ten hit for which band?
17 Who is the only Bryan to have had a record at No 1 for 16 weeks?
18 Which Lou wrote A Perfect Day?
19 Who had her first No 1 with Wuthering Heights?
20 Suzanne Vega was in who's Diner?
21 Which song was a No 1 for Nilsson and Mariah Carey?
22 Which film provided a best selling album for Whitney Houston?
23 Who recorded Riders On The Storm?
24 Who did Chrissie Hynde guest with for I Got You Babe?
25 Gazza sang with Lindisfarne about the fog on which river?

Answers

Pop Charts

1 Because We Want To. **2** Rotterdam. **3** Waterloo. **4** Red. **5** Knockin' On Heaven's Door. **6** Vogue. **7** Gym. **8** Cher. **9** Albatross. **10** Spice Girls. **11** Blondie. **12** Clive Dunn. **13** US. **14** Puff Daddy. **15** David Soul. **16** Verve. **17** Adams. **18** Reed. **19** Kate Bush. **20** Tom's. **21** Without You. **22** The Bodyguard. **23** The Doors. **24** UB40. **25** Tyne.

Quiz 28 Pot Luck

Level 1

1 A 1997 phenomenon, Hale-Bop was a type of what?
2 The charity Oxfam began in which city?
3 The sale of what was prohibited in America during prohibition?
4 Michael Owen scored a wonder World Cup goal against which country?
5 Which former British Prime Minister called for clemency for General Pinochet?
6 Which instrument was associated with Stephane Grapelli?
7 What was the name of the scandal that brought down US President Richard Nixon?
8 With which sport is Thierry Henry associated?
9 Who duetted with Kiki Dee on True Love?
10 In which decade was the battle of the Somme?
11 Former MP Neil Hamilton was involved in the cash for what scandal?
12 Which Ian created the character James Bond?
13 In movies, who or what were Lady and The Tramp?
14 What does the M stand for in MCC?
15 Which friend of Carla Lane and fellow campaigning vegetarian appeared in an episode of her sitcom *Bread* in 1988?
16 Which TV fox went 'Boom boom!'?
17 Which trials of 1946 dealt with Nazi war criminals?
18 Archibald Leach became known as which Hollywood actor?
19 The controversial James Pickles hit the headlines while serving as a what?
20 The New York Stock Exchange was established on which street?
21 In fiction, what was the name of Bertie Wooster's manservant?
22 Which American actor refused his Oscar awarded for *The Godfather*?
23 David Solberg became a famous actor/singer under which name?
24 Which country did Ray Houghton play soccer for?
25 Which British boxer won Olympic Gold at the Sydney Olympics and turned professional the following year?

Answers

Pot Luck

1 Comet. **2** Oxford. **3** Alcohol. **4** Argentina. **5** Margaret Thatcher. **6** Violin. **7** Watergate. **8** Soccer. **9** Elton John. **10** Second decade. **11** Questions. **12** Fleming. **13** Dogs. **14** Marylebone. **15** Linda McCartney. **16** Basil Brush. **17** Nuremberg. **18** Cary Grant. **19** Judge. **20** Wall Street. **21** Jeeves. **22** Marlon Brando. **23** David Soul. **24** Republic of Ireland. **25** Audley Harrison.

Quiz 29 70s Newsround

Level 1

1 What did Ceylon change its name to?
2 What was the name of the mansion where Elvis Presley died?
3 Which English soccer team did the only 70s FA Cup and League double?
4 Who had a Christmas special watched by an amazing 28 million people?
5 Who did Captain Mark Phillips marry at Westminster Abbey?
6 Which Brit won the ladies singles at Wimbledon?
7 Queen had their first No 1 with which record?
8 What was introduced in the 70s version of D-Day?
9 What was the nickname of Lord Lucan who vanished in the 70s?
10 Which Spare magazine was founded as part of the feminist movement?
11 Who was Satchmo who passed away in 1971?
12 The monarchy was restored to power in which European country?
13 Who or what was Chia Chia?
14 What type of Fields were linked with Cambodia?
15 The Aswan High Dam was opened in which country?
16 In 1976 which jockey won the Derby for a record seventh time?
17 In 1979 the Shah was forced to flee from which country?
18 Bobby Robson managed which soccer side to their first FA Cup triumph?
19 Sir Anthony Blunt was revealed to have led a secret life as what?
20 Which Czechoslovakian born sportswoman Martina defected to America?
21 What were the sea borne refugees fleeing Vietnam known as?
22 Who won the Eurovision Song Contest for Sweden?
23 In which country was a 2000 year old lifesize terracotta army discovered?
24 Johan Cruyff played in a World Cup Final for which country?
25 What was the name of the fashionable short pants worn by women?

Answers

70s Newsround

1 Sri Lanka. **2** Graceland. **3** Arsenal. **4** Morecambe & Wise. **5** Princess Anne. **6** Virginia Wade. **7** Bohemian Rhapsody. **8** Decimal coins. **9** Lucky. **10** Spare Rib. **11** Louis Armstrong. **12** Spain. **13** Giant Panda. **14** Killing. **15** Egypt. **16** Lester Piggott. **17** Iran. **18** Ipswich. **19** Spy. **20** Navratilova. **21** Boat People. **22** Abba. **23** China. **24** Netherlands. **25** Hot pants.

Quiz 30 CORONATION ST. Level 1

Pot Luck

1 Where did Curly propose to Emma?
2 What is Sarah Platt's daughter called?
3 What did Freshco used to be called before the takeover?
4 Who played Reg Holdsworth?
5 Which *Coronation Street* actress now stars in *Holby City*?
6 Which famous couple married in the same year as Ken and Deirdre?
7 Eileen Grimshaw rents the house belonging to whom?
8 What was Don Brennan's job?
9 Name the Freemason-like society which Weatherfield businessmen, including Fred Elliot and Alf Roberts, were members of.
10 What is Curly Watts' hobby?
11 What is Curly's real first name?
12 What is Spider Nugent's real first name?
13 Who married a French Count?
14 Where did Hilda Ogden go when she left *Coronation Street*?
15 Which actor-turned-pop-singer played the older Nick Tilsley?
16 How did Lisa Duckworth die?
17 Name Les Battersby's dodgy friend who lent him a mobile home.
18 Name the *Absolutely Fabulous* actress who played Ken Barlow's girlfriend.
19 What is Martin Platt's job?
20 Who had an affair with Raquel Wolstenhulme and Tania Pooley at the same time?
21 Who plays Maria Sutherland?
22 Who plays Vera and Jack's son, Terry?
23 Which *Coronation Street* actress appeared in *Carry on Cleo* and *Carry on Cabbie*?
24 Which street is Duggie Ferguson's new development situated on?
25 Name Rita's boyfriend.

Answers

Coronation Street – Pot Luck

1 On a boat on the Seine in Paris. **2** Bethany. **3** Firman's Freezers. **4** Ken Morley. **5** Angela Griffin. **6** Prince Charles and Lady Diana Spencer. **7** The McDonalds. **8** Cabbie. **9** The Square Dealers. **10** Astronomy. **11** Norman. **12**Geoffrey. **13** Raquel Wolstenhulme. **14** To work as a cleaner for Dr Lowther. **15** Adam Rickitt. **16** She was run over . **17** Charlie West. **18** Joanna Lumley. **19** Nurse. **20** Des Barnes. **21** Samia Ghadie. **22** Nigel Pivaro. **23** Amanda Barrie. **24** Victoria Street. **25** Anthony Stephens.

Quiz 31 Headline Makers

Level 1

1 Which MP David was exposed as having an affair in 1992?
2 Which rock legend Mick was David Bailey's best man?
3 Allan Lamb changed nationality from South African to what?
4 Which former actor and US President received an honorary knighthood?
5 Which Foreign Secretary did Gaynor Regan marry in 1998?
6 Which nanny was tried in the US over the death of a baby in her care?
7 What was the first name of Miss Lewinsky whose White House activities almost brought down Bill Clinton?
8 Who stormed off court at the end of the 1999 French Open and had to have her mother coax her back?
9 Who was South Africa's first black president?
10 In 1995 astronaut Michael Foale was the first Briton to walk where?
11 Which US President born in 1946 was called The Comeback Kid?
12 Which leader Boris succeeded Mikhail Gorbachev?
13 Which eastern European country did Pope John Paul II come from?
14 What was the name of Nelson Mandela's wife when he was released from prison?
15 Which Prime Minister was known as The Iron Lady?
16 Which tennis player famously yelled 'You cannot be serious!'?
17 Lord Lloyd Webber, Jim Davidson and Bob Monkhouse have all famously supported which political party?
18 Which Arthur was the miners' leader in the 1980s?
19 Which soccer star recorded a rap song called Geordie Boys?
20 Which PM's wife of the latter half of the 20th century was made a High Court judge?
21 What is the first name of Dr Mowlam?
22 Which Julia was the first to present the news on BBC and ITV?
23 What colour suit is Independent MP Martin Bell famous for wearing?
24 British nurses Lucille McLauchlan and Deborah Parry were accused of
25 murdering an Australian colleague in which country?
24 Matthew Simmons hit the headlines after he was kicked by which then Man Utd French footballer?

Answers

Headline Makers

1 Mellor. **2** Jagger. **3** British. **4** Ronald Reagan. **5** Robin Cook. **6** Woodward. **7** Monica. **8** Martina Hingis. **9** Nelson Mandela. **10** Space. **11** Bill Clinton. **12** Yeltsin. **13** Poland. **14** Winnie. **15** Margaret Thatcher. **16** John McEnroe. **17** Tory. **18** Scargill. **19** Gascoigne. **20** Cherie Booth. **21** Mo. **22** Somerville. **23** White. **24** Saudi Arabia. **25** Eric Cantona.

Quiz 32 Pot Luck

Level 1

1 Which Sinatra song manages to rhyme a line with 'shy way'?
2 Which politician was nicknamed 'Bambi'?
3 Henry Ford claimed that, 'History is...' what?
4 In the cost-a-lot-to-make movie *Waterworld* who played Mariner?
5 Rupert Murdoch comes from which country?
6 In 1996, which group of people voted themselves a 26% pay rise?
7 What name is shared by pop star sisters Dannii and Kylie?
8 Black activist Steve Biko died in which country in the 70s?
9 Which John was the star of the film *Grease*?
10 What colour are the Smurfs?
11 Mark Taylor played cricket for which country?
12 Which group had a 90s hit with These Are The Days of Our Lives?
13 What does the C stand for in LCD?
14 What did Tony and Cheri Blair call their youngest son?
15 Churchill, Sherman and Panzer were all developed as types of what?
16 Which motorway forms the Edinburgh to Glasgow route?
17 Who sang in the pop duo with Mel Appleby?
18 With which sport is Fred Couples associated?
19 Which Nigel was an 80s Chancellor?
20 What was the first name of jazz giant Ms Fitzgerald?
21 What is the occupation of Beryl Bainbridge?
22 Robert Menzies was Prime Minister of which country?
23 Which Irving penned the song White Christmas?
24 Who played Rachel Green in *Friends*?
25 Which country was racing's Niki Lauda born in?

Answers

Pot Luck

1 My Way. **2** Tony Blair. **3** Bunk. **4** Kevin Costner. **5** Australia. **6** MPs. **7** Minogue. **8** South Africa. **9** Travolta. **10** Blue. **11** Australia. **12** Queen. **13** Crystal. **14** Leo. **15** Tank. **16** M8. **17** Kim. **18** Golf. **19** Lawson. **20** Ella. **21** Novelist. **22** Australia. **23** Berlin. **24** Jennifer Aniston. **25** Austria.

Quiz 33 TV Comedy

Level 1

1 *Absolutely Fabulous* started life as a sketch on which comedy duo's show?
2 What was 'dropped' in the comedy about the Globelink newsroom?
3 How was David Jason's Sidney Charles Larkin known in *The Darling Buds of May*?
4 Which US actress Ellen was the star of *Ellen*?
5 Which sitcom was based in a French cafe in occupied France?
6 Who hosted *Fantasy Football League* with David Baddiel?
7 Which laconic comedian Dave first found fame on the Val Doonican show?
8 Which clerical sitcom was set on Craggy Island?
9 Which US series was about a lawyer called Ally?
10 Which Towers provided a comedy series for Torquay?
11 Who completed the trio with Filthy and Rich in the *Young Ones* styled comedy?
12 Who was Butt-Head's comedy partner?
13 Which female duo first found fame on *The Comic Strip Presents*?
14 How many friends were there in *Friends*?
15 Which Ruby was the American in *Girls On Top*?
16 Which Benny created Fred Scuttle and Professor Marvel in his saucy seaside postcard style show?
17 *Goodnight Sweetheart* was based in the 90s and which other decade?
18 Which 90s sitcom was about two sisters in Chigwell with a man-mad neighbour?
19 Which Tony lived at 23 Railway Cuttings, East Cheam?
20 Who accompanied Hale in the sketches of The Two Rons?
21 Which Mr Atkinson played Blackadder?
22 Which sitcom was based on writer Jimmy Perry's experiences in the Home Guard?
23 Which Harry created Wayne and Waynetta Slob?
24 In which city was *Bread* set?
25 Which 60s singer Adam played the title role in *Budgie*?

Answers

TV Comedy

1 French & Saunders. **2** The Dead Donkey. **3** Pop. **4** Ellen DeGeneres. **5** Allo Allo. **6** Frank Skinner. **7** Allen. **8** Father Ted. **9** Ally McBeal. **10** Fawlty Towers. **11** Catflap. **12** Beavis. **13** French & Saunders. **14** Six. **15** Wax. **16** Hill. **17** 1940s. **18** Birds of a Feather. **19** Hancock. **20** Pace. **21** Rowan. **22** Dad's Army. **23** Enfield. **24** Liverpool. **25** Faith.

Quiz 34 CORONATION ST. Level 1

1996

1 How many episodes did *Coronation Street* celebrate reaching this year: 3000, 4000 or 5000?
2 Who played Kelly Thomson?
3 Who was Sue Jeffers?
4 Who got married in a green dress from a charity shop and Doc Martens?
5 Who was punched by her husband and abandoned by the roadside?
6 Who was sent to Strangeways prison after becoming involved with Malcolm Fox?
7 Who did he try to persuade to take the blame for him?
8 Who became addicted to scratch cards and catalogue shopping?
9 Name the racehorse that Jack, Fred, Gary, Don Brennan collectively bought in a syndicate.
10 Who managed the Hourglass Wine Bar?
11 Who lent Fiona the money to buy the hair salon?
12 Who bought Gary Mallett's motorbike?
13 Who was sent to prison for non-payment of a TV licence fine?
14 Who received marriage proposals from Maud Grimes and Phyllis Pearce?
15 Who did Claire Palmer and daughter Becky move in with?
16 Whose house was featured in a local history tour as the site of Ernie Bishop's death?
17 Which local girl did Alec try to launch as a singer?
18 Who bought Number 5 from Nick Tilsley?
19 What did Nick spend the money on?
20 Who bought No. 12 from Reg Holdsworth?
21 Who left his wife for supermarket heiress Yvonne Bannister?
22 Who played policeman Alan McKenna?
23 How much did the Hortens pay Terry for Tommy Duckworth?
24 Who did Mike Baldwin trick into buying the garage at an inflated price?
25 Who did Vera believe was 'haunting' the Rovers?

Answers

Coronation Street – 1996

1 4000. **2** Sarah Moffett. **3** Weatherfield Comprehensive's headmistress. **4** Tracy Barlow-Preston. **5** Liz McDonald. **6** Steve McDonald. **7** Vicky. **8** Joyce Smedley. **9** Betty's Hot Shot. **10** Liz McDonald. **11** Her brother. **12** Samantha Failsworth. **13** Tricia Armstrong. **14** Percy. **15** Des. **16** The Wiltons. **17** Fiona. **18** Don. **19** Private education in Canada. **20** Alec Gilroy. **21** Reg. **22** Glen Hugill. **23** £10,000. **24** Don. **25** Ivy.

Quiz 35 Sporting Who's Who

Level 1

1 Who was the youngest Wimbledon women's champion of the century?
2 In which country was Greg Rusedski born?
3 Which manager was in charge of Nottm Forest for over 18 years?
4 Which boxer took to wearing a monocle?
5 Who was the first member of the Royal family to be BBC Sports Personality Of The Year?
6 Who was Man Utd's captain in the 1999 European Champions' Cup Final?
7 Who was the first rugby union player to reach 50 international tries?
8 Who was England's captain in cricket's 1999 World Cup?
9 Boxer Naseem Hamed was brought up in which English city?
10 Who didn't make England's World Cup squad for France after much publicised kebab-consuming sessions?
11 What nickname was given to basketball's Wilt Chamberlain?
12 Who was Edson Arantes do Nascimento?
13 Who is France's most successful motor racing driver of all time?
14 Who resigned as Welsh manager in 1999?
15 Which British runner became the oldest ever Olympic 100m winner?
16 Who was the first person to run a mile in under four minutes?
17 What was Dean's first name in the Torvill & Dean skating partnership?
18 Who was known as 'The Golden Bear'?
19 Who was the Joe who first defeated Muhammad Ali?
20 In the 90s who advertised Umbro, McDonalds and Lucozade?
21 In the 90s who was known as 'Bumble'?
22 Who was the first manager to have taken charge of both Australia and England?
23 In the 96 Olympics which Michael won both 200 and 400m?
24 What name was shared by motor racing's brothers Emerson and Wilson?
25 Which tennis player had a father named Peter who was jailed for tax irregularities?

Answers

Sporting Who's Who
1 Martina Hingis. **2** Canada. **3** Brian Clough. **4** Chris Eubank. **5** Princess Anne. **6** Schmeichel. **7** David Campese. **8** Alec Stewart. **9** Sheffield. **10** Paul Gascoigne. **11** The Stilt. **12** Pele. **13** Alain Prost. **14** Bobby Gould. **15** Linford Christie. **16** Roger Bannister. **17** Christopher. **18** Jack Nicklaus. **19** Frazier. **20** Alan Shearer. **21** David Lloyd. **22** Terry Venables. **23** Johnson. **24** Fittipaldi. **25** Steffi Graf.

Quiz 36 Pot Luck

Level 1

1 How was tycoon Robert Maxwell said to have died?
2 In the 90s what was Britain's busiest ferry passenger port?
3 What sort of Bottom did Noel Edmonds introduce to TV?
4 Which soccer side does former PM John Major support?
5 Which royal ship was decommissioned in 1997?
6 Under what name have Barry, Maurice and Robin been operating for over 30 years?
7 Which Kenneth was the independent prosecutor in the Bill Clinton affair?
8 In which country did Marilyn Monroe die?
9 Which team won the 1996 cricket World Cup?
10 Who was the first female presenter of the National Lottery?
11 What colour did guests wear for Mel B's wedding?
12 Nigel Short represented England at which indoor sport?
13 Preston is the administrative centre of which English county?
14 Which Kelvin used to edit *The Sun*?
15 What does the O stand for in HMSO?
16 What was Gary's surname in *Goodnight Sweetheart*?
17 In which city was Jan Smuts airport built?
18 With which sport is Vivian Richards associated?
19 Which Aretha has been dubbed the Queen Of Soul?
20 Which family feature in *The Darling Buds Of May*?
21 In which decade did Sir Cliff Richard receive his knighthood?
22 How many couples made up the main cast of *The Good Life*?
23 Fictional Grange Hill Comprehensive is set in which real city?
24 Peter Schmeichel played soccer for which country?
25 Which musical features the song As Long As He Needs Me?

Answers

Pot Luck

1 Drowned. **2** Dover. **3** Crinkley. **4** Chelsea. **5** Britannia. **6** The Bee Gees. **7** Starr. **8** United States. **9** Sri Lanka. **10** Anthea Turner. **11** White. **12** Chess. **13** Lancashire. **14** McKenzie. **15** Office. **16** Sparrow. **17** Johannesburg. **18** Cricket. **19** Franklin. **20** Larkins. **21** 90s. **22** Two. **23** London. **24** Denmark. **25** Oliver.

Quiz 37 Action Movies

Level 1

1 Which Steven directed *Saving Private Ryan*?
2 *Air Force One* deals with the holding to ransom of whom?
3 Which Tom played spy Ethan Hunt in *Mission: Impossible*?
4 Which 90s James Bond starred in *Dante's Peak*?
5 Which unlucky Apollo Mission was filmed in 1995 with Tom Hanks?
6 Which Judge from 2000 AD comic appeared on film in 1995?
7 Which Australian actor starred in and directed *Braveheart*?
8 Which Antarctic creature gives its name to the villain played by Danny De Vito in *Batman Returns*?
9 What type of creatures were Donatello, Raphael, Michaelangelo and Leonardo?
10 What is the profession of Harrison Ford in the Indiana Jones movies?
11 In which city does the action of Batman take place?
12 Which month is part of the title of the film where Tom Cruise plays war veteran Ron Kovic?
13 Which actor Daniel starred as Hawkeye in *The Last of the Mohicans*?
14 In which series of films were Danny Glover and Mel Gibson teamed in 1987, 1989, 1992 and 1998?
15 *Top Gun* is about which of the armed services?
16 The action of *The Killing Fields* takes place in which country?
17 What was the first Bond movie with Sean Connery?
18 Which actor, famous for spaghetti westerns, got the role in *Dirty Harry* after Frank Sinatra dropped out?
19 Which Gene played Popeye Doyle in *The French Connection*?
20 *The Poseidon Adventure* is about a disaster on what type of transport?
21 *Enter the Dragon* was the first US kung fu film of which Mr Lee?
22 In which city does Robert de Niro operate as a sinister Taxi Driver?
23 *The Shootist* was the last film to star which John, famous for his western roles?
24 Which creature was a threat to holidaymakers in *Jaws*?
25 In which 1999 film did Sean Connery star with Catherine Zeta Jones?

Answers

Action Movies

1 Spielberg. **2** US President. **3** Cruise. **4** Pierce Brosnan. **5** 13. **6** Dredd. **7** Mel Gibson. **8** Penguin. **9** Turtles. **10** Archaeologist. **11** Gotham. **12** July. **13** Day-Lewis. **14** Lethal Weapon. **15** Air Force. **16** Cambodia. **17** Dr No. **18** Clint Eastwood. **19** Hackman. **20** Ship. **21** Bruce. **22** New York. **23** Wayne. **24** Shark. **25** Entrapment.

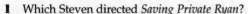

Quiz 38 CORONATION ST. Level 1

Pot Luck

1 Which comedienne and *Smack The Pony* star played a temptress who broke up Mike Baldwin's marriage to Alma?
2 What were the council planning to do to Coronation Street in December 2000, which prompted the 'Save Our Street' campaign?
3 What was on the top of Derek Wilton's company car?
4 Which 1970s pop star made a guest appearance in the live episode in December 2000 and wished the Street's residents a Merry Christmas?
5 Name Steve McDonald and Vik Desai's cab firm.
6 What is the name of the recreation ground in Weatherfield where Toyah, Emily and Spider climbed a tree in order to stop the council developing the land?
7 What is Maxine's job?
8 What stage name does the stripper Sam Kingston use?
9 PM Tony Blair has stood behind the bar of the Rovers: True or false?
10 What was Deirdre's maiden name?
11 What romantic gift did Curly buy for Raquel on their engagement?
12 What is the relationship between Toyah and Leanne Battersby?
13 Who lives on Grasmere Drive?
14 What garden ornaments did Derek Wilton have?
15 Where did Raquel go when she left Curly?
16 What is Kevin Webster's dad called?
17 What nationality is Jim McDonald?
18 What newspaper did Ken Barlow used to work on?
19 What sport did Duggie Ferguson used to play?
20 What garments are made in Mike Baldwin's factory?
21 Which actor plays Martin Platt?
22 Name either of the streets adjacent to Coronation Street.
23 Which Monkee appeared in *Coronation Street* as a child playing Ena Sharples' grandson?
24 Name all Ken's children and stepchildren.
25 What was Des Barnes' profession?

Answers

Coronation Street – Pot Luck

1 Fiona Allen. **2** Tarmac the cobbles. **3** A huge paper clip. **4** Noddy Holder from Slade. **5** Street Cars. **6** The Red Rec. **7** Hairdresser. **8** The Masked Python. **9** True. **10** Hunt. **11** A star called Mrs Raquel Watts. **12** Step sisters. **13** Audrey Roberts. **14** Gnomes. **15** Kuala Lumpur. **16** Bill Webster. **17** Irish. **18** The *Weatherfield Recorder*. **19** Rugby. **20** Lingerie. **21** Sean Wilson. **22** Viaduct Street or Rosamund Street. **23** Davy Jones. **24** Susan (deceased), Peter, Daniel, Tracy. **25** Bookie.

Quiz 39 On the Road

Level 1

1 Which city is the southernmost point of the A1?
2 What colour are the lines in a box junction?
3 How frequently must a three-year-old car have an MOT in Great Britain?
4 What colour Cross Code gives advice on crossing the road?
5 What does a red and amber traffic light mean?
6 On the road, what shape are most warning signs?
7 Which name for a very large truck gets its name from an Indian god?
8 Which London road race is held annually for professionals and those raising money for charity?
9 Which registration letter was the first to be introduced in a month other than August?
10 Which 24 Hour Race in France uses normal roads as part of the race track?
11 What is the minimum number of L plates a learner driver must have?
12 What is the type of driving licence a learner driver must have called?
13 Which government publication for all road users was first published in 1931?
14 Which Garages near Oxford originally produced the MG sports car?
15 The Milk Race is an annual race around Britain's roads on what form of transport?
16 How is the London Orbital Motorway also known?
17 An orange badge displayed in a car's windscreen means the driver is what?
18 Which Way begins West of Sheffield and stretches to Southern Scotland?
19 A memorial to which Queen stands in front of Buckingham Palace?
20 Which motoring association has an actual club in London, as its name implies?
21 Which national BBC Radio news and sport station broadcasts travel updates, usually every 15 minutes?
22 What colour card allows a motorist to travel abroad?
23 The letter H on a road sign means?
24 What does G stand for in HGV?
25 What colour is the background of motorway signs?

Answers

On the Road

1 London. **2** Yellow. **3** Once a year. **4** Green. **5** Stop. **6** Triangular. **7** Juggernaut. **8** Marathon. **9** T. **10** Le Mans. **11** Two. **12** Provisional. **13** Highway Code. **14** Morris. **15** Cycles. **16** M25. **17** Disabled. **18** Pennine Way. **19** Victoria. **20** RAC - Royal Automobile Club. **21** Radio 5 Live. **22** Green. **23** Hospital. **24** Goods. **25** Blue.

Quiz 40 Pot Luck

Level 1

1 In which Scottish town did Thomas Hamilton carry out a shooting atrocity?
2 Which Spice Girl wore a Union Jack dress?
3 Who resigned as Conservative Party leader in 2001?
4 What colour goes with white and red on the Bulgarian flag?
5 Soccer's Peter Nicholas won 73 international caps for which country?
6 Princess Grace of Monaco died after an accident in which form of transport?
7 In books and pop music, who tidied up on Wimbledon Common?
8 Who produced the car known as The Silver Ghost ?
9 Which TV Michael is linked with underestimating the 1987 hurricanes?
10 Which musical does Cabaret come from?
11 The driving test introduced a written section in which decade?
12 Who returned to run the Queen Vic in 2001?
13 With which sport is Helena Sukova associated?
14 Which country has B as its international vehicle registration letter?
15 The description situation comedy is usually shortened to what?
16 What does the S stand for in GCSE?
17 Matlock is the administrative centre of which English county?
18 How many Goodies were there?
19 Who was the British monarch at the start of the 20th century?
20 Which folksinger Joan featured in the civil rights and anti-Vietnam movements?
21 What does the letter S stand for in AIDS?
22 *Grace and Favour* was the sequel to which sitcom about Grace Brothers?
23 What instrument did 50s and 60s star Russ Conway play?
24 Which country did Bjorn Borg come from?
25 On TV, what colour was Inspector Morse's jag?

Answers

Pot Luck

1 Dunblane. **1** Geri Halliwell - Ginger Spice. **3** William Hague. **4** Green. **5** Wales. **6** Car. **7** The Wombles. **8** Rolls Royce. **9** Fish. **10** Cabaret. **11** 90s. **12** Sharon Watts. **13** Tennis. **14** Belgium. **15** Sitcom. **16** Secondary. **17** Derbyshire. **18** Three. **19** Victoria. **20** Baez. **21** Syndrome. **22**Are You Being Served? **23** Piano. **24** Sweden. **25** Red.

Quiz 41 Music - Who's Who

Level 1

1 Who wrote the lyrics for the 90s song Candle In The Wind?
2 Who is the Sid of Nancy and Sid notoriety?
3 Who is Blur's lead singer?
4 Who led the Blonde Ambition world tour of 1990?
5 Who wrote, sang and played the guitar on The Streets of London?
6 Which group's music featured in the frock horror film *Priscilla Queen Of The Desert* ?
7 Who had his first No 1 in the 70s with Maggie May?
8 Who first hit the top ten with Cornflake Girl?
9 Who said Go West in 1993?
10 Who was the Gary who sang with the Union Gap?
11 Who created the character Ziggy Stardust?
12 Who was 'The Boss'?
13 Under what name had the late Mary O'Brien been famous?
14 Who did Louise Nurding leave in 1995?
15 Who charted by saying Eh-Oh!?
16 Who had a singer Roger Daltrey and a drummer Keith Moon?
17 Which country does Bjork come from?
18 Who has been both Bad and Dangerous?
19 Who linked up with Aitken and Waterman?
20 Who was backed by Blockheads?
21 Who first charted back in the 70s with Seven Seas Of Rhye?
22 Who was Addicted to Love in the 80s?
23 Who had a hit with Orinoco Flow?
24 Who was backed by the Wailers?
25 Who was the big O?

Answers

Music – Who's Who

1 Bernie Taupin. **2** Sid Vicious. **3** Damon Albarn. **4** Madonna. **5** Ralph McTell. **6** Abba. **7** Rod Stewart. **8** Tori Amos. **9** Pet Shop Boys. **10** Puckett. **11** David Bowie. **12** Bruce Springsteen. **13** Dusty Springfield. **14** Eternal. **15** Teletubbies. **16** The Who. **17** Iceland. **18** Michael Jackson. **19** Stock. **20** Ian Dury. **21** Queen. **22** Robert Palmer. **23** Enya. **24** Bob Marley. **25** Roy Orbison.

Quiz 42 CORONATION ST.

Level 1

1997

1 Which pensioner made his final appearance this year?
2 Which controversial 'family from hell' moved into Number 5?
3 Who had an affair with Kevin Webster?
4 How did Billy Williams die?
5 Who tried to frame Samantha Failsworth for shoplifting from Firmans?
6 Angie Freeman dated Chris Collins this year: True or false?
7 Whose baby was born five weeks early?
8 Which character always called Derek Wilton 'Dirk' – even at his funeral?
9 Where did Mavis move to after Derek's death?
10 Which American city did Jack and Vera win a holiday to?
11 Who threw the Battersbys' CD player out of the window?
12 Who left Coronation Street with boyfriend Ray Thorpe?
13 What did Nick Tilsley study at the tech?
14 Who was 'Lazarus the Living Corpse'?
15 Who sold counterfeit K-bec goods on the market in a deal with Mike Baldwin?
16 Who did the Duckworths take on as a partner at the Rovers?
17 Who did Samantha Failsworth talk into doing a parachute jump with her?
18 Who ran a dating agency for older people called Golden Years?
19 Which ex-schoolteacher became one of his most popular male escorts?
20 Who had a secret husband called Ritchie Fitzgerald?
21 Who dated ex-con Frazer Henderson?
22 What was the cause of Judy Mallett's suspected infertility?
23 Who spent a night stranded on the golf course with a broken leg?
24 Whose baby did the Malletts buy, calling her Katie Joyce?
25 And what did her real mum change her name to when she took her back?

Answers

Coronation Street – 1997

1 Percy. **2** The Battersbys. **3** Natalie Horrocks. **4** Heart Attack. **5** Anne Malone. **6** True. **7** Tricia's baby, Brad Armstrong. **8** Norris. **9** The Lake District. **10** Las Vegas. **11** Curly. **12** Tricia Armstrong. **13** PE. **14** A friend of Alec's who helped him with a holiday competition scam. **15** Sally Webster. **16** Alec. **17** Des. **18** Alec. **19** Ken. 20 Samantha. **21** Liz McDonald. **22** An abortion at 16. **23** Fred Elliot. **24** Zoe Tattersall. **25** Shannon Jade.

Quiz 43 80s Newsround

Level 1

1 Which Scottish border town was the scene of a jumbo jet disaster?
2 Who or what was Mary Rose, making an appearance after 500 years?
3 Which soap had Britain asking, 'Who shot JR?'?
4 Which US President was linked with the 'Star Wars' policy?
5 An IRA car bomb was detonated outside which major London store?
6 Which Neil was elected leader of the Labour Party?
7 Who won the ladies' singles most times at Wimbledon in the 80s?
8 Which John portrayed The Elephant Man on film?
9 Solidarity was the mass movement of the people in which country?
10 Sarah Ferguson became Duchess of where?
11 What kind of disaster claimed some 100,000 lives in Armenia in 1988?
12 Which golfer Sandy triumphed at the US Masters?
13 In 1980 the SAS spectacularly freed hostages in which embassy in London?
14 Don't Die Of Ignorance was the message put out to combat which disease?
15 Which tennis ace completed his fifth successive Wimbledon singles triumph?
16 What did the L stand for in GLC?
17 Who became the world's youngest ever boxing heavyweight champion?
18 Which Jeffrey resigned as deputy chairman of the Tory party?
19 Which city was devastated by an earthquake in 1985 and then hosted the World Cup in 1986?
20 What was the so-called Black day for the City in the late 80s?
21 There was fighting around Port Stanley on which Islands?
22 Tiananmen Square was a scene of conflict in which country?
23 In which English city were Liverpool supporters crushed by crowds at an FA Cup semi final?
24 Which organisation had their ship the *Rainbow Warrior* sunk?
25 What type of disaster happened at Bradford City's stadium?

Answers

80s Newsround

1 Lockerbie. **2** Ship. **3** Dallas. **4** Reagan. **5** Harrods. **6** Kinnock. **7** Martina Navratilova. **8** Hurt. **9** Poland. **10** York. **11** Earthquake. **12** Lyle. **13** Iranian. **14** AIDS. **15** Bjorn Borg. **16** London. **17** Mike Tyson. **18** Archer. **19** Mexico. **20** Monday. **21** Falkland Islands. **22** China. **23** Sheffield. **24** Greenpeace. **25** Fire.

Quiz 44 Pot Luck

Level 1

1 Which 90s British political leader gave his marriage vows in Welsh?
2 With which sport is Shaquille O'Neal associated?
3 What type of skirt was the main fashion style of the 60s?
4 In *Notting Hill* what does the Hugh Grant character deal in?
5 In the 90s certain Newcastle Utd directors described the women of the area as being like which creatures?
6 Chancellor Helmut Kohl led which country in the 80s and 90s?
7 What does the G mean in GBH?
8 Which comedian Mike called himself The Rochdale Cowboy?
9 The William Tell Overture provided the title music to which TV western?
10 In finance what does the E in ERM stand for?
11 Which motorway links Carlisle to the Midlands?
12 What is the first name of sci-fi writer Asimov?
13 Which Hank played lead guitar with The Shadows?
14 Who did Jelena Dokic beat in the first round of Wimbledon 1999?
15 Who had a 90s No 1 with Don't Look Back In Anger?
16 In 1970 Germaine Greer produced the feminist book *The Female* what?
17 Keir Hardie was the first leader of which 20th C political party?
18 In which country is Archangel airport?
19 Quincy Jones was associated with which brass instrument?
20 Buster Mottram represented Britain at which sport?
21 What type of tragedy blighted Omagh in 1998?
22 What was the surname of Harry Enfield's creations Wayne and Waynetta?
23 Which Simon sang with Duran Duran?
24 Which Raymond wrote the detective novel *Farewell My Lovely*?
25 Relating to the TV show Auntie's Bloomers, who is Auntie?

Answers

Pot Luck

1 William Hague. **2** Basketball. **3** Mini. **4** Books. **5** Dogs. **6** Germany. **7** Grievous. **8** Harding. **9** The Lone Ranger. **10** Exchange. **11** M6. **12** Isaac. **13** Marvin. **14** Martina Hingis. **15** Oasis. **16** Eunuch. **17** Labour. **18** Russia. **19** Trumpet. **20** Tennis. **21** Bomb. **22** Slob. **23** Le Bon. **24** Chandler. **25** The BBC.

Quiz 45 Heroes & Villains

Level 1

1 In which US city was Al Capone crime king during the Prohibition?
2 Which US President George was the US's youngest ever pilot in WWII?
3 Which American leader did Lee Harvey Oswald assassinate?
4 What was the first name of Mr Waite held hostage in Beirut in the 1980s?
5 In 1987 Lester Piggott was jailed for not paying what?
6 In 1995 O.J. Simpson was cleared of murdering which of his relatives?
7 Pol Pot led the Khmer Rouge on which continent?
8 Archbishop Desmond Tutu fought for civil rights in which country?
9 Which ex-Minister Aitken was jailed in 1999 over a failed libel case?
10 Simon Weston became famous for his courage following horrific injuries in which war?
11 What nationality was Brian Keenan, held hostage with John McCarthy?
12 Which nickname was given to Boston murderer Albert de Salvo?
13 Which Lord vanished after his children's nanny was found murdered?
14 Which media magnate mysteriously disappeared off his yacht in 1991?
15 John Glenn became the oldest man to travel where when he boarded the *Discovery* in 1998?
16 Richard Bacon resigned from which TV show after drug allegations?
17 Which part of Evander Holyfield did Mike Tyson bite off during a fight?
18 Prosecutor Kenneth Starr was involved in impeachment proceedings against which US President?
19 Which French footballer David was chosen to publicise the dangers of landmines after the death of Diana Princess of Wales?
20 Which controversial politician Ann became Shadow Home Secretary in William Hague's 1999 Shadow Cabinet reshuffle?
21 Which colour precedes the name of Mr Adair, the firefighter who fought the Piper Alpha blaze in the 1980s?
22 What was the occupation of Nick Leeson when he brought down Barings?
23 Which Duchess had a satellite TV show called *Surviving Life*?
24 What was the nationality of the driver of the car in which Princess Diana died?
25 Who left his job on Radio 1 because he didn't want to work on Fridays?

Answers

Heoroes & Villains
1 Chicago. **2** Bush. **3** John F Kennedy. **4** Terry. **5** Taxes. **6** His wife. **7** Asia. **8** South Africa. **9** Jonathan. **10** Falklands. **11** Irish. **12** Strangler. **13** Lucan. **14** Robert Maxwell. **15** Space. **16** Blue Peter. **17** Ear. **18** Clinton. **19** Ginola. **20** Widdecombe. **21** Red. **22** Banker. **23** York. **24** French. **25** Chris Evans.

Quiz 46 CORONATION ST. Level 1

Pot Luck

1 Name the Welsh family consisting of Idris, Vera, Tricia and Megan who ran the Corner Shop in the 1970s.
2 Who played Ena Sharples?
3 Which number on Coronation Street do Janice and Les Battersby live at?
4 Who fathered Fiona Middleton's baby?
5 What was the name of Roy's Rolls when Alma Sedgewick owned it?
6 Who played Brian Tilsley?
7 Who played Phyllis Pearce?
8 What did Rita's husband, Ted Sullivan, do for a living?
9 Two popular longstanding *Coronation Street* actresses were awarded the MBE in 2000. Who were they?
10 What relation was Jenny Bradley to Rita?
11 Which actress, who later appeared in *Bad Girls*, played Zoe Tattersall?
12 What is Mike Baldwin's middle name?
13 Who died on Ashley and Maxine's wedding day?
14 What is the local hospital called?
15 How did Susan Barlow die?
16 Who played Maureen Holdsworth?
17 Whose autobiography is called *Ken and Me*?
18 Which former *Coronation Street* actor is married to Sue Nicholls?
19 Who played Don Brennan?
20 Which Barlow woman was *not* married to Ken: Valerie, Janet or Irma?
21 Which *Coronation Street* actress was an internationally famous singer in the 1940s?
22 Sally Webster was once a registered childminder: True or false?
23 In 1967, what vehicle crashed off the viaduct and into Coronation Street?
24 Which redheaded *Coronation Street* character was famous for wearing very short skirts?
25 How many husbands has Rita had?

Answers

Coronation Street – Pot Luck

1 The Hopkins family. **2** Violet Carson. **3** Number five. **4** Alan McKenna. **5** Jim's Cafe **6** Chris Quentin. **7** Jill Summers. **8** A sweets salesman (retired). **9** Liz Dawn and Betty Driver. **10** Foster daughter, then unofficial stepdaughter. **11** Joanne Froggatt. **12** Vernon. **13** Judy Mallett. **14** Weatherfield General. **15** In a car crash. **16** Sherrie Hewson. **17** William Roache. **18** Mark Eden. **19** Geoff Hinsliffe. **20** Irma. **21** Betty Driver. **22** True. **23** A train. **24** Liz McDonald. **25** Two – Len Fairclough and Ted Sullivan.

Quiz 47 TV Cops & Robbers

Level 1

1 Which US cop show was set in Hill Street Station?
2 PC Rowan upheld law and order in Aidensfield in which series?
3 Which Inspector was famous for his red Jag, crosswords and Wagner?
4 Which 80s hit was set on the island of Jersey?
5 Which John starred as Kavanagh QC?
6 Which crime series with Telly Savalas was known as *The Lion Without a Mane* in Germany?
7 Which 90s series was dubbed Between the Sheets because of its main character's personal affairs?
8 What was the profession of medieval sleuth Cadfael?
9 Where was the Vice tackled by Sonny Crockett and Ricardo Tubbs?
10 Which 80s/90s show once held a 30 minute slot three times a week?
11 Which unmarried female detective was created by Agatha Christie?
12 Which Lynda La Plante series featured DCI Jane Tennison?
13 In which country was *Prisoner: Cell Block H* set?
14 Which show featured private eye Jim Rockford?
15 Which Geordie actor Jimmy starred as Spender?
16 How was Ken Hutchinson known in the 70s series with David Soul and Paul Michael Glaser?
17 In which series did Robbie Coltrane play Fitz?
18 Which Hamish operated in Lochdubh?
19 On which channel was *LA Law* first broadcast in the UK?
20 Who was Dalziel's detective partner, from the novels by Reginald Hill?
21 Which series with Dennis Waterman and John Thaw got its name from the rhyming slang for Flying Squad?
22 What sort of Line was a police sitcom with Rowan Atkinson?
23 In which Dutch city did *Van der Valk* take place?
24 Which Cars provided police transport in the classic crime series of the 60s and 70s?
25 Which thriller series had a team of crime fighters with lots of electronic devices to help with their investigations?

Answers

TV Cops & Robbers

1 Hill Street Blues. **2** Heartbeat. **3** Morse. **4** Bergerac. **5** Thaw. **6** Kojak. **7** Between the Lines. **8** Monk. **9** Miami. **10** The Bill. **11** Miss Marple. **12** Prime Suspect. **13** Australia. **14** The Rockford Files. **15** Nail. **16** Hutch. **17** Cracker. **18** Macbeth. **19** ITV. **20** Pascoe. **21** The Sweeney. **22** Thin Blue. **23** Amsterdam. **24** Z Cars. **25** Bugs.

Quiz 48 CORONATION ST.

Level 1

Pot Luck

1. Which other soap has Gabrielle Glaister, who played Debs Brownlow, appeared in?
2. What was Linda Baldwin's maiden name?
3. *Coronation Street* was originally going to be called *Florizel Street*: True or false?
4. Which member of the Royal Family made a guest appearance in *Coronation Street* in October 2000?
5. Which actress plays Rita Sullivan?
6. Who killed Jez Quigley?
7. Roy Barraclough (Alec Gilroy) was once part of double act with which well-loved comedian?
8. Sarah Lancashire's father was once a writer on *Coronation Street*. True or false?
9. What religion was Ivy Tilsley?
10. Who had a budgie called Randy?
11. What pet did Mavis and Derek Wilton have?
12. Which *Coronation Street* actress is the daughter of a peer?
13. Which anniversary did *Coronation Street* celebrate in December 2000?
14. Who plays Sally Webster?
15. What was Hayley's first name before she became a woman?
16. Name the cruise company Alec Gilroy worked for.
17. Who was 'The Weatherfield One'?
18. Which McDonald male has *not* been in prison?
19. Who played Len Fairclough?
20. Which Alan Bleasdale drama did Jane (Leanne Battersby) Danson appear in as a child actress?
21. What was Mavis Wilton's maiden name?
22. What job did Vera Duckworth do when she first appeared in *Coronation Street*?
23. What job did Betty Williams' first husband do?
24. What sort of shop did Sally and Danny run?
25. What is Gail Platt's maiden name?

Answers

Coronation Street – Pot Luck

1 Brookside. **2** Sykes. **3** True. **4** Prince Charles. **5** Barbara Knox. **6** Jim McDonald. **7** Les Dawson. **8** True. **9** Catholic. **10** Percy Sugden. **11** A budgie. **12** Sue Nicholls. **13** Fortieth. **14** Sally Whittaker. **15** Harold. **16** Sunliners. **17** Deirdre Barlow. **18** Andy. **19** Peter Adamson. **20** GBH. **21** Riley. **22** Factory machinist. **23** Policeman. **24** Hardware. **25** Potter.

Quiz 49 Summer Sports

Level 1

1 How is British sportsman Francis Thompson more usually known?
2 Which county did Brian Lara first play for in England?
3 Which 30-plus player won his first golf Major at the 1998 US Masters?
4 Which country does tennis player Pat Rafter come from?
5 Which team play cricket at home at Grace Road?
6 Which golfer was Europe's leading moneywinner of 1998?
7 Who started his breakaway cricket 'Circus' in the 70s?
8 How many times did Ivan Lendl win Wimbledon singles?
9 Which cricketing county added Lightning to their name?
10 What is Denise Lewis's main athletic event?
11 Which British golfer regained the US Masters in 1996?
12 Who won Wimbledon in 1998 after twice losing in the final?
13 How many teams reached the second round of cricket's 1999 World Cup?
14 Which country does Goran Ivanisevic come from?
15 In which month is The Derby run?
16 What sport is the winner of the Harry Vardon trophy playing?
17 What is the specialist fielding position of India's Moin Khan?
18 Which Mark was captain of the European 1999 Ryder Cup team?
19 Which British Fred was a Wimbledon singles winner in the 1930s?
20 Athlete Zola Budd was born in which country?
21 Who captained the West Indies in the 1999 World Cup?
22 What sport is staged at the Roland Garros?
23 Which golfer split from his coach David Leadbetter in 1998?
24 How many Brits were in the top ten seeds for Wimbledon 1999?
25 Which phone company has sponsored the Derby?

Answers

Summer Sports

1 Daley Thompson. **2** Warwickshire. **3** Mark O'Meara. **4** Australia. **5** Leicestershire. **6** Colin Montgomerie. **7** Kerry Packer. **8** Never. **9** Lancashire. **10** Heptathlon. **11** Nick Faldo. **12** Jana Novotna. **13** Six. **14** Croatia. **15** June. **16** Golf. **17** Wicket keeper. **18** James. **19** Perry. **20** South Africa. **21** Brian Lara. **22** Tennis. **23** Nick Faldo. **24** Two. **25** Vodafone.

Quiz 50 CORONATION ST. Level 1

1998

1 Who had affairs with both Des Barnes and Chris Collins this year?
2 How long did Deirdre Rachid spend in prison?
3 What did Zoe Tattersall's baby die of?
4 Where did Alec Gilroy go to when he left Coronation Street this year?
5 Who fitted the leaky gas fire that almost killed Rita?
6 Who gave birth to twins on Christmas Day?
7 Who took a job as a nude model for Miranda Peters' art class?
8 Whose identity did Jon Lindsay assume in order to embezzle his money?
9 Who became trapped upstairs after refusing to pay Jim McDonald for work he did on their staircase?
10 Whose bed did Alec sneak into, believing it was Rita?
11 Who kidnapped Natalie Horrocks' cat?
12 Whose house did Jackie Dobbs break into and claim squatters' rights in?
13 Who ended up in a wheelchair after falling off some scaffolding?
14 Who pushed him off the scaffold?
15 Name the physiotherapist who ran off with his wife.
16 Who did Spider go out with after ditching his eco-warrior ex for eating a bacon sandwich?
17 Who did Des Barnes propose to and marry this year?
18 Who slept in a camper van on the street when his wife threw him out?
19 Who dated Dobber Dobson?
20 Who had an operation in Amsterdam?
21 Why was the Red Rec declared a site of historical interest?
22 How old was Leanne when she got married?
23 How did Des Barnes die?
24 Name the man who murdered Brian Tilsley and was released this year.
25 Who tried to set him up and resulted in him getting another prison sentence?

Answers

Coronation Street – 1998

1 Samantha Failsworth. **2** Three weeks. **3** Meningitis. **4** Brighton. **5** Steve McDonald. **6** Judy Mallett. **7** Nick Tilsley. **8** Captain Jenkins, a pilot. **9** The Duckworths. **10** Betty's. **11** Samantha. **12** Curly's. **13** Jim McDonald. **14** Steve McDonald. **15** Michael Wall. **16** Lorraine Brownlow. **17** Natalie Horrocks. **18** Les Battersby. **19** Toyah Battersby. **20** Hayley. **21** Roman remains were found there. **22** Sixteen. **23** He was beaten up by thugs looking for Tony Horrocks. **24** Darren Whately. **25** Nick and Leanne Tilsley.

Quiz 51 90s Movies

Level 1

1 Where are the Sliding Doors in the movie with Gwyneth Paltrow?
2 The action of *Saving Private Ryan* takes place during which war?
3 In which movie is Truman Burbank a popular character?
4 Which ex 007 played the Scottish villain in The Avengers?
5 In *Doctor Dolittle* Eddie Murphy has the ability to talk to whom?
6 Which Zorro film was released in 1998?
7 Which giant lizard was the star of the 1998 movie with Matthew Broderick?
8 Which star of ER played Batman in the 1997 *Batman & Robin*?
9 What was the first Spice Girls' film called?
10 Which part does Matt Damon play in *Good Will Hunting*?
11 Which 1996 remake replaced animated dogs with real ones and starred Glenn Close?
12 Which Fiennes starred in *The English Patient*?
13 Which 90s film of a Shakespeare play starred Leonardo DiCaprio and Claire Daines?
14 In which country of the UK was *Trainspotting* set?
15 In *Batman Forever* which villain was played by Jim Carrey?
16 What sort of animal was *Babe*?
17 Which Disney movie was based on the life of a native North American?
18 What was the occupation of Susan Sarandon in *Dead Man Walking*?
19 Which Story was the first ever completely computer animated movie?
20 Which knighted British pop star wrote the music for *The Lion King*?
21 *Philadelphia* became the first mainstream Hollywood film to tackle which disease?
22 Which blonde famously crossed her legs in *Basic Instinct*?
23 Who shared the title with Thelma in the 1991 film directed by Ridley Scott?
24 In which town was *The Full Monty* set?
25 Val Kilmer played Jim Morrison in the 1991 movie about which rock band?

Answers

90s Movies

1 Tube Train. **2** WWII. **3** The Truman Show. **4** Sean Connery. **5** Animals. **6** The Mask of Zorro. **7** Godzilla. **8** George Clooney. **9** Spiceworld: The Movie. **10** Will Hunting **11** 101 Dalmatians. **12** Ralph. **13** Romeo & Juliet. **14** Scotland. **15** The Riddler. **16** Pig . **17** Pocahontas. **18** Nun. **19** Toy Story. **20** Elton John. **21** AIDS. **22** Sharon Stone. **23** Louise. **24** Sheffield. **25** The Doors.

Quiz 52 Pot Luck

Level 1

1 Which MP John got a soaking at the Brit Awards?
2 Which cookery writer produced a Summer and a Winter Collection which rocketed to the top of the bestseller list?
3 Dock Of The Bay was a hit for which singer after his death?
4 Which Welshman Colin became a world record holder in hurdling?
5 The movie *Platoon* was about war in which country?
6 What was the nickname of US President Dwight Eisenhower?
7 White and what other colour feature on the Canadian flag?
8 An accident in which sporting activity claimed Sonny Bono's life?
9 Which sitcom has had elderly characters called Foggy Dewhurst, Seymour Utterthwaite and Wally Batty?
10 In which sport did John Lloyd represented Britain?
11 What does the D stand for in a DIY store?
12 In the 90s Paul Keating was Prime Minister of which country?
13 Which Melvyn is a TV arts presenter and a novelist?
14 The deepwater port of Alicante was built in which country?
15 Darren Gough plays cricket for which county?
16 How many Likely Lads were there?
17 What are the international vehicle registration letters of Australia?
18 With which sport is Corey Pavin associated?
19 First World War flying ace Manfred von Richtofen was what colour Baron?
20 Quick Draw McGraw was what kind of cartoon creature?
21 Which of the Marx Brothers never spoke on film?
22 Tom Thumb and Little Gem were developed as types of what?
23 Virginia Bottomley has represented which party in parliament?
24 Which British boxer successfully defended his WBC heavyweight title in 1997?
25 Ray Charles was associated with which musical instrument?

Answers

Pot Luck

1 Prescott. **2** Delia Smith. **3** Otis Redding. **4** Jackson. **5** Vietnam. **6** Ike. **7** Red. **8** Skiing. **9** Last of the Summer Wine. **10** Tennis. **11** Do. **12** Australia. **13** Bragg. **14** Spain. **15** Yorkshire. **16** Two. **17** AUS. **18** Golf. **19** Red. **20** Horse. **21** Harpo. **22** Lettuce. **23** Conservative. **24** Lennox Lewis. **25** Piano.

Quiz 53 World Tour

Level 1

1 Which city is called Kapstad in Afrikaans?
2 Which language apart from English is an official language of Canada?
3 Okinawa is a volcano in which country?
4 In which country is an Afghani a unit of currency?
5 Lesotho is a southern African kingdom surrounded by which country?
6 Madagascar is off which coast of Africa?
7 Antigua and Barbuda lie in which Sea?
8 Ottawa is which country's capital?
9 The Chinese city of Beijing was previously known as what?
10 Argentina's east coast lies on which ocean?
11 Which South American Canal joins the Atlantic to the Pacific ocean?
12 What is the largest country in South America?
13 Which two letters follow the name of the US capital Washington?
14 What is the Great Barrier Reef made from?
15 Which Chinese landmark was viewed from space?
16 For most of the 20th Century St Petersburg has been named after which Soviet hero?
17 Which US holiday state has the Everglades National Park?
18 How was the Cote d'Ivoire previously known?
19 Which northerly US state, one of four beginning with A, joined the Union in 1959?
20 In the USA what is a zip code?
21 The Victoria Falls are shared between Zimbabwe and which other country beginning with the same letter?
22 Which US state is famous for Disneyland and the film industry?
23 Manhattan is a part of which US city?
24 What are the Islas Canarias in English?
25 Which Australian province has New at the beginning of its name?

Answers

World Tour

1 Cape Town. **2** French. **3** Japan. **4** Afghanistan. **5** South Africa. **6** East. **7** Caribbean. **8** Canada. **9** Peking. **10** Atlantic. **11** Panama. **12** Brazil. **13** DC. **14** Coral. **15** Great Wall of China. **16** Lenin. **17** Florida. **18** Ivory Coast. **19** Alaska. **20** Post code. **21** Zambia. **22** California. **23** New York. **24** Canary Islands. **25** South Wales.

Quiz 54 CORONATION ST. Level 1

Pot Luck

1 What is the view on the opening credits of the programme?
2 What is the colour of the cat seen on the opening credits?
3 What is the surname of Eileen, who works at the taxi office?
4 What accessory is Deirdre famous for wearing?
5 Who had a 'muriel' in her living room?
6 What type of beauty therapy did Raquel specialise in?
7 Which Coronation Street couple – now divorced – once lodged with Hilda Ogden?
8 Where do Mike and Linda Baldwin live?
9 Who played Suzie Birchall in the 1970s?
10 Who was Miss Bettabuy?
11 Which ex-*Coronation Street* actress is now a policewoman in *Ballykissangel*?
12 What job does Charlie Ramsden do?
13 Which *Coronation Street* actors appeared in the hit film *East is East*?
14 Which young character is a vegetarian?
15 Who held Sally, Rosie and Sophie hostage?
16 What number do Jack and Vera live at?
17 Did Natalie Barnes have a baby boy or girl?
18 Who played Derek Wilton?
19 What colour was the Malletts' kitchen/living room?
20 Who played Des Barnes?
21 Whose baby did Alison Webster snatch when her own baby died?
22 And who snatched baby Morgan Middleton when she lost her baby?
23 Who gave Les Battersby his job at Street Cars?
24 What was the name of Natalie's niece?
25 Which character did she go out with for a while?

Answers

***Coronation Street* – Pot Luck**

1 The rooftops of Weatherfield. **2** Tabby and white. **3** Grimshaw. **4** Big glasses. **5** Hilda Ogden. **6** Aromatherapy. **7** Sally and Kevin Webster. **8** Weatherfield Quays. **9** Cheryl Murray. **10** Raquel Wolstenholme. **11** Catherine Cusack. **12** Teacher. **13** Jimmy Harkishin and Chris Bisson. **14** Toyah Battersby. **15** Greg Kelly. **16** Number 9. **17** A girl, Laura. **18** Peter Baldwin. **19** Purple. **20** Phil Middlemiss. **21** Sarah Platt's baby, Bethany. **22** Zoe Tattersall. **23** Steve McDonald. **24** Lorraine Brownlow. **25** Spider.

Quiz 55 Bands

Level 1

1 Which band included Phil Collins and Peter Gabriel?
2 Which band recorded the album The Joshua Tree?
3 Marti Pellow was the lead singer with which group?
4 In the 70s who put A Message In A Bottle?
5 Who fronted the Boomtown Rats?
6 Which boy band had No 1s with Babe and Sure?
7 Dave Gilmore and Roger Waters were in which long lasting group?
8 Which group became the first to have the word Pumpkins in their name?
9 Which group flew into the Hotel California?
10 Which Paul was in Style Council and Jam?
11 Who did Vic Reeves sing with?
12 Which US boys band featured three members of the Wilson family?
13 Which band recorded the album Parallel Lines?
14 How many members were there in the Eurythmics?
15 Which movement did The Sex Pistols begin?
16 What word was replaced by the letter T in T. Rex?
17 How many brothers were in the original Jackson family line-up?
18 How many boys were there in the Pet Shop Boys?
19 What was Adam backed by?
20 Which band actually had Noddy as lead singer?
21 What did the letter O stand for in ELO?
22 Pictures of Matchstick Men was the first hit for which veteran rockers?
23 Teeny boppers The Bay City Rollers were from which country?
24 Which band featured Paul McGuigan on bass?
25 Which all time great band featured Harrison and Starkey?

Answers

Bands

1 Genesis. **2** U2. **3** Wet Wet Wet. **4** Police. **5** Bob Geldof. **6** Take That. **7** Pink Floyd. **8** Smashing Pumpkins. **9** The Eagles. **10** Weller. **11** The Wonder Stuff. **12** The Beach Boys. **13** Blondie. **14** Two. **15** Punk. **16** Tyrannnosaurus. **17** Five. **18** Two. **19** The Ants. **20** Slade. **21** Orchestra. **22** Status Quo. **23** Teeny boppers. **24** Oasis. **25** The Beatles.

Quiz 56 Pot Luck

Level 1

1 In 1998 Freddie Shepherd resigned as club chairman of which soccer club?
2 Which parenting guru Doctor wrote *Baby and Child Care*?
3 Who was in charge of the Merry Men in the role reversal children's sitcom about Robin Hood?
4 At the end of the 20th C how many UK monarchs had been called Charles?
5 In which decade did Eric Morecambe die?
6 In pop music, what did the Police find In A Bottle?
7 In book and film, what was St Trinian's?
8 Paul McGrath played soccer for which international team?
9 Dutch-born spy Mata Hari was a dancer in which European city?
10 Which film was about the Olympic Games of 1924?
11 President Kennedy international airport is in which US city?
12 Which country does opera diva Lesley Garrett come from?
13 Whose name was part of a TV Experience where she would have certainly disapproved of the show's content?
14 Norwich is the administrative centre of which English county?
15 Louis B Mayer had which job in the film industry?
16 Australian singer Nellie Melba had a dish named after her containing which fruit?
17 Who was Speaker of the House of Commons for the greater part of the 90s?
18 With which sport is Nick Price associated?
19 In which city was the Marco Polo airport built?
20 Which entertainer said, 'Nice to see you, to see you - nice'?
21 Which Raymond wrote the novel *The Big Sleep*?
22 In 1990 Lithuania declared its independence from what?
23 At the end of the 20th C how many UK monarchs had been called George?
24 Who teamed up with Hanna to form a studio producing cartoon films?
25 What is the last word of the James Herriot book *It Shouldn't Happen To A ______*?

Answers

Pot Luck

1 Newcastle. **2** Spock. **3** Maid Marian. **4** Two. **5** 80s. **6** Message. **7** School. **8** Republic Of Ireland. **9** Paris. **10** Chariots of Fire. **11** New York. **12** England. **13** Mary Whitehouse. **14** Norfolk. **15** Producer. **16** Peach. **17** Betty Boothroyd. **18** Golf. **19** Venice. **20** Bruce Forsyth. **21** Chandler. **22** USSR. **23** Six. **24** Barbera. **25** Vet.

Quiz 57 Leaders

Level 1

1 Bob Hawke and Paul Keating were Prime Ministers of which country?
2 In which country did Gadaffi seize power in the 60s?
3 Who was British Prime Minister at the time of the Gulf War?
4 What was the last name of Ferdinand and Imelda, leaders of the Philippines?
5 Who was Prime Minister of the UK throughout the 80s?
6 Who seized power in Cuba in the late 50s?
7 Which words did Winston Churchill use to describe the East and West divide in Europe?
8 Diana, Princess of Wales' led the campaign against the use of which explosive devices?
9 Haile Selassie ruled in which country?
10 How many general elections did Mrs Thatcher win?
11 Which 90s leader said, 'I did not have sexual relations with that woman'?
12 Who was the leader of the brutal Khmer Rouge government?
13 In which decade was Nelson Mandela sent to prison in South Africa?
14 What did the letter A stand for in Mandela's ANC?
15 Who became Britain's youngest Prime Minister of the century?
16 The death of which General led to the restoration of the monarchy in Spain?
17 In the 90s Silvio Berlusconi won the general election in which country?
18 David Ben-Gurion was the first Prime Minister of which new state?
19 In which country did Lech Walesa lead the conflict against the communist government?
20 Which Chris was the last British governor of Hong Kong?
21 Who was known as Il Duce ?
22 Ayatollah Khomeini ordered a death threat on which UK-based writer?
23 Which US President had a daughter named Chelsea?
24 Nicholas II was the last person to hold which title in Russia?
25 Idi Amin became president of which country?

Answers

Leaders

1 Australia. **2** Libya. **3** John Major. **4** Marcos. **5** Margaret Thatcher. **6** Castro. **7** Iron Curtain. **8** Land mines. **9** Ethiopia. **10** Three. **11** Bill Clinton. **12** Pol Pot. **13** 60s. **14** African. **15** Tony Blair. **16** Franco. **17** Italy. **18** Israel. **19** Poland. **20** Patten. **21** Mussolini. **22** Salman Rushdie. **23** Clinton. **24** Tsar. **25** Uganda.

Quiz 58 CORONATION ST. Level 1

1999

1 Which blond actor left *Coronation Street* this year to pursue a career in pop music?
2 Which well-loved actor died this year, only weeks after his screen character died of a heart attack at a New Year's Eve party?
3 Where were the six spin-off programmes featuring Reg, Bet, Vikram, Vicky and Steve filmed?
4 Which couple married this year in the cafe?
5 Who tipped off the journalist that hounded them out of their planned church wedding?
6 Who had an unrequited crush on Nita Desai?
7 Who won custody of Rosie and Sophie?
8 Who played machinist Alison Wakefield?
9 Who did Danny Hargreaves date before Sally?
10 Who camped out on the Red Rec to watch the eclipse and then missed it because they were so wrapped up in each other?
11 Who had a scam smuggling tobacco into the country?
12 What was Vinny's Velvet?
13 Who did Maxine employ at the salon in Audrey's absence?
14 What was the name of the rival salon the two of them set up in Maxine's flat?
15 Who played Danny Hargreaves?
16 Who dated Gwen Loveday?
17 What was Danny's occupation when he met Sally?
18 Who did Fred first tell about his secret son?
19 What was the name of Fred's sister, who brought Ashley up and pretended to be his mother?
20 Who spent the night with Colin Barnes?
21 Who took a job at Weatherfield Vale Old Folks Home after resigning from his old job?
22 Who became engaged to pensioner Sidney Templeton?
23 Who were the godparents to the Mallett twins?
24 What was the theme of the Valentine's Disco at the Flying Horse: 1960s, 1970s or 1980s?
25 Which unlikely character took a job as a claims officer at the DSS?

Answers

Coronation Street – 1999

1 Adam Rickitt. **2** Bryan Mosley. **3** Brighton and France. **4** Roy and Hayley. **5** Les Battersby. **6** Spider Nugent. **7** Sally. **8** Naomi Radcliffe. **9** Sharon Gaskell. **10** Toyah and Spider. **11** Steve McDonald. **12** Stout brewed by Rovers' drayman Vinny Sorrell. **13** Tom Ferguson. **14** A Cut Above. **15** Richard Standing. **16** Jim McDonald. **17** Market Trader. **18** Audrey. **19** Beryl Peacock. **20** Natalie. **21** Martin Platt. **22** Maud Grimes. **23** Vera and Jack and Ken Barlow. **24** 1970s. **25** Spider.

Quiz 59 Personalities

Level 1

1 What is David Bailey famous for?
2 What colour was Barbara Cartland most seen in?
3 Which Max is famous as a PR man?
4 Dr Stefan Buczacki is an expert in what?
5 Which large opera star launched a perfume for men named after him?
6 What is the name of Joan Collins' novelist sister?
7 Which part of his body did goalkeeper David Seaman insure for £1 million?
8 Which actor Kenneth was Emma Thompson's first husband?
9 Who is Gloria Hunniford's TV presenter daughter?
10 Brooklyn Beckham is the son of which Spice Girl?
11 What is Hillary Clinton's daughter called?
12 What type of dance was Rudolf Nureyev famous for?
13 How did US Ambassador Shirley Temple Black earn fame as a child?
14 Which singer Cleo is married to Johnny Dankworth?
15 What is the name of Wendy Turner's older TV presenter sister?
16 What is the name of the MEP who is Neil Kinnock's wife?
17 Unlike his name suggests, who is the oldest daily presenter on BBC Radio 2?
18 Which Yorkshire cricketer Geoffrey was born the same day as Manfred Mann?
19 What is the birthday of Mario Andretti, who only has a real birthday every four years?
20 Which musical was based on Wild West star Annie Oakley?
21 Who has a catchphrase 'You'll like this – not a lot!'?
22 Which comedy duo were 'the one with the glasses and the one with the short fat hairy legs'?
23 Which cricket commentator was known as Johnners?
24 Which Prime Minister's wife became a Dame in the 1999 Queen's birthday honours?
25 Eileen Drewery was a spiritual healer who helped which England football manager?

Answers

Personalities
1 Photography. **2** Pink. **3** Clifford. **4** Gardening. **5** Luciano Pavarotti. **6** Jackie. **7** Hands. **8** Branagh. **9** Caron Keating. **10** Victoria. **11** Chelsea. **12** Ballet. **13** Film star. **14** Laine. **15** Anthea. **16** Glenys. **17** Jimmy Young. **18** Boycott. **19** 29th February. **20** Annie Get Your Gun. **21** Paul Daniels. **22** Morecambe & Wise. **23** Bryan Johnston. **24** Norma Major. **25** Glenn Hoddle.

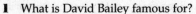

Quiz 60 Pot Luck

Level 1

1 Dana International won the Eurovision Song Contest for which country?
2 The disastrous poison gas leak at Bhopal took place in which country?
3 In the US what became known as a 'greenback'?
4 In advertising, PAL was said to prolong active what?
5 In which country is Ciampino airport?
6 In Julie Andrews' first film she played which nanny?
7 Who or what was Piper Alpha?
8 What is the main colour on the Chinese flag?
9 The UK's Summer Bank Holiday falls in which month?
10 Sir Anthony Hopkins was born in which part of the UK?
11 The TV special *Men Behaving Very Badly Indeed* concentrated on the lads' fixation with which Australian singer/actress?
12 Which stage musical was set in the Paris Opera House?
13 With which sport is Cedric Pioline associated?
14 Carlisle is the administrative centre of which English county?
15 Which two words did Churchill use to dub the Battle of Britain pilots?
16 What is the first name of Zimbabwean statesman Mugabe?
17 On what type of vehicle did Rupert Murdoch remarry in 1999?
18 Claude Oscar Monet was famous for what ?
19 Lord Mountbatten was murdered off the coast of which country?
20 In the 80s Shirley Williams left which political party to launch the SDP?
21 Freddie Laker set up low cost travel in what type of transport?
22 In which decade did Elvis Presley die?
23 Mike Denness captained England in which sport?
24 The deepwater port of Gdansk was developed in which country?
25 Which veteran stand up comic Bob had his own show, *On the Spot*, in the mid 90s?

Answers

Pot Luck

1 Israel. **2** India. **3** Dollar. **4** Life. **5** Italy. **6** Mary Poppins. **7** An oil rig. **8** Red. **9** August. **10** Wales. **11** Kylie Minogue. **12** The Phantom Of The Opera. **13** Tennis. **14** Cumbria. **15** The Few. **16** Robert. **17** Yacht. **18** Paintings. **19** Ireland. **20** Labour. **21** Aeroplanes. **22** 70s. **23** Cricket. **24** Poland. **25** Monkhouse.

Quiz 61 TV Famous Faces

Level 1

1 Which comedian Paul shares his surname with campaigner Mary?
2 Which Royal read one of his own stories on *Jackanory* in 1983?
3 Which Kenny's shows were 'in the best possible taste'?
4 Which June was married to Terry in a series of classic sitcoms?
5 Which Alan was a character created by Steve Coogan?
6 Which *New Faces* winner created the characters PC Ganga and Theophilus P Wildebeeste?
7 Which female Radio DJ succeeded Emma Forbes on *Live & Kicking*?
8 Which actress Alex played Moll Flanders then moved to the US for *ER*?
9 Which former tennis player and sports presenter hosted the BBC coverage of the last Royal Wedding of the century?
10 Which Pamela was the female comedian on *Not the Nine O'Clock News*?
11 Which Sean starred as Sharpe in the series about the Napoleonic Wars?
12 Which pop drummer narrated *Thomas the Tank Engine* on TV?
13 Dawn French played the Vicar of which English village in the sitcom of the same name?
14 Which comedienne and writer Victoria had a series *As Seen on TV*?
15 In which Files would Mulder and Scully appear?
16 Which knighted Cabinet Secretary was played by Nigel Hawthorne in *Yes Minister*?
17 Colin Firth played Darcy in which classic Jane Austen adaptation in 1995?
18 Which four brothers, Joe, Mark, Paul and Stephen, starred in the drama set in Ireland, *The Hanging Gale*?
19 Which Attenborough brother presented *The Private Life of Plants*?
20 What was the occupation of Jemma Redgrave in the Victorian drama *Bramwell*?
21 Which Paula featured on *Cue Paula* on The Big Breakfast?
22 Which Jonathan replaced Barry Norman on BBC's film programme in 1999?
23 Which newsreader Trevor received a knighthood in the last Queen's Birthday Honours of the century?
24 Which Nick was the first presenter of *Crimewatch UK*?
25 Which Charlton advertised Shredded Wheat on TV?

Answers

TV Famous Faces

1 Whitehouse. **2** Prince Charles. **3** Everett. **4** Whitfield. **5** Partridge. **6** Lenny Henry. **7** Zoe Ball. **8** Kingston. **9** Sue Barker. **10** Stephenson. **11** Bean. **12** Ringo Starr. **13** Dibley. **14** Wood. **15** The X Files. **16** Sir Humphrey. **17** Pride & Prejudice. **18** McGann. **19** David. **20** Doctor. **21** Yates. **22** Ross. **23** McDonald. **24** Ross. **25** Jack.

Quiz 62 CORONATION ST. Level 1

Pot Luck

1 What is the surname of Dennis, Eileen's boyfriend?
2 What is the name of Linda's brother, who works at Underworld?
3 What is the name of their brother who was killed in the Frescho seige?
4 What does Matt Ramsden do for a living?
5 Which two business partners and friends fell out over Karen Phillips?
6 And who plays Karen Phillips?
7 Which accessory was Reg Holdsworth's trademark?
8 Why did Des and Steph Barnes split up?
9 Who set fire to Baldwin's factory, before killing himself?
10 Who plays Fred Elliot?
11 Where did Gary Mallett go to live when he left Coronation Street?
12 Who plays Steve McDonald?
13 Which of these positions has Audrey Roberts never held: Hairdresser, shop assistant or barmaid?
14 Which cantankerous pensioner claimed to have 'made gravy under shellfire' during the war?
15 What linked Derek Wilton and Norris Cole?
16 Who joined a computer dating agency as 'Vince St Clair' only to end up being paired up with his wife?
17 Which bitchy barmaid sent Raquel on an 'Armani' modelling assignment to R. Marney's fruit and veg stall?
18 Which actress played Vicky Arden?
19 Which two jobs did Judy Mallett have when she lived in Coronation Street?
20 What job did Judy's mum Joyce do?
21 Who conned Tyrone and Jason over the stolen stereo scam?
22 What was the name of Alf Roberts' second wife?
23 How many times was Alf Roberts Mayor of Weatherfield?
24 And who was his mayoress the first time around?
25 Which young actress plays Sarah Platt?

Answers

Coronation Street – Pot Luck

1 Stringer. **2** Ryan. **3** Dean. **4** Doctor. **5** Steve McDonald and Vikram Desai. **6** Suzanne Jones. **7** Coloured specs. **8** She had an affair. **9** Don Brennan. **10** John Savident. **11** Blackpool. **12** Simon Gregson. **13** Barmaid. **14** Percy Sugden. **15** Angela Hawthorne was married to both men. **16** Jack Duckworth. **17** Tanya Pooley. **18** Chloe Newsome. **19** Amusement arcade attendant and barmaid. **20** Pub cleaner. **21** Ryan Sykes. **22** Renee Bradshaw. **23** Twice. **24** Annie Walker. **25** Tina O'Brien.

Quiz 63 Darts & Snooker

Level 1

1 Who was snooker's world champion most times in the 80s?
2 What does the letter O stand for in BDO?
3 Cliff Thorburn – 'The Grinder' – came from which country?
4 Which ball is worth one point less than a black?
5 Which John scored the first nine-dart 501 in a major tournament?
6 Moving anti-clockwise on a dartboard, which number is after 1?
7 Which snooker player was nicknamed 'Whirlwind'?
8 Which Sunday paper ran a darts competition from the 40s to the early 90s?
9 In which decade was snooker's World Championship first staged at The Crucible?
10 Which Leighton became darts' first World Professional Championship?
11 Who took over No 1 ranking from Stephen Hendry?
12 Which English darts player was awarded an MBE in 1989?
13 Which London soccer team is Barry Hearne connected with?
14 Dennis Priestley plays for which country?
15 Which snooker player was known as 'Hurricane'?
16 On a dartboard, which number is directly opposite the 6?
17 Which 'veteran' sensationally beat Stephen Hendry in the first round of the 1998 World Championship?
18 What's the smallest three-dart score made with three trebles all in different even numbers?
19 Which player broke up Hendry's World Championship monopoly of the early 90s?
20 What does the B stand for in the WPBSA?
21 Which darts player is known as 'Barney Rubble'?
22 Who is Gary Lineker's big mate in the snooker world?
23 Can you raise a glass and name the sponsor of the WDC Darts Championship?
24 Which ball is worth one point more than a blue?
25 Who is the first Ken to win snooker's World Championship?

Answers

Darts & Snooker

1 Steve Davis. **2** Organisation. **3** Canada. **4** Pink. **5** Lowe. **6** 20. **7** Jimmy White. **8** News Of The World. **9** 70s. **10** Rees. **11** John Higgins. **12** Eric Bristow. **13** Leyton Orient. **14** England. **15** Alex Higgins. **16** 1. **17** Jimmy White. **18** 36. **19** John Parrott. **20** Billiards. **21** Raymond Van Barneveld. **22** Willie Thorne. **23** Skol. **24** Pink. **25** Docherty.

Quiz 64 Pot Luck

Level 1

1 The Louise Woodward affair was tried in which country?
2 In its early days what was offered for sale 'in any colour as long as it's black'?
3 Which Russian leader had a pronounced birthmark on his forehead?
4 Which Joe wrote the play *Entertaining Mr Sloane*?
5 Which country was readmitted into international rugby fixtures in 1993?
6 Which future superstar Robin played Mork in *Mork and Mindy*?
7 Which Private magazine led the 60s satire boom?
8 David Owen, now Lord Owen, was trained in what profession before becoming a politician ?
9 In the world of plants and gardening, what type of Royal Society is the RHS?
10 Tony Doyle represented Britain at which sport?
11 What do players try to collect in the board game Trivial Pursuit?
12 What is the name of Neil Kinnock's wife?
13 The influential Russian figure Rasputin followed which profession?
14 Mary Robinson became the first woman president of which country in 1990?
15 Which nickname did fighter Ray Robinson have?
16 Geoff Boycott has had which kind of plant named after him?
17 Paul Boateng has represented which party in parliament?
18 Which royal married Lord Snowdon?
19 In the cookery world, what relation is Albert to Michel Roux?
20 Mrs Merton took her chat show – and her pensioner audience – to which US entertainment venue for a series of her shows?
21 Warren Beatty was born in which decade of the century?
22 With which sport is Grant Hill associated?
23 Maud Grimes is a character from which soap?
24 Brian Mulrooney was Prime Minister of which country in the 80s and 90s?
25 Early in the century who wrote the novels *Lord Jim* and *Heart of Darkness*?

Answers

Pot Luck

1 United States. **2** Motor car. **3** Gorbachev. **4** Orton. **5** South Africa. **6** Williams. **7** Eye. **8** Doctor. **9** Horticultural. **10** Cycling. **11** Wedges. **12** Glenys. **13** Monk. **14** Ireland. **15** Sugar. **16** Rose. **17** Labour. **18** Princess Margaret. **19** Brother. **20** Las Vegas. **21** 30s. **22** Basketball. **23** Coronation Street. **24** Canada. **25** Joseph Conrad.

Quiz 65 Actresses

Level 1

1 Who cried during her Oscar acceptance speech for *Shakespeare in Love*?
2 Who starred in *Mermaids* and went to No 1 with The Shoop Shoop Song?
3 Which pop star Lisa made her movie debut in *Swing*?
4 Sigourney Weaver in *Alien II* and Demi Moore in *G.I. Jane* shaved what?
5 Who won an Oscar for her first film role in *Mary Poppins*?
6 Which actress and fitness guru Jane married CNN mogul Ted Turner?
7 Which actress appeared on the cinema poster for *Titanic*?
8 In *The Seven Year Itch* whose white skirt is billowing around because of hot air blowing up from a grating?
9 Which superstar was nicknamed 'The Swedish Sphinx'?
10 What is Goldie Hawn's real name?
11 How is Mary Elizabeth Spacek known in the film world?
12 Who was cast as Princess Leia in *Star Wars* after her film debut in *Shampoo* with Warren Beatty?
13 Melanie Griffith married which star of *Evita* and *The Mask of Zorro*?
14 Which Oscar winning black actress played the medium Oda Mae Brown in *Ghost*?
15 For which role did Michelle Pfeiffer wear 63 catsuits in *Batman Returns*?
16 Which plant was Uma Thurman named after in *Batman & Robin*?
17 Which actress has children called Scout and Rumer from her marriage to Bruce Willis?
18 In which 1979 film with Bo Derek was the title simply a number?
19 Which actress who starred in *Fatal Attraction* won a Tony for her role in *Sunset Boulevard* on Broadway?
20 Which star of *Sliding Doors* split with fiance Brad Pitt in 1997?
21 Which wife of Paul Newman played Tom Hanks' mother in *Philadelphia*?
22 Which Ms Smith played the Mother Superior opposite Whoopi Goldberg in *Sister Act*?
23 Which Redgrave was Oscar nominated for *Gods and Monsters*?
24 Janet Leigh played one of the most horrific scenes where in a motel?
25 Which French sex symbol became an animal rights campaigner later in her life?

Answers

Actresses

1 Gwyneth Paltrow. **2** Cher. **3** Stansfield. **4** Heads. **5** Julie Andrews. **6** Fonda. **7** Kate Winslet. **8** Marilyn Monroe. **9** Greta Garbo. **10** Goldie Hawn. **11** Sissy. **12** Carrie Fisher. **13** Antonio Banderas. **14** Whoopi Goldberg. **15** Catwoman. **16** Ivy. **17** Demi Moore. **18** 10. **19** Glenn Close. **20** Gwyneth Paltrow. **21** Joanne Woodward. **22** Maggie. **23** Lynn. **24** Shower. **25** Brigitte Bardot.

Quiz 66 CORONATION ST. Level 1

2000

1 Who had sex with Jez Quigley in order to stop a planned raid on the Rovers?
2 What was the name of Natalie's sister?
3 What was her profession?
4 Whose estranged wife came back for a visit and told him he had a daughter?
5 Who was badly beaten up by Jez Quigley's cronies after borrowing £8,000 from him?
6 Who slept with his ex-wife on the eve of his wedding?
7 Who attempted to steal £35,000 from Jim McDonald?
8 Who ruined his father's wedding with a shocking confession?
9 Who almost missed the birth of his granddaughter because he was in bed with his mistress?
10 Who reverted to her maiden name of Halliwell this year?
11 How did Alison Webster die?
12 Who left Coronation Street for a year-long spiritual trek to India?
13 Who plays bookstore owner Anthony Stephens?
14 Which *Coronation Street* character did he begin dating this year?
15 Who was tormented by disturbed ex-girlfriend Amy Goskirk?
16 Who met his girlfriend when he was being stalked by one of her colleagues?
17 Which cast member also played Denis Rutledge in the old series of *Crossroads*?
18 Who underwent drug counselling?
19 Where did Tyrone ask Maria to marry him?
20 Who dated creepy councillor Bob Bradshaw?
21 Who had to serve 150 hours community service for defrauding the DHS?
22 Who went to see a masseuse for back pain but became the subject of local gossip when the premises were raided by the vice police?
23 What was the name of Rebecca Hopkins' violent estranged husband?
24 What was Sally and Danny's shop called?
25 Who plays Tyrone Dobbs?

Answers

Coronation Street – 2000
1 Leanne. **2** Debs Brownlow. **3** Hairdresser. **4** Curly (Raquel). **5** Steve McDonald. **6** Kevin Webster. **7** Gwen Loveday. **8** Mark Redman. **9** Martin Platt. **10** Alma. **11** She was run over. **12** Spider. **13** John Quayle. **14** Rita. **15** Dev. **16** Curly (met Emma). **17** Bryan Mosley. **18** Leanne. **19** Blackpool Tower. **20** Alma. **21** Les. **22** Fred. **23** Jerry. **24** D & S Hardware. **25** Alan Halsall.

Quiz 67 Books

Level 1

1 Which *Book of Records* was first published in 1955?
2 Which book by Peter Benchley made into a film by Spielberg, was originally called *The Summer of the Shark*?
3 Which tennis player Martina wrote a novel called *Total Zone*?
4 Which MP Tony wrote lengthy diaries of his years in office?
5 James Alfred Wright was better known as James who, when writing about his experiences as a Yorkshire vet?
6 In *Peter Pan* what sort of animal was Nana?
7 What was Thomas Harris's sequel to *Silence of the Lambs* called?
8 Cornish restaurateur Rick Stein's books are about what type of food?
9 Which novelist Barbara was Princess Diana's step-grandmother?
10 Which King's novels such as *Carrie* and *The Shining* have been made into successful films?
11 Which children's books were made into a film in 2001?
12 Which offbeat fictional detective was created by R.D. Wingfield and was played on TV by David Jason?
13 Which crime-writing Dame is the best selling fiction author in the world?
14 What was the name of Martin Amis's famous author father?
15 Who wrote *Hollywood Wives*?
16 Novelist Jeffrey Archer was once Chairman of which political party?
17 Which Jaguar-driving, crossword fanatic detective was created by Colin Dexter?
18 Whose autobiography, written with the help of Andrew Morton, was about the Clinton White House Scandal?
19 Jamie Oliver wrote a book about his work called *The Naked* what?
20 Which tycoon and entrepreneur in the fields of music, airlines and cola wrote *Losing My Virginity*?
21 Which Bill wrote *Notes From a Small Island*?
22 Pongo was one of 101 what in the novel by Dodie Smith?
23 The novel *The Sheep Pig* was turned into a movie called what?
24 Which Cooper followed *Polo* and *Riders* with *Score!*?
25 One of the Famous Five was what type of pet animal?

Answers

Books
1 Guinness. **2** Jaws. **3** Navratilova. **4** Benn. **5** Herriot. **6** Dog. **7** Hannibal. **8** Fish. **9** Cartland. **10** Stephen. **11** The Harry Potter books. **12** Frost. **13** Agatha Christie. **14** Kingsley. **15** Jackie. **16** Tory. **17** Morse. **18** Monica Lewinsky. **19** Chef. **20** Richard Branson. **21** Bryson. **22** Dalmatians. **23** Babe. **24** Jilly. **25** Dog.

Quiz 68 Pot Luck

Level 1

1 Which Derek was finally cleared of murder 45 years after he was hanged?
2 Which Godfrey was an England wicket keeper?
3 In a Spice Girls hit what follows 'swing it, shake it, move it...'?
4 What is the main colour featured on the flag of Denmark?
5 What did Britain stage in 1908 and 1948?
6 What does the letter S stand for in SAE?
7 Who appeared with Peter Cook in *Not Only... But Also*?
8 Which Tory became Deputy Prime Minister in 1995?
9 The world's longest tunnel, the Seikan tunnel, was built in which country?
10 Rachel Heyhoe Flint played for England at which sport?
11 Garrett Fitzgerald was Prime Minister of which country?
12 Who wrote the thriller novel *The Day Of The Jackal*?
13 With which sport is Marcelo Salas associated?
14 Albert and Michael are which brothers in the world of food?
15 Magician Paul Daniels was born in which decade?
16 Michael Dukakis missed out in his attempts to become President of where?
17 The American *Not Necessarily the News* was based on which UK show with Pamela Stephenson, Mel Smith and others?
18 In the 80s which country was responsible for ethnic attacks on the Kurds?
19 Despite owning an airline and a railway, Richard Branson makes headlines travelling by what means?
20 What was Stalin's first name?
21 Which Shroud was declared a fake in the 80s?
22 Which West Indian cricketer had the first names Garfield St Auburn?
23 What was the Sopwith Camel?
24 Which Rugby League side became Warriors in the late 90s?
25 Remembrance Day is in which month?

Answers

Pot Luck

1 Bentley. **2** Evans. **3** Make it. **4** Red. **5** Olympic Games. **6** Stamped. **7** Dudley Moore. **8** Michael Heseltine. **9** Japan. **10** Cricket. **11** Ireland. **12** Frederick Forsyth. **13** Soccer. **14** Roux. **15** 20s. **16** USA. **17** Not the Nine O'Clock News. **18** Iraq. **19** Hot-air balloon. **20** Joseph. **21** Turin. **22** Sobers. **23** Plane. **24** Wigan. **25** November.

Quiz 69 Musical Superstars

Level 1

1 Who recorded the Immaculate Collection?
2 What was certainly the debut album by Oasis?
3 Which Lionel sang with The Commodores?
4 In which US state was Elvis Presley's mansion?
5 What was the title of the first album from The Spice Girls?
6 I Will Always Love You was an early 90s hit for which superstar?
7 Alan, Jay and Donny were part of which 70s group?
8 Who first charted as a solo performer with Careless Whisper?
9 Which group is made up of Gibbs?
10 What instrument does Charlie Watts play in the Rolling Stones?
11 Who was the first to leave Take That?
12 Who teamed up with Barbra Streisand for Tell Him?
13 Who was the original lead singer with The Supremes?
14 How many people were in the original Queen?
15 Who became the most famous group formed in Colchester?
16 In which decade was Elton John's original Candle In The Wind a hit?
17 Baker, Bruce and Clapton formed which 60s supergroup?
18 In 1996 Robert Hoskins was convicted of stalking which star?
19 Which supergroup contains The Edge?
20 Who has recorded with Elton John, Queen, Lisa Stansfield and Toby Bourke?
21 Which band produced the mega-selling album Rumours?
22 What was the first All Saints record to sell a million?
23 Visions Of Love was the first British top ten hit for which female superstar?
24 Which Hotel gave Elvis his first British chart hit?
25 Which group wrote the songs for the movie *Saturday Night Fever*?

Answers

Musical Superstars
1 Madonna. **2** Definitely Maybe. **3** Richie. **4** Tennessee. **5** Spice. **6** Whitney Houston. **7** The Osmonds. **8** George Michael. **9** The Bee Gees. **10** Drums. **11** Robbie Williams. **12** Celine Dion. **13** Diana Ross. **14** Four. **15** Blur. **16** 70s. **17** Cream. **18** Madonna. **19** U2. **20** George Michael. **21** Fleetwood Mac. **22** Never Ever. **23** Mariah Carey. **24** Heartbreak. **25** The Bee Gees.

Quiz 70 CORONATION ST. Level 1

Pot Luck

1 How many times was Alf Roberts married?
2 Where does Raquel now live?
3 Which famous actor played Ravi Desai?
4 Which member of the *Fawlty Towers* cast once played a bus conductress in *Coronation Street*?
5 Who plays Janice Battersby?
6 Who did Janice kiss last year after throwing Les out?
7 Where does Les Battersby currently work?
8 Why did Leanne Battersby have to leave Coronation Street?
9 Who lost his taxi in a poker game?
10 Who did Judy's mother, Joyce Smedley, enjoy a romantic weekend with in 1996?
11 Which McDonald brother dated Anne Malone?
12 Which McDonald brother ran away with Joanne Khan?
13 In which year did Hilda Ogden leave Coronation Street?
14 What was the name of Fred Gee's second wife?
15 Who played her?
16 And which soap is she currently appearing in?
17 Who fell through the ceiling of No 5 onto Leanne Battersby and Nick Tilsley?
18 Where did Percy Sugden and Maud Grimes move to after leaving Coronation Street?
19 How did Don Brennan die?
20 Who plays Roy Cropper?
21 Which job did Derek Wilton once have at Weatherfield Comprehensive?
22 What was the name of Betty Williams' last husband
23 Who does Malcolm Hebden play?
24 Liz Dawn and Bill Tarmey used to be extras on *Coronation Street* before becoming famous characters: True or false?
25 Who played Bet Gilroy?

Answers

Coronation Street – Pot Luck

1 Three. **2** France. **3** Saeed Jaffrey. **4** Prunella Scales. **5** Vicky Entwistle. **6** Dennis Stringer. **7** Streetcars. **8** She was stalked by Jez Quigley. **9** Don Brennan. **10** Alec Gilroy. **11** Andy. **12** Steve. **13** 1987. **14** Eunice Nuttall. **15** Meg Johnson. **16** *Brookside*. **17** Ken Barlow. **18** Mayfield Court. **19** He drove his car into a wall. **20** David Neilson. **21** Caretaker. **22** Billy. **23** Norris Cole. **24** True. **25** Julie Goodyear.

Quiz 71 Rich & Famous

Level 1

1 Which Knightsbridge store did Mohammed Al-Fayed buy by outwitting rival Tiny Rowland?
2 Who was the first Beatle to be knighted?
3 Habitat was founded by which Terence?
4 What was the profession of Margaret Thatcher's father?
5 Which Princess was the youngest daughter of Mrs Frances Shand Kydd?
6 Which Rupert launched the satellite TV station which became Sky?
7 To the nearest five years, how old would Marilyn Monroe have been in 2000?
8 Which Swedish tennis player was John McEnroe's best man?
9 How many Beatles were not known by their real names?
10 Which opera singer gave her name to a kind of peach dessert?
11 Which tennis player was nicknamed Pistol Pete?
12 The ship *Queen Elizabeth* was named after who?
13 Which MP was immortalised in Madame Tussaud's in 1995 shortly after becoming leader of his party?
14 Dame Shirley Porter is heiress to which major supermarket chain?
15 Which Spice Girl sang Happy Birthday to Prince Charles at his 50th birthday party?
16 Whose head was due to be lost on banknotes when Britain joined the single European currency?
17 Who was engaged to Michael Hutchence of INXS when he died?
18 What was Camilla Shand's surname after her first marriage?
19 In which country did Princess Anne marry for the second time?
20 Which skinny Sixties model married actor Leigh Lawson?
21 Carol Vorderman agreed a multi-million pound contract to do sums on which TV show?
22 William Henry Gates III amassed his fortune from which source?
23 Which British PM's father was a trapeze artist?
24 Which Duchess had a weeping Jana Novotna on her shoulder after the Czech player lost her Wimbledon final?
25 Which 90s Wimbledon champion married actress Brooke Shields?

Answers

Rich & Famous

1 Harrods. **2** Paul McCartney. **3** Conran. **4** Grocer. **5** Diana. **6** Murdoch. **7** 74. **8** Bjorn Borg. **9** One. **10** Melba. **11** Pete Sampras. **12** Queen Mother. **13** Tony Blair. **14** Tesco. **15** Geri. **16** The Queen. **17** Paula Yates. **18** Parker-Bowles. **19** Scotland. **20** Twiggy. **21** Countdown. **22** Computer software. **23** John Major. **24** Kent. **25** Andre Agassi.

Quiz 72 Pot Luck

Level 1

1 Which Eddie was a 90s governor of the Bank of England?
2 In the game Monopoly, what colour are both Mayfair and Park Lane?
3 What type of mask was issued to all people in Britain in 1939?
4 Which Charles appears on the back of a £10 note?
5 Imagine was a hit for which singer after his death?
6 Whose business vehicle has New York, Paris, Peckham written on the side?
7 Albert Schweitzer is best remembered for his work on which continent?
8 What does the H stand for in the world organization WHO?
9 Where was the action of *Please Sir!* set?
10 Keith Fletcher captained England at which sport?
11 In which country did the Bolsheviks seize power?
12 Which actress Mirren was the star of TV's *Prime Suspect*?
13 What letter is used for numbers relating to food additives?
14 John Lee Hooker is associated with which type of music?
15 Who or what was the Flying Scotsman?
16 Who wrote *Animal Farm*?
17 The deepwater port of Faro was developed in which country?
18 With which sport is Ronan Rafferty associated?
19 Chrissie Hynde first had a No 1 as lead singer with which group?
20 How was Arkwright's shop described in the title of the sitcom with Ronnie Barker and David Jason?
21 Which car manufacturer introduced the Robin?
22 Who wrote the play *The Importance of Being Earnest*?
23 The Tamil Tigers were fighting for a separate state within which country?
24 In which decade was Radio 1 launched?
25 The Pompidou centre was built in which European city?

Answers

Pot Luck

1 George. **2** Dark blue. **3** Gas mask. **4** Dickens. **5** John Lennon. **6** The Trotters. **7** Africa. **8** Health. **9** School. **10** Cricket. **11** Russia. **12** Helen. **13** E. **14** Blues. **15** Steam train. **16** George Orwell. **17** Portugal. **18** Golf. **19** The Pretenders. **20** Open All Hours. **21** Reliant. **22** Oscar Wilde. **23** Sri Lanka. **24** 60s. **25** Paris.

Quiz 73 TV Quiz & Game Shows

Level 1

1 Wolf, Amazon and Saracen competed in which show?
2 Which satirical show hosted by Angus Deayton was derived from Radio 4's *The News Quiz*?
3 Which knockabout game show spawned a version with The Duke & Duchess of York, Princess Anne and Prince Edward as contestants?
4 Which show first hosted by Terry Wogan gave losers a model of a cheque book and pen?
5 Which show named after Superman's home planet tried to find the 'Super-being of Great Britain'?
6 Which show introduced the phrase 'I've started so I'll finish.'?
7 Which Cilla Black show was called *The Dating Game* in the USA?
8 What is reduced from fifteen to one in *Fifteen to One*?
9 On *Blockbusters* who was often asked 'Can I Have a P please Bob'?
10 Who presented the first series of *The Generation Game* on UK TV?
11 Which Marti hosted *New Faces*?
12 Which Stars programme featured the catchphrase 'Ulrika-ka-ka-ka-ka'?
13 How was Michael Barrymore's show *Strike It Lucky* renamed?
14 Which afternoon programme was based on the French show *Les Chiffres et les Lettres* – Numbers and Letters?
15 Which Ms Rice led contestants in *Treasure Hunt*?
16 Which student quiz had a starter for ten?
17 In which show did one contestant throw darts and one answer questions?
18 Which Ian edits *Private Eye* and is a regular on *Have I Got News For You*?
19 What was the name of the National Lottery show which included a quiz?
20 Who first hosted *Who Wants to be A Millionaire*?
21 In which show hosted by Roy Walker did contestants try to guess well known phrases from computerised images?
22 Which group of people make up the audience of *Man O Man*?
23 What is *Masterchef* for young contestants called?
24 In the title of the cookery challenge show what follows *Can't Cook*?
25 Which Sue was the first regular female presenter of *A Question of Sport*?

Answers

TV Quiz & Game Shows

1 Gladiators. **2** Have I Got News For You. **3** It's A Knockout. **4** Blankety Blank. **5** The Krypton Factor. **6** Mastermind. **7** Blind Date. **8** Number of contestants. **9** Bob Holness. **10** Bruce Forsyth. **11** Caine. **12** Shooting Stars. **13** Strike It Rich. **14** Countdown. **15** Anneka. **16** University Challenge. **17** Bullseye. **18** Hislop. **19** Winning Lines. **20** Chris Tarrant. **21** Catchphrase. **22** Women. **23** Junior Masterchef. **24** Won't Cook. **25** Barker.

Quiz 74 CORONATION ST.

Level 1

Pot Luck

1 Who did Mike Baldwin marry in 1991?
2 How long did the marriage last?
3 When did Alma first appear in Coronation Street?
4 What was the name of her first husband?
5 In which year did Mike marry Alma?
6 What did Alma buy for herself when her ex-husband left her some money?
7 What was Alma's catering company called?
8 When did Mike first appear in *Coronation Street*?
9 Who is Mark Redman's mother?
10 What did she do for a living?
11 Which other Coronation Street resident did she date some years later?
12 Where is Mike and Linda's flat?
13 Which barmaid did Mike install as his 'housekeeper' in the 1970s?
14 Name the boutique Mike owned in the 1970s.
15 Who was the estate agent that Mike went out with in 1989?
16 Her brother tricked Mike into buying some land that was worthless: Where?
17 What did Alma do when Mike dumped her for Jackie?
18 Which police series did Claire McGlynn (Charlie Ramsden) appear in before *Coronation Street*?
19 Who played two timing Ian Bentley?
20 Which long-running series did he star in before *Coronation Street*?
21 Who played Tony Horrocks?
22 Which *Coronation Street* producer became known as 'the axeman'?
23 Who was Coronation Street's longest serving Producer?
24 Why was Tina Fowler sacked from the Rovers?
25 What was the name of Tina's boyfriend who jilted her on her hen night?

Answers

Coronation Street – Pot Luck

1 Jackie Ingrams. **2** A week. **3** 1981. **4** Jim Sedgewick. **5** 1992. **6** A sports car. **7** ABC Catering. **8** 1976. **9** Maggie Dunlop. **10** Florist. **11** Ken Barlow. **12** Weatherfield Quays **13** Bet Lynch. **14** Western Front. **15** Dawn Prescott. **16** Spain. **17** She slashed Jackie's duvet. **18** Cops. **19** Jonathan Guy Lewis. **20** *London's Burning*. **21** Lee Warburton. **22** Brian Park. **23** Bill Podmore. **24** She was rude to customers when she began dating brewery boss Nigel Ridley. **25** Eddie Ramsden.

Quiz 75 Sporting Chance

Level 1

1 Wentworth Golf Club is in which English county?
2 Susan Brown was the first woman to take part in which race?
3 Which country was captained by Dunga?
4 Which sporting ground has a Nursery End and a Pavilion End?
5 In which sport does the Fastnet Race take place?
6 What is the colour of the stage leader's jersey in the Tour de France?
7 Who did England have to beat to stay in cricket's 1999 World Cup – and didn't?
8 In what year was soccer's World Cup last held in the 80s?
9 Rugby is played at Ellis Park in which city?
10 Mark Spitz landed how many golds in the 1972 Olympics?
11 Yapping Deng was a world champion in which sport?
12 Who captained South Africa in cricket's 1999 World Cup?
13 In which sport were Lonsdale Belts awarded?
14 Who was England's first Italian Footballer Of The Year?
15 Andy Caddick played for England at which sport?
16 In which decade did Man Utd players die in the Munich Air Disaster?
17 Which baseball team are Giants?
18 In a nickname, what rank of the peerage was given to Ted Dexter?
19 The Australian Dawn Fraser was famous for which sport?
20 Which soccer team used to play at Ayresome Park?
21 Who or what became known as The Crafty Cockney?
22 The final of which tennis Grand Slam tournament is played in a Meadow?
23 At which circuit does the San Marino Grand Prix take place?
24 The Fosbury Flop was developed in which sport?
25 In which country in mainland Europe did Ian Rush play club soccer?

Answers

Sporting Chance

1 Surrey. **2** The Boat Race. **3** Brazil. **4** Lord's. **5** Yachting. **6** Yellow. **7** India. **8** 1986. **9** Johannesburg. **10** Seven. **11** Table tennis. **12** Hanse Cronje. **13** Boxing. **14** Gianfranco Zola. **15** Cricket. **16** 50s. **17** San Francisco. **18** Lord. **19** Swimming. **20** Middlesbrough. **21** Eric Bristow. **22** US Open. **23** Imola. **24** High jump. **25** Italy.

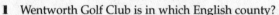

Quiz 76 CORONATION ST. Level 1

Pot Luck

1 Who assaulted Sally on New Year's Eve 1998?
2 Who rescued Sally from the attack?
3 Which adult character had to be baptised in 1999 in order to become a godparent?
4 Who went to bed with Freshco boss James Kitching?
5 Who played Jez Quigley?
6 Who told Ken Barlow that university had made him a 'stuck up little snob' in the first ever episode of *Coronation Street*?
7 Who set fire to all his furniture in the middle of Coronation Street ?
8 Who played Sean Skinner in the 90s and Terry Goodwin in the 70s?
9 Who was Tom the hairdresser's father?
10 Who had a budgie called Jarvis Cocker?
11 Who played both Joyce Smedley in the 90s and Brenda Summers in the 70s?
12 Who played Anne Malone?
13 Which *Coronation Street* actress once appeared in a film alongside Morecambe and Wise?
14 Whose first ex-wife was called Joyce Crosby?
15 Who played Gwen Loveday?
16 Which *Coronation Street* actor provided the voice of Paul McCartney in the animated version of *Yellow Submarine*?
17 On which nights was *Coronation Street* screened from 1961–1989?
18 Whose wedding on *Coronation Street* warranted a 32-page supplement to commemorate the occasion in 1967?
19 Which *Coronation Street* actress also appeared in a film called *The Slipper and the Rose*?
20 Who is afraid of flying and had to return from his honeymoon on a boat?
21 What did Alma die of?
22 Who did Natalie rent her house to straight after Des died?
23 Who said of the Rovers 'This pub isn't a democracy – I run it!'?
24 Who does Georgia Taylor play?
25 Which madcap *Coronation Street* actor also appeared as a General in the comedy *´Allo ´Allo*?

Answers

Coronation Street – Pot Luck

1 Greg Kelly. **2** Nick Tilsley. **3** Jack Duckworth. **4** Nita Desai. **5** Lee Boardman. **6** Albert Tatlock. **7** Jim McDonald. **8** Terence Hillier. **9** Duggie Ferguson. **10** Becky Palmer. **11** Anita Carey. **12** Eve Steele. **13** Amanda Barrie. **14** Alec Gilroy. **15** Annie Hulley. **16** Geoff Hughes. **17** Monday and Wednesday. **18** Elsie and Steve Tanner. **19** Sherrie Hewson. **20** Ashley. **21** Cancer. **22** Sally. **23** Duggie Ferguson. **24** Toyah. **25** Ken Morley.

Quiz 77 Comedies

Level 1

1 Which Jim played Truman in *The Truman Show*?
2 Who was the near silent subject of *The Ultimate Disaster Movie* in 1997?
3 Which 90s movie told of a group of stripping Sheffield steel workers?
4 In the 1994 movie what did Jim Carrey find that turned him from a bank clerk into a comic book character, in the film of the same name?
5 Which *Blackadder* star played the vicar in *Four Weddings and a Funeral*?
6 Which 1994 movie was based on a TV cartoon and was set in Bedrock?
7 In *Forrest Gump*, his mum says Life is like a box of what?
8 What was A Fish called in the movie with Michael Palin and John Cleese?
9 Which blonde country star had a cameo role in *The Beverly Hillbillies*?
10 What is the name of the nanny Robin Williams becomes to look after his estranged children in the 1993 film?
11 Where did Deloris, played by Whoopi Goldberg, find refuge in *Sister Act*?
12 Whose World was a 1992 film with Mike Myers and Dana Carvey?
13 Which *Carry On* film was released in the 500th anniversary year of Columbus' arrival in the Americas?
14 *Postcards From the Edge* was based on the life of which actress Carrie?
15 In which movie did Macaulay Culkin first play abandoned child Kevin McCallister?
16 Which Bruce is the voice of Mikey in *Look Who's Talking*?
17 Why was Mick Dundee nicknamed Crocodile?
18 Which Michael played teenager Marty in *Back to the Future*?
19 In which 80s comedy did Dustin Hoffman play an actor who pretends to be a woman to get a part in a soap?
20 Which member of Arthur's staff was played by John Gielgud in the 80s film with Dudley Moore?
21 *There's Something About* whom in the politically incorrect comedy with Cameron Diaz?
22 Which crawling insects are the major stars of *A Bug's Life*?
23 Which spinach-eating cartoon character was played by Robin Williams?
24 Which silent movie star created the comic character The Little Tramp?
25 Which brothers starred in *Monkey Business* and *A Night at the Opera*?

Answers

Comedies

1 Carrey. **2** Bean. **3** The Full Monty. **4** The Mask. **5** Rowan Atkinson. **6** The Flintstones. **7** Chocolates. **8** Wanda. **9** Dolly Parton. **10** Mrs Doubtfire. **11** Convent. **12** Wayne's. **13** Carry on Columbus. **14** Fisher. **15** Home Alone. **16** Willis. **17** He survived a crocodile attack. **18** J Fox. **19** Tootsie. **20** Valet. **21** Mary. **22** Ants. **23** Popeye. **24** Charlie Chaplin. **25** Marx Brothers.

Quiz 78 CORONATION ST. Level 1

Pot Luck

1 Name the actor who plays Duggie Ferguson.
2 Which *Coronation Street* writer had great success with the series *Family at War*?
3 Name the acclaimed Ken Loach film that Bruce Jones appeared in.
4 Who did Vinny Sorrell sleep with while he was seeing Natalie?
5 Why was Audrey in financial trouble after Alf died?
6 Which two ladies went to the 1999 Valentine's Disco as Debbie Harry?
7 Who played Nita Desai?
8 Which *Coronation Street* actress was once a hostess on *Double Your Money* and presented a pop music show in the 1960s?
9 Who rescued Elsie Tanner when her house nearly caught fire?
10 Which *Coronation Street* actress once appeared in *The Wheeltappers and Shunters Social Club*?
11 What was the name of the race conflict sitcom that *Coronation Street* writers Harry Driver and Vince Powell penned in the 1970s?
12 Which actor who became the star of this series also appeared as Johnny Webb, Eddie Yeats' binman pal in *Coronation Street*?
13 Has *Coronation Street* ever been transmitted on a Saturday?
14 Which actress played Debbie Webster?
15 Which *Coronation Street* actress appeared in the film *Rita, Sue and Bob Too*?
16 Who wrote the book *The Lights Of Manchester*?
17 Which *Coronation Street* actor was also a talented fencer?
18 Who introduced a video library into the Kabin in 1987?
19 Who played Colin Barnes?
20 On which Bank Holiday did Emily and Ernest Bishop get married?
21 Who was locked in the van when Vikram Desai drove from Calais to Brighton?
22 Chris Oakes, Chris Cook and Paul Fox have all played which character?
23 Which *Coronation Street* actress also appeared in the film *Penny Paradise*?
24 Which actress released an album called *On the Street Where I Live*?
25 Whose boarding house did the Duckworths take over?

Answers

Coronation Street – Pot Luck
1 John Bowe. **2** John Finch. **3** *Raining Stones*. **4** Her sister Debs. **5** He let his insurance policy lapse. **6** Janice Battersby and Jackie Dobbs. **7** Rebecca Sarker. **8** Amanda Barrie. **9** Hilda Ogden. **10** Liz Dawn. **11** *Love Thy Neighbour*. **12** Jack Smethurst. **13** Yes, once on Christmas Day 1999. **14** Sue Devaney. **15** Michelle Holmes (Tina Fowler). **16** Tony Warren. **17** Bryan Mosley. **18** Alan Bradley. **19** Ian Embleton. **20** Easter Monday. **21** Reg Holdsworth. **22** Mark Redman. **23** Betty Driver. **24** Barbara Knox. **25** Eunice Gee's.

Quiz 79 Media

Level 1

1 In which city is Anglia TV based?
2 In 1991 which BBC World Service was added to the radio service?
3 Which flagship BBC TV programme for children began in 1958?
4 GMTV broadcasts on which TV channel?
5 Which major independent radio station opened in 1973 to broadcast to London?
6 Which classical radio station has its own magazine?
7 Granada TV is based in which city?
8 *Grandstand* is chiefly broadcast on which day of the week?
9 Which city name did the *Guardian* have in its name until 1961?
10 Which magazine is an English version of the Spanish celebrity mag Hola!?
11 Which sister paper to the *Independent* is not published Monday to Friday?
12 What did J stand for in the music station JFM?
13 What did W stand for in LWT?
14 Which UK soccer club was the first to have its own TV station?
15 In spring 1999 which late evening news programme disappeared from our TV screens?
16 What does E stand for in the music paper NME?
17 In which newspaper were 'Page 3' girls first seen?
18 What name is given to papers like the *Sun* and the *Mirror* as opposed to broadsheets?
19 What is the subject of The Nigel Dempster pages in the *Daily Mail*?
20 Which major TV listings magazine does not have TV or television in its title?
21 Which radio programme comes from Borsetshire?
22 What does the second B stand for in BSkyB?
23 Where is Channel TV based?
24 Border TV is based on the borders of which two countries?
25 In which decade of the 20th century was *GQ* magazine founded?

Answers

Media

1 Norwich. **2** TV. **3** Blue Peter. **4** ITV. **5** Capital Radio. **6** Classic FM. **7** Manchester. **8** Saturday. **9** Manchester. **10** Hello. **11** Independent on Sunday. **12** Jazz. **13** Weekend. **14** Manchester Utd. **15** News At Ten. **16** Express. **17** The Sun. **18** Tabloids. **19** Celebrity gossip. **20** Radio Times. **21** The Archers. **22** Broadcasting. **23** Channel Islands. **24** England & Scotland. **25** 80s.

Quiz 80 Pot Luck

Level 1

1 Who declared, 'The lady's not for turning'?
2 In the 90s film, who played *G I Jane*?
3 Who won the Eurovision Song Contest along with the Waves?
4 In February 1996 the Princess of Wales agreed to Prince Charles' request for what?
5 Who won a Grammy for Kiss From A Rose?
6 Who stepped down as Lib Dem leader in 1999?
7 What does the I stand for in CBI?
8 Rowan Atkinson was born in which decade of the century?
9 In which country was John Lennon murdered?
10 Johnny Giles represented the Republic of Ireland at which sport?
11 Which singer David starred in *The River* in the 80s sitcom?
12 Chernobyl witnessed a disaster at what type of power station?
13 With which sport is Peter Ebdon associated?
14 Winchester is the administrative centre of which English county?
15 Dennis Skinner has represented which party in parliament?
16 Which item of clothing introduced by Mary Quant symbolised the Swinging Sixties ?
17 Robert Carlyle was born in which part of the UK?
18 In which decade did the sitcom *Roseanne* begin?
19 Who had a 90s No 1 with A Different Beat?
20 At which seaside town was an 80s Tory party conference victim of an IRA bomb?
21 Which sport did Fred Perry take up after becoming world champion at table tennis?
22 Double agent Harold Philby was known by which first name?
23 In which country was Pablo Picasso born?
24 In which decade of the 20th century did Elvis Presley shoot to fame?
25 What followed the names of Rowan and Martin in the classic 60s comedy series?

Answers

Pot Luck

1 Margaret Thatcher. **2** Demi Moore. **3** Katrina. **4** Divorce. **5** Seal. **6** Paddy Ashdown. **7** Industry. **8** 50s. **9** United States. **10** Soccer. **11** Essex. **12** Nuclear power. **13** Snooker. **14** Hampshire. **15** Labour. **16** Miniskirt. **17** Scotland. **18** 1980s. **19** Boyzone. **20** Brighton. **21** Tennis. **22** Kim. **23** Spain. **24** 50s. **25** Laugh In.

Quiz 81 80s

Level 1

1 Duran Duran were part of which New movement?
2 What Purple thing topped the US album charts for 20 weeks?
3 What was the second name of the group starting Spandau?
4 Which pop singer starred in the movie *The Jazz Singer*?
5 Who was Shaky?
6 Who had the best selling album Diva?
7 What number featured in the name of the Fun Boy band?
8 Which Belinda sang that Heaven Is A Place On Earth?
9 Who sang – in Australian – Je Ne Sais Pas Pourquoi?
10 Which King was back in the charts with the re-issued When I Fall In Love?
11 What colour of Box recorded Ride On Time?
12 Who teamed up with Barbara Dickson for I Know Him So Well?
13 Which Bunny had a string of dance successes?
14 What was Diana Ross' only 80s No 1?
15 Who duetted with David Bowie on the No 1 hit Dancing In The Street?
16 Which female solo singer had most chart weeks in 1985, 1986 and 1987?
17 How many hits did Rolf Harris have in the 80s?
18 According to Michael Ball, Love Changes what?
19 Who charted with the old Supremes hit You Can't Hurry Love?
20 Who duetted with Kylie Minogue for a No 1?
21 Which Jennifer sang about The Power of Love?
22 Which charity song was a hit for Band Aid?
23 Every Loser Wins was a winner for which soap actor?
24 Which Sledge had a hit with Frankie?
25 Who was Saving All My Love For You?

Answers

80s

1 Romantics. **2** Rain. **3** Ballet. **4** Neil Diamond. **5** Shakin' Stevens. **6** Annie Lennox. **7** Three. **8** Carlisle. **9** Kylie Minogue. **10** Nat King Cole. **11** Black. **12** Elaine Paige. **13** Jive Bunny. **14** Chain Reaction. **15** Mick Jagger. **16** Madonna. **17** None. **18** Everything. **19** Phil Collins. **20** Jason Donovan. **21** Rush. **22** Do They Know It's Christmas?. **23** Nick Berry. **24** Sister Sledge. **25** Whitney Houston.

Quiz 82 CORONATION ST.

Level 1

Pot Luck

1 Which actor – more famous as Pete Beale in *Eastenders* – once played a character called Fangio Bateman in *Coronation Street*?
2 Which character did Alan Rothwell (David Barlow) play in *Brookside*?
3 Who did Sergei Kasparov propose to before being shopped to immigration officials by a jealous Fred Elliot?
4 Which *Coronation Street* actress also appeared in *Russ Abbott's Madhouse*?
5 Which *Coronation Street* actress also makes fitness videos?
6 Which young character has been played by both Darryl Edwards and Joseph Aston?
7 Who played Tom Ferguson?
8 Who were Sharon Gaskell's witnesses at her wedding to Ian Bentley?
9 Which *Coronation Street* actor also played George Fairchild in the 1980s comedy series *Brass*?
10 Who did Dev help to escape an arranged marriage?
11 Who began dating Linda Sykes' mother, not realising who she was?
12 Who stood first as campaign manager for and then as rival to Audrey in the local elections in 2001?
13 Who was stripped of his winner's title after allegedly entering a vegetarian product in the sausage making contest?
14 Who raped Toyah Battersby?
15 Which *Coronation Street* actress went on to appear as a factory worker in *Clocking Off*?
16 What did Sharon Gaskell start selling in the Kabin in 1999?
17 Which *Coronation Street* actress wrote a book called *All My Burning Bridges*?
18 Which factory girl is played by Naomi Russell?
19 Who does Jason Grimshaw work for?
20 Who kidnapped Arthur the Gnome?
21 Which couple are Weatherfield First Aiders?
22 On which day of the week was *Coronation Street* first transmitted?
23 Who once threw Des Barnes out into the street in his underwear?
24 Who wrote a book called I *Was Ena Sharples' Father*?
25 What was the name of Jim and Liz McDonald's baby daughter?

Answers

Coronation Street – Pot Luck

1 Peter Dean. **2** Nicholas Black. **3** Audrey Roberts. **4** Sherrie Hewson. **5** Beverley Callard. **6** Tommy Duckworth. **7** Tom Wisdom. **8** Sally and Danny. **9** Don Brennan. **10** Sunita Parekh. **11** Fred Elliot. **12** Curly Watts. **13** Ashley Peacock. **14** Phil Simmonds. **15** Sarah Lancashire. **16** Fireworks. **17** Pat Phoenix. **18** Bobbi Lewis. **19** Sally Webster. **20** Norris Cole. **21** Roy and Hayley. **22** Friday. **23** Samantha Failsworth. **24** Tony Warren. **25** Katie.

Quiz 83 Famous Firsts

Level 1

1 Which type of transport was designed by Christopher Cockerell in the 50s?
2 C-Curity was the name of the first type of what?
3 Who was the first man to set foot on the moon?
4 Ruud Gullit became the Premiership's first black manager at which club?
5 Golda Meir was the first female Prime Minister of which country?
6 In which country did the Grunge movement first begin?
7 Helen Sharman was the first British woman to go where?
8 The Bates Motel first appeared in which film?
9 Christiaan Barnard carried out which medical first?
10 Who was the first Spanish golfer to win the British Open?
11 In which decade did the first wheel clamps arrive in Britain?
12 Which Charles first flew non-stop across the Atlantic?
13 Who was the first of Tony Blair's MPs to have won a film Oscar?
14 In 1975, which Arthur became the first black champion in the Men's Singles at Wimbledon?
15 Who starred in the first talkie movie?
16 The first successful cloning of an adult took place with what type of animal?
17 Which major sporting contest first took place in 1930?
18 Which Alexander discovered the first antibiotic?
19 Who was the leader of the first successful expedition to the South Pole?
20 Who were the first group seen on Channel 5?
21 In Jan 1974 professional football in Britain was played for the first time on which day?
22 Which brothers made the first powered plane flight?
23 Which famous first is claimed by Hillary and Tenzing?
24 Who was the first British monarch to abdicate in this century?
25 Which country was the first to send a woman into space?

Answers

Famous Firsts

1 Hovercraft. **2** Zip fastener. **3** Neil Armstrong. **4** Chelsea. **5** Israel. **6** United States. **7** Space. **8** Psycho. **9** Heart transplant. **10** Severiano Ballesteros. **11** 80s. **12** Lindbergh. **13** Glenda Jackson. **14** Ashe. **15** Al Jolson. **16** Sheep. **17** Soccer World Cup. **18** Fleming. **19** Roald Amundsen. **20** Spice Girls. **21** Sunday. **22** Wright. **23** Climbing Everest. **24** Edward VIII. **25** USSR.

Quiz 84 CORONATION ST. Level 1

Pot Luck

1 Who played Vinny Sorrell?
2 Which *Coronation Street* actress has a famous daughter called Rebecca who has appeared in *Band Of Gold* and *The Borrowers*?
3 Who has written nine books about *Coronation Street* ?
4 Who has a van with a sausage on the top of it?
5 Who plays Sunita Parekh?
6 Name Ashley Peacock's assistant who defected to work for Fred Elliot.
7 Who plays Gail Platt?
8 Which of the following characters has not owned the hair salon – Audrey, Denise, Maxine, Fiona?
9 Who plays Todd Grimshaw?
10 Which *Coronation Street* actress was voted Britain's fourth most popular woman in 1982?
11 Who played nurse Wendy Farmer before returning to a more permanent role in the street as a blonde barmaid?
12 Who is Rita's assistant at the Kabin and Post Office?
13 Which 1980s ITV comedy, starring Timothy West, was scripted by *Coronation Street* writers John Stephenson and Julian Roach?
14 Which rival soap started in 1985?
15 What did Harriet the budgie die of?
16 Who played Liz McDonald's boyfriend Frazer Henderson?
17 Who did Angela Griffin, Holly Newman, Gaynor Faye, Tracy Shaw and Jane Danson appear as in *Celebrity Stars in Their Eyes*?
18 Who played Chris Collins?
19 Which chat show host said 'There was life before *Coronation Street* but it didn't add up to much'?
20 Who owned Onyx Fashions in the 1990s?
21 Who took over the print shop from Mike Baldwin in 1994?
22 Who played Douglas Wormold, but later became famous as Boon?
23 Who delivered Brad Armstrong?
24 What are the two main ingredients of hot pot?
25 Who played Darren Whateley?

Answers

Coronation Street – Pot Luck
1 James Gaddas. **2** Beverley Callard. **3** Daran Little. **4** Fred Elliot. **5** Shobna Gulati. **6** Boris Weaver. **7** Helen Worth. **8** Maxine. **9** Bruno Langley. **10** Jean Alexander. **11** Sarah Lancashire. **12** Norris Cole. **13** Brass. **14** *Eastenders*. **15** Shock. **16** Glyn Grain. **17** The Spice Girls. **18** Matthew Marsden. **19** Russell Harty. **20** Hanif Ruparell. **21** Steve McDonald. **22** Michael Elphick. **23** Betty Williams. **24** Lamb and potatoes. **25** Andy Robb.

Quiz 85 The Royals

Level 1

1 John Bryan was reputedly what type of adviser to the Duchess of York?
2 Which prince is the Queen's youngest son?
3 What is Prince Harry's real first name?
4 How is Prince Michael of Kent's wife known?
5 Which princess had a holiday villa on Mustique?
6 What is Prince Charles' Gloucestershire home called?
7 Who was Princess Diana referring to when she said her marriage was 'a bit crowded'?
8 Which Prince was born on the Greek island of Corfu?
9 Which Scottish school did Princes Charles, Andrew and Edward all attend?
10 Which Princess is the mother of Peter Phillips?
11 How many daughters does the Queen Mother have?
12 In which cathedral did Prince Charles marry Lady Diana Spencer?
13 Who celebrated their 80th birthday in June 2001?
14 Anthony Armstrong-Jones took an Earldom named after which mountain after his marriage to Princess Margaret?
15 Which hair colour is shared by Earl Spencer and his nephew Prince Harry?
16 What is the name of the Spencer ancestral home in Northamptonshire?
17 With which royal's name was Koo Stark's linked in the early 80s?
18 Which name of a castle does Prince Edward use as a professional surname when working in the media?
19 At which English university did Prince Charles study?
20 Which school did Princes William and Harry attend in the late 90s?
21 In which 80s war did Prince Andrew serve?
22 Major Ronald Ferguson is the father of which Duchess?
23 Which Royal wrote *The Old Man of Lochnagar*?
24 Which branch of the construction industry is Viscount Linley involved in?
25 Which Royal has had a collection of his paintings exhibited?

Answers

The Royals

1 Financial. **2** Edward. **3** Henry. **4** Princess Michael of Kent. **5** Margaret. **6** Highgrove. **7** Camilla Parker Bowles. **8** Philip. **9** Gordonstoun. **10** Anne. **11** Two. **12** St Paul's. **13** Prince Philip. **14** Snowdon. **15** Red. **16** Althorp. **17** Prince Andrew. **18** Windsor. **19** Cambridge. **20** Eton. **21** Falklands. **22** York. **23** Prince Charles. **24** Carpentry. **25** Prince Charles.

Quiz 86 CORONATION ST.

Level 1

Pot Luck

1 Which actress played Annie Walker?
2 Who is the current cleaner of the Rovers?
3 Which *Brookside* actress played barmaid Gloria Todd in the 1980s?
4 Who celebrated 30 years' service at the Rovers in 1999?
5 Who suffered a fatal heart attack in the Rovers in 1964?
6 What was the name of Ken's mother?
7 What was the name of Ken's father?
8 Where were Ken's twins Susan and Peter brought up?
9 Who was the first person Deirdre was ever engaged to?
10 What is the name of Tracy's husband?
11 How did Eddie Yeats meet his fiancée Marion Willis, aka 'Stardust Lil'?
12 What was the name of Emily's first husband?
13 Who did Ashley Peacock go out with before marrying Maxine?
14 Who was Deirdre's first husband?
15 Who did Linda Baldwin have an affair with before marrying Mike?
16 Who was Maureen Holdsworth's mother?
17 What is the relationship between Natalie Barnes and Debs Brownlow?
18 What was the name of Jack Duckworth's brother?
19 Name Gail Platt's eldest son.
20 How did Brian Tilsley die?
21 Which of the following famous people have not appeared on *Coronation Street*: Joanna Lumley, Robbie Coltrane or Ben Kingsley?
22 Where did Reg Holdsworth move to when he left the Street?
23 What was the name of the Malletts' dog?
24 Which Liverpool actress played Tyrone Dobbs' mum, Jackie?
25 Who was Judy Mallett's mother?

Answers

Coronation Street – Pot Luck

1 Doris Speed. **2** Edna Miller. **3** Sue 'Jackie Corkhill' Jenkins. **4** Betty Williams. **5** Martha Longhurst. **6** Ida. **7** Frank. **8** Glasgow. **9** Billy Walker. **10** Robert Preston. **11** On CB radio. **12** Ernest Bishop. **13** Zoe Tattersall. **14** Ray Langton. **15** His son, Mark Redman. **16** Maud Grimes. **17** Sisters. **18** Clifford. **19** Nick. **20** He was stabbed outside a nightclub. **21** Robbie Coltrane. **22** Lowestoft. **23** Scamper. **24** Margi Clarke. **25** Joyce Smedley.

Quiz 87 TV Trivia

Level 1

1. Who with Greg Dyke was credited with saving TV am?
2. Which model advertised Pizza Hut with Jonathan Ross?
3. Who found fame in the docusoap about a driving school?
4. Which TV personality appeared on The Archers – as himself – for their 10,000th episode?
5. From which part of her house did Delia Smith present her 90s TV series?
6. Which duo began as stand-up comics called The Menopause Sisters?
7. Which airline did Jeremy Spake from *Airport* work for?
8. In which supermarket ad did Jane Horrocks play Prunella Scales' daughter?
9. Fred Housego shot to fame as a winner on which TV show?
10. Who replaced Danny Baker on *Pets Win Prizes*?
11. Who provided the music for *The Wombles*?
12. Who or what did Barbara Woodhouse train?
13. Which *Ready Steady Cook* regular was also a regular presenter on *Breakfast Time*?
14. What is the subject of the Quentin Wilson show *All the Right Moves*?
15. What was Keith Floyd's TV show based on Far East cooking called?
16. Who interviewed Prince Edward and Sophie Rhys Jones in a pre wedding programme?
17. Who wrote and sang the theme music to *Spender*?
18. Which early presenter of the *Big Breakfast* wore glasses?
19. Who was the original presenter of *Gladiators* with Ulrika Jonsson?
20. Which drama series was based on the Constable novels by Nicholas Rhea?
21. Which series had the tag line 'The truth is out there....'?
22. Who worked together on *The Frost Report* and went on to have their own successful series together?
23. Which quiz began with 'Your starter for ten..'?
24. Which work of reference do the celebrity and the expert possess in *Countdown*?
25. Which soap powder did Robbie Coltrane advertise?

Answers

TV Trivia

1 Roland Rat **2** Caprice **3** Maureen Rees **4** Terry Wogan **5** Conservatory **6** French & Saunders **7** Aeroflot **8** Tesco **9** Mastermind **10** Dale Winton **11** Mike Batt **12** Dogs **13** Fern Britton **14** Property **15** Far Flung Floyd **16** Sue Barker **17** Jimmy Nail **18** Chris Evans **19** John Fashanu **20** Heartbeat **21** The X Files **22** The Two Ronnies **23** University Challenge **24** Oxford Dictionary **25** Persil

Quiz 88 Pot Luck

Level 1

1 Robert Mugabe was the first Prime Minister of which country?
2 Boy George fronted which Club?
3 Which Nazi died in jail after being imprisoned for 46 years?
4 In fiction what is the last name of Dr Hannibal – the Cannibal?
5 Who sang Little Donkey with Nina?
6 How did Allen Stewart Konigsberg become better known?
7 Brown-Eyed Handsome Man was a hit for which singer after his death?
8 Chelmsford is the administrative centre of which English county?
9 Which Jeremy was a 90s *University Challenge* presenter?
10 What was developed in the 40s Manhattan Project?
11 Which character did Johnny Briggs play in *Coronation Street*?
12 Which group sacked drummer Pete Best before they hit the big time?
13 In medicine, what does the D stand for in CJD?
14 Fluck & Law were famous for their puppets on which show?
15 Which William wrote the novel *Lord Of The Flies*?
16 Which sitcom with Rowan Atkinson was set in Gasforth Police station?
17 Who had a 90s No 1 with Back For Good?
18 What was the surname of the father and son rag and bone men who lived at Mews Cottage, Oil Drum Lane?
19 What is the first name of best selling sci fi writer Pratchett?
20 Cookery writer and TV presenter Loyd Grossman hails from which country?
21 Which late comedian had 'short, fat, hairy legs'?
22 Which motorway links London to Cambridge?
23 Timothy Dalton and Pierce Brosnan have both played which character?
24 Which sport in the Olympics includes pikes, tucks and twists?
25 Which Freddie, born Freddie Fowell, earned a reputation as one of Britain's most outrageous comedians?

Answers

Pot Luck

1 Zimbabwe. **2** Culture. **3** Rudolf Hess. **4** Lecter. **5** Frederick . **6** Woody Allen. **7** Buddy Holly. **8** Essex. **9** Paxman. **10** Atomic Bomb. **11** Mike Baldwin. **12** The Beatles. **13** Disease. **14** Spitting Image. **15** Golding. **16** The Thin Blue Line. **17** Take That. **18** Steptoe. **19** Terry. **20** USA. **21** Ernie Wise. **22** M11. **23** James Bond. **24** Diving. **25** Starr.

Quiz 89 TV Soaps

Level 1

1 Which Grove was a popular teen soap?
2 In which soap was Blake married to Alexis, then Krystle?
3 Which member of the Mitchell family was killed on New Year's Eve 1998?
4 Which soap community has the postcode E20?
5 In which soap was the body of a wife-beater famously buried under the patio?
6 Which day of the week is the *EastEnders* omnibus edition?
7 Which chocolate makers first sponsored *Coronation Street* in 1996?
8 Which doomed BBC soap was set in Spain?
9 *The Colbys* was a spin-off from which US soap?
10 What was *Emmerdale* called when it was first screened in the afternoon?
11 *Knots Landing* was a spin-off from which oil based soap?
12 As opposed to oil, *Falcon Crest* was about which commodity California is famous for?
13 Which Ken is the only original member of the *Coronation Street* cast?
14 In which Ward was the Emergency in TV's first medical soap?
15 In 1993 *Emmerdale* suffered an air disaster similar to which real life tragedy?
16 Which late comedian Larry was Meg Richardson's wedding chauffeur in *Crossroads*?
17 Which soap launched the pop careers of Kylie Minogue and Jason Donovan?
18 Which soap ran the classic cliff-hanger 'Who shot J.R.?'?
19 How did *Take The High Road* change its name from 1995 onwards?
20 Which blonde replaced Vera behind the bar at the Rovers Return?
21 In *Coronation Street*, what does Mike Baldwin's factory make?
22 In *EastEnders*, who did Peggy marry in 1999?
23 In which Cheshire location was *Hollyoaks* set?
24 Which soap from Down Under was created to rival *Neighbours*?
25 Which soap for children was set in a London comprehensive?

Answers

TV Soaps
1 Byker. **2** Dynasty. **3** Tiffany. **4** Walford. **5** Brookside. **6** Sunday. **7** Cadbury's. **8** ElDorado. **9** Dynasty. **10** Emmerdale Farm. **11** Dallas. **12** Wine. **13** Barlow. **14** 10. **15** Lockerbie. **16** Grayson. **17** Neighbours. **18** Dallas. **19** High Road. **20** Natalie. **21** Underwear. **22** Frank. **23** Chester. **24** Home & Away. **25** Grange Hill.

Quiz 90 Pot Luck

Level 1

1 Which Earl was the brother of Diana, Princess of Wales?
2 In music who 'just called to say I love you'?
3 A Swedish car displays which international vehicle registration mark?
4 Which of the Barrymore family featured in the film *Batman Forever*?
5 What type of beer is served in *Coronation Street*'s Rovers' Return?
6 Derek Underwood played which sport for England?
7 The MRLP is what kind of Raving Loony Party?
8 Marion Morrison become famous under which name?
9 Who wrote the novel *The Shining*?
10 What does the B stand for in SCUBA diving?
11 On which day was the midweek Lottery first drawn?
12 Which Welsh city had a millennium sports stadium built?
13 The deepwater port of Kagoshima was built in which country?
14 In advertising, Fry's Turkish Delight was described as being 'Full of Eastern' what?
15 Which soccer team does Jo Brand follow?
16 Which Joseph was Hitler's minister of propaganda?
17 On which Isle was Ronaldsway airport built?
18 With which sport is Curtis Strange associated?
19 Cheery entertainer Jim Davidson was born in which decade?
20 General Pinochet was a former ruler of which country?
21 Who lost part of his ear to the teeth of Mike Tyson in 1997?
22 Which Liverpool comedian Jimmy went to the same school as John Lennon?
23 BB King is associated with which musical instrument?
24 Lord Mountbatten was the last viceroy of which country?
25 In which chapel did Edward and Sophie Rhys-Jones get married?

Answers

Pot Luck

1 Spencer. **2** Stevie Wonder. **3** S. **4** Drew. **5** Newton and Ridley. **6** Cricket. **7** Monster. **8** John Wayne. **9** Stephen King. **10** Breathing. **11** Wednesday. **12** Cardiff. **13** Japan. **14** Promise. **15** Crystal Palace. **16** Goebbels. **17** Isle of Man. **18** Golf. **19** 50s. **20** Chile. **21** Evander Holyfield. **22** Tarbuck. **23** Guitar. **24** India. **25** St George's.

Quiz 91 Horse Racing

Level 1

1 Who returned to racing in 1990 when he was over 50?
2 Which horse was first to win the Grand National three times?
3 Where is the William Hill Lincoln Handicap held?
4 Trainers Lynda and John Ramsden won a libel case against which paper?
5 In which country was Shergar captured?
6 In which month is the Melbourne Cup held?
7 Who was National Hunt champion jockey from 1986 to 1992?
8 Which horse Benny won the 1997 Derby?
9 Which English classic is held at Doncaster?
10 What is a £500 bet known as?
11 Why was the Cheltenham Festival cancelled in 2001 ?
12 The Prix du Jockey-Club is held at which race course?
13 Which horse had the nickname Corky?
14 Which Gordon, a trainer of over 2000 winners, died in September 1998?
15 Which country hosts the Belmont and Preakness Stakes?
16 Who chartered a train from Victoria to Epsom to watch the 1997 Derby at a cost of over £11,000?
17 Which race meeting is described as Glorious?
18 The 12th Earl of where gave his name to a famous race?
19 Which horsewoman was the first Mrs Mark Phillips?
20 After a Saturday bomb threat in 1997 on which day was the National run?
21 The Curragh is in which Irish county?
22 Which horse was the first to win Horse of the Year four times?
23 Where did Frankie Dettori have his record-breaking seven wins?
24 Which horse won the Derby by a record distance in 1981?
25 In which country is Flemington Park race course?

Answers

Horse Racing

1 Lester Piggott. **2** Red Rum. **3** Doncaster. **4** The Sporting Life. **5** Ireland. **6** November. **7** Peter Scudamore. **8** The Dip. **9** St Leger. **10** Monkey. **11** Because of Foot and Mouth Disease. **12** Chantilly. **13** Corbiere. **14** Richards. **15** United States. **16** The Queen. **17** Goodwood. **18** Derby. **19** Princess Anne. **20** Monday. **21** Kildare. **22** Desert Orchid. **23** Ascot. **24** Shergar. **25** Australia.

Quiz 92 The Oscars

Level 1

1 Which veteran actress Katharine was the first actress to win four Oscars?
2 Which 1997 movie equalled *Ben Hur*'s record 11 Oscars?
3 Which Emma won an Oscar for her screenplay of *Sense and Sensibility*?
4 Who won his second Oscar in successive years for *Forrest Gump*?
5 Judi Dench won an Oscar as which Queen in *Shakespeare in Love*?
6 Who won Best Actor and Best Director Oscar for *Dances With Wolves*?
7 Who won his second Oscar for the autistic Raymond in *Rain Man*?
8 In the 70s which gangster film won an Oscar, as did its sequel?
9 In 1997 James Cameron won an Oscar for which blockbuster?
10 Geoffrey Rush won an Oscar for *Shine*, as what type of musician?
11 For which film about a Scottish hero did Mel Gibson win his first Oscars for Best Picture and Best Director?
12 Which Nick won an Oscar for *The Wrong Trousers*?
13 Which lyricist who has worked with Elton John and Andrew Lloyd Webber won an award for A Whole New World from *Aladdin*?
14 In which film did Jodie Foster play FBI agent Clarice Starling?
15 Who won an Oscar wearing an eye patch in *True Grit*?
16 Which film with Ralph Fiennes won Anthony Minghella an Oscar?
17 Which Jessica was the then oldest Oscar winner for *Driving Miss Daisy*?
18 Nigel Hawthorne was Oscar nominated for The Madness of which King?
19 Which Oscar nominated film had You Sexy Thing as its theme song?
20 The multi-Oscar winning *The Deer Hunter* was about steelworkers who went to fight where?
21 Which Julie won an Oscar for *Darling* in 1965 and was Oscar nominated in 1998 for *Afterglow*?
22 For which 80s film was Pauline Collins nominated for playing a bored Liverpool housewife?
23 Which Oscar winner from *The Silence of the Lambs* campaigned to save Snowdonia in 1998?
24 Which musical based on Romeo & Juliet was a 60s Oscar winner?
25 Raindrops Keep Falling On My Head was an Oscar winner from which movie with Robert Redford & Paul Newman?

Answers

The Oscars

1 Hepburn. **2** Titanic. **3** Thompson. **4** Tom Hanks. **5** Elizabeth I. **6** Kevin Costner. **7** Dustin Hoffman. **8** The Godfather. **9** Titanic. **10** Pianist. **11** Braveheart. **12** Park. **13** Tim Rice. **14** The Silence of the Lambs. **15** John Wayne. **16** The English Patient. **17** Tandy. **18** George. **19** The Full Monty. **20** Vietnam. **21** Christie. **22** Shirley Valentine. **23** Anthony Hopkins. **24** West Side Story. **25** Butch Cassidy & The Sundance Kid.

Quiz 93 On Line

Level 1

1 What does the first W stand for in WWW?
2 If you surf the Internet what do you do?
3 Which page of a Web site is called a Home Page?
4 In addition to the computer, what else must a modem be plugged into?
5 What does Q mean in FAQ?
6 What does S mean in ISP?
7 In which country did the Internet start?
8 A small a in a circle (@) is pronounced how?
9 What name is given to the software program needed to access the Web?
10 What goes after Netscape in the name of a popular Internet browser?
11 If you have an active Internet connection you are said to be on what?
12 What is the opposite of downloading?
13 What is freeware?
14 If you log off, what do you do?
15 What is netiquette?
16 What is the minimum number of computers which can be networked?
17 What letter appears on the computer screen when you are using Microsoft Internet Explorer?
18 Which name of something used by avid readers is the Netscape Navigator name for Favorites?
19 Where does bounced e-mail return to?
20 Which 'space' refers to the Internet and all that goes with it?
21 What does offline mean?
22 A newbie is a new what?
23 In an e-mail address how is a symbol like a full stop said out loud?
24 What name is given to a program designed to cause damage by attaching itself to other programs?
25 What is Microsoft's browser software called?

Answers

On Line
1 World. **2** Look around. **3** First. **4** Phone. **5** Question. **6** Service. **7** USA. **8** At. **9** Browser. **10** Navigator. **11** Line. **12** Uploading. **13** Free software. **14** Disconnect. **15** Good behaviour on the net. **16** Two. **17** E. **18** Bookmarks. **19** Sender. **20** Cyberspace. **21** Not connected. **22** Internet user. **23** Dot. **24** Virus. **25** Internet Explorer.

Quiz 94 Pop 90s

Level 1

1 What was finally a top ten hit for Ce Ce Peniston on its 1992 re-release?
2 Who recorded the album Nevermind?
3 Who had a Christmas No 1 in 1996, 1997 and 1998?
4 Who had a hit with the old song I Believe?
5 What kind of Doll did Aqua sing about?
6 Whose debut album was called Doggystyle?
7 Which girl group led the 1995 Party In The Park for the Prince's Trust?
8 Edele and Keavy Lynch were together in which group?
9 What is Billie's surname?
10 Which film revived the 70s song You Sexy Thing?
11 How did Kurt Kobain end his life?
12 Which team do the Gallagher brothers support?
13 What was the first single of The Spice Girls?
14 Which soccer team sang Come On You Reds?
15 Whose debut album was Talk On Corners?
16 Norman Cook is better known as which club DJ?
17 Which group's first No 1 was Some Might Say?
18 Richie Edwards vanished in 1995 leaving behind which group?
19 Who had success with Abba-esque?
20 Who was Mrs Bob Geldof when the 90s started?
21 Which alternative dance group first charted with Charly?
22 Which Heather sang with M People?
23 Which chart topper was pink, tall, spotted and very destructive?
24 Whose Nothing Compares 2 U made No 1 in both the UK and the US?
25 An advert for which drink led to Perez Prado being back in the charts?

Answers

Pop 90s

1 Finally. **2** Nirvana. **3** Spice Girls. **4** Robson & Jerome. **5** Barbie. **6** Snoop Doggy Dog. **7** All Saints. **8** B*Witched. **9** Piper. **10** The Full Monty. **11** He shot himself. **12** Man City. **13** Wannabe. **14** Man Utd. **15** The Corrs. **16** Fatboy Slim. **17** Oasis. **18** Manic Street Preachers. **19** Erasure. **20** Paula Yates. **21** Prodigy. **22** Small. **23** Mr Blobby. **24** Sinead O'Connor. **25** Guinness.

Quiz 95 Technology

Level 1

1 What does the G stand for in WYSIWYG?
2 In which decade was the Sony Walkman stereo launched?
3 Oftel regulates which industry?
4 Which phone company adopted a colour name before going into the red?
5 Which UK motor company produced the Prefect?
6 What kind of codes did American supermarkets introduce in the mid 70s?
7 What does the B stand for in IBM?
8 The Three Mile Island nuclear leak in the 70s was in which country?
9 What did pirate radio stations broadcast?
10 Which Bill formed Microsoft?
11 Which 'unsinkable' craft sank in 1912?
12 Which Clarence pioneered quick freezing in the food industry?
13 The tallest tower of the 70s, the Sears Tower, was built in which country?
14 Foods will not brown in what type of oven?
15 What used to go round at thirty three and a third r.p.m.?
16 In which decade was the Channel Tunnel first opened?
17 What did Lazlo Biro invent in the 30s?
18 The wide-bodied passenger-carrying Boeing 747 became known as what type of jet?
19 Which popular small car was introduced by Austin Morris at the end of the 50s?
20 Which country combined with Britain in building Concorde?
21 What touches the surface of a CD when playing?
22 What does the F stand for in FM?
23 The Sony company originated in which country?
24 Modulator-Demodulator is usually shortened to what?
25 What was the middle name of TV pioneer John Baird?

Answers

Technology

1 Get. **2** 70s. **3** Telecommunications. **4** Orange. **5** Ford. **6** Bar codes. **7** Business. **8** United States. **9** Pop music. **10** Gates. **11** Titanic. **12** Birdseye. **13** United States. **14** Microwave. **15** Long playing records. **16** 90s. **17** Ballpoint pen. **18** Jumbo. **19** Mini. **20** France. **21** Nothing. **22** Frequency. **23** Japan. **24** Modem. **25** Logie.

Quiz 96 CORONATION ST. Level 1

Pot Luck

1 What house number does Emily Bishop live at?
2 Who is Emily Bishop's lodger?
3 *Coronation Street* creator Tony Warren is now an MBE: True or false?
4 Mike and Alma are now officially divorced: True or false?
5 What is Fred Elliot's catchphrase?
6 Who plays Sarah Louise Platt's younger brother?
7 Which famous musical star made a 'phantom' appearance as an extra on *Coronation Street* in the 1990s?
8 And which famous singer and fan of the show once appeared anonymously in the Rovers bar?
9 Who did Vera donate a kidney to last year?
10 What is the name of Curly and Raquel's daughter?
11 Where does Eileen Grimshaw work?
12 Where does Bobbi Lewis work?
13 Who lives at Number 7?
14 Who is godfather to Natalie Barnes' baby?
15 Who was known as the nanny from hell?
16 Which actor – now a writer – played Eddie Ramsden?
17 Which series about binmen, starring Tim Healey and Edward Woodward, did he write?
18 Which *Coronation Street* actress is married to Tim Healey?
19 In which year did the Duckworths take over the Rovers?
20 What did Kevin and Alison Webster call their son?
21 Who was Kelly Thomson's boyfriend?
22 Who did pensioner Lily Dempsey throw an egg at during the battle for Mayfield Court?
23 What did the Wiltons fear Norris had buried on their allotment?
24 Who got Tricia Armstrong pregnant?
25 Fred Elliot once proposed to Rita Sullivan, true or false?

Answers

Coronation Street – Pot Luck
1 Number three. **2** Norris Cole. **3** True. **4** True. **5** 'I say'. **6** Jack P Shepherd. **7** Michael Crawford. **8** Cliff Richard. **9** Paul Clayton. **10** Alice. **11** Street Cars. **12** Underworld. **13** Curly and Emma. **14** Kevin Webster. **15** Carmel Finnan. **16** William Ivory. **17** Common as Muck. **18** Denise Welch. **19** 1995. **20** Jake. **21** Ashley Peacock. **22** Audrey. **23** His wife Angela's body. **24** Terry Duckworth. **25** True.

Quiz 97 TV Times

Level 1

1 In which country was *Due South* set?
2 Which George played Doug Ross in *ER*?
3 Which show was set in a Boston bar 'Where everybody knows your name'?
4 In which decade was the first Eurovision Song Contest?
5 In which Yorkshire location was *Band of Gold* set?
6 Which ex-Bond Girl Jane played *Dr Quinn: Medicine Woman*?
7 Which animated series was originally to have been called *The Flagstones*?
8 Which other Kelly presented the first series of *Game For A Laugh* with Henry?
9 Henry Winkler's Arthur Fonzarelli was better known as what?
10 How many sisters established *The House of Elliot*?
11 Which Jim might have fixed it for you?
12 What was the first name of arch snob Mrs Bucket – pronounced Bouquet?
13 The *Larry Sanders Show* was a spoof of what type of show?
14 In Last of the Summer Wine what wrinkled part of Nora Batty was a source of fascination for Compo?
15 Which action drama centred on Blue Watch B25, Blackwall?
16 *The Mary Whitehouse Experience* came to TV from which radio station?
17 I Could Be So Good for You was a Dennis Waterman hit from which show he starred in with George Cole?
18 Caroline Aherne was the alter ego of which pensioner chat show hostess?
19 Which cult sci fi series was originally to have been called *Wagon Train to the Stars*?
20 Which show featured Noo Noo the vacuum cleaner?
21 Which so called yuppie drama series was set in Philadelphia and was first shown in the UK on Channel 4?
22 Which East London football team did Alf Garnett support?
23 In the 70s series what followed *Tinker, Tailor, Soldier* in the title?
24 Which line followed 'It's goodnight from me...' on *The Two Ronnies*?
25 What was the job of Hudson in *Upstairs Downstairs*?

Answers

TV Times

1 Canada. **2** Clooney. **3** Cheers. **4** 50s. **5** Bradford. **6** Seymour. **7** The Flintstones. **8** Matthew. **9** The Fonz. **10** Two. **11** Saville. **12** Hyacinth. **13** Chat show. **14** Stockings. **15** London's Burning. **16** Radio 1. **17** Minder. **18** Mrs Merton. **19** Star Trek. **20** Teletubbies. **21** Thirtysomething. **22** West Ham. **23** Spy. **24** And it's goodnight from him. **25** Butler.

Quiz 98 Sports Bag

Level 1

1 What is 'Magic' Johnson's first name?
2 How many attempts at the target does a player get in curling?
3 In which Spanish city were the 1992 Olympics held?
4 Eric Cantona joined Man Utd from which club?
5 The Vince Lombardi trophy is awarded in which sport?
6 Gabriela Sabatini comes from which country?
7 In which event did Bob Beaman hold an Olympic record for over 20 years?
8 Graeme Le Saux was born in which group of islands?
9 What did Dionico Ceron win three years in a row in England's capital city?
10 In which month of the year is the Super Bowl held?
11 In 1999 Ian McGeechan became coach of which international rugby team?
12 What word can follow American, Association or Gaelic to name a sport?
13 Which sport has a team that plays at a Cottage?
14 Which country won cricket's 1996 World Cup?
15 In which sport is the Cowdray Park Cup awarded?
16 In American Football, where do the Colts come from?
17 What was athlete Florence Griffith-Joyner usually known as?
18 Rugby's William Henry Hare was better known by what nickname?
19 In athletics, what does the first A stand for in the initials IAAF?
20 Which team did Jock Stein lead to European Cup success?
21 Micky Mantle played which sport?
22 Which Nigel was BBC Sports Personality in 1992?
23 In which city does the Tour de France finish?
24 Norman Whiteside became the youngest soccer player of the century for which international side?
25 Who played Australia in cricket's drawn 1999 World Cup semi-final?

Answers

Sports Bag

1 Earvin. **2** Two. **3** Barcelona. **4** Leeds. **5** American Football. **6** Argentina. **7** Long jump. **8** Channel. **9** Marathon. **10** January. **11** Scotland. **12** Football. **13** Soccer – Fulham. **14** Sri Lanka. **15** Polo. **16** Baltimore. **17** Flo-Jo. **18** Dusty. **19** Amateur. **20** Celtic. **21** Baseball. **22** Mansell. **23** Paris. **24** N Ireland. **25** S Africa.

Quiz 99 Screen Greats

Level 1

1 Boris Karloff starred as which monster in one of the first horror movies?
2 Which actor is the father of actress Jamie Lee Curtis?
3 Arnold Schwarzenegger married the niece of which US president?
4 Which TV soap was Rock Hudson a star of shortly before his death?
5 Which actress born Ruth Elizabeth Davis was the first female president of the Academy of Motion Picture Arts & Sciences?
6 Which Ford of *Star Wars* was voted Film Star of the century by a panel of critics in 1994?
7 In which city did Steve McQueen take part in the car chase in *Bullitt*?
8 Richard Gere is a follower of which eastern religion?
9 Which screen great was Lauren Bacall married to at the time of his death?
10 In which country was Marlene Dietrich born?
11 Who found fame as *Alfie*?
12 Which Oscar winner for From *Here To Eternity*, more famous as Ol' Blue Eyes the singer, died in 1998?
13 In which country was Cary Grant born as Archie Leach?
14 Which star of *The Godfather* in the 70s played opposite Vivien Leigh in *A Streetcar Named Desire* in the 50s?
15 Which dancing duo's first film together was called *Flying Down to Rio*?
16 Which dancer, the star of *Singing in the Rain*, never won an Oscar?
17 *Rebel Without A Cause* made a star of which actor whose life was cut short in a car accident?
18 Grace Kelly became Princess of which principality where her film *To Catch a Thief* was set?
19 In which movie did Alec Guinness first appear as Ben Obi Wan Kenobi?
20 Which comedian starred with Bing Crosby in the *Road* films?
21 What is the name of Michael Douglas's father?
22 Which star Joan was the subject of the movie *Mommie Dearest*?
23 Which Jack won an Oscar for *One Flew Over the Cuckoo's Nest*?
24 Which Russian Doctor was played in the 60s by Omar Sharif?
25 Who found fame trying to resist the charms of Mrs Robinson in *The Graduate*?

Answers

Screen Greats

1 Frankenstein's. **2** Tony. **3** John F Kennedy. **4** Dynasty. **5** Bette Davis. **6** Harrison. **7** San Francisco. **8** Buddhism. **9** Humphrey Bogart. **10** Germany. **11** Michael Caine. **12** Frank Sinatra. **13** England. **14** Marlon Brando. **15** Fred Astaire/Ginger Rogers. **16** Gene Kelly. **17** James Dean. **18** Monaco. **19** Star Wars. **20** Bob Hope. **21** Kirk. **22** Crawford. **23** Nicholson. **24** Zhivago. **25** Dustin Hoffman.

Quiz 100 CORONATION ST.

Level 1

Who's Who

1 Who deliberately flooded Natalie Horrocks' house?
2 Which famous comedy actress from *Open All Hours* played amorous Renee Turnbull?
3 Who married Maureen in a big wedding complete with barbershop quartet?
4 Who did Kenneth Farrington play?
5 Name the arcade boss that Judy Mallett had sex with for £2000.
6 Who became shop steward at Mike's factory in 1980?
7 Who played Don Watkins, but was more famous for his role in *The Bill*?
8 Who was the landlady of the White Swan?
9 Who played Rebecca Hopkins?
10 What was the name of the actor who played Jon Lindsay?
11 Who went in search of her real father and ended up being kidnapped by Neil Flynn?
12 Who threw herself into a canal in a suicide attempt?
13 Who played Greg Kelly?
14 Who broke his toe while stealing cobbles from the Street?
15 Who went to a hypnotist to stop smoking and adopted the seventeenth century persona of 'Lusty Jack'?
16 Who sold Vera the car that she was driving when she crashed with Judy as a passenger?
17 What did Judy subsequently die of?
18 Who found Judy's body?
19 Which two rival families were furious to find themselves staying on the same caravan site on holiday in Wales?
20 Which popular character underwent a triple bypass after suffering a heart attack brought on by the amorous advances of Eunice Gee?
21 Who travelled to the Far East to scatter Sidney Templeton's ashes over the bridge he helped build as a POW?
22 What did Rita give Sharon Gaskell as a birthday present in 1999?
23 Which comedy series did Sue Nicholls appear in as secretary Joan?
24 Who had an abortion in 1999 at the insistence of her husband?
25 Which actress from *Coronation Street* can also be seen in the BBC2 comedy *Two Pints of Lager and a Packet of Crisps*?

Answers

Coronation Street – Who's Who

1 Sally Webster. **2** Lynda Baron. **3** Fred Elliot. **4** Billy Walker. **5** Paul Fisher. **6** Ivy Tilsley. **7** Kevin Lloyd. **8** Stella Rigby. **9** Jill Halfpenny. **10** Owen Aaronovitch. **11** Toyah. **12** Zoe Tattersall. **13** Stephen Billington. **14** Les Battersby. **15** Jack Duckworth. **16** Terry Duckworth. **17** An embolism brought on by the impact of the crash. **18** Emily. **19** The Platts and the Battersbys. **20** Jack. **21** Emily and Maud. **22** The Kabin. **23** *The Rise and Fall of Reginald Perrin*. **24** Leanne Battersby. **25** Beverley Callard.

The Medium Questions

This next selection of questions is getting a little more like it. For an open entry quiz then you should have a high percentage of medium level questions – don't try to break people's spirits with the hard ones. Just make sure that they play to their ability.

Like all questions, these can be classed as either easy or impossible depending on whether you know the answer or not, and although common knowledge is used as the basis for these questions, there is a sting in the tail of quite a few. Also, if you have a serious drinking squad playing, then they can more or less say goodbye to the prize, but that isn't to say they will feel any worse about it.

Specialists are the people to watch out for, as those with a good knowledge of a particular subject will doubtless do well in these rounds, so a liberal sprinkling of pot-luck questions is needed to flummox them.

Quiz 1 CORONATION ST. Level 2

What Year Was It?

1 When did Jerry Booth marry Myra Dickenson?
2 When did Suzie Birchall move into Coronation Street?
3 When did Steve McDonald marry Vicky Arden?
4 When did Steph and Des Barnes move to Coronation Street?
5 When did Fred Gee marry Eunice Nuttall?
6 When was Tommy Duckworth born?
7 When did Martha Longhurst die?
8 When was Nicky Tilsley born?
9 When did Curly move into Coronation Street?
10 When did Jack Walker die?
11 When was Ernie Bishop shot?
12 When did Bet and Alec get married?
13 When did Marion Willis first appear in Coronation Street?
14 When were Steve and Elsie Tanner married?
15 When did Lisa Duckworth die?
16 When did Minnie Caldwill leave Coronation Street?
17 When did Len Fairclough die?
18 When was *Coronation Street* filmed in colour for the first time?
19 When did Ken Barlow marry Janet Reid?
20 When were Peter and Susan Barlow born?
21 When did Maggie Clegg leave Coronation Street?
22 When were Emily and Ernie Bishop married?
23 When did Ken Barlow marry Valerie Tatlock?
24 When did Ena Sharples leave Coronation Street?
25 When did Kevin and Sally buy Number 13 Coronation Street?

Answers

Coronation Street – What Year Was It?

1 1963. **2** 1977. **3** 1995. **4** 1990. **5** 1981. **6** 1992. **7** 1964. **8** 1980. **9** 1983. **10** 1970. **11** 1978 **12** 1987. **13** 1982. **14** 1967. **15** 1993. **16** 1976. **17** 1983. **18** 1969. **19** 1973. **20** 1965. **21** 1974. **22** 1972. **23** 1962. **24** 1980. **25** 1988.

Quiz 2 20th C Who's Who

Level 2

1 Who did Pope John Paul II succeed as Pope?
2 What did the letter F stand for in the name of President J F Kennedy?
3 Gitta Sereny courted controversy for writing a book about which convicted killer?
4 Who became the first woman prime minister of an Islamic nation?
5 Who said, 'The Trent is lovely too. I've walked on it for 18 years'?
6 Tom Whittaker was the first man to climb Everest in what circumstances?
7 Who was posthumously pardoned in 1998 after being hanged for the murder of a policeman in 1953?
8 Who replaced Mary Robinson as president of Ireland in 1997?
9 Which American president had the middle name Baines?
10 Which Russian dictator imposed a reign of terror throughout the 30s and 40s?
11 On TV who originally asked contestants to Take Their Pick?
12 Who was the only female MP in The Gang of Four?
13 Who made the official speech opening the Scottish Parliament?
14 Who once described his paintings as 'hand-painted dream photographs'?
15 Donald Woods escaped which country in 1979, a story later made into the film *Cry Freedom*?
16 What was the name of the Chinese leader whose widow was arrested for trying to overthrow the government in the 1970s?
17 Where was Ronnie Biggs arrested in 1974 after over eight years on the run?
18 Which manager signed the first Catholic player for Glasgow Rangers?
19 In 1968 The Oscars were postponed for 48 hours because of whose death?
20 Who succeeded Lal Bahadur Shastri as Prime Minister of India?
21 In the 1960s the Queen dedicated an acre of ground in the UK to the memory of whom?
22 Who created Fantasyland, Adventureland and Frontierland?
23 Who led so-called witch hunts against communists in the USA after WWII?
24 Which kidnap victim was involved in a bank raid, brandishing a gun, even after a ransom had been paid?
25 Who was Master of the Rolls from 1962 to 1982?

Answers

20th C Who's Who

1 John Paul I. **2** Fitzgerald. **3** Mary Bell. **4** Benazir Bhutto. **5** Brian Clough. **6** He only has one leg. **7** Derek Bentley. **8** Mary McAleese. **9** Lyndon Johnson. **10** Stalin. **11** Michael Miles. **12** Shirley Williams. **13** The Queen. **14** Salvador Dali. **15** South Africa. **16** Mao Tse Tung. **17** Brazil. **18** Graeme Souness. **19** Martin Luther King. **20** Indira Gandhi. **21** President Kennedy. **22** Walt Disney. **23** McCarthy. **24** Patty Hearst. **25** Lord Denning.

Quiz 3 CORONATION ST. Level 2

The Platts and The Tilsleys

1. In which year did Martin Platt join *Coronation Street*?
2. Who was Martin's first girlfriend on the programme?
3. Whose sister did Martin used to go out with?
4. And what was her name?
5. Which *Coronation Street* villain did Martin used to work for?
6. In which year did he marry Gail?
7. Name the nurse he had a one night stand with one Christmas.
8. When was Gail's first appearance in *Coronation Street*?
9. Who was her red-haired landlady back in the 1970s?
10. And which house number did they live at?
11. Name Gail's dark-haired friend whose family owned the Corner Shop.
12. Who played her?
13. Who was Gail's red-haired best friend?
14. Who did Gail marry in 1979?
15. And who did she marry in 1988?
16. Who did Gail have an affair with during this marriage?
17. And where was he from?
18. Which of Gail's children did Brian wrongly suspect might have been fathered by someone else?
19. Which of Gail's children is Martin's?
20. What was Martin's job when he first appeared in *Coronation Street*?
21. What number Coronation Street does Gail live at?
22. Why did Martin lose his job at Weatherfield hospital in the 1990s?
23. How old was Sarah when she became pregnant?
24. Who played Gail's half-brother Stephen Reid?
25. Who made a clumsy pass at him, believing herself to be in love with him?

Answers

Coronation Street – The Platts and The Tilsleys
1 1985. **2** Jenny Bradley. **3** Sally's. **4** Gina Seddon. **5** Alan Bradley. **6** 1991. **7** Cathy Power. **8** 1975. **9** Elsie Tanner. **10** Number 11. **11** Tricia Hopkins. **12** Kathy Jones. **13** Suzie Birchall. **14** Brian Tilsley. **15** Brian Tilsley – they divorced and remarried. **16** Ian Latimer. **17** Australia. **18** Sarah Louise. **19** David. **20** Washing up in the café. **21** Number 8. **22** Les Battersby falsely accused him of trying to kill him. **23** 13. **24** Todd Boyce. **25** Alma Baldwin.

Quiz 4 Diana, Princess of Wales

Level 2

1 Who designed Diana's wedding dress?
2 Who coined the phrase The People's Princess about Diana?
3 What was the name of the kindergarten where Diana worked before her marriage?
4 What colour suit did Diana wear in her engagement photograph?
5 Which film star did Diana famously dance with at The White House?
6 Diana became an ambassador for which charity's campaign to ban land mines?
7 Which auctioneers auctioned Diana's dresses in 1997?
8 Which Palace was Diana's home in the last year of her life?
9 Who interviewed Diana during her famous *Panorama* interview?
10 With which ballet dancer did Diana dance to Uptown Girl at a charity gala in 1985?
11 In 1996 Diana visited the Shaukat Kanum cancer hospital in Pakistan which was built in the memory of whose mother?
12 What was the name of Diana's mother at the time of Diana's marriage?
13 In which hospital was Diana photographed watching a heart operation?
14 Which official title did Diana have after her divorce?
15 To the nearest £3 million, what was Diana's divorce settlement?
16 In which city did the auction of Diana's dresses take place?
17 What was the name of the driver of the car in which Diana met her death?
18 Who wrote the 1992 biography, written with Diana's knowledge, which revealed personal details of Charles and Diana's married life?
19 In early July 1997 Diana and her sons were on holiday on whose yacht?
20 What are Diana's two sisters called?
21 In 1987 what special ward, the first in Britain, was opened by Diana?
22 At which theme park was Diana photographed, soaking wet, with William and Harry in 1994?
23 On which Royal estate was Diana born?
24 In what capacity was Paul Burrell employed by Diana?
25 Whose book in 1998 criticised Diana and was itself disapproved of by Prince Charles and Camilla Parker-Bowles?

Answers

Diana, Princess of Wales

1 The Emanuels. **2** Tony Blair. **3** Young England. **4** Blue. **5** John Travolta. **6** Red Cross. **7** Christie's. **8** Kensington. **9** Martin Bashir. **10** Wayne Sleep. **11** Imran Khan. **12** Frances Shand Kydd. **13** Harefield. **14** Diana, Princess of Wales. **15** £15 Million. **16** New York. **17** Henri Paul. **18** Andrew Morton. **19** Mohammed Al Fayed's. **20** Sarah & Jane. **21** Aids. **22** Thorpe Park. **23** Sandringham. **24** Butler. **25** Penny Junor.

Quiz 5 Pot Luck

Level 2

1. Opened in June 1999, the Matthew Street Gallery in Liverpool was dedicated to the works of who?
2. Neil Armstrong was a pilot in which war?
3. Which international soccer keeper of the 90s also played cricket for Scotland?
4. Who wrote *The Scarlet Pimpernel*?
5. In 1997 which long running TV quiz had started so it finished?
6. Who had an 80s No 1 with Frankie?
7. Which snooker star has a son called Blain?
8. Which series was based on the 'Constable' novels by Nicholas Rhea?
9. Which item of clothing cost Isadora Duncan her life?
10. Which soccer country beat the Republic of Ireland in the play-off for France 98?
11. In which country was Ursula Andress born?
12. Zoe Redhead was headmistress of which school in the news in the 90s?
13. Who wrote the novels *Spy Hook* and *Spy Line*, published in the 80s?
14. What was the first UK Top Ten hit for 911?
15. At which sport did Gary Armstrong represent Scotland?
16. Which motorway goes from London to Winchester?
17. In the summer of 1999 Anna Kournikova signed a lucrative contract to model what?
18. In which decade did Belgium join the European Union?
19. In which series did Neil Pearson play Tony Clark?
20. In which city did Man Utd win the 1999 European Champions' Cup Final?
21. Louis Armstrong sang the title song for which Bond film?
22. What did Clarice Cliff create?
23. To the nearest million, what is the population of London?
24. In Rugby League, what did Wigan add to their name in the 90s?
25. Which city is the home of Yorkshire TV?

Answers

Pot Luck

1 John Lennon. **2** Korean. **3** Andy Goram. **4** Baroness Orczy. **5** Mastermind. **6** Sister Sledge. **7** Stephen Hendry. **8** Heartbeat. **9** Scarf – it was caught in a moving car wheel. **10** Belgium. **11** Switzerland. **12** Summerhill. **13** Len Deighton. **14** Don't Make Me Wait. **15** Rugby Union. **16** M3. **17** Bras. **18** 50s. **19** Between The Lines. **20** Barcelona. **21** On Her Majesty's Secret Service. **22** Pottery. **23** 7 million. **24** Warriors. **25** Leeds.

Quiz 6

CORONATION ST.

Level 2

The Barlows

1 Name Ken's second wife.
2 Which actress played her?
3 And how did she die?
4 What job did Ken's dad do?
5 Which actor played him?
6 What was the source of tension between them?
7 Who played Ken's mother?
8 How did Ida die?
9 What was Valerie Barlow's profession?
10 Which family member took the twins after Valerie's death?
11 Ken's brother David was a professional footballer: True or false?
12 Which actor played David?
13 Whose daughter did David marry, and what was her name?
14 Which actress played her?
15 Where did the couple emigrate to?
16 And how did David die?
17 Name all three actresses who have played Tracy Barlow.
18 In which year was Tracy born?
19 What is Tracy's middle name?
20 In which year did Deirdre marry Ray Langton?
21 Why did Ray split up with Deirdre?
22 Where did he go to after leaving Deirdre?
23 Which actor played Ray?
24 Where did Ray work, and who for?
25 What did Ken recently discover about Fred Elliot?

Answers

Coronation Street – The Barlows
1 Janet Reid. **2** Judith Barker. **3** She committed suicide. **4** Postman. **5** Frank Pemberton. **6** He thought Ken had become a snob. **7** Noel Dyson **8** She was hit by a bus. **9** Hairdresser. **10** Her mum. **11** True. **12** Alan Rothwell. **13** Stan and Hilda Ogden's daughter, Irma. **14** Sandra Gough. **15** Australia. **16** In a car crash. **17** Holly Chamarette, Christabel Finch, Dawn Acton. **18** 1977. **19** Lynette. **20** 1975. **21** He had an affair. **22** Holland. **23** Neville Buswell. **24** Len Fairclough's yard. **25** One of his ancestors was a murderer.

Quiz 7 Pot Luck

Level 2

1. Nick Leeson hid his debts in a secret account with which number?
2. Louis Washkansky was the first recipient of what?
3. Which musical featured the song Hello Young Lovers?
4. In cricket what did Yorkshire add to their name in the 90s?
5. In which country was Mel Gibson born?
6. Which Spice Girl teamed with Bryan Adams on When You're Gone?
7. Where is the Glasgow terminus of the M8?
8. Canaan Banana was the first president of which country?
9. What was Britain's first breakfast TV programme called?
10. Which athlete was the BBC Sports Personality the year after Steve Ovett won the award?
11. What did the W H stand for in the name of the poet W H Auden?
12. In TV ads, who shared a glass of Cinzano with Joan Collins?
13. Who made No 1 with Breakfast At Tiffany's?
14. In which sport could the Trailblazers take on the Warriors?
15. 1999 is the Chinese year of which creature?
16. What was the name of Natalie's drug dealer son in *Coronation Street*?
17. Which sporting event was featured in the first outside TV broadcast?
18. Who wrote the novel *Brave New World*?
19. Asturias international airport is in which country?
20. In which decade was Jenny Agutter born?
21. Goalkeeper Bernard Lama has played for which country?
22. What did the Q originally stand for in the magazine *GQ*?
23. East Pakistan has become known as what?
24. Who married Mickey Rooney, Artie Shaw and Frank Sinatra?
25. Which dog clocked up an amazing 550 plus hours of air time on BBC TV?

Answers

Pot Luck

1 88888. **2** Heart transplant. **3** The King And I. **4** Phoenix. **5** USA. **6** Mel C. **7** Airport. **8** Zimbabwe. **9** Breakfast Time. **10** Sebastian Coe. **11** Wystan Hugh. **12** Leonard Rossiter. **13** Deep Blue Something. **14** Basketball. **15** Hare. **16** Tony. **17** The Derby. **18** Aldous Huxley. **19** Spain. **20** 50s. **21** France. **22** Quarterly. **23** Bangladesh. **24** Ava Gardner. **25** Petra.

Quiz 8 Soccer

Level 2

1 Peter Schmeichel joined Man Utd from which club?
2 Which side finished fourth in the 1998 World Cup?
3 In 1999's European Champions' Cup Final which player scored the first goal?
4 Which soccer club began the century known as Newton Heath?
5 What was the half-time Argentina v England score in the 1998 World Cup?
6 Pierluigi Casiraghi joined Chelsea in 1998 from which club?
7 At which club did Ron Atkinson replace Dr Josef Venglos as manager?
8 Which club became Britain's first to have an all-seater stadium?
9 Who was the first England manager to be born in Worksop?
10 In the 60s and 70s Ron Harris set an appearance record at which soccer club?
11 Who scored Scotland's only goal from outfield play in France 98?
12 Darren Anderton first played league soccer with which club?
13 Which British club in the 1980s became the first to install an artificial pitch?
14 Who was the first 50-plus player to turn out in a top flight league game in England?
15 Who became the first Croatian international to play for an English club?
16 Which German team were first to win the European Cup?
17 Who was the first World Cup-winning skipper to play in the Premiership?
18 Which manager took Peter Beardsley to Newcastle?
19 With 96 caps, Jan Ceulemans set an appearance record for which country?
20 In the 90s, which British manager won successive titles with PSV Eindhoven?
21 Which Scottish international played for Barcelona in the 80s?
22 Who were England's first opponents in the 1998 World Cup in France?
23 Who was the first keeper to captain an FA Cup winning team at Wembley?
24 Who followed Bill Shankly as Liverpool manager?
25 Coventry first won the FA Cup in which decade?

Answers

Soccer

1 Brondby. **2** Holland. **3** Basler. **4** Man Utd. **5** 2-2. **6** Lazio. **7** Aston Villa. **8** Aberdeen. **9** Graham Taylor. **10** Chelsea. **11** Craig Burley. **12** Portsmouth. **13** QPR. **14** Stanley Matthews. **15** Igor Stimac. **16** Bayern Munich. **17** Deschamps. **18** Kevin Keegan. **19** Belgium. **20** Bobby Robson. **21** Steve Archibald. **22** Tunisia. **23** Dave Beasant. **24** Bob Paisley. **25** 80s.

Quiz 9 CORONATION ST. Level 2

1960 and 1961

1 Who owned the Corner Shop when *Coronation Street* first began?
2 Who took over from her when she sold up and retired?
3 What was Elsie Tanner's daughter called?
4 And which actress played her?
5 What was the name of Ena Sharples' daughter?
6 And who played her?
7 Which character died from a brain tumour in 1960 after a spell in a psychiatric hospital?
8 What was Harry Hewitt's daughter called?
9 Ken Barlow has been in *Coronation Street* since the first episode, but who arrived in 1961 and is still living on the street today?
10 On what date was *Coronation Street* first broadcast?
11 The early shows used to be transmitted live – True or False?
12 Which famous film director was photographed in the Rovers in 1961?
13 Who did Elsie Tanner wrongly accuse of sending her hate mail in 1961?
14 What were Annie and Jack Walker's children called?
15 Who did Concepta Riley marry?
16 Where had Dennis Tanner been before arriving in Coronation Street?
17 Who was Leonard Swindley's assistant?
18 Who briefly took over from Ena as caretaker at the Mission of Glad Tidings when she was caught drinking in the Rovers and was fired as a result?
19 Name the librarian that Ken Barlow dated.
20 What was Jed Stone's trademark item of clothing?
21 Who was Harry Hewitt's sister?
22 What was Ivan and Linda Cheveski's son called?
23 What country did the Cheveski's emigrate to?
24 Who played Christine Hardman?
25 Name the Naval Officer that Elsie Tanner dated in 1961.

Answers

Coronation Street – 1960 and 1961
1 Elsie Lappin. **2** Florrie Lindley. **3** Linda Cheveski. **4** Anne Cunningham. **5** Vera Lomax. **6** Ruth Holden. **7** May Hardman. **8** Lucille. **9** Emily. **10** 9 December, 1960. **11** True. **12** Alfred Hitchcock. **13** Ena Sharples. **14** Joan and Billy. **15** Harry Hewitt. **16** Prison. **17** Emily Nugent. **18** Albert Tatlock. **19** Marion Lund. **20** Cap. **21** Alice Burgess. **22** Paul. **23** Canada. **24** Christine Hargreaves. **25** Bill Gregory.

Quiz 10 20th C Blockbusters

Level 2

1 What was Anna Chancellor's nickname in *Four Weddings and a Funeral*?
2 Which member of the Corleone family did Al Pacino play in The *Godfather*?
3 In which film did Michael Douglas and Glenn Close play Dan Gallagher and Alex Forrest?
4 Who played Amon Goeth in *Schindler's List*?
5 Which of his characters did Robin Williams say was a cross between Bill Forsyth, Alastair Sim and the Queen Mother?
6 *The Third Man* was set in which European city?
7 The action of which 70s movie revolves around the Kit Kat Club in Berlin?
8 In which part of New York did *Shaft* take place?
9 Which trilogy of films with Michael J Fox featured a De Lorean sports car?
10 Who played the role on film in *Shadowlands* which Nigel Hawthorne had made his own on the stage?
11 What was the first name of Private Ryan?
12 Which Orson Welles movie was voted top US movie of all time by the US Film Institute in 1998?
13 The action of *Trainspotting* takes place in Edinburgh, but where was the movie filmed?
14 Which Scottish hero was released on video to coincide with the opening of the 90s Scottish Parliament?
15 Who played the villainous Sir August de Wynter in *The Avengers*?
16 What was the sequel to *Jurassic Park* called?
17 Which actor was the narrator in *Evita*?
18 *Dante's Peak* featured which type of natural disaster?
19 In which country does the action in *The Piano* take place?
20 In which blockbusting 60s musical did the Sharks meet the Jets?
21 How many tunnels were built in *The Great Escape*?
22 Who was Julius Caesar in *Cleopatra* with Elizabeth Taylor in the title role?
23 What was the second Bond movie with Sean Connery?
24 Who played the architect of the skyscraper in *The Towering Inferno*?
25 Who played Dr Zhivago's wife in *Dr Zhivago*?

Answers

20th C Blockbusters

1 Duckface. **2** Michael. **3** Fatal Attraction. **4** Ralph Fiennes. **5** Mrs Doubtfire. **6** Vienna. **7** Cabaret. **8** Harlem. **9** Back To The Future. **10** Anthony Hopkins. **11** James. **12** Citizen Kane. **13** Glasgow. **14** Braveheart. **15** Sean Connery. **16** The Lost World: Jurassic Park. **17** Antonio Banderas. **18** Volcano. **19** New Zealand. **20** West Side Story. **21** Three. **22** Rex Harrison. **23** From Russia With Love. **24** Paul Newman. **25** Geraldine Chaplin.

Quiz 11 Pot Luck

Level 2

1. Who lived under the pseudonym of Harriet Brown in New York from the 40s to the 90s?
2. In baseball where do the Red Sox come from?
3. What was Wham's first No 1?
4. In which year was Bloody Sunday in Londonderry?
5. What was the main colour of a Stormtrooper in *Star Wars*?
6. Which club did Stan Collymore join when he left Nottm Forest?
7. Which country did Albert Einstein move to as the Nazis rose to power?
8. Which lawyer made Raymond Burr famous?
9. Who joined The Wonder Stuff on the UK No 1 Dizzy?
10. Who was Prime Minister when England won the World Cup?
11. If I Were A Rich Man was a big hit from which stage show?
12. Sir Leslie Porter is a former chairman of which supermarket chain?
13. Which TV reporter's stories of the famine in 1984 inspired Bob Geldof to set up Band Aid?
14. Who made No 1 with Boom Boom Boom?
15. At which sport did Nigel Aspinall win international success?
16. Which musical featured the song You'll Never Walk Alone?
17. Which EastEnders actress directed Barbara Windsor in her harrowing cancer scare scenes in the soap?
18. Who wrote the novels on which BBC's classic series *The Forsythe Saga* was based?
19. Luxor international airport is in which country?
20. In the 90s how many points have been awarded for finishing first in a Grand Prix?
21. Which footballer was the BBC Sports Personality of 1990?
22. *Which?* is the magazine of which Association?
23. Who played Private Godfrey in *Dad's Army*?
24. David Seaman first played for England when he was with which club?
25. What was the name of Gene Autry's horse?

Answers

Pot Luck

1 Greta Garbo. **2** Boston. **3** Wake Me Up Before You Go Go. **4** 1972. **5** White. **6** Liverpool. **7** America. **8** Perry Mason. **9** Vic Reeves. **10** Harold Wilson. **11** Fiddler on the Roof. **12** Tesco. **13** Michael Buerk. **14** Outhere Brothers. **15** Croquet. **16** Carousel. **17** Susan Tully. **18** John Galsworthy. **19** Egypt. **20** 10. **21** Paul Gascoigne. **22** Consumers. **23** Arnold Ridley. **24** QPR. **25** Champion.

Quiz 12 Around The UK

Level 2

1 The research laboratories at Porton Down are near which cathedral town?
2 To the nearest 100ft, how tall is the Canary Wharf Tower?
3 Where did the Royal Mint move to from Tower Hill, London, in 1968?
4 According to a University of East Anglia report, which year of the 90s was the hottest ever recorded in the UK?
5 Where did the National Horseracing Museum open in 1983?
6 Where was the site of the Millennium Exhibition and the Millennium Dome chosen to be?
7 Which Cheshire village was the home of nanny Louise Woodward?
8 Which castle was restored by the end of 1997 at a cost of £37 million?
9 Which English county has the place with the longest name – Sutton-Under-Whitestonecliffe ?
10 Where is the annual music festival founded by Benjamin Britten held?
11 The first of a chain of which holiday centres opened in Skegness in 1936?
12 Which branch of the armed services is trained at Cranwell in Lincolnshire?
13 Where is the Government Communications Headquarters?
14 In the 1990s which theatre was rebuilt on the site of an Elizabethan theatre?
15 Which military museum was established by Act of Parliament in 1920?
16 Which airport in the English capital was built in 1987?
17 Which social organisation's name is the Latin word for table?
18 Metrolink operates a train service around which city?
19 Which city has a railway station called Temple Meads?
20 Beaulieu in Hampshire has a famous museum of what?
21 In 1991 the Sainsbury Wing was built as an extension to which Gallery?
22 The Burrell Gallery is in which Scottish city?
23 In which inner city was the first National Garden Festival held in 1984?
24 Which company merged with Stena to face the cross-Channel competition for services through the Channel Tunnel?
25 Where is the Open University based?

Answers

Around the UK

1 Salisbury. **2** 800ft. **3** Cardiff. **4** 1995. **5** Newmarket. **6** Greenwich. **7** Elton. **8** Windsor. **9** North Yorkshire. **10** Aldeburgh. **11** Butlin's. **12** RAF. **13** Cheltenham. **14** Globe. **15** Imperial War Museum. **16** London City Airport. **17** Mensa. **18** Manchester. **19** Bristol. **20** Cars. **21** National Gallery. **22** Glasgow. **23** Liverpool. **24** P & O. **25** Milton Keynes.

Quiz 13 CORONATION ST. Level 2

Pot Luck

1 Who took up junk sculpture but had his works taken away by bin men?
2 Who was Maggie Clegg's sister?
3 And who was Gordon Clegg's mum?
4 Who left *Coronation Street* and appeared in *Harbour Lights*?
5 Which burly builder did Janet Reid date long before Ken Barlow?
6 In which year did Elsie Tanner marry Alan Howard?
7 Who produced *Coronation Street* twice?
8 Who told Candice's two boyfriends about her two-timing ways?
9 How many episodes were celebrated in March 2001?
10 Which chat show host was a famous *Coronation Street* fan?
11 Who married two husbands with the same surname?
12 And what were their first names?
13 Whose son is an actor who appeared in the film *Priest*?
14 And what is his name?
15 What creatures did Toyah and Spider sabotage Firman's Freezers for?
16 What instrument did Gary Mallett play?
17 What links Pat Phoenix to Tony Blair?
18 What did Jack's glasses used to be held together with?
19 Which married couple had a tandem in the 1970s?
20 What instrument of Spider's did Emily play?
21 Which of the ducks on Hilda's wall was crooked?
22 What did Mavis Wilton cook for Derek, believing it to have aphrodisiac properties?
23 What accent does Adam Barlow have?
24 Who threw a brick through Emma Watts' window?
25 Who missed his own surprise 60th birthday party in March 2001?

Answers

Coronation Street – Pot Luck
1 Stan Ogden. **2** Betty Turpin. **3** Betty Turpin. **4** Tina Hobley. **5** Len Fairclough. **6** 1970. **7** HV Kershaw. **8** David Platt. **9** 5000. **10** Russell Harty. **11** Elsie Tanner. **12** Steve and Arnold (Tanner). **13** Bill Roache. **14** Linus. **15** Norwegian prawns. **16** Drums. **17** Pat married Cherie Blair's father, Tony Booth. **18** A Plaster. **19** The Ogdens. **20** Didgeridoo. **21** The middle one. **22** Parsnips. **23** Scottish (Glasgwegian). **24** Ryan Sykes. **25** Norris Cole.

Quiz 14 Music - Girl Power

Level 2

1 How many of The Corrs are female?
2 In which decade was vocalist Karen Carpenter born?
3 Whose real name is Gaynor Hopkins?
4 Which soap star had a 1990 hit with Just This Side of Love?
5 Shout was the first hit for which solo female star?
6 Which comedienne featured on the B side of the Comic Relief hit The Stonk?
7 In 1995 the album Daydream topped the charts for which female vocalist?
8 How many girls were in the group Ace of Base?
9 In which decade was vocalist Lisa Stansfield born?
10 Who released an album called Jagged Little Pill?
11 Who asked Unbreak My Heart in 1997?
12 Which Spice Girls hit was No 1 at the beginning of 1997?
13 In 1995 which soapstar was Happy Just to Be with You?
14 Who was a Professional Widow according to her 1997 hit?
15 What was Madonna's third UK No 1?
16 In which country was Neneh Cherry born?
17 What was Whitney Houston's first UK top ten hit?
18 Who released a UK No 1 album in 1992 called Shepherd Moons?
19 Which country was represented by Celine Dion at the Eurovision Song Contest?
20 Which female vocalist said All I Want for Christmas is You in 1994?
21 Who duetted with Peter Gabriel on Don't Give Up?
22 Who got to No 1 in 1994 in her first-ever week in the UK charts?
23 Who released the top selling album Guilty in 1980?
24 Which female artist had huge success with the album The Kick Inside?
25 Who won a US Song of the Year Award in 1995 for Breathe Again ?

Answers

Music - Girl Power

1 Three. **2** 1950s. **3** Bonnie Tyler. **4** Malandra Burrows. **5** Lulu. **6** Victoria Wood. **7** Mariah Carey. **8** Two. **9** 60s. **10** Alanis Morisette. **11** Toni Braxton. **12** 2 Become 1. **13** Michelle Gayle. **14** Tori Amos. **15** La Isla Bonita. **16** Sweden. **17** Saving All My Love For You. **18** Enya. **19** Switzerland. **20** Mariah Carey. **21** Kate Bush. **22** Whigfield. **23** Barbra Streisand. **24** Kate Bush. **25** Toni Braxton.

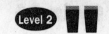

Quiz 15 Pot Luck

Level 2

1 In which country did the notorious security force the Tontons Macoutes operate?
2 Which producer of *Kavanagh QC* has been a regular on *Food & Drink*?
3 In cricket, which English team became Royals in the 90s?
4 What was the first UK Top Ten hit for the Smashing Pumpkins?
5 What became the capital of Australia during the 20th century?
6 On which Caribbean island did Princess Diana spend her first Christmas after her divorce was announced?
7 Which musical featured the song Thank Heaven For Little Girls?
8 What breed of dog did Columbo own?
9 In basketball, where do the Mavericks come from?
10 British Honduras has become known as what?
11 Which song was released to raise funds for *Children in Need* in 1997?
12 For many years Fred Basset has been a regular of which Daily paper?
13 To the nearest million what is the population of Australia?
14 Who made No 1 with Deeply Dippy?
15 Who wrote *The Good Companions*?
16 Which Prime Minister replaced Anthony Eden?
17 Who did Liz leave Coronation Street with?
18 The *Queen Elizabeth* liner was destroyed by fire in the 70s in which harbour?
19 Gracie Fields sang about the Biggest what In The World?
20 Who took over as President of the European Commission in January 1985?
21 Malpensa international airport is in which country?
22 What were the initials of *Doctor Finlay* creator Cronin?
23 Who was Cohen's fullback partner in England's World Cup winning team?
24 1998 is the Chinese year of which creature?
25 Which country does musician Alfred Brendel come from?

Answers

Pot Luck

1 Haiti. **2** Chris Kelly. **3** Worcestershire. **4** Tonight Tonight. **5** Canberra. **6** Barbuda. **7** Gigi. **8** Basset hound. **9** Dallas. **10** Belize. **11** Perfect Day. **12** Mail. **13** 18 million. **14** Right Said Fred. **15** J B Priestley. **16** Harold Macmillan. **17** Michael. **18** Hong Kong. **19** Aspidistra. **20** Jacques Delors. **21** Italy. **22** A J. **23** Wilson. **24** Tiger. **25** Austria.

Quiz 16 War Zones

Level 2

1 Which US General along with Schwarzkopf was leader in the Gulf War?
2 The Taliban were a guerrilla group in which country?
3 How long did the Arab–Israeli War of 1967 last?
4 Who during the Vietnam war was known as Hanoi Jane?
5 Which breakaway Russian republic had Grozny as its capital?
6 Which country's 'Spring' was halted by the arrival of Soviet tanks in 1968?
7 Where is the Bay of Pigs whose invasion sparked a world crisis in the 60s?
8 Which country pulled out of Vietnam in the 1950s?
9 Where did the *Enola Gay* drop a devastating bomb in WWII?
10 In which country is Passchendaele, scene of battle in WWI?
11 Whose forces were defeated at the Battle of Midway in 1942?
12 Who were defeated along with the Germans at El Alamein?
13 During World War I what kind of gas was used in the trenches?
14 What Operation was the codename for the D-Day landings?
15 Which major weapon of war was used for the first time in 1916?
16 The Tamil Tigers were fighting for a separate state on which island?
17 Muhammad Ali refused to fight in which war?
18 War broke out in Biafra in the 60s when it broke away from which country?
19 Where did Nazi leader Rudolf Hess crashland in 1941?
20 Which 'Lord' was executed for treason in 1946 for broadcasting Nazi propaganda?
21 During which war was OXFAM set up?
22 In WWII who was in charge of the Afrika Korps?
23 The EOKA were a terrorist group operating on which island?
24 What was the number of the British Armoured Division known as The Desert Rats?
25 Which city was besieged by German troops for over 900 days in WWII?

Answers

War Zones
1 Powell. **2** Afghanistan. **3** Six Days. **4** Jane Fonda. **5** Chechenia. **6** Czechoslovakia. **7** Cuba. **8** France. **9** Hiroshima. **10** Belgium. **11** Japan. **12** Italians. **13** Mustard gas. **14** Overlord. **15** Tank. **16** Sri Lanka. **17** Vietnam. **18** Nigeria. **19** Scotland. **20** Lord Haw-Haw. **21** WWII. **22** Rommel. **23** Cyprus. **24** 8th. **25** Leningrad.

Quiz 17 CORONATION ST. Level 2

Name The Grooms of These Brides

1 Renee Bradshaw.
2 Maggie Clegg.
3 Sally Seddon.
4 Irma Ogden.
5 Christine Hardman.
6 Joan Walker.
7 Concepta Riley.
8 Myra Dickinson.
9 Valerie Tatlock.
10 Jenny Sutton.
11 Eunice Nuttall.
12 Marion Willis.
13 Elaine Prior.
14 Audrey Potter.
15 Susan Barlow.
16 Ivy Tilsley.
17 Jackie Ingram.
18 Lisa Horton.
19 Alma Sedgewick.
20 Vicky Arden.
21 Leanne Battersby.
22 Natalie Horrocks.
23 Maxine Heavey.
24 Hayley Patterson.
25 Sharon Gaskell.

Answers

Coronation Street – Name The Grooms of These Brides
1 Alf Roberts. **2** Ron Cooke. **3** Kevin Webster. **4** David Barlow. **5** Colin Appleby. **6** Gordon Davies. **7** Harry Hewitt. **8** Jerry Booth. **9** Ken Barlow. **10** Dennis Tanner. **11** Fred Gee. **12** Eddie Yeats. **13** Bill Webster. **14** Alf Roberts. **15** Mike Baldwin. **16** Don Brennan. **17** Mike Baldwin. **18** Terry Duckworth. **19** Mike Baldwin. **20** Steve McDonald. **21** Nick Tilsley. **22** Des Barnes. **23** Ashley Peacock. **24** Roy Cropper. **25** Ian Bentley.

Quiz 18 20th C Famous Names

Level 2

1 Which British Dame became the first woman to win two Olivier awards for best actress in the same year – in 1996?
2 Israel Moses Sieff was head of which British chain of stores?
3 Who was Deep Blue, Gary Kasparov's famous chess opponent?
4 Which comic became the BBC's youngest scriptwriter in 1980, aged 21?
5 Which chef opened a restaurant called Woz?
6 Which MP announced in 1996 that she had been reunited with the son she gave up for adoption 31 years before?
7 What relation was the Queen's Private Secretary Robert Fellowes to the late Diana Princess of Wales?
8 Who is the great-granddaughter of Prime Minister Herbert Asquith?
9 What is the name of gourmet Egon Ronay's designer daughter?
10 In 1991 who was voted 'the most successful Australian to get to the top with least ability' by students in Adelaide?
11 What was the first name of the baby in the Louise Woodward case?
12 Which Rugby player did Julia Smith marry in 1994?
13 What is Tony Blair's daughter called?
14 Which musical instrument does astronomer Patrick Moore play?
15 Gerald Scarfe is famous as what?
16 What was the name of Mrs Neil Hamilton who forcefully defended her husband over sleaze allegations?
17 Ulrich Salchow was the first Olympic medallist in his sport and gave his name to one of its jumps; what sport is it?
18 Which veteran DJ's autobiography was called *As It Happens*?
19 Which photographer have Catherine Deneuve and Marie Helvin married?
20 Which cartoon strip was Charles Schulz' most famous creation?
21 Who was the sole survivor of the car crash in which Princess Diana died?
22 Who sold the story of David Mellor & Antonia de Sancha to the papers?
23 In which area of London did Ronnie Scott open his jazz club in 1959?
24 Which singer and comedian published a volume of autobiography in 1989 called *Arias and Raspberries*?
25 David Sheppard, the Bishop of Liverpool, was famous for what sport?

Answers

20th C Famous Names
1 Judi Dench. **2** Marks & Spencer. **3** Computer. **4** Ben Elton. **5** Anthony Worrall-Thompson. **6** Claire Short. **7** Brother-in-law. **8** Helena Bonham Carter. **9** Edina. **10** Kylie Minogue. **11** Matthew. **12** Will Carling. **13** Kathryn. **14** Xylophone. **15** Cartoonist. **16** Christine. **17** Skating. **18** Jimmy Savile. **19** David Bailey. **20** Peanuts. **21** Trevor Rees-Jones. **22** Max Clifford. **23** Soho. **24** Harry Secombe. **25** Cricket.

Quiz 19 CORONATION ST. Level 2

1980

1 Which *Coronation Street* matriarch left in April, when her character went to live in St Annes?
2 *Coronation Street* had a big anniversary in this year: How many episodes did it celebrate?
3 Which female character said 'I were fourteen when I first decided me face didn't suit me.'
4 Which baby was born on New Year's Eve?
5 Who walked out on her husband because he wouldn't decorate their house?
6 Where did Gail and Brian begin their married life?
7 Who temporarily moved into the newlywed Tilsleys' new home, causing Brian to be sacked from the garage?
8 Name the lorry driver lodger who had a relationship with Elsie Tanner.
9 Which barmaid did he two-time her with?
10 Whose knickers were run up the town hall flagpole?
11 Who did Dora Entwistle leave £100 and two china dogs to in her will?
12 Which two characters opened the Coronation Street Secretarial Bureau?
13 Who married Arnold Swain?
14 Why was the marriage dissolved?
15 Who won a holiday to Blackpool playing bingo?
16 Who became manageress of Jim's Cafe this year?
17 Who was tormented by obscene phone calls?
18 Who was falsely arrested when the police set a trap for the caller?
19 What was Hilda's Christmas treat to herself?
20 Who locked herself in the toilet of the Corner Shop flat?
21 How did Renee Roberts die?
22 Name Elsie Tanner's grandson, who stayed with her in this year.
23 Who took him on as an apprentice?
24 Alf, Bert, Eddie and Fred temporarily joined ranks to form what sort of group?
25 Who won a date with Mike Baldwin in a raffle?

Answers

Coronation Street – 1980

1 Ena Sharples. **2** 2000. **3** Hilda Ogden. **4** Nicky Tilsley. **5** Rita Fairclough. **6** Living with Bert and Ivy at Number 5. **7** Audrey Potter. **8** Dan Johnson. **9** Bet Lynch. **10** Vera Duckworth's. **11** Stan Ogden. **12** Emily and Deirdre. **13** Emily. **14** He was a bigamist. **15**5 Vera. **16** Elsie Tanner. **17** Mavis Riley. **18** Eddie Yeats. **19** She hired her own cleaner. **20** Tracy Barlow. **21**1 A lorry crashed into her car. **22** Martin Cheveski. **23** Len Fairclough. **24** Barber Shop Quartet. **25** Hilda Ogden.

Quiz 20 20th C Famous Faces

Level 2

1 Scott Chisholm found fame promoting what type of TV programmes?
2 Who left *News At Ten* to help launch the *BBC's Breakfast Time*?
3 Who was the antiques expert on the 1999 series of *Going For a Song*?
4 Trude Mostue found fame in a docu soap about which profession?
5 Which Dingle from Emmerdale presented *You've Been Framed*?
6 Which *They Think It's All Over* regular has a beard?
7 Which extrovert TV chef was a member of the Calypso Twins?
8 How is Meg Lake better known?
9 On which show did Jane McDonald shoot to fame?
10 Who was the *Six O'Clock News* anchorman when the programme was revamped in 1999?
11 Who was *The Naked Chef*?
12 Who replaced Peter Sissons as host of *Question Time*?
13 Who presented the BBC's daytime Wimbledon coverage in the late 1990s?
14 *My Kind of People* was LWT talent spotting show fronted by whom?
15 Who played gamekeeper Mellors opposite Joely Richardson in the D H Lawrence TV adaptation?
16 In 1997 who played Max de Winter in a TV adaptation of Daphne Du Maurier's Rebecca?
17 Who moved from *Whose Line Is It Anyway* to *Call My Bluff*?
18 Who was the sole regular male team member in *Victoria Wood – As Seen on TV*?
19 Which ex-Blue Peter presenter introduced *Mad About Pets*?
20 Who was the team captain opposing Jack Dee in the first series of *It's Only TV but I Like It*?
21 Which character had a hit single with a song of the theme music from *EastEnders*?
22 Who presented the very first edition of *Top of the Pops*?
23 David Jason's first long running serious TV role was as which character?
24 Who was behind the yoof series *DEF II*?
25 Who became *Gardener's World*'s regular presenter after the death of Geoff Hamilton?

Answers

20th C Famous Faces

1 Children's. **2** Selina Scott. **3** Eric Knowles. **4** Vets. **5** Mandy. **6** Rory McGrath. **7** Ainsley Harriott. **8** Mystic Meg. **9** The Cruise. **10** Huw Edwards. **11** Jamie Oliver. **12** David Dimbleby. **13** Desmond Lynam. **14** Michael Barrymore. **15** Sean Bean. **16** Charles Dance. **17** Sandi Toksvig. **18** Duncan Preston. **19** John Noakes. **20** Julian Clary. **21** Angie. **22** Jimmy Savile. **23** Jack Frost. **24** Janet Street Porter. **25** Alan Titchmarsh.

Quiz 21 Pot Luck

Level 2

1 In which decade was the last hanging of a woman in the UK?
2 Inspector Slack was always on the case with which amateur sleuth?
3 Robert Gallo was one of the pioneers in the identification of which virus?
4 In cricket, what did Derbyshire add to their name in the 90s?
5 What is the home state of ex-US President Jimmy Carter?
6 Who had an 80s No 1 with Respectable?
7 In *Only Fools and Horses* what does Trigger call Rodney?
8 Where is the HQ of the multinational Samsung?
9 Until his death in 1969, Brian Jones was in which pop band?
10 Which speed star was the BBC Sports Personality of the Year in 1986 and 1992?
11 Who wrote the *Father Brown* novels?
12 Where in the UK was Tom Conti born?
13 Which Bond girl was played by Maud Adams?
14 Which mountain range to the west of Sydney was badly damaged by bush fires in 1993?
15 Which flowers gave the title to a No 8 UK hit in 1982 for Patrice Rushen?
16 Which Irish presenter works on *Animal Hospital*?
17 In which decade did Austria join the European Union?
18 Which Raymond created *The Snowman*?
19 Which US President was inaugurated in 1969?
20 In the patriotic World War I song what should we Keep the Home Fires doing?
21 Translated as *The People's Daily*, in which country is this a major seller?
22 Vehicles from which country use the international registration letter Z?
23 In finance, what does the letter P stand for in APR?
24 In which decade was comic actor Frank Thornton born?
25 In TV ads, which breakfast cereal did Jackie Charlton and his grandson tuck into?

Answers

Pot Luck

1 50s. **2** Miss Marple. **3** HIV. **4** Scorpions. **5** Georgia. **6** Mel and Kim. **7** Dave. **8** South Korea. **9** The Rolling Stones. **10** Nigel Mansell. **11** J K Chesterton. **12** Paisley. **13** Octopussy. **14** The Blue Mountains. **15** Forget Me Nots. **16** Shauna Lowry. **17** 90s. **18** Briggs. **19** Richard Nixon. **20** Burning. **21** China. **22** Zambia. **23** Percentage. **24** 20s. **25** Shredded Wheat.

Quiz 22 Sport - 90s Action Replay Level 2

1 Which English bowler took a 90s hat trick against the West Indies?
2 In which US state were the last summer Olympics of the century held?
3 Who were the opponents in Schmeichel's last league game for Man Utd?
4 Who beat Tim Henman in his first Wimbledon singles semi-final?
5 Who missed England's last penalty in the Euro 96 shoot-out v Germany?
6 In 1995, which England captain was sacked and then reinstated within a few days?
7 Who inflicted Nigel Benn's first defeat as a professional?
8 Who was the last team to be relegated from the Premiership in the 20th century?
9 Which team won cricket's county championship in 1990 and 1991?
10 Yuan Yuan was caught carrying drugs for which Chinese team?
11 Which Grand Slam did Pete Sampras not win in the century?
12 Man Utd bought Gary Pallister from and sold him back to which club?
13 In baseball who set a record with 70 home runs?
14 In 1998 Tegla Loroupe set a new world record in the women's section of which event?
15 Which soccer team moved to Pride Park in the 90s?
16 How long was swimmer Michelle de Bruin banned for attempting to manipulate a drugs test?
17 Who did Mike Atherton replace as England's cricket captain?
18 In which sport did Andy Thomson become a world champion?
19 Which legendary American golfer played his last British Open in 1995?
20 The scorer of Romania's last minute winner v England in the 98 World Cup played with which English club?
21 Which cricketing county won a sideboard full of trophies with Dermot Reeve as skipper?
22 Which jockey rode over 200 winners in both 1997 and 1998?
23 Who won a record ninth Wimbledon singles title in 1991?
24 In 1995 Man Utd set a record Premier score by beating which team 9-0 ?
25 Which English wicket keeper set a new record of 11 dismissals in a test in 1995?

Answers

Sport - 90s Action Replay

1 Dominic Cork. **2** Georgia. **3** Spurs. **4** Pete Sampras. **5** Gareth Southgate. **6** Will Carling. **7** Chris Eubank. **8** Charlton Athletic. **9** Essex. **10** Swimming. **11** French. **12** Nottm Forest. **13** Mark McGwire. **14** Marathon. **15** Derby. **16** 4 years. **17** Graham Gooch. **18** Bowls. **19** Arnold Palmer. **20** Chelsea - it was Dan Petrescu. **21** Warwickshire. **22** Kieren Fallon. **23** Martina Navratilova. **24** Ipswich. **25** Jack Russell.

Quiz 23 CORONATION ST. Level 2

1981

1 How old was Ken in this year when he married 26-year-old Deirdre Langton?
2 Who gave Deirdre away at her wedding?
3 Who was the matron of honour?
4 Where was the honeymoon?
5 Who was chosen as Nicky Tilsley's godmother, to the objection of Ivy?
6 Why did Albert Tatlock object to nephew Ken's new car?
7 Who was the disastrous relief manager sent by the brewery to run the Rovers while Annie was away?
8 Who found himself the subject of a DSS investigation?
9 Who swapped a washing machine for an accordion?
10 Who had her house ransacked by a boyfriend's jealous wife?
11 Who fostered 13-year-old John Spencer?
12 Who took over from Elsie as manageress of Jim's Cafe?
13 Who held Emily hostage?
14 Who agreed to pose nude for artist Maurice Dodds but backed out at the last minute?
15 Who lodged with Elsie Tanner for a while after leaving her boyfriend and moving into Coronation Street?
16 Who married and separated within a year?
17 Who fixed up a blind date with sales rep Bobby Simpson over the telephone?
18 Who went on the date in her place when she couldn't go through with it?
19 Who talked Alf into buying an MG?
20 What was the name of Eunice Nuttall's daughter?
21 Name the actor who played Wally Randall – and was later to resurface in the *Street* as a much nastier character?
22 Which female character did Wally reject as being too old for him?
23 Why were the Fairclough turned down by the adoption board?
24 Who collapsed in the street, believing nobody wanted him?
25 Did Deirdre wear her glasses on her wedding day?

Answers

Coronation Street – 1981

1 42. **2** Alf Roberts. **3** Emily. **4** Corfu. **5** Elsie Tanner. **6** It was a German Volkswagen. **7** Gordon Lewis. **8** Bert Tilsley. **9** Eddie Yeats. **10** Elsie Tanner. **11** The Faircloughs. **12** Alma Sedgewick. **13** Arnold Swain. **14** Mavis Riley. **15** Audrey Potter. **16** Fred Gee and Eunice Nuttall. **17** Mavis Riley. **18** Bet Lynch. **19** Audrey Potter. **20** Debbie. **21** Mark Eden. **22** Elsie Tanner. **23** They were too old. **24** Albert Tatlock. **25** No.

Quiz 24 Movies Who's Who

Level 2

1 Who has the nickname Sly?
2 Which Richard found fame in *Withnail and I*?
3 Who won best actress at the 1997 Cannes Film festival for her role in *Nil By Mouth*?
4 Which activist did Denzel Washington play in *Cry Freedom*?
5 Which actress's official title is Lady Haden-Guest?
6 Which actor shot to fame in 1980 with *American Gigolo*?
7 Who briefly changed his name to Lenny Williams but returned to his Italian sounding name?
8 Who could not accept the offer to play 007 first time round as he was committed to playing Remington Steele?
9 What is the name of John Travolta's son – so called because of the actor's passion for aeroplanes?
10 How was Joanne Whalley known after her marriage to her husband?
11 Actress Glenda Jackson became MP for which constituency?
12 Who dubbed Kenneth Branagh's voice for the French version of *Henry V*?
13 Who reputedly was in discussion with Diana, Princess of Wales about making a sequel to *The Bodyguard* shortly before her death?
14 How did Christopher Reeve suffer the appalling injuries which brought about his paralysis in 1995?
15 Which Oscar-winning actor was the voice of John Smith in *Pocahontas*?
16 Who is Jason Gould's mum who starred with him in *Prince of Tides*?
17 Which James Bond appeared in *Spiceworld: The Movie*?
18 Who did Antonio Banderas marry after they met on the set of *Two Much*?
19 Who wrote the novel on which *Trainspotting* was based?
20 Which actress won an Oscar for her screenplay adaptation of Jane *Austen's Sense & Sensibility*?
21 In which city was Hugh Grant arrested with Divine Brown?
22 Which English actor was the voice of Scar in *The Lion King*?
23 Which child star appeared in *Richie Rich*?
24 Who or what was Clyde in Clint Eastwood in *Any Which Way You Can*?
25 Who played the doctor who cared for John Merrick in *The Elephant Man*?

Answers

The Movies Who's Who

1 Sylvester Stallone. **2** E. Grant. **3** Kathy Burke. **4** Steve Biko. **5** Jamie Lee Curtis. **6** Richard Gere. **7** Leonardo DiCaprio. **8** Pierce Brosnan. **9** Jett. **10** Joanne Whalley Kilmer. **11** Hampstead & Highgate. **12** Gerard Depardieu. **13** Kevin Costner. **14** Fell from a horse. **15** Mel Gibson. **16** Barbra Streisand. **17** Roger Moore. **18** Melanie Griffith. **19** Irvine Welsh. **20** Emma Thompson. **21** Los Angeles. **22** Jeremy Irons. **23** Macaulay Culkin. **24** Orang Utan. **25** Anthony Hopkins.

Quiz 25 Pot Luck

Level 2

1 Who moved up to No 1 ranking for snooker's 1998–99 season?
2 Whose clothes shop Bazaar was a trendsetter in the 60s?
3 Which detective lived on a boat called St Vitus Dance?
4 NUPE was the National Union of what?
5 In WWII where did the Bevin Boys work?
6 Who had an 80s No 1 with Like A Prayer?
7 In which eastern country were the Moonies founded in 1954?
8 In *Coronation Street* what was the surname of Colin and the late Des?
9 Truman Capote wrote about Breakfast at which place?
10 Abyssinia has become known as what?
11 Which US singer said, 'You're not drunk if you can lie on the floor without holding on'?
12 What are the international registration letters of a vehicle from India?
13 What is the name of the USA's main space exploration centre in Florida?
14 How long is Indianapolis's most famous motor race?
15 Who was the first female to have three consecutive US No 1 albums?
16 On which river was the Grand Coulee built?
17 Which star of Are *You Being Served?* became a regular panellist on radio's *Just A Minute*?
18 In the Arab world what does the letter E stand for in UAE?
19 In which decade was Ewan McGregor born?
20 What kind of orchard did Chekhov write a play about?
21 In Rugby League what did Widnes add to their name in the 90s?
22 On a computer keyboard which letter on the same line is immediately right of the O?
23 To the nearest million what is the population of New York?
24 In TV advertising which beer was said to 'work wonders'?
25 In American Football where do the Saints come from?

Answers

Pot Luck

1 John Higgins. **2** Mary Quant. **3** Crockett. **4** Public Employees. **5** Mines. **6** Madonna. **7** Korea. **8** Barnes. **9** Tiffany's. **10** Ethiopia. **11** Dean Martin. **12** IND. **13** Cape Canaveral. **14** 500 miles. **15** Donna Summer. **16** Columbia. **17** Wendy Richard. **18** Emirates. **19** 70s. **20** Cherry. **21** Vikings. **22** P. **23** 7 million. **24** Double Diamond. **25** New Orleans.

Quiz 26 Euro Tour

Level 2

1 What colour did Air France repaint some Concorde jets to advertise Pepsi?
2 How was Eurotunnel known before its name change in 1998?
3 Where is the French terminus for the Hoverspeed service?
4 Which European town gave its name to a Treaty which symbolises closer economic links between European countries?
5 In which European country did Victoria Adams marry David Beckham?
6 What is the oldest university in Northern Ireland called – founded in 1908?
7 Sullom Voe is famous for exporting which commodity?
8 How are Belgian World Airlines also known?
9 Which country lies to the north of Austria and to the south of Poland?
10 How many independent 'Baltic states' are there?
11 On which date in 1999 did Duty Free Shopping dramatically change?
12 Where is the Belgian terminus for Eurostar trains?
13 When did Euro Disney – now Disneyland Paris – open?
14 In 1998 a new breed of mosquito was discovered on which underground system?
15 Where is the Donana National Park?
16 In which country was the Angel of the North erected in 1998?
17 Which home of champagne in France was also where the German High Command surrendered in WWII?
18 What name is given to the popular holiday area between Marseille and La Spezia?
19 Which British architect was responsible with Renzo Piano for the famous Pompidou Centre in Paris?
20 In which European city is The Atomium?
21 Which tourist islands include the lesser known Cabrera and Formentera?
22 Which winter sports venue, home of the Cresta Run, has hosted two Olympic Games in the 20th century?
23 What is Ireland's longest river and greatest source of electric power?
24 The Simplon Tunnel links Italy with which country?
25 On which Sea does Croatia stand?

Answers

Euro Tour

1 Blue. **2** Le Shuttle. **3** Boulogne. **4** Maastricht. **5** Ireland. **6** Queen's University. **7** Oil. **8** SABENA. **9** Czech Republic. **10** Three. **11** 30th June. **12** Brussels Midi. **13** 1992. **14** London. **15** Spain. **16** England. **17** Reims. **18** Riviera. **19** Richard Rogers. **20** Brussels. **21** Balearics. **22** St Moritz. **23** Shannon. **24** Switzerland. **25** Adriatic.

Quiz 27 CORONATION ST. Level 2

1982

1 Which pastel-haired old lady made her *Coronation Street* debut this year?
2 Which members of the Royal Family attended the opening of the newly built outdoor set?
3 Who had an affair with married man Wilf Stockwell?
4 Who did Stan get to send Hilda a Valentine card, so she wouldn't recognise the writing?
5 Who did Jack Duckworth have a fling with this year?
6 Who took a job in Quatar for six months this year?
7 Where did his wife work in his absence?
8 What job did Mike Baldwin give to Emily?
9 How did the factory girls save Cleo the cat from being given to the RSPCA?
10 Who moved house from Number 9 to Number 7?
11 Who had their name changed from Harry to Harriet?
12 What was Chalkie Whitely's job?
13 Which married man did Sharon Gaskell fall for?
14 Where did Mavis meet Victor Pendlebury?
15 What was the name of Chalkie Whitely and Phyllis Pearce's grandson?
16 Marion Willis left Eddie Yeats twice this year: Once for an old flame but what was the other reason?
17 What did Sharon Gaskell do when she left Weatherfield?
18 Whose father died, leaving him £3000?
19 Who got drunk accompanying Anne Walker to the Licensed Victuallers Ball?
20 Who left Emily an unwanted inheritance?
21 Why did Bert Tilsley risk losing his new job?
22 Who refused to give his girlfriend, Maggie, a business loan, saying she was a bad risk?
23 Who was Ted Farrell?
24 Why did Gordon Clegg's wedding upset Betty?
25 Who did Joyce Lomas pursue this year?

Answers

Coronation Street – 1982

1 Phyllis Pearce. **2** The Queen and Prince Philip. **3** Elsie Tanner. **4** Alf Roberts. **5** Bet Lynch. **6** Brian Tilsley. **7** Jim's Café. **8** Wages clerk. **9** They made it a member of their union. **10** The Faircloughs. **11** Mavis' budgie. **12** Bin man. **13** Brian Tilsley **14** At an English class. **15** Craig. **16** He lost their savings. **17** She became a kennel maid. **18** Mike's dad, Frankie Baldwin. **19** Fred Gee. **20** Arnold Swain. **21** The start date clashed with his court case. **22** Mike Baldwin. **23** Gordon Clegg's father. **24** He didn't invite her. **25** Alf Roberts.

Quiz 28 Charts

Level 2

1 Which all boy group's first No 1 in 1989 was You Got It (The Right Stuff)?
2 Denis was the first UK hit for which group?
3 Who had an album in the 90s called Said and Done?
4 Which film featured the No 1 UK hit Take My Breath Away?
5 What was the Osmonds' only UK No 1 hit?
6 Who had an 80s hit with Good Tradition?
7 Which decade saw the introduction of the Grammy award?
8 Which group's first hit was Labour of Love?
9 What was Simply Red's first top ten single?
10 How many centimetres did an LP measure across?
11 In which decade did Imagine by John Lennon reach No 1 in the UK?
12 Who wrote the UK chart topper I Will Always Love You?
13 Which artist has had the most chart album hits in the US?
14 Who spent most weeks in the UK singles charts in 1996?
15 Who topped the album charts in 1990 with But Seriously?
16 Which American's first Top Ten album was 52nd Street?
17 Which game was in the title of a Pet Shop Boys hit from 1988?
18 During which decade did CDs officially go on sale in Europe?
19 Which group topped the album charts with Turtle Power?
20 Whose first hit in the 90s was End of the Road?
21 Who released an album in 1996 called Travelling Without Meaning?
22 Which country singer from the 80s sang Thank God I'm a Country Boy?
23 Who had an album called Take Two released in 1996?
24 Roxy Music had their first UK hit in which decade?
25 Which group topped the album charts in 1995 with Nobody Else?

Answers

Charts

1 New Kids On The Block. **2** Blondie. **3** Boyzone. **4** Top Gun. **5** Love Me For A Reason. **6** Tanita Tikaram. **7** 50s. **8** Hue and Cry. **9** Holding Back The Years. **10** 30. **11** 80s. **12** Dolly Parton. **13** Elvis Presley. **14** Oasis. **15** Phil Collins. **16** Billy Joel. **17** Dominoes. **18** 80s. **19** Partners In Kryme. **20** Boyz II Men. **21** Jamiroquai. **22** John Denver. **23** Robson and Jerome. **24** 1970s. **25** Take That.

Quiz 29 CORONATION ST. Level 2

1983

1 Which cantankerous pensioner first joined *Coronation Street* this year?
2 Why was Albert Tatlock's daughter, Beattie, furious with Ken this year?
3 How did Annie's Rover 2000 meet its end?
4 Who did Terry Goodwin track down to Coronation Street from London?
5 Why did Eddie and Marion bring their wedding forward?
6 What sort of holiday did Victor Pendlebury treat Mavis to on her birthday?
7 Who tried to seduce Brian to prove to Gail that he wasn't a good husband?
8 Who had an affair with married man Des Foster?
9 Jack's pseudonym at the Bill and Coo dating agency was Vince St Clair. What was Vera's *nom de plume*?
10 Who originally owned the pigeons that Jack inherited in 1983?
11 Who bought Stan Ogden's window cleaning round?
12 When Curly Watts arrived in Coronation Street he moved in to lodge with which elderly lady?
13 Who left Hilda a chip shop in his will?
14 How did Len Fairclough die?
15 What did Rita discover about her husband at his funeral?
16 Which of Elsie Tanner's old flames showed up this year?
17 Who celebrated their Ruby Wedding Anniversary?
18 Which young mechanic made his debut this year?
19 And who did he begin working for?
20 Who drove Bet and Betty into a lake?
21 Who went into a psychiatric hospital?
22 Where did Victor Pendlebury buy a cottage and ask Mavis to move to?
23 Who won over £3,500 on a five-horse accumulator and moved to Australia?
24 Who won Bet Lynch's weight loss challenge: Eddie, Alf or Fred?
25 Who wanted to mate with Mavis' budgie Harriet?

Answers

Coronation Street – 1983

1 Percy Sugden. **2** He bought Number One from Albert. **3** Eddie Yeats reversed over it in the bin lorry. **4** His wife, Suzie Birchall. **5** She was pregnant. **6** A camping trip in the Lakes. **7** Suzie Birchall. **8** Bet Lynch. **9** Carole Monroe. **10** Chalkie Whitely. **11** Eddie Yeats. **12** Emily Bishop. **13** Archie Crabtree. **14** He crashed his van. **15** He'd been having an affair. **16** Bill Gregory. **17** The Ogdens. **18** Kevin Webster. **19** Brian Tilsley. **20** Fred Gee. **21** Bert Tilsley. **22** Saddleworth. **23** Chalkie Whitely. **24** Alf. **25** Percy's budgie, Randy.

Quiz 30 80s Newsround

Level 2

1 The world was first aware of the Chernobyl disaster after detectors were triggered at a nuclear plant in which country?
2 Christa McAuliffe died in an accident in what type of vehicle in 1986?
3 Where was John Paul II when an attempt was made on his life in 1981?
4 Which form of death penalty was abolished by Francois Mitterand?
5 Who succeeded Brezhnev as Soviet premier?
6 Which drink did the Cocoa Cola Company launch in 1982?
7 Which film actor became mayor of Carmel, California, in 1986?
8 How did James F Fixx, promoter of jogging for good health, die in 1984?
9 Where did teenager Mathias Rust land his plane in 1987 much to the surprise of the country's authorities?
10 What colour wedding gown, veil and train did Paula Yates wear for her wedding to Bob Geldof?
11 Where did Torvill and Dean win Olympic gold with their Bolero routine?
12 Where did the US side of the Band Aid concert take place?
13 Natan Sharansky was released from prison in the USSR to begin a new life where?
14 Which country was the first to make catalytic convertors compulsory?
15 Which organ was transplanted with heart and lungs in the first triple transplant operation in the UK?
16 How were the balls at Wimbledon different in 1986 from previous years?
17 In which country was the first permanent bungee jumping site situated?
18 Which capital city was the scene of a major summit between Reagan and Gorbachev in 1986?
19 Proceedings in which House were first on TV in January 1985?
20 Who co-wrote the Band Aid song with Bob Geldof?
21 Virgin Atlantic flights first went to New York from which UK airport?
22 Which keeper was beaten by Maradona's 'hand of God' 1986 World Cup goal?
23 Which oil tanker disastrously ran aground off Brittany in 1987?
24 In which year did the £1 note cease to be legal tender in England?
25 Which country celebrated its bicentenary in 1988?

Answers

80s Newsround

1 Sweden. **2** Space Shuttle. **3** Rome. **4** Guillotine. **5** Andropov. **6** Diet Coke. **7** Clint Eastwood. **8** Heart attack while jogging. **9** Red Square. **10** Scarlet. **11** Yugoslavia. **12** Philadelphia. **13** Israel. **14** Switzerland. **15** Liver. **16** Yellow. **17** New Zealand. **18** Reykjavik. **19** House of Lords. **20** Midge Ure. **21** Gatwick. **22** Peter Shilton. **23** Amoco Cadiz. **24** 1988. **25** Australia.

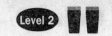

Quiz 31 Pot Luck

Level 2

1 Andy Warhol's 60s exhibition featured cans of which product?
2 Which doubles partner of Martina Navratilova commentated for the BBC at Wimbledon during the 1990s?
3 Who became US vice-president when Spiro Agnew resigned?
4 What claimed the life of the singer Kathleen Ferrier?
5 Which George invented the Kodak roll-film camera?
6 In TV ads which coffee did Gareth Hunt and Diane Keen drink?
7 What type of pens did Pentel create?
8 Which children's show had a pink hippo called George?
9 Which writer created the series *Prime Suspect* which starred Helen Mirren?
10 Ezzard Charles was a world champion in which sport?
11 Who was the first woman to make a solo flight across the Atlantic?
12 Harold Larwood's bowling for England v Australia ensured the series was known as what ?
13 Who or what was Schnorbitz?
14 Who made No 1 with Ebeneezer Goode?
15 Who along with Philips developed the CD in the late 70s?
16 San Giusto international airport is in which country?
17 Where is the multinational Nestlé based?
18 Who was in goal for Man Utd in the 1990 FA Cup Final replay but not in the original Final?
19 1996 is the Chinese year of which creature?
20 In the 90s how many points have been awarded for finishing second in a Grand Prix?
21 Rita Coolidge sang the title song for which Bond film?
22 Who hosted a TV Madhouse and played Fagin on stage in the 1990s?
23 In which decade of the century was Sir John Hall born?
24 Who wrote the novel *Brideshead Revisited*?
25 Which country became the first in the world to issue the dreaded parking ticket?

Answers

Pot Luck

1 Soup. **2** Pam Shriver. **3** Gerald Ford. **4** Cancer. **5** Eastman. **6** Nescafe. **7** Felt tips. **8** Rainbow. **9** Lynda La Plante. **10** Boxing. **11** Amelia Earhart. **12** Bodyline. **13** St Bernard dog. **14** Shamen. **15** Sony. **16** Italy. **17** Switzerland. **18** Les Sealey. **19** Rat. **20** 6. **21** Octopussy. **22** Russ Abbot. **23** 30s. **24** Evelyn Waugh. **25** France.

Quiz 32 20th C Celebs

Level 2

1 Who did Myte Garcia marry in 1996 by pointing to his symbol?
2 What did Bob Geldof and Paula Yates agree to swap as part of their divorce settlement?
3 In 1992 whose name was linked with then Tory minister David Mellor?
4 What is the name of Prince Edward's TV production company?
5 Who in 1994 put an ad in *The Times* with Richard Gere to say their marriage was still strong?
6 Which perfume house did Madonna advertise in the late 1990s?
7 Who accused Bill Clinton of sexual harassment after an incident in a hotel in 1991?
8 Model Ms Bourret is usually known by her first name alone; what is it?
9 Which royal spouse designed the Aviary at London Zoo?
10 Sir Richard Attenborough was a director of which London soccer side from 1969–1982?
11 Who did Anthea Turner say she was leaving husband Pete Powell for in 1998?
12 Which film producer is the father-in-law of Loyd Grossman?
13 Which gourmet and wit described Margaret Thatcher as Attila the Hen?
14 In 1998 Cristina Sanchez became the first woman to become what?
15 Which celebrity restaurants do Stallone, Willis and Schwarzenegger own?
16 Derrick Evans is better known as which Mr?
17 How many brothers and sisters does Dale Winton have?
18 Who protested about Michael Jackson during the Brit Awards in 1996?
19 Which British redhead did *Paris Match* sign as a regular writer in 1996?
20 Who has Patsy tattooed on his arm?
21 Which racing driver has a wife called Georgie?
22 Sir Magdi Yacoub became famous in which medical field?
23 In 1997 who did Kelly Fisher claim she was engaged to when photos of him with someone else appeared in the papers?
24 Where in London was the house Peter Mandelson bought with the help of a loan from Geoffrey Robinson?
25 Where was Nick Leeson released from jail in July 1999?

Answers

20th C Celebs

1 Prince. **2** Houses. **3** Antonia de Sancha. **4** Ardent. **5** Cindy Crawford. **6** Max Factor. **7** Paula Jones. **8** Caprice. **9** Lord Snowdon. **10** Chelsea. **11** Grant Bovey. **12** David Puttnam. **13** Clement Freud. **14** Matador. **15** Planet Hollywood. **16** Motivator. **17** None. **18** Jarvis Cocker. **19** The Duchess of York. **20** Liam Gallagher. **21** Damon Hill. **22** Heart transplants. **23** Dodi Fayed. **24** Notting Hill. **25** Singapore.

Quiz 33 CORONATION ST. Level 2

1984

1 Where did Elsie Tanner go to when she left Coronation Street?
2 What was Kevin Webster's sister called?
3 What business was Bill Webster in?
4 Who lent Bill money to fund his first job?
5 Whose niece did Bill Webster fall in love with?
6 Who won Fred Gee's car for £1 in a raffle?
7 Who won the egg-and-spoon race in the 1984 Pub Olympics?
8 Who tried to blackmail Emily Bishop for £600?
9 Who attempted to sue the council after her husband stubbed his toe on a paving stone?
10 Who did Christine Glover develop an obsession with?
11 Who was attacked by her mother's fiancé, George Hepworth?
12 Name the two male journalists Sally Waterman become involved with this year.
13 Which European country did Alma Sedgewick move to?
14 Who became the centre of attention after allegedly spotting a UFO?
15 Who received two marriage proposals this year?
16 Who had a fling with Dulcie Froggatt?
17 Three well-loved male characters died this year: Name them.
18 Who started up a neighbourhood watch scheme?
19 Who was sacked for thumping Billy Walker?
20 Who played Curly's girlfriend, Elaine Pollard?
21 Who offered a £10 reward for returning his missing budgie?
22 And who tried to pass off another budgie as the missing pet to claim the money?
23 Who became manager of Jim's Cafe after Alma's departure?
24 Who was Gordon Lewis?
25 Who was banned from driving after failing a breath test?

Answers

Coronation Street – 1984

1 Portugal. **2** Debbie. **3** Building. **4** Rita. **5** Percy's (Elaine Prior). **6** Percy. **7** Hilda. **8** Billy Walker. **9** Hilda. **10** Ken. **11** Gail. **12** Billy Walker and Ken Barlow. **13** Spain. **14** Curly. **15** Mavis. **16** Jack. **17** Albert Tatlock, Stan Ogden and Bert Tilsley. **18** Percy. **19** Fred Gee. **20** Janette Beverley. **21** Percy. **22** Jack Duckworth. **23** Gail. **24** Relief manager at the Rovers. **25** Jack.

Quiz 34 20th C TV Presenters

Level 2

1 Who first presented *The Good Sex Guide*?
2 Who interviewed Tony Blair at the launch of *5 News* on Channel 5?
3 Who went on from being a researcher on *Kilroy* to co-presenting *Watchdog* with Anne Robinson?
4 Who replaced Gaby Roslin on *The Big Breakfast*?
5 Carol Vorderman was dropped from the BBC's *Tomorrow's World* for advertising what commodity?
6 Which GMTV presenter is the wife of its chief reporter Martin Frizell?
7 Which duo, who were successful on TV am, provided BBC opposition to Richard & Judy on the morning sofa?
8 Which sport is Chris Tarrant's main hobby?
9 Who presented *Blue Peter* and *The Money Programme*?
10 Which news presenter went to school with Paul McCartney?
11 Which regular stand-in for Wogan had her own – unsuccessful – show *Saturday Matters*?
12 Which 90s news presenter bemoaned the fact that there was too little good news on TV?
13 Who was the first regular presenter of *Nine O'Clock Live* on GMTV?
14 *Paradise Gardens* was the last series made by which TV favourite?
15 Who was the first presenter of *Don't Forget Your Toothbrush*?
16 Who was dubbed TV's Mr Sex?
17 Whose third wife is former Puerto Rican beauty queen Wilnelia Merced?
18 Who was the presenter of *The Cook Report*?
19 Who moved on from *Newsround* to The *Travel Show*?
20 Which lady presented *Sunday Sunday* for LWT for eight years in the 80s?
21 *On Breakfast Time* what feature did The Green Goddess always present?
22 Who presented LWT's long time Saturday night celebrity show from 1984-1993?
23 Which knight presents *Through the Keyhole*?
24 Which former *Blue Peter* presenter took over from Sean Maguire as Marty in *Dangerfield*?
25 Which TV and radio journalist wrote and broadcast the *Letter to Daniel*?

Answers

20th C TV Presenters
1 Margi Clarke. **2** Kirsty Young. **3** Alice Beer. **4** Zoe Ball. **5** Soap powder. **6** Fiona Phillips. **7** Anne & Nick. **8** Fishing. **9** Valerie Singleton. **10** Peter Sissons. **11** Sue Lawley. **12** Martyn Lewis. **13** Lorraine Kelly. **14** Geoff Hamilton. **15** Chris Evans. **16** Angus Deayton. **17** Bruce Forsyth. **18** Roger Cook. **19** Juliet Morris. **20** Gloria Hunniford. **21** Keep fit. **22** Michael Aspel. **23** David Frost. **24** Tim Vincent. **25** Fergal Keane.

Quiz 35 CORONATION ST. Level 2

1985

1 Which *Coronation Street* regular joined this year, washing up at the cafe?
2 Who did Kevin Webster lodge with before moving in with Hilda?
3 Who became manageress of the Rovers this year?
4 At which seaside resort did Mavis and Rita take a holiday?
5 Who lost the Brainiest Pub Competition for the Rovers team?
6 Who had an affair with barman Frank Mills?
7 Who became a grandma when Peter Clegg was born?
8 Who took in lodger Henry Wakefield?
9 Why was Henry sacked from the factory?
10 Who started up the 'Cheap and Cheerful' removal business?
11 Who won a second honeymoon when she wasn't even married?
12 Which house did the Clayton family move in to?
13 What was Harry Clayton's job?
14 Which Clayton sister fell for Terry Duckworth?
15 Who did machinist Shirley Armitage begin dating?
16 Who played a bowls match with Percy Sugden to win the affections of Phyllis Pearce?
17 Who ran away to Newcastle and was brought home by Susan Barlow?
18 Who began a romance with Ivy Tilsley?
19 Why did Ivy refuse his marriage proposal?
20 Who upset his wife by spending his savings on his business rather than a home for his young family?
21 Who offered to buy Hilda's house to expand his business?
22 What was the first name of the youngest Clayton sister?
23 Why did the Claytons leave Coronation Street?
24 What was the name of Kevin's posh tennis-playing girlfriend?
25 Who broke his ankle falling off a ladder?

Answers

Coronation Street – 1985

1 Martin Platt. **2** Emily. **3** Bet. **4** Blackpool. **5** Percy. **6** Bet. **7** Betty. **8** Hilda. **9** The union found out he had been a scab at his previous workplace. **10** Terry and Curly. **11** Mavis. **12** Number 11. **13** Milkman. **14** Andrea. **15** Curly. **16** Sam Tindall. **17** Tracy. **18** George Wardle. **19** He was divorced and she was a Catholic. **20** Brian Tilsley. **21** Alf Roberts. **22** Sue. **23** Andrea was pregnant with Terry's baby. **24** Michelle Robinson. **25** Jack.

Quiz 36 Sporting Legends

Level 2

1 Which jockey was born on Bonfire Night?
2 Michael Jordan was a super scorer for which team?
3 Who was the Louiseville Lip?
4 Cricket's Alfred Freeman was known by which nickname?
5 In which decade was Daley Thompson born?
6 Who won swimming gold in the 100m freestyle at the 56, 60 and 64 Olympics?
7 Sergey Bubka has broken the world record on over 30 occasions in which event?
8 Ian Botham made his England debut while playing for which county?
9 How old was Nadia Comaneci when she won Olympic Gold as a gymnast?
10 Joe DiMaggio was known as what kind of Joe?
11 Apart from sprinting, in which event did Carl Lewis twice take Olympic gold?
12 Who was the first Brit to be British and US Open champion at the same time?
13 Gary Sobers hit six sixes in an over against which county?
14 Walter Swinburne won his first Derby on which legendary horse?
15 Who was the first British soccer player to be transferred to a foreign club?
16 Racing's Juan Manuel Fangio came from which country?
17 What did the G stand for in W G Grace's name?
18 Who was the first Scottish soccer player to gain 100 caps?
19 What position did Bill Beaumont play?
20 Who is Pakistan's all time leading Test wicket taker?
21 Which England soccer World Cup winner was knighted in 1998?
22 Which country did long distance runner Emil Zatopek come from?
23 Who was the first batsman to hit over 500 in a first class cricket game?
24 Who did Pete Sampras beat in the final to take his sixth Wimbledon singles title?
25 Who has been champion jockey on the flat most times this century?

Answers

Sporting Legends

1 Lester Piggott. **2** Chicago Bulls. **3** Muhammad Ali – born as Cassius Clay. **4** Titch. **5** 50s. **6** Dawn Fraser. **7** Pole vault. **8** Somerset. **9** 14. **10** Joltin'. **11** Long jump. **12** Tony Jacklin. **13** Glamorgan. **14** Shergar. **15** John Charles. **16** Argentina. **17** Gilbert. **18** Kenny Dalglish. **19** Lock. **20** Wasim Akram. **21** Geoff Hurst. **22** Czechoslovakia. **23** Brian Lara. **24** Andre Agassi. **25** Gordon Richards.

Quiz 37 Pot Luck

Level 2

1 Who had sidekicks called Eric and Tinker?
2 Which physicist was involved in the development of nuclear weapons in the USSR but became a dissident under Communist rule?
3 What type of plays did Georges Feydeau specialise in writing?
4 Which French brothers invented the first films?
5 What does A stand for in GATT?
6 Who had an 80s No 1 with Rock Me Amadeus?
7 Who was boxing's heavyweight champion throughout the 40s?
8 Who presented News Swap on *Multi Coloured Swap Shop*?
9 Which musical featured the song When I Marry Mr Snow?
10 In TV ads Shane Ritchie knocked at doors holding a packet of what?
11 What did the W C stand for in W C Fields' names?
12 Field Marshal Montgomery became Viscount Montgomery of where?
13 Who first sang the theme music to *Heartbeat*?
14 Who was Queen Elizabeth II's paternal grandfather?
15 In which city was Sean Connery born?
16 Where would you see the Dow Jones index?
17 Vehicles from which country use the international registration letter N?
18 Early in the century who wrote the novel *The Lost World*?
19 Who was the first person to interview George Michael about his arrest?
20 Which member of the Gibb family made a cameo appearance on *Only Fools and Horses*?
21 What does the letter F stand for in ASLEF?
22 In which decade did Denmark join the European Union?
23 Which group used a Bond film title for a 1996 top ten hit?
24 In American Football where do the Falcons come from?
25 Which language does the word ombudsman derive from?

Answers

Pot Luck

1 Lovejoy. **2** Andrei Sakharov. **3** Farce. **4** Lumiere Brothers. **5** Agreement. **6** Falco. **7** Joe Louis. **8** John Craven. **9** Carousel. **10** Daz. **11** William Claude. **12** Alamein. **13** Nick Berry. **14** George V. **15** Edinburgh. **16** Wall Street. **17** Norway. **18** Arthur Conan Doyle. **19** Michael Parkinson. **20** Barry. **21** Firemen. **22** 70s. **23** Ash – it was Goldfinger. **24** Atlanta. **25** Swedish.

Quiz 38 Sci Fi& Fantasy Movies

Level 2

1 Who played Dr Who in the 90s movie made for TV?
2 Who starred in the lead role in the *The Fly* opposite Geena Davis?
3 What was the fourth Alien film called?
4 Who received $3 million to recreate her five year TV role on film with her male partner?
5 Who tries to save the world from virtual reality in *The Matrix*?
6 Which spin off from a 60s sitcom was a 1999 movie with Jeff Daniels and Christopher Lloyd?
7 Who played Batman immediately before George Clooney?
8 In which 1998 film did Bruce Willis lead a team to confront a deadly threat from outer space?
9 Which tough guy played Mr Freeze in *Batman & Robin*?
10 Which 1996 film has its climax on 4th July?
11 In which sci fi classic did the space ship Nostromo first appear?
12 Which important US building has its roof ripped off in *Superman II*?
13 What was the first sequel to *Star Wars*?
14 What was the name of Drew Barrymore's character in *E.T.*?
15 Who played Rick Deckard in *Blade Runner*?
16 What number Star Trek movie was called *The Wrath of Khan*?
17 Which UK pop singer and environmental campaigner appeared in *Dune*?
18 Which decade does Michael J Fox go back to in *Back to the Future*?
19 Which Star Trek star directed *Three Men and a Baby*?
20 Who played the young Obi-Wan Kenobi in the Star Wars prequel?
21 Which 1968 sci fi classic was based on *The Sentinel* by Arthur C Clarke?
22 What was the subtitle of *Terminator 2*?
23 In which city does the action of the 1998 movie *Godzilla* take place?
24 What is the name of Darth Vader in Episode 1 _ *The Phantom Menace*?
25 Who did Jane Fonda play in the 60s movie of the same name where she constantly lost her clothes?

Answers

20th C The Movies Sci Fi & Fantasy
1 Paul McGann. **2** Jeff Goldblum. **3** *Alien Resurrection*. **4** Gillian Anderson - in *The X Files*. **5** Keanu Reeves. **6** *My Favourite Martian*. **7** Val Kilmer. **8** *Armageddon*. **9** Arnold Schwarzenegger. **10** *Independence Day*. **11** *Alien*. **12** The White House. **13** *The Empire Strikes Back*. **14** Gertie. **15** Harrison Ford. **16** II. **17** Sting. **18** 50s. **19** Leonard Nimoy. **20** Ewan McGregor. **21** *2001: A Space Odyssey*. **22** *Judgment Day*. **23** New York. **24** Anakin Skywalker. **25** Barbarella.

Quiz 39 CORONATION ST. Level 2

1986

1 Who made her first appearance on *Coronation Street*, meeting her future husband when he drove past and splashed her tights?
2 Which well-loved actress died of cancer two years after leaving *Coronation Street*?
3 Why did Jenny Bradley move in with Rita?
4 Who dyed Hilda's hair bright orange?
5 Who won a Vauxhall Nova in a magazine competition?
6 Who gave Susan Barlow a car for her 21st birthday?
7 Whose ex-fiancé, Derek, turned up and announced he was married to someone else?
8 Who started the Rovers fire when he changed a fuse?
9 Who attempted to rescue Bet Lynch from the flames?
10 Who opened the pub after its refurbishment?
11 Who did Kevin Webster punch when he found him kissing Sally?
12 Who did Tom Hopwood woo with free vegetables from his greengrocers?
13 Which barmaid did Alan Bradley have a fling with while seeing Rita?
14 What item of Curly's was stolen when burglars broke into Number 3?
15 Who formed a children's clothing business called Hopscotch?
16 Who changed her name to Barlow?
17 Who did Curly and Terry employ as their bookkeeper?
18 Who inherited a cat called Rommel?
19 Who dated Liz Turnbull?
20 Who played Jenny Bradley?
21 Who wanted to manage Jenny as a nightclub singer?
22 Which couple married in October?
23 Which couple married in May?
24 Whose ex-boyfriend was jailbird Steve Holt?
25 Which house did Alf and Audrey buy?

Answers

Coronation Street – 1986

1 Sally. **2** Pat Phoenix. **3** Rita fostered her when her mother died. **4** Audrey. **5** Vera. **6** Mike. **7** Mavis. **8** Jack. **9** Kevin. **10** Hilda. **11** Terry. **12** Hilda. **13** Gloria Todd. **14** Telescope. **15** Susan Baldwin. **16** Tracy Langton, when Ken adopted her. **17** Emily. **18** Hilda. **19** Brian. **20** Sally Ann Matthews. **21** Alec Gilroy. **22** Kevin and Sally. **23** Mike and Susan. **24** Gloria Todd. **25** Number 11.

Quiz 40 On the Road

Level 2

1 Which rules of the road for children were first published in 1971?
2 GT after a car's name means what?
3 Which margarine company sponsored the 1997 London Marathon?
4 How is a pedestrian light-controlled crossing more commonly known?
5 How many National Parks does the Pennine Way pass through?
6 Which illegal act is committed most frequently in cars?
7 What is London's Middlesex Street called on Sundays?
8 In 1974 roads in Rutland became roads in which county?
9 How was Sellafield known before 1981?
10 Which motorway crosses the estuary of the river Severn?
11 Which county saw the protests about the building of the Newbury bypass in the mid 90s?
12 What was the car toll for the new Severn Bridge when it opened in 1996?
13 What name is given to low bumps in the road which slow down traffic?
14 In which Road is the headquarters of the Labour Party?
15 How is a Denver boot also known?
16 How many yellow lines show that you can never park or unload in that location?
17 What letter or letters make up the sign for a Tourist Information office?
18 The Scilly Isles come under the authority of which English county?
19 What is the maximum speed limit in kilometres on a motorway?
20 What name is given to a short narrow road which links an A road to a motorway?
21 Which two counties do the North Downs run through?
22 What is the maximum custodial penalty for causing death by dangerous driving?
23 30 inside a blue circle with no red border means what when on the road?
24 What is the administrative centre of Cornwall?
25 What colour is a sign indicating an English Heritage site?

Answers

On the Road

1 Green Cross Code. **2** Gran turismo. **3** Flora. **4** Pelican crossing. **5** Three. **6** Speeding. **7** Petticoat Lane. **8** Leicestershire. **9** Windscale. **10** M4. **11** Berkshire. **12** £3.80. **13** Sleeping policeman. **14** Walworth. **15** Wheel clamp. **16** Two. **17** I. **18** Cornwall. **19** 113. **20** Slip road. **21** Kent & Surrey. **22** 10 years. **23** Minimum speed 30. **24** Truro. **25** Brown.

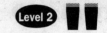

Quiz 41 CORONATION ST. Level 2

1987

1 Which well-loved character made her final appearance on Christmas Day of this year?
2 Who was driving Rita's car when Martin Platt was knocked unconscious?
3 Who moved in with Rita as her common law husband?
4 Who had an affair with his friend's wife, Linda Jackson?
5 Which *Coronation Street* baby was born this year, four months early?
6 Who organised the over-60s' tea dance?
7 Why did Mike and Susan Barlow split up?
8 What was the name of Vera's mum who moved into Number 9 this year?
9 Who became engaged to Frenchman Patric Podevin?
10 Which two ladies fought over pensioner Tom Hopwood?
11 Where did Kevin and Sally move to this year?
12 Who ruined Kevin and Sally's new chair by spilling red wine on it at their flat-warming party?
13 Who lent Bet the money to buy the tenancy of the Rovers?
14 Where did Bet run away to when she couldn't meet the repayments?
15 Who kidnapped Nicky Tilsley?
16 Who helped Gail to find Nicky?
17 Who hired a private detective to follow her husband?
18 And who did she threaten to name as co-respondent in the divorce?
19 Who tried to sweep his own chimney and covered the lounge in soot?
20 Who began an affair with Jack's old flame Dulcie Froggatt?
21 Which character lost his council seat and had a heart attack this year?
22 Which cabbie made his first appearance?
23 Who was lured to the registry office for a surprise wedding but refused to go through with it?
24 Who sacked his own wife from his factory?
25 Who played jilted husband Pete Jackson?

Answers

Coronation Street – 1987
1 Hilda. **2** Jenny Bradley. **3** Alan Bradley. **4** Terry. **5** Sarah Louise Tilsley. **6** Percy. **7** She told him she'd aborted their child. **8** Amy Burton. **9** Jenny Bradley. **10** Phyllis and Hilda. **11** The Corner Shop flat. **12** Alf. **13** Alec Gilroy. **14** Spain. **15** Brian. **16** Alan Bradley. **17** Angela Hawthorne/Wilton. **18** Mavis. **19** Jack. **20** Terry. **21** Alf. **22** Don Brennan. **23** Rita. **24** Mike. **25** Ian Mercer.

Quiz 42 Who's Who

Level 2

1 Which female vocalist was a member of the Eurythmics?
2 Which vocalist's real name is Michael Barratt?
3 Paul Weller was the lead singer of which group in the early 80s?
4 Which Gibb brother is the eldest?
5 Who played Aiden Brosnan in *Eastenders*?
6 Who duetted with Peabo Bryson on Beauty and the Beast?
7 What is Paul McCartney's real first name?
8 Who sang on If You Ever with East 17 in 1996?
9 Which country does Eddy Grant originate from?
10 Sting's Englishman in New York was used to advertise which make of car?
11 The Kemp brothers were in which 80s group?
12 Who was the lead singer of Yazoo?
13 William Broad became better known under which name?
14 Morten Harket was part of which 80s group?
15 Who accompanied Boyz II Men on the hit One Sweet Day?
16 Which liquid refreshment was advertised by Bob Geldof in 1987?
17 Who duetted on the '93 hit I've Got You Under My Skin with Frank Sinatra?
18 Who said drug taking was as normal as having a cup of tea in 1997?
19 Who Lost her Heart to a StarShip Trooper?
20 Which popular singer duetted with Elton John on Slow Rivers?
21 Vincent Furnier became better known as whom?
22 Who sang with Phil Collins on the 1985 hit Separate Lives?
23 In which decade was female vocalist Annie Lennox born?
24 Who sang with Kenny Rogers on We've Got Tonight?
25 Whose debut single in 1996 was called Anything?

Answers

Who's Who

1 Annie Lennox. **2** Shakin' Stevens. **3** The Jam. **4** Barry. **5** Sean Maguire. **6** Celine Dion. **7** James. **8** Gabrielle. **9** Guyana. **10** Rover. **11** Spandau Ballet. **12** Alison Moyet. **13** Billy Idol. **14** A-ha. **15** Mariah Carey. **16** Milk. **17** Bono. **18** Noel Gallagher. **19** Sarah Brightman. **20** Cliff Richard. **21** Alice Cooper. **22** Marilyn Martin. **23** 50s. **24** Sheena Easton. **25** 3T.

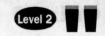

Quiz 43 Pot Luck

Level 2

1 Mark O'Meara first won the British Open at which course?
2 Which country designated Chachoengsao as its new capital?
3 Who had an 80s hit with Golden Brown?
4 Which village is the home of Agatha Christie sleuth Miss Marple?
5 The Duke of Wellington appeared on the back of which British banknote?
6 What was Mahatma Gandhi's profession outside politics?
7 In cricket, which English team turned into Eagles in the 90s?
8 What rose from the Solent in 1982?
9 Which musical featured the song Sunrise Sunset?
10 Sergey Golubitsky has been a world champion in which sport?
11 What was Take That's first UK No 1?
12 In which sport could the Bucks take on the Raptors?
13 Who presented *Football Focus* before moving to ITV in the mid 90s?
14 What is the second of Prince William's four names?
15 In which decade did Germany join the European Union?
16 In which city was Michael Jackson a Stranger in 1996?
17 Which actress wrote the novel *Prime Time* in the 1980s?
18 Vigo international airport is in which country?
19 Who said, 'When you are as great as I am, it's hard to be humble'?
20 Which jazz trumpeter hosted radio's *I'm Sorry I Haven't A Clue*?
21 On which river was the Hoover dam built?
22 If you lose on *Ready Steady Cook* what do you receive?
23 1995 was the Chinese year of which creature?
24 Shearer and who else scored when England beat Scotland in Euro 96?
25 The train in the Great Train Robbery was making which journey?

Answers

Pot Luck

1 Birkdale. **2** Thailand. **3** Stranglers. **4** St. Mary Mead. **5** £5. **6** Law. **7** Essex. **8** Mary Rose. **9** Fiddler On The Roof. **10** Fencing. **11** Pray. **12** Basketball. **13** Bob Wilson. **14** Arthur. **15** 50s. **16** Moscow. **17** Joan Collins. **18** Spain. **19** Muhammad Ali. **20** Humphrey Lyttleton. **21** Colorado. **22** Food Hamper. **23** Bear. **24** Paul Gascoigne. **25** Glasgow to London.

Quiz 44 90s Newsround

Level 2

1 Which hotel had Princess Diana and Dodi Fayed just left when they were involved in their fatal car crash?
2 Who ran against Bill Clinton in the 1996 US election?
3 Ian Botham and Allan Lamb lost a libel case against which other cricketer?
4 Who in 1997 met an old school friend in the *Big Issue* office?
5 13 year old Sarah Cook hit the headlines after marrying a waiter while on holiday where?
6 Sandra Gregory was given a 25 year sentence for drug smuggling where?
7 In 1999 what sort of savings plan replaced Tessa?
8 In which city was Mother Teresa buried?
9 Which English city was blasted by an IRA bomb in June 1996?
10 Which Club finally voted in 1998 to admit women members?
11 In which city did Louise Woodward's US trial take place?
12 Which toy was the panic buy of Christmas 1997 due to a shortage in supply?
13 Who recorded Monica Lewinsky's conversations about her affair with Bill Clinton?
14 In '98 the US Embassy was bombed in which country with many fatalities?
15 Legal proceedings began against Scotsman Jim Sutherland for flouting a ban on what?
16 The Duchess of York's mother was killed near her home in which country?
17 How was eco warrior Daniel Hooper better known?
18 Which American was the first US pop star to perform in a sanction-free South Africa?
19 What was the name of the low fat burger launched by McDonalds?
20 Neil & Jamie Acourt were involved in the court case about which victim?
21 Which politician said her boss, 'had something of the night about him'?
22 Which Building Society was floated in 1997 with members each receiving a windfall?
23 Which former MP did William Hague make Party Chairman in 1997?
24 In which town was Gianni Versace shot?
25 In 1991 which country mourned the loss of King Olaf?

Answers

90s Newsround

1 Ritz. **2** Bob Dole. **3** Imran Khan. **4** Prince Charles. **5** Turkey. **6** Thailand. **7** Isa. **8** Calcutta. **9** Manchester. **10** MCC. **11** Boston. **12** Teletubbies. **13** Linda Tripp. **14** Kenya. **15** Selling beef on the bone. **16** Argentina. **17** Swampy. **18** Paul Simon. **19** McLean. **20** Stephen Lawrence. **21** Ann Widdecombe. **22** Halifax. **23** Lord Parkinson. **24** Miami. **25** Norway.

Quiz 45 CORONATION ST. Level 2

1988

1. Who moved in to Number 13 this year?
2. Who proposed to his girlfriend through the letter box of the Kabin?
3. Which couple remarried this year?
4. Who became unexpectedly pregnant but suffered a miscarriage?
5. Who shocked Gail by revealing she had a secret son?
6. Who stole the deeds of Rita's house to secure a bank loan?
7. What job did newcomer Sandra Stubbs take?
8. Who punched Malcolm Reid on a coach to Blackpool?
9. Whose sister was convicted as an accessory to theft?
10. Who had an affair with Carole Burns?
11. Who dated both Gloria Todd and Linda Farrell this year?
12. Who was banned from driving after Ida Clough tipped off the police about him being over the limit?
13. Who broke his nose when his wife crashed their car into a lamppost?
14. Who moved in to Number 3 with Emily?
15. Which formidable pensioner dated Arnold Swift?
16. Who did Curly move into the Corner Shop flat with?
17. Why was Alf Roberts exposed as a bigot this year?
18. Who had a guard dog called Rover?
19. Who was in trouble for shoplifting from the Corner Shop and Rovers?
20. Who played Percy Sugden?
21. Who was beaten up by Gina Seddon's jealous boyfriend?
22. Why was there a paper boys' rebellion at the Kabin?
23. Who took his girlfriend out in Mike's Jaguar, resulting in it being vandalised?
24. Who was imprisoned in Brian Roscoe's flat?
25. Who employed Martin Platt as an assistant but sacked him for being too friendly with his daughter?

Answers

Coronation Street – 1988

1 Sally and Kevin. **2** Derek. **3** Gail and Brian. **4** Bet. **5** Audrey. **6** Alan Bradley. **7** Rovers cleaner. **8** Alf. **9** Sally's sister Gina. **10** Alan Bradley. **11** Mike. **12** Mike. **13** Jack. **14** Percy. **15** Phyllis. **16** Shirley Armitage. **17** He objected to Shirley moving in because she was black. **18** Bet. **19** Amy Burton. **20** Bill Waddington. **21** Martin Platt. **22** Mavis employed a pensioner, Harry Ashton. **23** Terry. **24** Deirdre. **25** Alan Bradley.

Quiz 46 20th C Brat Pack

Level 2

1 Nigel Short was the youngest champion in which game in 1984?
2 What did Woody Allen call his son as a tribute to Louis 'Satchmo' Armstrong?
3 Which comedian is the father of Lucy David who plays Hayley in *The Archers*?
4 Linus Roache's father plays which character in a TV soap?
5 Which 80s Wimbledon Men's Singles champion is the father of twins?
6 Which soul singer is Whitney Houston's godmother?
7 Who was the most famous Head Girl at Kesteven and Grantham Girls' School?
8 What did Mel B call her baby with Jimmy Gulzar?
9 Where did Princess Anne's daughter Zara famously sport a stud in 1998?
10 What type of car did Prince William receive for his 17th birthday?
11 What is the name of Paul and Linda McCartney's only son?
12 Which son of Camilla Parker Bowles was exposed in a drugs scandal in the summer of 1999?
13 Which pop star has a son called Prince Michael?
14 Which politician is writer Vera Brittain's daughter?
15 What relation is Joely Richardson to Vanessa Redgrave?
16 What are the first names of the Sawalha sisters of *AbFab* and *EastEnders* fame?
17 Melanie Molitor is the mum of which former tennis world No 1?
18 How is John Major's celebrity brother known?
19 Finty Williams is the daughter of which film and theatre Dame?
20 Which Biblical name does Boris Becker's older son have?
21 Princess Anne's son Peter Phillips was Head Boy at which famous school?
22 Who is Julian Lennon's stepmother?
23 Which university did Tony Blair and Bill Clinton both attend in their younger days?
24 How many sisters and half sisters combined does Cherie Booth have?
25 Which footballer had his baby's name printed on his football socks?

Answers

20th C Brat Pack

1 Chess. **2** Satchel. **3** Jasper Carrott. **4** Ken Barlow. **5** Pat Cash. **6** Aretha Franklin. **7** Margaret Thatcher. **8** Phoenix Chi. **9** Tongue. **10** Golf. **11** James. **12** Tom. **13** Michael Jackson. **14** Shirley Williams. **15** Daughter. **16** Julia & Nadia. **17** Martina Hingis. **18** Terry Major-Ball. **19** Judi Dench. **20** Noah. **21** Gordonstoun. **22** Yoko Ono. **23** Oxford. **24** Six. **25** David Beckham.

Quiz 47 CORONATION ST. Level 2

1989

1 Which bespectacled retail manager made his debut this year?
2 Which anniversary did *Coronation Street* celebrate this year – 1000, 2000 or 3000 episodes?
3 What big change occurred this year in the way *Coronation Street* was scheduled?
4 Which new family moved in to Number 11?
5 Which house received a face-lift in the form of stone cladding?
6 Who was given a pregnant greyhound called Harry's Luck?
7 Who was killed outside a nightclub?
8 Who did Mark Casey work for?
9 Who broke her ankle driving in a banger race?
10 Who hit Martin on finding out he was dating Gail?
11 Who moved in with Jack and Vera after splitting up with his girlfriend?
12 What was the name of builder Eddie Ramsden's son?
13 Who played Liz McDonald?
14 Whose intervention saved Rita from being suffocated by Alan Bradley?
15 Where did Rita run away to after Alan's trial?
16 Who employed an exotic dancer and a troupe of performing budgies for a Middle East tour?
17 Who took a job at Chuckle's Novelties?
18 Who was the council mole, and Ken Barlow's lover?
19 Who thought he had seen the real Father Christmas, after spotting Derek on the warehouse roof after a Christmas party?
20 Who was wrongly suspected of having an affair with Paul Rigby?
21 Who kicked a football through Alf Roberts' shop window?
22 Who played Mark Casey?
23 Who tried to rape Dawn Prescott?
24 Who played Jim McDonald?
25 Who did Jack tell Vera he had taken out, prompting her to cut up all his trousers?

Answers

Coronation Street – 1989

1 Reg Holdsworth. **2** 3000. **3** A third weekly episode was introduced on Fridays. **4** The McDonalds. **5** Number 9. **6** Don Brennan. **7** Brian. **8** Kevin. **9** Sally. **10** Ivy. **11** Curly. **12** Jamie. **13** Beverley Callard. **14** Jenny Bradley's. **15** Blackpool. **16** Alec. **17** Derek. **18** Wendy Crozier. **19** Jack. **20** Bet. **21** The McDonald twins. **22** Stuart Wolfenden. **23** Alan Bradley. **24** Charles Lawson. **25** Tina Fowler.

Quiz 48 20th C TV Classics

Level 2

1 Who was *News At Ten*'s first woman presenter?
2 What was Kojak's first name?
3 In which English county was *Lovejoy* filmed?
4 Which Olympic Games were the first to be televised?
5 Who was Edina's PA in *AbFab*?
6 Who was the astrologer on the BBC's *Breakfast Time*?
7 How much were the 'cheapest' questions worth in the first series of *Sale of the Century*?
8 What was the name of the 70s comedy series based on the *Carry On* films?
9 Which game was *Celebrity Squares* based on?
10 Which ship featured in *Sailor*?
11 *When the Boat Comes In* was set in which part of the UK?
12 Which classic 80s drama series shot Anthony Andrews and Jeremy Irons to fame?
13 Which actor was *The Bounder*?
14 What was the name of the David Attenborough series set in the south Atlantic?
15 Which character in *The X Files* is the name of a mystery person implicated in the Watergate affair?
16 Which cult series asked, "Who killed Laura Palmer?"?
17 Which classic British sitcom spawned the catchphrase 'you dirty old man!'?
18 Which show was blamed by a British police chief for making police officers 'drive like maniacs'?
19 Who plays the nurse in Hancock's classic *The Blood Donor*?
20 In the early 80s if David McCallum was Steel who was Sapphire?
21 What was Rumpole's first name?
22 Which drama series featured a ship called The Charlotte Rhodes?
23 Which actress played the scatty mum in *Not In Front of the Children*?
24 Which future husband of Demi Moore found fame in the TV series *Moonlighting*?
25 How many Monkees were there?

Answers

20th C TV CLassics

1 Anna Ford. **2** Theo. **3** Suffolk. **4** 1948. **5** Bubbles. **6** Russell Grant. **7** £1. **8** Carry on Laughing. **9** Noughts & Crosses. **10** Ark Royal. **11** North East England. **12** Brideshead Revisited. **13** Peter Bowles. **14** Life in the Freezer. **15** Deep Throat. **16** Twin Peaks. **17** Steptoe and Son. **18** Starsky & Hutch. **19** June Whitfield. **20** Joanna Lumley. **21** Horace. **22** The Onedin Line. **23** Wendy Craig. **24** Bruce Willis. **25** Four.

Quiz 49 Pot Luck

Level 2

1 Which month in 1914 did WWI begin?
2 Who was Princes William and Harry's nanny after their parents' separation?
3 Who had an 80s No 1 with Beat Surrender?
4 In cricket what did Glamorgan add to their name in the 90s?
5 What was Crockett's pet in *Miami Vice*?
6 What stopped Suzanne Lenglen playing at Wimbledon after 1926?
7 What was the nickname of Klaus Barbie, the Nazi war criminal?
8 Which veteran DJ used to advertise Brentford Nylons?
9 Who wrote the Inspector Alleyn mysteries?
10 Which Australian city hosted its final Formula 1 race in 1995?
11 Which actress gave birth to twins at the age of 44 in 1995?
12 What are the international registration letters of a vehicle from Peru?
13 On TV who interviewed Earl Spencer at length several months after Princess Diana's death?
14 With which sport is Said Aouita associated?
15 In which city was Robbie Coltrane born?
16 Which company used the Hollies' hit I'm Alive to advertise in 1997?
17 In which decade did Portugal join the European Union?
18 In which country was Jean Claude van Damme born?
19 Who wrote the novel *Eating People Is Wrong*?
20 Who presented *You've Been Framed* before Lisa Riley?
21 The name Stanley Gibbons has become associated with what?
22 In which country is the deepwater port of Dampier?
23 Which city has a team of Reds and a team of Bengals?
24 In which decade was Andie MacDowell born?
25 How did the German V-1 flying bomb become known?

Answers

Pot Luck

1 August. **2** Tiggy Legge-Bourke. **3** Jam. **4** Dragons. **5** Alligator. **6** She became a professional. **7** Butcher Of Lyons. **8** Alan Freeman. **9** Ngaio Marsh. **10** Melbourne. **11** Jane Seymour. **12** PE. **13** Sally Magnusson. **14** Athletics. **15** Glasgow. **16** Boots. **17** 80s. **18** Belgium. **19** Malcolm Bradbury. **20** Jeremy Beadle. **21** Stamps. **22** Australia. **23** Cincinnati. **24** 50s. **25** Doodlebug.

Quiz 50 Cricket

Level 2

1 Who followed Viv Richards as West Indian captain?
2 Who along with Mark Waugh accepted money from an Indian bookmaker for 'weather forecasts'?
3 Who was the last man out in the Australia v S Africa semi-final tie in 1999?
4 Who were England playing in the Atherton 'ball tampering' incident?
5 What was the nickname of England pace bowler David Lawrence?
6 Who were the opponents in Mike Atherton's last series as England skipper?
7 Who was man of the match in the 1999 World Cup final?
8 Administrator Lord MacLaurin was a former chairman of which supermarket group?
9 Who was the first bowler since Laker to take all ten wickets in the same Test innings?
10 Which county was the last to be admitted to the County circuit in the century?
11 Which team won the 1992 World Cup?
12 Which visiting bowler took nine wickets in a Test in England in the 90s?
13 At which ground did Atherton and Donald have their famous 'battle' of 1998?
14 Who preceded Ray Illingworth as chairman of the Test selectors?
15 England batsman Aftab Habib managed only one first class game for which county?
16 Who was England's leading wicket taker on the 97–98 W Indies tour?
17 What was Clive Lloyd's middle name?
18 Where are the Eden Gardens?
19 In what year did Graham Gooch first play for England?
20 Which Minor County did England keeper Chris Read play for?
21 Steve James was playing for which county when first capped for England?
22 Which team have won the county championship most in the century?
23 What colour were the Australian trousers in the 1999 World Cup final?
24 Who was the first player to score 100 and take eight wickets in an innings in the same Test?
25 Which English keeper had the middle names Philip Eric?

Answers

Cricket

1 Richie Richardson. **2** Shane Warne. **3** Allan Donald. **4** South Africa. **5** Syd. **6** W Indies. **7** Shane Warne. **8** Tesco. **9** Anil Kumble. **10** Durham. **11** Pakistan. **12** Muttiah Muralitharan. **13** Trent Bridge. **14** Ted Dexter. **15** Middlesex. **16** Angus Fraser. **17** Hubert. **18** Calcutta. **19** 1975. **20** Devon. **21** Glamorgan. **22** Yorkshire. **23** Yellow. **24** Ian Botham. **25** Alan Knott.

Quiz 51 CORONATION ST. Level 2

1990

1. Who said of Alma Sedgewick, 'Alma's sort don't like work – they like to find a man who'll do it all'?
2. Which newlywed couple moved into Number 6 this year?
3. Who sprayed their car with the slogan 'Get lost you yupies' (sic)?
4. Which Coronation Street babies were both born this year, within a day of each other?
5. Who set fire to her home while cooking chips?
6. Who sought out his estranged daughter Sandra Arden?
7. Who owned a recycling plant called Pendlebury's Paper Products?
8. Who was Flick Khan's housemate at Number 7?
9. Who was given the garage business for his 21st birthday?
10. What was Angie Freeman studying at college?
11. Who shaved off Kevin Webster's moustache?
12. Who thew a piece of stone cladding through the Wiltons' window?
13. Who became engaged to frumpy Kimberley Taylor?
14. Who organised a free bus to Bettabuy, upsetting Alf as it stopped outside the Corner Shop?
15. Who did Derek catch massaging Mavis feet?
16. Which two young women took jobs promoting the cider drink *Pomme de Lite*?
17. Who bought a holiday from Alec Gilroy only to find the company had gone bankrupt?
18. Who played Jackie Ingram?
19. Who lied about his age to get a job as a lollipop man?
20. Who bought a dog called Boomer which ate their Christmas Dinner?
21. Who played Angie Freeman?
22. Who had an identity crisis after visiting a spiritualist church?
23. Who had an affair with Nigel Ridley?
24. Who opened a motorbike repair shop under the viaduct?
25. Who had a dalliance with Lester Fontayne?

Answers

Coronation Street – 1990

1 Audrey. **2** Steph and Des Barnes. **3** The Duckworths. **4** Rosie Webster and David Platt. **5** Tracy Barlow. **6** Alec. **7** Victor Pendlebury. **8** Jenny Bradley. **9** Mark Casey. **10** Fashion Design. **11** Steph Barnes. **12** Vera Duckworth. **13** Curly. **14** Reg Holdsworth. **15** Victor Pendlebury. **16** Jenny Bradley and Steph Barnes. **17** The Wiltons. **18** Shirin Taylor. **19** Percy. **20** The Duckworths. **21** Deborah McAndrew. **22** Ivy Brennan. **23** Tina Fowler. **24** Jim McDonald. **25** Vera Duckworth.

Quiz 52 20th C 90s Movies

Level 2

1 Which *ER* star played opposite Jenny Seagrove in *Don't Go Breaking My Heart*?
2 *Beloved* in 1999 was whose first movie since *The Color Purple* in 1985?
3 In *Stepmom* who played Susan Sarandon's daughter?
4 Who played the colliery band leader in *Brassed Off*?
5 In which 90s movie did Al Pacino play retired Colonel Frank Slade?
6 Which sitcom star appeared on the big screen in *The Object of My Affection*?
7 Who played Drew Barrymore's stepmother in *Ever After*?
8 Which US president did Anthony Hopkins play in a film whose title was simply his name?
9 Which Schwarzenegger movie about a man who gets pregnant was originally titled *Oh Baby*?
10 In which movie did Jane Horrocks play a girl who can sing like the great musical stars?
11 Which star of *Cheers* co starred with Whoopi Goldberg in *Made in America*?
12 Which *The Bridges of Madison County* star became a father again aged 65?
13 Who was the star of the dark thriller 8mm?
14 Where was the 1990s version of Dickens' *Great Expectations* set?
15 Which King did Leonardo DiCaprio play in *The Man in the Iron Mask*?
16 Which regular member of the *Friends* cast starred in *Lost in Space*?
17 Which role did Rupert Everett play in *The Madness of King George*?
18 Which animation film was originally a 50s musical set in Siam?
19 What is the name of Kate Winslet's character in *Titanic*?
20 Who played the title role in *Emma*?
21 Which character did Julia Roberts play in Steven Spielberg's *Hook*?
22 Which movie was a biopic about the life of David Helfgott?
23 Which Apollo mission was filmed in 1995 with Tom Hanks?
24 In which film did Susan Sarandon play Sister Helen Prejean?
25 What was Pierce Brosnan's first outing as 007?

Answers

20th C 90s Movies
1 Anthony Edwards. **2** Oprah Winfrey. **3** Julia Roberts. **4** Pete Postlethwaite. **5** Scent of a Woman. **6** Jennifer Aniston. **7** Anjelica Houston. **8** Nixon. **9** Junior. **10** Little Voice. **11** Ted Danson. **12** Clint Eastwood. **13** Nicolas Cage. **14** New York. **15** Louis XIV. **16** Matt LeBlanc. **17** The Prince of Wales. **18** The King and I. **19** Rose. **20** Gwyneth Paltrow. **21** Tinkerbell. **22** Shine. **23** 13. **24** Dead Man Walking. **25** Goldeneye.

Quiz 53 CORONATION ST. Level 2

1991

1 Who was accused of having an affair with Vivian Barford during the council elections?
2 Who renovated a boat in his back garden?
3 Who left Coronation Street to become the mistress of a dentist?
4 Who rigged a trolley dash at Bettabuy, allowing Rita to win?
5 Who had an affair with Simon Beatty?
6 Who was in trouble for fencing car stereos after selling Alf Roberts' model to Derek Wilton?
7 Who had a rival in love called Adrian Gosthorpe?
8 Who claimed to be the illegitimate grandson of Edward VII?
9 Who was orphaned and came to live in the Rovers?
10 Whose garden did Freddie The Fox appear in?
11 Who was accused of sexual harrassment by his office cleaner after slapping her bottom whilst under the influence of 'aphrodisiac' vegetables?
12 Who did Phyllis Pearce clean for?
13 Who was Angie Freeman's house-mate this year?
14 Who was Bacchus on the Bettabuy carnival float?
15 Who sent Vera a card from the Queen as an April Fools joke?
16 Who was best man at Mike's wedding to Jackie Ingrams?
17 Who was sacked as Bettabuy's Santa for being too grumpy?
18 Where did Ivy work after being sacked from Ingrams?
19 Kevin Webster and Alma Sedgewick were witnesses at whose wedding?
20 Who had an affair with Julie Dewhurst?
21 Who threatened Mike with a loaded shotgun?
22 Who opened a charity shop in aid of Friends Of Weatherfield General?
23 Name the Bettabuy Head Office manager played by Milton Johns.
24 Who moved into the flat at Number 12 after his wife threw him out?
25 Who had an adolescent crush on Steph Barnes?

Answers

Coronation Street – 1991

1 Alf. **2** Des. **3** Jenny Bradley. **4** Reg Holdsworth. **5** Steph Barnes. **6** Steve McDonald. **7** Curly. **8** Joss Shackleton. **9** Vicky Arden. **10** Mavis and Derek's. **11** Derek. **12** Des. **13** Curly. **14** Reg. **15** Jack. **16** Phil Jennings. **17** Percy. **18** The Corner Shop. **19** Gail and Martin's. **20** Don Brennan. **21** Jackie Ingrams-Baldwin. **22** Emily. **23** Brendan Scott. **24** Reg **25** Steve McDonald.

Quiz 54 20th C World Tour

Level 2

1 In which country are the world's tallest buildings, the Petronas Towers?
2 In 1997 which airline replaced the flag on its tail fin with ethnic designs from around the world?
3 Where is there the Valley of the Kings, scene of a terrorist attack in 1997?
4 In which decade of the 20th century did the first scheduled passenger air service begin?
5 What was Ethiopia called before it was called Ethiopia?
6 What is California's answer to Scotland's Silicon Glen called?
7 What name was given to the effect which warmed the waters of the Pacific, notably in the 1990s?
8 Andy Elson's world tour by balloon was thwarted in 1998 because he could not cross which country's air space?
9 What was Ho Chi Minh city before it was called Ho Chi Minh city?
10 In which continent is over half of the world's rainforests?
11 What was replaced by Brasilia as Brazil's capital in the 60s?
12 Which country is known as the Land of the Long White Cloud?
13 Which desert expanded by 251,000 sq miles between 1940 and 1990?
14 What was St Petersburg called for most of the 20th century?
15 On which island will you find Bondi Beach?
16 Which Californian resort is famous for its Golden Gate bridge?
17 In which country is the headquarters of the Save the Children Fund?
18 Which country contains the Biblical rivers of the Tigris and the Euphrates?
19 Transamazonica is a roadway across which large South American country?
20 Which German airport has 'am main' after its name?
21 If a car's index mark is GBA, where does it come from?
22 What is the Pacific terminus of the Trans Siberian Railway?
23 In which US state did skateboards originate as an alternative to surfing?
24 Which items essential for world travel, are made in Seattle?
25 To the nearest thousand, how many islands does Indonesia have?

Answers

20th C World Tour

1 Malaysia. **2** British Airways. **3** Egypt. **4** 2nd decade - it was 1914. **5** Abyssinia. **6** Silicon Valley. **7** El Nino. **8** China's. **9** Saigon. **10** America. **11** Rio de Janeiro. **12** New Zealand. **13** Sahara. **14** Leningrad. **15** Australia. **16** San Francisco. **17** England. **18** Iraq. **19** Brazil. **20** Frankfurt. **21** Alderney. **22** Vladivostok. **23** California. **24** Jets. **25** 13.

Quiz 55 Pot Luck

Level 2

1 Which former Tory MP lost the Derbyshire South seat in 1997?
2 In *NYPD Blue* who played Bobby Simone?
3 Barbara Castle was a long-standing PM for which constituency?
4 Who wrote the *Clayhanger* series of novels?
5 Who had an 80s No 1 with Making Your Mind Up?
6 In baseball where do the Tigers come from?
7 Who founded Body Shop?
8 Whose secret agent partner was Penfold?
9 In cricket, which English team became Bears in the 90s?
10 Which group had a No 1 album in 1986 titled Once Upon A Time?
11 Jonathan Power has been a world champion in which sport?
12 What are the international registration letters of a vehicle from Switzerland?
13 How much in old pence was a tanner worth in predecimal days?
14 In Germany what are strumpfhose?
15 1994 was the Chinese year of which creature?
16 Who were the first landlords of the Rovers Return in *Coronation Street*?
17 'Adopt, adapt, improve' was adopted as which group's motto?
18 Which actor's real name was Walter Matasschansayasky?
19 Who sailed solo round the world in *Gipsy Moth IV* in 1966-67?
20 What did Tic-Tac throw in the Bond movies with deadly results?
21 In S Africa what does the I stand for in IFP?
22 In TV ads which drink claimed, 'It's what your right arm's for'?
23 Which Rugby League team became Bulldogs in the 90s?
24 What is the motto of the Scout movement?
25 In which decade was Hugh Grant born?

Answers

Pot Luck

1 Edwina Currie. **2** Jimmy Smits. **3** Blackburn. **4** Arnold Bennett. **5** Bucks Fizz. **6** Detroit. **7** Anita Roddick. **8** Dangermouse. **9** Warwickshire. **10** Simple Minds. **11** Squash. **12** CH. **13** Six. **14** Tights. **15** Dog. **16** Jack and Annie Walker. **17** The Round Table. **18** Walter Matthau. **19** Francis Chichester. **20** Bowler hat. **21** Inkatha. **22** Courage. **23** Batley. **24** Be prepared. **25** 60s.

Quiz 56 Bands

Level 2

1 The Proclaimers were King of the what in 1990?
2 Chrissie Hynde was the female member of which successful band?
3 Which band had a 90s album titled Our Town - Greatest Hits?
4 Which Irish group has a name which means family?
5 Which groups first hit was titled House of Love?
6 Who rereleased the 1984 No 8 hit Young At Heart in 1993?
7 Which group recorded the track that Welsh soccer fans changed to Bobby Gould Must Go?
8 Which group was founded by Ian Broudie?
9 Which hit-making band featured Andy Summers and Stewart Copeland?
10 In which city were Pulp formed?
11 Falco's Rock Me Amadeus was sung in which language?
12 How many songs by the Bee Gees were in the film *Saturday Night Fever*?
13 Which Status Quo hit opened the 1985 Live Aid concert?
14 Who released an album in 1996 called A Different Beat?
15 Who told us to Keep On Running in a 60s No 1 hit?
16 Who had an insect-sounding hit with The Fly in 1991?
17 Siobhan Fahey and Marcella Detroit were in which band in the 90s?
18 How many members are in the group Boyz II Men?
19 Where is the native home country of Bjorn Again?
20 Which 60s group included Pete Quaife and Mick Avory?
21 Which all-girl group were first to sell more than a million copies of an album in the UK?
22 Who were Naked In The Rain in a No. 4 hit from July 1990?
23 Who formed a rock band in 1989 called Tin Machine?
24 What was 2 Unlimited's first UK No 1 from 1993?
25 Which company used Queen's I Want To Break Free in TV commercials?

Answers

Bands

1 Road. **2** Pretenders. **3** Deacon Blue. **4** Clannad. **5** East 17. **6** Bluebells. **7** Manic Street Preachers. **8** The Lightning Seeds. **9** The Police. **10** Sheffield. **11** German. **12** 7. **13** Rockin' All Over The World. **14** Boyzone. **15** Spencer Davis Group. **16** U2. **17** Shakespear's Sister. **18** Four. **19** Australia. **20** The Kinks. **21** Eternal. **22** Blue Pearl. **23** David Bowie. **24** No Limit. **25** Shell.

Quiz 57 UK Leaders

Level 2

1 For how long did the UK's first woman Prime Minister hold this office?
2 How old was Tony Blair when he became PM?
3 Who did Paul Gascoigne describe as 'nice and cuddly'?
4 What position in government did John Major hold before he became PM?
5 Who won Leon Brittan's parliamentary seat when he became an EC Commissioner?
6 Which Tory Party Chairman and MP for Chingford's wife was paralysed in the Brighton bombing of 1984?
7 Who was Education Secretary, Home Secretary and Chancellor in the 90s?
8 Who was the first Labour Prime Minister?
9 In the 1990 Tory leadership who first stood against Margaret Thatcher?
10 As Prime Minister Andrew Bonar Law represented which party?
11 Former Labour leader Neil Kinnock was a European Commissioner in charge of which department?
12 Who was the last prime minister to be created an earl?
13 Which left wing MP and former council leader wrote *If Voting Changed Anything They'd Abolish It*?
14 Who was sacked as Deputy Leader of the Tory Party in William Hague's first major reshuffle?
15 Baroness Margaret Jay is the daughter of which ex-PM?
16 Who delivered the first Budget speech to be televised – in March 1990?
17 Who did George Carey replace as Archbishop of Canterbury?
18 Which MP shared a beefburger with his young daughter to try and prove British beef was safe to eat?
19 Whose resignation speech in 1990, with allusions to a game of cricket, precipitated the downfall of Margaret Thatcher?
20 Who was Britain's second youngest PM this century?
21 Who was Mrs Thatcher's press secretary during her last years as PM?
22 What was John Major's constituency when he was PM?
23 On leaving No 10 Margaret Thatcher became which Baroness?
24 Which middle name did Winston Churchill share with Charlie Chaplin?
25 Who is the century's longest serving MP for Old Bexley and Sidcup?

Answers

UK Leaders

1 11 years. **2** 43. **3** Margaret Thatcher. **4** Chancellor of the Exchequer. **5** William Hague. **6** Norman Tebbit. **7** Kenneth Clarke. **8** Ramsay MacDonald. **9** Michael Heseltine. **10** Conservative. **11** Transport. **12** Harold Macmillan. **13** Ken Livingstone. **14** Peter Lilley. **15** James Callaghan. **16** John Major. **17** Robert Runcie. **18** John Gummer. **19** Geoffrey Howe. **20** John Major. **21** Bernard Ingham. **22** Huntingdon. **23** Kesteven. **24** Spencer. **25** Edward Heath.

Quiz 58 CORONATION ST. Level 2

1992

1 Who was sacked from the Rovers for throwing a pint over Des?
2 Whose baby only lived for one day?
3 Who married Terry Duckworth?
4 Who married Alma?
5 And who married Rita?
6 Which hairdresser joined *Coronation Street* and was called 'the new Elsie Tanner' by the tabloids?
7 Who fell for student Paula Maxwell?
8 What job did Jim McDonald take after closing the bike shop?
9 Who said 'Mike Baldwin is like a vampire, draining the life out of people'?
10 Which couple revived their engagement after being matched by a computer dating agency?
11 Who had a nervous breakdown and went missing in her slippers?
12 Who got drunk with ex-POW Klaus Muller?
13 Who bought a mouse-eating spider to attract customers, but came unstuck when it escaped?
14 Who got a place at Sheffield University?
15 Who upset his fiancée by buying a telescope?
16 Who lent Mike £10,000?
17 Who did Caroline Milmoe play?
18 Who dated football player Wayne Farrell?
19 Who was Denise Osbourne's estranged husband?
20 Who did he begin a relationship with?
21 Who moved in with the Platts as a babysitter?
22 Who tried to kill himself but only succeeded in losing a foot?
23 Who was victimised at work by Harold Potts?
24 Who was put on a diet by his wife after eating a whole Christmas Pudding?
25 Who took a second job as a pallbearer?

Answers

Coronation Street – 1992

1 Angie Freeman. **2** The McDonalds **3** Lisa Horten. **4** Mike Baldwin. **5** Ted Sullivan. **6** Denise Osbourne. **7** Andy McDonald. **8** Security Guard. **9** Ken. **10** Curly and Kimberley. **11** Emily. **12** Percy. **13** Alec Gilroy. **14** Andy McDonald. **15** Curly. **16** Emily. **17** Lisa Horten. **18** Raquel. **19** Neil Mitchell. **20** Angie. **21** Carmel Finnan. **22** Don. **23** Derek. **24** Alf. **25** Jack.

Quiz 59 20th C Headline Makers

Level 2

1 Fleur Lombard was the first woman to die on duty in which profession?
2 Who took out an injunction against Martin Steenning after he tried to take photographs of her?
3 How many babies did Mandy Allwood expect when she sold her story?
4 What was the occupation of Philip Lawrence, who was killed outside his place of work in December 1995?
5 What was the name of the NATO spokesman in the 1999 Kosovo crisis?
6 Which former Tory MP hosts a late night Radio 5 Live phone-in show?
7 Which British player moved to Chelsea in July 1999 for a cool £10 million?
8 Nicoletta Mantovani hit the headlines through her relationship with which big figure in the entertainment world?
9 Released on June 22nd 1999, Patrick Magee was known as which Bomber?
10 Timothy McVeigh was convicted for which bombing?
11 Who was dubbed Red Ken?
12 Which First Lady had to give evidence over the Whitewater scandal?
13 Which outgoing MP in the 1997 General Election had the initials MDX?
14 What movement for the terminally ill was begun by Cicely Saunders?
15 Which woman space traveller published *The Space Place* in 1997?
16 Marc Dutroux hit the headlines over a 'house of horrors' in which country?
17 Who penned a ballad from Belmarsh Gaol?
18 What was the surname of the couple who disappeared with their foster daughters after they feared they would be taken away from them?
19 What was Clive Sinclair's personal transport vehicle called?
20 Which party leader once made a pop video with Tracey Ullman?
21 Who defended her nursery children from a machete attack in 1995?
22 Which sports commentator said, 'Do my eyes deceive me or is Senna's Lotus sounding a bit rough!'?
23 About which British politician did Francois Mitterand say, 'She has the mouth of Marilyn Monroe and the eyes of Caligula'?
24 Who was convicted of murdering her fiance Lee Harvey after she alleged he had been killed in a road rage attack?
25 Who was the last British Wimbledon singles champion of the 20th century?

Answers

20th C Headline Makers

1 Fire fighter. **2** Princess Diana. **3** Eight. **4** Head teacher. **5** Jamie Shea. **6** Edwina Currie. **7** Chris Sutton. **8** Luciano Pavarotti. **9** Brighton Bomber. **10** Oklahoma. **11** Ken Livingstone. **12** Hillary Clinton. **13** Michael Portillo. **14** Hospice Movement. **15** Helen Sharman. **16** Belgium. **17** Jonathan Aitken. **18** Bramley. **19** C5. **20** Neil Kinnock. **21** Lisa Potts. **22** Murray Walker. **23** Margaret Thatcher. **24** Tracie Andrews. **25** Virginia Wade.

Quiz 60 Pot Luck

Level 2

1 What was the frequency of Radio Luxembourg?
2 What is the set of fans at the front of a jet engine called?
3 On TV who presented *Saturday Night Armistice*?
4 In cricket, what did Sussex add to their name in the 90s?
5 Who had a national airline called Garuda?
6 Which British PM imposed a 10.30pm TV curfew in 1973?
7 Which musical featured the song Rhythm Of Life?
8 Who was the first tennis player to be BBC Sports Personality in the 1990s?
9 In which month of the year is Battle of Britain week?
10 How is Declan McManus better known?
11 What is the largest genus of flower?
12 Who was the first US golfer to win the US amateur title in three consecutive years?
13 Which British entertainer used the catchphrase, 'She knows, you know'?
14 Who made No 1 with Boombastic?
15 In American Football where do the Chiefs come from?
16 Where in Devon is the railway station St. David's?
17 What was advertised by persuading you that your fingers should do the walking?
18 Entebbe international airport is in which country?
19 What is David Frost's middle name?
20 What does the letter C stand for in the media organisation CNN?
21 Who said, "I married beneath me. All women do"?
22 What relation is TV cook Sophie Grigson to late cookery expert Jane?
23 Which American novelist wrote *For Whom the Bell Tolls*?
24 Andy Linnighan scored a last minute FA Cup winner for which team?
25 Sheryl Crow sang the title song for which Bond film?

Answers

Pot Luck

1 208. **2** Compressor. **3** Armando Iannucci. **4** Sharks. **5** Indonesia. **6** Heath. **7** Sweet Charity. **8** Greg Rusedski. **9** September. **10** Elvis Costello. **11** Orchid. **12** Tiger Woods. **13** Hylda Baker. **14** Shaggy. **15** Kansas City. **16** Exeter. **17** Yellow pages. **18** Uganda. **19** Paradine. **20** Cable. **21** Nancy Astor. **22** Daughter. **23** Ernest Hemingway. **24** Arsenal. **25** Tomorrow Never Dies.

Quiz 61 20th C TV Sitcoms

Level 2

1 Who was Patsy's boss in *Absolutely Fabulous*, as played by Kathy Burke?
2 Which member of the cast of *Friends* has a son called Julian in real life?
3 Which star of the sitcom *Babes in the Wood* represented the UK in the Eurovision Song Contest in 1991?
4 Which premature pensioner played Denise in *The Royle Family*?
5 Which actor from *Only Fools and Horses* is the father of Emily Lloyd?
6 What was the surname of the couple who lived next door to the Goods in *The Good Life*?
7 Which *They Think It's All Over* regular starred in *Holding the Baby*?
8 Which sitcom was based in the restaurant Le Chateau Anglais?
9 Where was *It Ain't Half Hot Mum* set?
10 What was the occupation of Gladys Emmanuel in *Open All Hours*?
11 In the first series of *Yes Minister* what was Jim Hacker's department?
12 Which elderly relative did the Trotters live with in the first series of *Only Fools and Horses*?
13 What was Blackadder called in *Blackadder's Christmas Carol*?
14 What was Tracey's son called in *Birds of a Feather*?
15 Who was the brother of Hyacinth Bucket's neighbour Elizabeth?
16 Which two sitcom stars advertised Surf soap powder?
17 In which sitcom did Margaret Thatcher read a scene with its stars at an awards ceremony in 1984?
18 Which series revolved around Diana and Tom in a retirement home?
19 Which ex Bond girl played the mother-in-law in *The Upper Hand*?
20 Which sitcom centred on Bill and Ben and their family?
21 What was Alf Garnett's film star nickname for his son-in-law?
22 Which series with Rowan Atkinson and James Dreyfus was set in the fictitious town of Gasforth?
23 Miss Jones was the only female lodger in which sitcom with Leonard Rossiter?
24 Who was the shop owner in *Open All Hours*?
25 Grantleigh, in the village Cricket St Thomas, was the setting for which series?

Answers

20th C TV Sitcoms

1 Magda. **2** Lisa Kudrow. **3** Samantha Janus. **4** Caroline Aherne. **5** Roger Lloyd Pack. **6** Leadbetter. **7** Nick Hancock. **8** *Chef!*. **9** India. **10** Nurse. **11** Administrative Affairs. **12** Grandad. **13** Ebenezer Blackadder. **14** Garth. **15** Emmet. **16** Pauline Quirke & Linda Robson. **17** *Yes Minister*. **18** *Waiting For God*. **19** Honor Blackman. **20** *2 Point 4 Children*. **21** Shirley Temple. **22** *The Thin Blue Line*. **23** *Rising Damp*. **24** Arkwright. **25** *To The Manor Born*.

Quiz 62 CORONATION ST. Level 2

1993

1. Which young hairdressers' assistant made her debut this year?
2. Who declared his unrequited love for Angie Freeman?
3. Who began a relationship with Hanif Ruparell?
4. Who left home to move in with her first boyfriend, delivery boy Craig Lee?
5. Who dated Doug Murray?
6. Who pushed Carmel Finnan downstairs?
7. Who became obsessed with Denise Osbourne, plaguing her with phone calls?
8. Where was Tracy Barlow's first job?
9. Who left Coronation Street for Mexico?
10. Which two men came to blows over Lisa Duckworth's death bed?
11. Who asked Rita for a £30,000 loan and was turned down?
12. Who paid for the car insurance on Steve McDonald's Ford Escort?
13. Name Reg Holdsworth's old flame who began working at Bettabuy.
14. Who bought the Corner Shop from Alf?
15. And how did he die after only a few months in the business?
16. Name the single mum that Andy McDonald fell in love with.
17. Why did they split up?
18. Who dated Gordon Blinkhorn?
19. Who played Maud Grimes?
20. Who was Curly's ambitious deputy manager at Bettabuy?
21. Who fell for Sally and begged her to leave Kevin?
22. Who stole Mike Baldwin's Jag?
23. Who had a 'magic tree' in his garden?
24. Who played Fiona Middleton?
25. Who played Charlie Whelan?

Answers

Coronation Street – 1993

1 Fiona Middleton. **2** Curly. **3** Denise Osbourne. **4** Tracy Barlow. **5** Deirdre. **6** Gail. **7** Don. **8** Maggie Redman's flower shop. **9** Angie. **10** Terry and Des. **11** Jenny Bradley. **12** Vicky Arden. **13** Maureen Naylor. **14** Brendan Scott. **15**. Heart Attack on the shop floor. **16** Amy Nelson. **17**. She was reunited with her son's father in Trinidad. **18**. Raquel. **19**. Elizabeth Bradley. **20**.Elaine Fenwick. **21**. Joe Broughton. **22**. Doug Murray. **23**. Derek. **24**. Angela Griffin. **25**. John St Ryan.

Quiz 63 Motor Sports

Level 2

1 In which 98 Grand Prix did David Coulthard move aside to let Mika Hakkinen win?
2 In which decade did Frank Williams launch his own racing team?
3 Which British driver got himself in the money stakes with deals with Sauber and Sony Playstation?
4 On which race track was Jim Clark killed?
5 Heinz-Harlad Frentzen moved to Jordan from which team?
6 Which motor race was first held on the old Sarthe circuit?
7 Who was the first Brit to claim the World Rally title?
8 In which US state is the Daytona Beach circuit?
9 Which Grand Prix provided Damon Hill's only victory in 1998?
10 In which decade was the Le Mans 24 hour race first held?
11 Which team did Nigel Mansell drive with when he was Formula 1 champ?
12 Who was the last Finn before Mika Hakkinen to be Formula 1 champion?
13 Which team did Johnny Herbert move to for the 1999 Grand Prix season?
14 Mika Hakkinen ended up with how many points in becoming 1998 world champion?
15 Which Grand Prix has been held at Mosport and Mont Tremblant?
16 In 1998 the Algerian government claimed which top driver was in fact an Algerian?
17 James Hunt was born in and died in which city?
18 Who was the first person to clock up over 250 Grand Prix starts?
19 Rod Dennis has been managing director of which team?
20 Who was the first Brit to be Formula 1 champion?
21 In the 90s how many points have been awarded for finishing third in a Grand Prix?
22 What was the last Grand Prix outside Britain in which Damon Hill raced?
23 Which team did Jim Clark drive for at Formula 1?
24 In which year was Nigel Mansell Indy Car champion?
25 When Michael Schumacher was first Formula 1 champ he was with which team?

Answers

Motor Sports

1 Australian. **2** 70s. **3** Johnny Herbert. **4** Hockenheim. **5** Williams. **6** Le Mans 24 Hours. **7** Colin McRae. **8** Florida. **9** Belgian. **10** 20s. **11** Williams. **12** Keke Rosberg. **13** Stewart. **14** 100. **15** Canadian. **16** Michael Schumacher. **17** London. **18** Riccardo Patrese. **19** McLaren. **20** Mike Hawthorn. **21** 4. **22** Hungarian. **23** Lotus. **24** 1993. **25** Benetton.

Quiz 64 Pot Luck

Level 2

1 Which politician was involved in charges made by male model Norman Scott ?
2 English writer P G Wodehouse took out citizenship in which country?
3 What type of disaster took place in Skopje in 1963?
4 John George Diefenbaker was once PM of where?
5 Under what name did Thomas Hicks become a famous entertainer?
6 What is 50 mph in kilometres per hour?
7 Which musical featured the song My Favourite Things?
8 In WWI according to the Germans, who were the Ladies from Hell?
9 Which drink was advertised with the song I'd Like To Teach The World To Sing?
10 James Braddock was a world champion in which sport?
11 How did Virginia Woolf's life end?
12 What was the surname of underwater film makers Hans and Lotte?
13 What was the title of Dick Francis's first novel set in the horse racing world?
14 In which sport could the Heat take on the Magic?
15 In advertising what type of service was promoted using a giant letter X?
16 Who made No 1 with Killer?
17 Who said, 'Talking jaw to jaw is better than going to war'?
18 In which decade did Luxembourg join the European Union?
19 Ian Wright has scored FA Cup Final goals for Arsenal and who else?
20 Who won a Booker Prize for *Paddy Clarke Ha Ha Ha*?
21 Klagenfurt international airport is in which country?
22 What did the letter A stand for in GATT?
23 Which Red Indian tribe featured in *Dances With Wolves*?
24 Which golf course includes the Rabbit and the Seal?
25 Father's Day was first celebrated in which country?

Answers

Pot Luck

1 Jeremy Thorpe. **2** US. **3** Earthquake. **4** Canada. **5** Tommy Steele. **6** 80. **7** The Sound Of Music. **8** Highland soldiers in kilts. **9** Coca Cola. **10** Boxing. **11** Drowned herself. **12** Hass. **13** Dead Cert. **14** Basketball. **15** Building Society – The Halifax. **16** Adamski. **17** Winston Churchill. **18** 50s. **19** Crystal Palace. **20** Roddy Doyle. **21** Austria. **22** Agreement. **23** Sioux. **24** Troon. **25** USA.

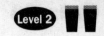

Quiz 65 Movie Moguls

Level 2

1 Which blonde actress made her debut as a producer in *Private Benjamin*?
2 On which Isle was Anthony Minghella born?
3 Who directed the first three *Godfather* films?
4 Which *Indecent Proposal* star made a directorial debut in *Ordinary People*?
5 Who directed *Celebrity*, the 1998 movie whose stars included Leonardo DiCaprio?
6 Which director sacked Harvey Keitel from the cast of *Apocalypse Now*?
7 *That Thing You Do* was the directorial debut of which double Oscar winner?
8 Who directed Oscar-nominated John Travolta in *Pulp Fiction*?
9 Out of 11 films, how many did Grace Kelly make for Hitchcock?
10 *Sliding Doors* director Peter Howitt starred in which Liverpool sitcom?
11 Which celebrity couple co-founded the production company Simian Films?
12 Who directed *Tea With Mussolini*?
13 Which actor, whose name was linked with Catherine Zeta Jones in 1999, co-produced *One Flew Over the Cuckoo's Nest*?
14 Based on a novel by Nicholas Evans, what was Robert Redford's first film as director and star?
15 Who directed the original *Rear Window*, remade in the 90s with Christopher Reeve?
16 Which woman starred in and directed *The Prince of Tides*?
17 Which 'man with no name' directed *The Bridges of Madison County*?
18 What was Quentin Tarantino's follow up to *Reservoir Dogs*?
19 Which actor/director founded The Sundance Film Festival?
20 Which director adapted Stephen King's *The Shining* for the big screen?
21 Which hugely successful director co-wrote and produced *Poltergeist*?
22 Taylor Hackford is the husband of which 50-plus British actress?
23 Who directed Ben Kingsley in his first Oscar-winning role as a civil rights hero?
24 Which novel by E M Forster did David Lean make into a film in 1984 with Peggy Ashcroft and Judy Davis?
25 Which director of *Titanic* gave Arnold Schwarzenegger his big break in *The Terminator*?

Answers

Movie Moguls
1 Goldie Hawn. **2** Isle of Wight. **3** Francis Ford Coppola. **4** Robert Redford. **5** Woody Allen. **6** Francis Ford Coppola. **7** Tom Hanks. **8** Quentin Tarantino. **9** Three. **10** Bread. **11** Hugh Grant & Liz Hurley. **12** Franco Zeffirelli. **13** Michael Douglas. **14** The Horse Whisperer. **15** Alfred Hitchcock. **16** Barbra Streisand. **17** Clint Eastwood. **18** Pulp Fiction. **19** Robert Redford. **20** Stanley Kubrick. **21** Steve Spielberg. **22** Helen Mirren. **23** Richard Attenborough – for Gandhi. **24** A Passage to India. **25** James Cameron.

Quiz 66 CORONATION ST. Level 2

1994

1 Which baby was born this year?
2 Which portly purveyor of meat products made his *Coronation Street* debut?
3 Which famous *Coronation Street* actress died, aged 95?
4 Why did Alf stop using the mayoral Limo?
5 Who bought the Corner Shop in this year?
6 Which couple got married?
7 Who proposed to Maud Grimes but later broke off the engagement?
8 Who gave the Websters £5000?
9 Who did Mike Baldwin take advantage of in a business deal to do with t-shirt printing?
10 Who discovered her real father was an American serviceman?
11 What did the Websters originally call Sophie before Rosie persuaded them to change her name?
12 Who became a driver at Mike Baldwin's executive taxi firm?
13 Who did Nick Tilsley move in with after a series of rows at home?
14 Who was the 'birdman of Weatherfield'?
15 Who got left behind on his own coach trip to see *Miss Saigon*?
16 Who played Alex Christie?
17 Whose boyfriend entered her in a Dolly Parton look-alike contest?
18 Who introduced Derek to pyramid selling with Envirosphere?
19 Who collapsed and was rushed to hospital for an emergency appendectomy?
20 Where did Jon Welch work?
21 Who had her portrait painted by artist and librarian Roger Crompton?
22 Where did Deirdre meet Samir Rachid?
23 Who played Jack's brother Clifford?
24 Who bought a star for Raquel?
25 Who became engaged to Emily?

Answers

Coronation Street – 1994

1 Sophie Webster. **2** Fred Elliot. **3** Doris Speed. **4** Audrey fancied the chauffeur. **5** Reg Holdsworth. **6** Reg and Maureen. **7** Percy Sugden. **8** Rita. **9** Steve McDonald. **10** Maureen. **11** Lauren. **12** Jim McDonald. **13** Don. **14** Jack. **15** Derek. **16** Gavin Richards. **17** Bet's boyfriend Charlie Whelan. **18** Norris Cole. **19** Sarah Louise Platt. **20** The hairdressers. **21** Mavis. **22** Morocco. **23** Dave King. **24** Curly. **25** Rev. Bernard Morten

Quiz 67 Books

Level 2

1 How did the barrister Rumpole refer to his wife Hilda?
2 Which county did Catherine Cookson come from and write about?
3 Who won a Booker Prize for *Midnight's Children*?
4 In which decade of the century did H G Wells die?
5 Under which name did American author Samuel Langhorne Clemens write?
6 At the very end of the 19th C who wrote the novel that produced the most filmed horror character of the 20th C?
7 Whose sports-based novels of the 90s include *Comeback* and *To The Hilt*?
8 Aunt Agatha and Bingo Little feature in the escapades of which man about town?
9 Which writer of horrific happenings was himself involved in a road accident while out walking in 1999?
10 In which decade was *The Lord Of The Rings* first published?
11 Who is Frank Richards' most famous creation?
12 Who penned the airport lounge best seller titled *Airport*?
13 Which writer was influenced by his upbringing in Slad, Gloucestershire?
14 In 1917 which Joseph endowed an annual literary prize in America?
15 David John Cornwell wrote spy stories under which name?
16 What type of jungle animal was Shere Khan?
17 Georges Simenon created which character known by one name?
18 In bookselling what does the N stand for in NBA?
19 Which American novelist with an English place surname wrote *White Fang*?
20 Who wrote the children's classic *Swallows And Amazons*?
21 What was the first name of New Zealand novelist Ms Marsh?
22 Which fictional detective refers to using the little grey cells?
23 What was the particular link between Jean Plaidy, Phillipa Carr, Victoria Holt?
24 Which of the Mitfords wrote *Love In A Cold Climate*?
25 In the books as opposed to the TV series, where did Morse's sidekick Lewis come from?

Answers

Books

1 She who must be obeyed. **2** Durham. **3** Salman Rushdie. **4** 40s. **5** Mark Twain. **6** Bram Stoker. **7** Dick Francis. **8** Bertie Wooster. **9** Stephen King. **10** 50s. **11** Billy Bunter. **12** Arthur Hailey. **13** Laurie Lee. **14** Pulitzer. **15** John Le Carre. **16** Tiger. **17** Maigret. **18** Net. **19** Jack London. **20** Arthur Ransome. **21** Ngaio. **22** Hercule Poirot. **23** They are the same person. **24** Nancy. **25** Wales.

Quiz 68 Pot Luck

Level 2

1 Who was the first MP elected for the SDP?
2 Which song says, 'The words of the prophet are written On the subway halls'?
3 In which country did General Jaruzelski impose martial law in 1981?
4 On which channel did Nigel Slater cook up *Real Food*?
5 Which chair was kidnapped by students from the Cranfield Institute of Technology in 1978?
6 Devon Malcolm took nine wickets in a Test innings against which country?
7 Which musical featured the song The Street Where You Live?
8 Henley was the 80s and 90s seat of which prominent politician?
9 In cricket, which English team became Hawks in the 90s?
10 How is John Virgo known on *Big Break*?
11 Who sang the title song for the Bond film *A View To A Kill*?
12 The Cod War of the 70s was between Britain and which country?
13 Which Desmond wrote the 80s book studying fans' behaviour called *The Soccer Tribe*?
14 What's Alvin Stardust's real name?
15 At which sport did Karen Brown win international success?
16 Which family were the subject of *Two Point Four Children*?
17 Which Disney film had the theme tune A Whole New World?
18 Hellenikon international airport is in which country?
19 In TV ads, who has sung the praises of Kenco Coffee and Renault cars?
20 Who was the target of the failed 'Bomb Plot' of 1944?
21 Who made No 1 with Young At Heart?
22 In basketball where do the Celtics come from?
23 In honours what does the G stand for in GC?
24 Who wrote the novel *The Go Between*?
25 In which Gloucester street was the Wests' House of Horrors?

Answers

Pot Luck

1 Shirley Williams. **2** Sound of Silence. **3** Poland. **4** Channel 4. **5** Mastermind chair. **6** South Africa. **7** My Fair Lady. **8** Michael Heseltine. **9** Hampshire. **10** Mr Trick Shot. **11** Duran Duran. **12** Iceland. **13** Morris. **14** Bernard Jewry. **15** Hockey. **16** The Porters. **17** Aladdin. **18** Greece. **19** Lesley Garrett. **20** Hitler. **21** Bluebells. **22** Boston. **23** George. **24** L P Hartley. **25** Cromwell Street.

Quiz 69 Solo Singers

Level 2

1 In which decade was singer Bruce Springsteen born?
2 Who had a hit with You're All That Matters to Me in 1992?
3 Stevie Wonder was given the keys to which city in recognition of his talents in 1984?
4 Which costume was worn by David Bowie on his Ashes to Ashes video?
5 Who, in 1994, did a cover of Jennifer Rush's The Power of Love?
6 George Michael was brought up in which city?
7 Who had a hit with Mysterious Girl in 1996?
8 Whose first album was titled Soul Provider?
9 Who was Dancing on the Ceiling in 1986?
10 Which senior star released an album in 1996 called Strong Love Affair?
11 Which American city links songs by Bruce Springsteen and Elton John?
12 What type of creature is Michael Jackson's pet Muscles?
13 Which record label did David Bowie sign to in 1995?
14 How old was Elvis Presley when he died?
15 What was the first UK top ten hit from March 1997 for Sash!?
16 What is in brackets in the title of Cher's The Shoop Shoop Song?
17 Spice Girl Mel C joined which artist on the hit When You're Gone?
18 Which hit got to No 2 for former *Neighbours* star Natalie Imbruglia in 1997?
19 Who is the oldest female solo singer to top the UK charts?
20 Who was Old Before I Die in 1997?
21 Who made it big in 1996 with Flava?
22 In which decade was superstar Michael Bolton born?
23 What was Louise's first UK top ten hit?
24 Which American rapper was Loungin' in a UK No 7 from 1996?
25 What was Bjork's first UK top ten hit?

Answers

Solo Singers

1 1940s. **2** Curtis Stigers. **3** Detroit. **4** Pierrot. **5** Celine Dion. **6** London. **7** Peter Andre. **8** Michael Bolton. **9** Lionel Richie. **10** Ray Charles. **11** Philadelphia. **12** Snake. **13** Virgin. **14** 42. **15** Encore Une Fois. **16** It's In His Kiss. **17** Bryan Adams. **18** Torn. **19** Cher. **20** Robbie Williams. **21** Peter Andre. **22** 1950s. **23** Light Of My Life. **24** LL Cool J. **25** Army of Me.

Quiz 70 CORONATION ST. Level 2

1995

1 Which character died off-screen in a religious retreat?
2 Name the baby born in this year.
3 Who married her old wartime sweetheart, Billy Williams?
4 Which house did the Malletts buy?
5 Who bought a Mile Muncher?
6 Who went to Buckingham Palace?
7 Who inherited £240,000 on her 18th birthday?
8 Where did Raquel and Curly get married?
9 What was Denise Osbourne's sister called?
10 Who collapsed after taking esctasy?
11 Who had a relationship with Josie Clark?
12 Who were Mike Baldwin's tenants at Number 1?
13 What did they do when he tried to evict them?
14 Who was Rodney Bostock?
15 Who annoyed his wife by buying a drum kit?
16 Who owned Crimea Flats, home to Deirdre, Roy Cropper and Tricia Armstrong?
17 Which famous boat did Raquel and Curly take their honeymoon on?
18 Who did they bump into on their cruise?
19 Who had a vasectomy?
20 Who tried to rape Raquel in the storeroom of Firman's Freezers?
21 Who had a neon sign outside their home saying 'Santa's Nookie Nest'?
22 Why was Councillor Harry Potts sent to prison?
23 Who was blacklisted by local bookies after running up huge debts?
24 Who played Tricia Armstrong?
25 Who bought a wig to make himself look younger?

Answers

Coronation Street – 1995

1 Ivy. **2** Daniel Osbourne. **3** Betty. **4** Number 9. **5** Derek. **6** Alf Roberts and Betty Turpin. **7** Vicky Arden. **8** In the Register Office. **9** Alison Dunkley. **10** Tracy Barlow. **11** Don Brennan. **12** Jamie and Tricia Armstrong. **13** Barricaded themselves in and threw water over him. **14** Relief manager at the Rovers. **15** Gary Mallett. **16** Mike Baldwin. **17** The QEII. **18** Rita, Mavis and Alec. **19** Jim. 20 Leo Firman. **21** The Malletts. **22** For embezzling mayoral funds. **23** Steve McDonald. **24** Tracy Brabin. **25** Reg.

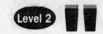

Quiz 71 Scandals & Disasters

Level 2

1 Which politician got entangled with Antonia de Sancha?
2 Which Open Tennis tournament was John McEnroe expelled from?
3 Robert Maxwell drowned near which islands?
4 Which disaster took place in Kobe, Japan, in 1995?
5 Charles Rolls of Rolls Royce fame was actually in what type of vehicle when he died?
6 In 1996 Stephen Cameron became the first fatality of which increasingly violent trend?
7 Whose downfall and disgrace revolved round a stay at the Paris Ritz in September 1993?
8 Bandleader Glenn Miller was last seen in an aircraft leaving which country?
9 In 1998 the Festina team was banned from what over drug allegations?
10 Where was the USA's worst nuclear accident, in 1979?
11 On which of the Canary Islands did a collision of two jumbo jets take place, making it one of the worst air disasters in history?
12 Who was the first US President to resign while in office?
13 Where in Wales was a school engulfed by a slag heap in 1966?
14 Which Olympic Games were the scene of a terrorist attack by Palestinian guerrillas?
15 Onto which road did a British Midlands aeroplane crash in 1990?
16 What was the first name of Dr Crippen's wife?
17 Ernest Saunders and Gerald Ronson were convicted for their roles in the scandal in which company?
18 Who were Liverpool's opposition when the Hillsborough disaster took place?
19 The *Herald of Free Enterprise* capsized outside which port?
20 How did 40s murderer John Haigh dispose of his victims' bodies?
21 Policewoman Yvonne Fletcher was shot outside which London embassy?
22 What was the nationality of the jet shot down in Russian air space in 1983?
23 Who or what was Sefton, injured in a bomb blast in Hyde Park in 1982?
24 Which year was known as the 'winter of discontent'?
25 Which Brighton hotel was bombed during a Tory Party conference in 1984?

Answers

Scandals & Disasters

1 David Mellor. **2** Australian. **3** Canary Islands. **4** Earthquake. **5** Aeroplane. **6** Road rage. **7** Jonathan Aitken. **8** England. **9** Tour de France. **10** Three Mile Island. **11** Tenerife. **12** Richard Nixon. **13** Aberfan. **14** Munich. **15** M1. **16** Cora. **17** Guinness. **18** Nottm Forest. **19** Zeebrugge. **20** Acid bath. **21** Libya. **22** Korean. **23** Horse. **24** 1979. **25** Grand.

Quiz 72 Pot Luck

Level 2

1 Who kept saying that it was time for bed in *The Magic Roundabout*?
2 The sinking of which ship prompted the Sun's 'Gotcha!' headline?
3 Who was Sean Penn married to for 27 months before divorce was filed?
4 From which show does Love Changes Everything come?
5 In *EastEnders*, what were Cindy & Ian Beale's twins called?
6 In baseball, where do the Royals come from?
7 What colour is Laa Laa?
8 For what did Georgia O'Keefe become famous?
9 St Albans has been the 90s seat of which prominent Tory politician?
10 In economics, what does the letter G stand for in GNP?
11 The Spanish soccer team Real Betis play at home in which city?
12 Which character brought the phrase, 'You silly old moo' to TV?
13 To the nearest million, what is the population of the USA?
14 Who made No 1 with Spaceman?
15 In which country was Michael J Fox born?
16 How much was the top prize on Cilla Black's *The Moment of Truth*?
17 Under what name did Leonard Slye ride across the silver screen?
18 On which movies soundtrack from the 90s did Brenda Lee feature?
19 Who did Harry Enfield play in the first series of *Men Behaving Badly*?
20 Which politician said, 'He got on his bike and looked for work...'?
21 A-Ha sang the title song for which Bond film?
22 In advertising, who or what was 'Your flexible friend'?
23 Which German soccer striker was known as The Bomber?
24 Which writer came up with *Catch 22* in the 60s?
25 Bourgas international airport is in which country?

Answers

Pot Luck

1 Zebedee. **2** General Belgrano. **3** Madonna. **4** Aspects of Love. **5** Peter & Lucy. **6** Kansas City. **7** Yellow. **8** Painting. **9** Peter Lilley. **10** Gross. **11** Seville. **12** Alf Garnett. **13** 265 million. **14** Babylon Zoo. **15** Canada. **16** £20,000. **17** Roy Rogers. **18** Dick Tracy. **19** Dermot. **20** Norman Tebbit. **21** The Living Daylights. **22** Access Card. **23** Gerd Muller. **25** Joseph Heller. **25** Bulgaria.

Quiz 73 20th C Rich & Famous

Level 2

1 Which golfer announced he was leaving his wife and three children for Brenna Cepalak in 1996?
2 Marina Mowatt is the daughter of which British Princess?
3 Fitness trainer Carlos Leon was the father of which singer/actress's child?
4 Whose portrait in 1996 was described by Brian Sewell as looking like 'a pensioner who is about to lose her bungalow.'?
5 In which North African country was Mohammed Al-Fayed born?
6 Longleat is the stately home of which Marquess?
7 What is Madonna's daughter called?
8 In addition to becoming Earl of Wessex, Prince Edward became Viscount of where on his marriage?
9 Lady Sarah Chatto is the daughter of which famous lady?
10 Caroline Conran, once wife of Sir Terence, is a writer in her own right on which subject?
11 In 1996 who did The Spice Girls say was their Girl Power role model?
12 What is Frankie Dettori's real first name?
13 How did Sir Ranulph Twisleton-Wykeham-Fiennes achieve fame?
14 Madeleine Gurdon is the third wife of which millionaire?
15 Who was the first Princess to appear on *The Archers*?
16 What is the first name of Charles' brother of Saatchi & Saatchi?
17 In which country was Earl Spencer's acrimonious divorce settlement heard?
18 Who did Stella McCartney dedicate her first collection for Chloe to?
19 In which North African country was Yves St Laurent born as Henri Donat Mathieu?
20 Which child of Princess Grace of Monaco competed in the 1988 Olympics?
21 Which former England captain was Viv Richards' best man?
22 Which member of the Royal Family suffered a mild stroke when in the Caribbean in 1998?
23 Which multimillion pound sport is Bernie Ecclestone associated with?
24 How many brothers and sisters does Tony Blair have?
25 Which member of the Royal Family converted to Catholicism in the 1990s?

Answers

20th C Rich and Famous

1 Nick Faldo. **2** Alexandra. **3** Madonna. **4** The Queen. **5** Egypt. **6** Bath. **7** Lourdes Maria. **8** Severn. **9** Princess Margaret. **10** Cookery. **11** Margaret Thatcher. **12** Lanfranco. **13** Explorer. **14** Andrew Lloyd Webber. **15** Margaret. **16** Maurice. **17** South Africa. **18** Her mother Linda. **19** Algeria. **20** Prince Albert. **21** Ian Botham. **22** Princess Margaret. **23** Motor racing. **24** None. **25** The Duchess of Kent.

Quiz 74 CORONATION ST. Level 2

Pot Luck

1 Who plays Ashley Peacock?
2 Who currently lives in the flat above the bookies?
3 Which underage girl did Vik Desai once date?
4 What animal do Ashley and Maxine have as a pet?
5 Which *Coronation Street* character developed an unfortunate allergy to beer?
6 When did Tracy Barlow get married?
7 When did Suzie Birchall leave Coronation Street?
8 When was Tricia Hopkins injured in a warehouse fire?
9 In what year did Ida Barlow die?
10 When did The Rovers catch fire?
11 What was the name of Stephen Reid's garment business in Canada?
12 Ivy Brennan left her house to Nick Platt on what condition?
13 Who played the younger Nick?
14 Where did Gail once have a bedsit in the 1970s?
15 What was the name of the married man that Gail had an affair with in 1970s?
16 Whose working practices did Ken recently criticise publicly, acting on information from Edna Miller?
17 Did Ken attend his daughter Susan's wedding to Mike Baldwin or not?
18 What was Deirdre's first job in Coronation Street?
19 Who did Ken buy his house from in 1995?
20 Who played Ken's girlfriend and mother of Daniel, Denise Osbourne?
21 What was the name of Elsie's first husband?
22 Whose was the first wedding in *Coronation Street*?
23 What was Esther Hayes' troublesome brother called?
24 What was the name of Ida's mother, Ken Barlow's grandmother?
25 What sort of business did Leonard Swindley run?

Answers

***Coronation Street* – Pot Luck**

1 Steven Arnold. **2** Kevin Webster. **3** Candice Stowe. **4** Cat. **5** Stan Ogden. **6** 1996. **7** 1983. **8** 1975. **9** 1961. **10** 1986. **11** K-Bec. **12** That he changed his name to Tilsley. **13** Warren Jackson. **14** Above the Corner Shop. **15** Roy Thornley. **16** Mike Baldwin's. **17** Yes, he gave her away at the last minute. **18** Secretary at Len's yard. **19** Mike Baldwin. **20** Denise Black. **21** Arnold Tanner. **22** Joan Walker and Gordon Davies'. **23** Tom. **24** Nancy Leathers. **25** Haberdashery.

Quiz 75 20th C TV Drama

Level 2

1 Which TV and Movie actor played Dr Phillip Chandler in *St Elsewhere*?
2 In which series did Paul Nicholls play *Terry Sydenham*?
3 How did Assumpta perish in *Ballykissangel*?
4 Who did Charlie marry in *Casualty*?
5 In *Heartbeat* who was Nick's second wife?
6 In which capital city did the action of *The Ambassador* take place?
7 Which TV detective was obsessed with his little grey cells?
8 What is Sam's profession in *Silent Witness*?
9 Who co-starred with Robson Green in *Grafters*?
10 Which actor replaced Nigel Le Vaillant in *Dangerfield*?
11 How many *Talking Heads* were there in the first series in 1988?
12 What was the name of the doctor played by Simon Shepherd in *Peak Practice*?
13 Which writer links *Soldier, Soldier*, *Peak Practice* and *Bramwell*?
14 Who played opposite Francesca Annis in *Reckless*?
15 Which drama series takes place in Skelthwaite in Yorkshire?
16 In which serial did Colin Firth shoot to fame opposite Jennifer Ehle?
17 For which drama did John Thaw win the Best Actor BAFTA in 1999?
18 In *Juliet Bravo*, what was Juliet Bravo?
19 *Why Didn't They Ask Evans* was the first in a murder mystery series by which famous author?
20 Charlie Hungerford was which detective's ex-father in law?
21 Which famous detective did Jeremy Brett play for many years on TV?
22 Lucy Gannon's drama series *Hope and Glory* was set where?
23 Which 80s drama mini series was based on Paul Scott's *Raj Quartet*?
24 In which south coast county was *Howard's Way* set?
25 In which series did Saskia Wickham play Dr Erica Matthews?

Answers

20th C TV Drama
1 Denzel Washington. **2** City Central. **3** Electrocuted. **4** Baz. **5** Jo. **6** Dublin. **7** Poirot. **8** Pathologist. **9** Stephen Tompkinson. **10** Nigel Havers. **11** Six. **12** Will Preston. **13** Lucy Gannon. **14** Robson Green. **15** Where the Heart Is. **16** Pride & Prejudice. **17** Goodnight Mister Tom. **18** Radio call sign. **19** Agatha Christie. **20** Bergerac's. **21** Sherlock Holmes. **22** School. **23** The Jewel in the Crown. **24** Hampshire. **25** Peak Practice.

Quiz 76 Pot Luck

Level 2

1 Dying in 1972, under what name was Emmanuel Goldberg better known?
2 Dav Whatmore left Lancashire to coach which cricket team?
3 Who played the Rev Tony Blair in *Sermon From St Albions*?
4 What has been the commonest name for Popes through the millennium?
5 Which great entertainer made his film debut in *Pennies From Heaven*?
6 Who was David Beckham's best man at his wedding to Posh?
7 Which musical featured the song Ol' Man River?
8 Who wrote *The Camomile Lawn*, seen on TV starring Felicity Kendal and Tara Fitzgerald?
9 Blackburn has been the 90s seat of which prominent politician?
10 Who sang the theme to *One Foot in the Grave*?
11 Peter Gilchrist has been a world champion in which sport?
12 Who made No 1 with Return Of The Mack?
13 What was the name of Tom Mix's horse?
14 In which country is the deepwater port of Townsville?
15 Who wrote *My Family And Other Animals*?
16 Whose one line was 'Nice hat' in *Friends*?
17 In which country was Keanu Reeves born?
18 In which decade did Sweden join the European Union?
19 In which sport could the Knicks take on the Nets?
20 Which politician stated, 'Read my lips: no new taxes'?
21 Which famous Michael has promoted Kwik Save in TV ads?
22 The Irish dramatist Samuel Beckett settled in which city?
23 Long Beach airport was built in which US state?
24 Who followed Matt Busby as Man Utd manager?
25 In which decade did Alcatraz close?

Answers

Pot Luck

1 Edward G Robinson. **2** Sri Lanka. **3** Harry Enfield. **4** John. **5** Louis Armstrong. **6** Gary Neville. **7** Showboat. **8** Mary Wesley. **9** Jack Straw. **10** Eric Idle. **11** Billiards. **12** Mark Morrison. **13** Tony. **14** Australia. **15** Gerald Durrell. **16** Sarah, Duchess of York. **17** Lebanon. **18** 90s. **19** Basketball. **20** George Bush. **21** Barrymore. **22** Paris. **23** California. **24** Wilf McGuinness. **25** 60s.

Quiz 77 Sporting Chance

Level 2

1 Which city has a team of Bulls and a team of Bears?
2 Which Man Utd player was replaced by Solskjaer in the 1999 European Champions' Cup Final?
3 What is the nickname of record-breaking sprinter Maurice Greene?
4 Who was the first boxer to twice regain the world heavyweight title?
5 For which county did Edmonds and Emburey form a lethal spin attack?
6 What was Sue Barker's best placing in the Wimbledon singles?
7 Which sport do Essex Metropolitan play?
8 Ballustrol, Medinah and Oakmont are all types of what?
9 In basketball, where do the Rockets come from?
10 Who was the first Scot to captain England at cricket?
11 Which country does tennis player Marcelo Rios come from?
12 What was the sport of Stirling Moss's sister Pat?
13 Which country does marathon man Abel Anton come from?
14 How was Walker Smith Robinson better known?
15 Who captained India in cricket's 1999 World Cup?
16 The Melbourne Cup is run at which ground?
17 Peter Nichol became the first Brit in 25 years to win the British Open in which sport?
18 Who told a Wimbledon umpire, 'You are the pits of the world'?
19 Which Robin was the first yachtsman to sail non-stop around the world?
20 Which player has played the most league games for Man Utd?
21 Allan Lamb first played in England for which county?
22 Who fought George Foreman in the Rumble In The Jungle?
23 Who had Derby victories riding Troy, Henbit, Nashwan and Erhaab?
24 With which athletics event was Geoff Capes particularly associated?
25 Teddy Sheringham was with which club when he was the top league scorer in England?

Answers

Sporting Chance

1 Chicago. **2** Cole. **3** Kansas Cannonball. **4** Muhammad Ali. **5** Middlesex. **6** Semi finals. **7** Netball. **8** American golf course. **9** Houston. **10** Mike Denness. **11** Chile. **12** Rallying. **13** Spain. **14** Sugar Ray Robinson. **15** Azharuddin. **16** Flemington Park. **17** Squash. **18** John McEnroe. **19** Knox-Johnson. **20** Bobby Charlton. **21** Northants. **22** Muhammad Ali. **23** Willie Carson. **24** Shot. **25** Spurs.

Quiz 78 CORONATION ST. Level 2

Pot Luck

1 Who was photographed sitting on top of a bin during the Rovers Return's dispute with the refuse collectors?
2 Whose father visited him, and conned Fred Gee out of £70?
3 Name Eddie's binman-mate who lodged with the Ogdens in this year.
4 Who fell for the charms of barmaid Arlene Jones this year?
5 Who was barred from the factory girls' pools syndicate?
6 What job did Elsie take after leaving Jim's cafe?
7 Which actor, currently playing a leading character in *Coronation Street*, made his debut as troublesome paperboy Neil Grimshaw in 1981?
8 Why was Nicky Platt's name changed at the last minute from Daniel David?
9 What was Mike's clothing factory called?
10 Who temporarily moved in with Bert and Ivy after her husband discovered she'd been having an affair?
11 Who painted their house with 'Jamaican Sun' brown paint?
12 Who was viciously mugged?
13 Who did Ron Sykes offer a business partnership to?
14 Who went on a date with lorry driver Les Charlton?
15 Which singer who had one hit in the late 70s played Les Charlton?
16 Which famous *Coronation Street* actress died in 1980, aged 85?
17 Which well-loved *Coronation Street* actor got an MBE in the 1983 New Year's Honours list?
18 Who baked a 'mystery cake' full of sage for the Autumn Fair?
19 Which unusual venue broke with tradition by announcing Ken and Deirdre's reconciliation on its electronic scoreboard at half time?
20 What was the name of the club Mike Baldwin, Alf Roberts and Len Fairclough opened?
21 In 1984, who gave a home and bed to convict Vinny Morris and then found out he was an impostor?
22 Who crashed into Jack's taxi in 1984?
23 Which two ladies were involved with policeman Tony Cunliffe?
24 Who played Bill Webster?
25 Who passed himself off as Mike Baldwin in a money-making scam?

Answers

***Coronation Street* – Pot Luck**

1 Bet Lynch. **2** Mike's father, Frankie Baldwin. **3** Johnny Webb. **4** Fred Gee. **5** Hilda Ogden. **6** Machinist at the factory. **7** Michael Le Vell. **8** His initials would have been DDT. **9** Baldwin's Casuals. **10** Vera Duckworth. **11** The Ogdens and Eddie Yeats. **12** Betty Turpin. **13** Brian Tilsley. **14** Gail Tilsley. **15** Graham Fellowes/Jilted John. **16** Violet Carson. **17** Jack Howarth. **18** Mavis Riley. **19** Old Trafford Football Club. **20** The Graffiti Club. **21** Bet Lynch. **22** Mavis. **23** Bet and Rita. **24** Peter Armitage. **25** Fred Gee.

Quiz 79 20th C Movies Comedies Level 2

1 What was dubbed 'an equal, not a sequel' to *Four Weddings and a Funeral*?
2 What was the first name of Truman in *The Truman Show*?
3 Which 1997 film was the then most successful British movie of all time?
4 Mike Nichols' *The Birdcage* was a remake of which musical?
5 Who played the Nutty Professor in the 1996 remake of Jerry Lewis's film?
6 Which wife of Laurence Olivier appeared in *101 Dalmatians*?
7 What type of shop does Wendowlene own in *A Close Shave*?
8 Who or what is Priscilla in *The Adventures of Priscilla, Queen of the Desert*?
9 In the original *Pink Panther* movie what is the Pink Panther?
10 Which Monty Python film contains 'Always Look on the Bright Side of Life'?
11 Who was Elwood's brother in *The Blues Brothers*?
12 Which country singer starred in *9 to 5*?
13 Where does Goldie Hawn's husband die in *Private Benjamin*?
14 Which member of the Arquette family starred in *Desperately Seeking Susan* with Madonna?
15 What is Crocodile Dundee's real first name?
16 Who was the male star of *The Witches of Eastwick* who famously said 'I'm a horny little devil'?
17 Of the *Three Men and a Baby*, who had appeared in Cheers?
18 Who scripted as well as starring in *A Fish Called Wanda*?
19 Who was the *Working Girl* of the title in the film in which Harrison Ford also starred?
20 Which 1988 film with Michelle Pfeiffer was about Mafia wives?
21 Who played the private eye hired by Roger Rabbit?
22 What is Jim Carrey's profession in *Liar Liar*?
23 Where does the most infamous scene in *When Harry Met Sally* take place?
24 Inside what toy does a love scene in *Honey I Shrunk The Kids* take place?
25 In which 80s film did Arnold Schwarzenegger play Danny De Vito's brother?

Answers

20th C Movies Comedies

1 Notting Hill. **2** Truman. **3** The Full Monty. **4** La Cage aux Folles. **5** Eddie Murphy. **6** Joan Plowright. **7** Wool. **8** Bus. **9** Diamond. **10** Life of Brian. **11** Jake. **12** Dolly Parton. **13** In bed. **14** Rosanna. **15** Mick. **16** Jack Nicholson. **17** Ted Danson. **18** John Cleese. **19** Melanie Griffith. **20** Married to the Mob. **21** Bob Hoskins. **22** Lawyer. **23** Restaurant. **24** Lego brick. **25** Twins.

Quiz 80 Pot Luck

Level 2

1. What do Bluebell, Severn Valley and Watercress have in common?
2. Who was Edward VII's Queen?
3. Which country recorded 17 straight wins in Rugby Union in the late 90s?
4. Why were Hope and Crosby 'like Webster's Dictionary'?
5. What is the RAF equivalent to the army rank of Major?
6. In which decade of the 20th century was Jack Nicholson born?
7. Which musical featured the song I Talk To The Trees?
8. What was held for the first time on 11th Nov, 1921?
9. In basketball, where do the Kings come from?
10. Who made No 1 with Should I Go Or Should I Stay?
11. What did the second E stand for in Premium Bonds' ERNIE?
12. Which country did tennis-playing sisters Katerina and Manuela Maleeva originally come from?
13. In which year did Bill Hayley's Rock Around The Clock top the charts?
14. In advertising which chocolates were said to 'Grow on you'?
15. At which sport did Ken Buchanan win international success?
16. Spiro Agnew was vice-president to which US President?
17. Who sang the title song for the Bond film *The Spy Who Loved Me*?
18. Calgary International airport is in which country?
19. Ansel Adams worked in which field in America?
20. Which politician stated that, 'A week is a long time in politics'?
21. Which Liverpool legend was manager of the year six times from 1976 to 1983?
22. Who wrote the novel *Doctor Zhivago*?
23. In which decade did the Netherlands join the European Union?
24. Who created the, 'Ooh, you are awful, but I like you' character Mandy?
25. In which country is the Francorchamps race track?

Answers

Pot Luck

1 (Preserved) railways. **2** Alexandra. **3** South Africa. **4** They were Morocco bound. **5** Squadron Leader. **6** 30s. **7** Paint Your Wagon. **8** Poppy Day. **9** Sacramento. **10** The Clash. **11** Equipment. **12** Bulgaria. **13** 1955. **14** Roses. **15** Boxing. **16** Nixon. **17** Carly Simon. **18** Canada. **19** Photographer. **20** Harold Wilson. **21** Bob Paisley. **22** Boris Pasternak. **23** 50s. **24** Dick Emery. **25** Belgium.

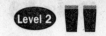

Quiz 81 Sport: Who's Who? Level 2

1 Jennifer Susan Harvey is better known by what name?
2 Who was the female competitor excused a sex test in the 1976 Olympics?
3 Which Italian said he could not 'understand a word Dennis Wise was saying?
4 Which Andy won rugby's Lance Todd Award in 1988 and 1990?
5 Who was skipper of Middlesbrough's 1997 FA Cup Final team?
6 Who was the English captain of the 1980 British Lions tour?
7 Which Spanish player interrupted Graf's reign as women's singles champion at Wimbledon?
8 Who took second division Wycombe Wanderers to the FA Cup semi-final in 2001?
9 Who was first to win the US Masters five times?
10 Who managed Frank Bruno?
11 Who scored Southampton's FA Cup winner in the 70s?
12 Who had a set to with umpire Shakoor Rana at Faisalabad in 1987?
13 Who retired in the 90s after 15 years as chairman of the FA?
14 Who was Marvellous Man?
15 Who were rowed into the record books with Steve Redgrave in the coxless fours at the Sydney Olympics?
16 Which Englishman used to manage the Australian national football team?
17 Who did Gerard Houllier take over from at Liverpool?
18 Who became the youngest woman to sail solo round the world in 2001?
19 Which left-handed batsman scored the most test runs for England?
20 Which cups did Liverpool win to secure a unique treble in 2001?
21 Allan Lamb first played in England for which county?
22 Which cricket umpire wrote a surprise bestseller?
23 Who managed QPR to relegation in 1996?
24 Which boxer was born in Bellingham, London, on May 3 1934?
25 What is the name of Michael Schumacher's younger brother?

Answers

Sporting Chance

1 Jenny Pitman. **2** Princess Anne. **3** Gianfranco Zola. **4** Gregory. **5** Nigel Pearson. **6** Bill Beaumont. **7** Conchita Martinez. **8** Lawrie Sanchez. **9** Jack Nicklaus. **10** Terry Lawless. **11** Bobby Stokes. **12** Mike Gatting. **13** Sir Bert Millichip. **14** Marvin Hagler. **15** Matthew Pinsent, James Cracknell, Tim Foster. **16** Terry Venables. **17** Roy Evans. **18** Ellen MacArthur. **19** David Gower. **20** Worthington, FA, UEFA. **21** Northants. **22** Dickie Bird. **23** Ray Wilkins. **24** Henry Cooper. **25** Ralph.

Quiz 82 CORONATION ST. Level 2

Pot Luck

1 Who formed a business partnership with fashion designer Christine Millward?
2 Who opened the revamped Corner Shop as Miss Weatherfield 1955?
3 Who proposed to Rita whilst drunk?
4 Who was left behind when his family moved to Southampton?
5 Who married Alf Roberts?
6 Who took driving lessons and passed first time?
7 Sally Webster worked as a barmaid at the Rovers: True or false?
8 Who played Sam Tindall?
9 Who was sacked by Mike Baldwin for going shopping in company time?
10 Who was cautioned as a public nuisance after locking a water board official in Hilda's outside loo?
11 Which unlikely couple married in September 1987?
12 Who proposed to Gail and was turned down in 1987?
13 Who enrolled on a business studies course when his removal business folded?
14 Who held a fête to raise £500 to send a local boy for an operation in America?
15 Who dated plumber Jeff Singleton when her husband left her?
16 Which character had a son called Jason and a violent ex called Ronnie?
17 Which couple married at St Luke's Catholic Church?
18 Who started up a sandwich delivery business from Jim's Cafe?
19 What was Percy's budgie called?
20 Who played Shirley Armitage?
21 What was Curly's position at Bettabuy when he first passed his HND?
22 In which month in 1989 was Alan Bradley killed?
23 Who bought Mike's factory in order to develop the land?
24 Who led the fight for redundancy pay for the factory workers in 1989?
25 Who gave retired ventriloquist Charlie Bracewell a job at the Rovers?

Answers

Coronation Street – Pot Luck

1 Mike Baldwin. **2** Bet. **3** Alf. **4** Kevin. **5** Audrey Potter. **6** Vera. **7** True. **8** Tom Mennard. **9** Vera. **10** Percy. **11** Alec and Bet. **12** Ian Latimer. **13** Curly. **14** Emily. **15** Gail. **16** Sandra Stubbs. **17** Ivy and Don. **18** Gail. **19** Randy. **20** Lisa Lewis. **21** Trainee Assistant Manager. **22** December. **23** Maurice Jones. **24** Emily. **25** Alec.

Quiz 83 TV Selection

Level 2

1. Who played John Wilder in *The Power Game*?
2. The original presenters of the BBC'S *Breakfast Time* were Frank Bough, Selena Scott, and one other. Who?
3. Who introduced *It'll be Alright on the Night*?
4. Which artist played a digeridoo?
5. *The Simpsons* became the longest-running cartoon family in 1997, replacing whom?
6. Who was the original weatherman on BBC's *Breakfast Time*?
7. Which character in *EastEnders* was Mark's wife?
8. In which year did the BBC TV schools service begin?
9. Which actress had to survive on her own on a desert isle?
10. Who was Jennifer Paterson's cooking partner?
11. What was the name of the first space ship used by *Blake's 7*?
12. Which fictional village was *Heartbeat* set in?
13. Which rodent starred on TVAM?
14. What was an Admag, banned by Parliament in 1963?
15. Who presented *The Human Body*?
16. What was the profession of the major characters in *This Life*?
17. What did the ARP Warden call Captain Mainwaring?
18. In which decade was *Hi-De-Hi!* first set?
19. Which early evening programme did Mel and Sue introduce?
20. Who is the current host of *Going for a Song*?
21. Which actress played *The Sculptress*?
22. Who was Lovejoy's original love interest?
23. Which actor was Maxwell Smart?
24. Who played Tom Howard's wife in *Howard's Way*?
25. In which city was PI Daniel Pike based?

Answers

TV Selection

1 Patrick Wymark. **2** Nick Ross. **3** Dennis Norden. **4** Rolf Harris. **5** *The Flintstones*. **6** Francis Wilson. **7** Ruth. **8** September 1957. **9** Joanna Lumley. **10** Clarissa Dickson-Wright. **11** The Liberator. **12** Aidensfield. **13** Roland Rat. **14** An advertisement broadcast in the guise of a genuine programme. **15** Sir Robert Winston. **16** Lawyers. **17** Napoleon. **18** 1950s. **19** Late Lunch. **20** Michael Parkinson. **21** Pauline Quirke. **22** Lady Jane Felsham. **23** Don Adams. **24** Jan Harvey. **25** Glasgow.

Quiz 84 Pot Luck

Level 2

1 In 1954 what was tested at Bikini Atoll?
2 Who wrote *Dinnerladies*?
3 Which city is snooker player Willie Thorne's home town?
4 Who was the BBC's royal correspondent at the time of Princess Diana's death?
5 Eurostar will take you to which station in Paris?
6 In which decade of the century did a woman first sit in the Commons?
7 Which musical featured the song Food, Glorious Food?
8 According to the advertising campaign, Ian Botham couldn't eat three what?
9 Who was US President when America entered World War II?
10 Who became the first black athlete to captain the British team?
11 Who was appointed Vice President of the European Commission in July 1999?
12 Who made No 1 with Dreams?
13 What was being advertised by Lorraine Chase's Luton Airport character?
14 In which country is the deepwater port of Valparaiso?
15 What was the name of Fitz's wife in *Cracker*?
16 What was the third Bond film for which Shirley Bassey sang the title song?
17 In the 90s how many points have been awarded for finishing sixth in a Grand Prix?
18 In which decade was Kenneth Branagh born?
19 Who had a No 1 in the 60s with Mike Sarne before becoming a TV actress?
20 Which animal appeared on British eggs in 1957?
21 Which instrument is particularly associated with bandleader Buddy Rich?
22 Which English soccer international was known as 'Crazy Horse'?
23 Findel international airport is in which country?
24 Who wrote *East Of Eden*?
25 Whose motto is, 'Let not the deep swallow me up'?

Answers

Pot Luck

1 Hydrogen bomb. **2** Victoria Wood. **3** Leicester. **4** Jennie Bond. **5** Gare Du Nord. **6** Second decade. **7** Oliver. **8** Shredded Wheat. **9** Franklin Roosevelt. **10** Kriss Akabusi. **11** Neil Kinnock. **12** Gabrielle. **13** Campari. **14** Chile. **15** Judith. **16** Moonraker. **17** 1. **18** 60s. **19** Wendy Richard. **20** Lion. **21** Drums. **22** Emlyn Hughes. **23** Luxembourg. **24** John Steinbeck. **25** RNLI.

Quiz 85 Media

Level 2

1 Which former Soviet Communist Party newspaper was relaunched as a tabloid in 1996?
2 In 1997 The Duchess of York was signed up by which US newspaper to write a weekly column?
3 Who bought Virgin Radio from Richard Branson in 1997?
4 What was the original target audience for Sky's UK Living?
5 Where is the HQ of the BBC World Service?
6 In which decade was *Cosmopolitan* magazine launched in the UK?
7 How frequently is *Private Eye* published?
8 What did CMTV stand for?
9 Where did *The Times* offices move to in 1986?
10 What did G stand for in GLR?
11 What did C stand for in the shopping channel QVC?
12 Which national radio station was launched by the BBC in the 1990s?
13 In which decade of the century did radio's *Desert Island Discs* begin ?
14 Who took over from Zoe Ball on the Radio One Breakfast Show?
15 At the end of the century *Test Match Special* was broadcast on which national radio network?
16 In which decade could *Radio Times* and *TV Times* first publish details of programmes on all channels?
17 How is Sianel Pedwar Cymru – Channel 4 in Wales – abbreviated?
18 In which county were Pinewood Studios?
19 Meridian broadcast to which area of the UK ?
20 What does I stand for in ILR?
21 In which decade was *Radio Times* first published?
22 *Tribune* supported which political party?
23 Which magazine paid around £1 million for the exclusive rights to David Beckham and Victoria Adams' wedding photos?
24 Which sitcom characters have guest edited *Marie Claire*?
25 In which decade was *The Sun* first published?

Answers

Media
1 Pravda. **2** New York Times. **3** Chris Evans. **4** Women. **5** Bush House. **6** 70s. **7** Fortnightly. **8** Country Music Television. **9** Wapping. **10** Greater. **11** Convenience. **12** Radio 5 Live. **13** 40s. **14** Sara Cox. **15** Radio 4 Long Wave. **16** 1990s. **17** S4C. **18** Buckinghamshire. **19** S & SE England. **20** Independent. **21** 1920s. **22** Labour. **23** O.K. **24** Edina & Patsy. **25** 60s.

Quiz 86

Pot Luck

1 Who played Steph Barnes?
2 Who was charged with assault after hitting a joyrider who stole his cab?
3 Who got a job as a TV repair man and was chased by amorous Audrey?
4 Who took Deirdre to Paris for New Year?
5 How did Peter Ingram die?
6 Who played Des Barnes?
7 Who had a one night stand with Curly after too much red wine?
8 Who reported Gail to Social Services for being an unfit mother?
9 Who started their own pirate radio station?
10 Who was the real character behind their creation Captain Kenny?
11 Name the baby born on the street in 1992.
12 Who played Hanif Ruparell?
13 Name the Flying Pickets' singer who played Doug Murray.
14 How did Ted Sullivan die?
15 Who moved in with Des, then moved out again when Steph returned home?
16 Who befriended Rev. Bernard Morten?
17 Who made an effigy of Percy for their bonfire?
18 Who thumped Brewery boss Richard Willmore, believing he was seeing his wife?
19 Who had a one night stand with Don Brennan?
20 Who told Mark Redman that Mike Baldwin was his dad?
21 Why did Reverend Bernard Morten break off his engagement to Emily Bishop?
22 Who played Jamie Armstrong?
23 Why was Curly sacked from Bettabuy?
24 Where did he work next?
25 Who asked Vera to leave Jack for a bungalow in Filey?

Answers

Coronation Street – Pot Luck

1 Amelia Bulmore. **2** Don Brennan. **3** Jim. **4** Phil Jennings. **5** Heart attack. **6** Phil Middlemiss. **7** Angie Freeman. **8** Ivy. **9** Steve and Andy. **10** Ken Barlow. **11** Tommy Duckworth. **12** Ayub Khan Din. **13** Brian Hibbard. **14** Brain Tumour. **15** Raquel. **16** Emily. **17** The Platt kids. **18** Jim McDonald. **19** Bet. **20** Tracy Barlow.**21** He found out she'd had a breakdown. **22** Joseph Gilgun. **23** Elaine Fenwick made a sexual harassment case against him. **24** Soopa Scoopa. **25** Lester Fontayne.

Quiz 87 80s

Level 2

1 Which Michael had a 1989 hit with Love Changes Everything?
2 Which coloured day of the week was a hit for New Order in 1983 and 1988?
3 Who had a man in 1986 who was So Macho?
4 Which Radio 1 DJ would not play Relax by Frankie Goes to Hollywood on his early morning show?
5 Which actor had a hit with Under The Boardwalk in 1987?
6 Which group had a hit in 1988 with Harvest for the World?
7 Which TV weatherperson was celebrated in a 1988 hit for the Tribe of Toffs?
8 Who gave Lessons in Love in 1986?
9 Which group made Private Investigations in a 1982 hit?
10 According to the 1984 hit by Pat Benatar, Love is a what?
11 Which Summer gave Bryan Adams a hit in 1985?
12 Who had a hit with You Take Me Up in 1984?
13 Singers of Heartache, Pepsi and Shirley were backing singers to who?
14 Who did a cover of Everything I Own in the 80s?
15 Who had a hit in 1988 with The Only Way Is Up?
16 Which American lady had a hit in 1989 with The Wind Beneath My Wings?
17 Who had a hit in 1981 with Oh Superman?
18 Which group had a hit in 1989 about The Living Years?
19 Who took Ride On Time to the UK Top Spot for six weeks in 1989?
20 Which rock band had a UK No 1 in 1986 with The Final Count Down?
21 Which group were Going Back To My Roots in a No 4 hit from 1981?
22 Which group asked Don't Get Me Wrong in 1986?
23 Whose only Top Ten UK hit was Your Love Is King from 1984?
24 Who had a hit in 1987 with Never Can Say Goodbye?
25 In 1980 who were All Out of Love?

Answers

80s

1 Ball. **2** Blue Monday. **3** Sinitta. **4** Mike Read. **5** Bruce Willis. **6** Christians. **7** John Kettley. **8** Level 42. **9** Dire Straits. **10** Battlefield. **11** 69. **12** The Thompson Twins. **13** Wham!. **14** Boy George. **15** Yazz. **16** Bette Midler. **17** Laurie Anderson. **18** Mike and the Mechanics. **19** Black Box. **20** Europe. **21** Odyssey. **22** Pretenders. **23** Sade. **24** The Communards. **25** Air Supply.

Quiz 88 Pioneers

Level 2

1 What was the first name of the world's first test tube baby?
2 Jane Couch was the first woman to be granted a professional licence to do what?
3 In which city did the original Wallace and Gromit models get lost in 1996?
4 What sort of radio was designed by British inventor Trevor Baylis?
5 The Ishihara Test is a test for what?
6 Which pioneer in men's appearance had the first names King Camp?
7 Air flight pioneer Amy Johnson vanished over which river?
8 What was the name of Clive Sinclair's electric trike?
9 Reaching which place led to the quote, 'Great God, this is an awful place'?
10 Who accompanied Dr Michael Stroud on the first unsupported crossing of the Antarctic?
11 In 1993 Barbara Harmer became the first woman pilot of what?
12 Who was the first racing driver to win the world drivers' championship in his own car?
13 Which country was the first in the world to have a woman Prime Minister?
14 What was the first item of non-stick cookware marketed by Teflon?
15 Which flags along with that of the UN were planted on the top of Everest by Hillary and Tensing?
16 In the Whitbread Round the World Race, who skippered the all-women crew of *Maiden*?
17 David Scott and James Irwin were the first people to drive where?
18 Who introduced the first personal stereo ?
19 In which decade were camcorders introduced?
20 Which items of sports equipment were developed by US ice hockey players Scott and Brennan Olson?
21 Gro Harlem Brundtland was the first woman PM in which country?
22 Who was the USA's first spacewoman?
23 Who was the first black archbishop of Cape Town?
24 What sort of wave was seen for the first time at a sporting fixture in 1986?
25 Which Scandinavian country was the first to ban aerosol sprays because of the potential damage to the environment?

Answers

Pioneers

1 Louise. **2** Box. **3** New York. **4** Clockwork radio. **5** Colour blindness. **6** Gillette. **7** Thames. **8** C5. **9** The South Pole. **10** Ranulph Fiennes. **11** Concorde. **12** Jack Brabham. **13** Ceylon, later Sri Lanka. **14** Frying pan. **15** Britain & Nepal. **16** Tracey Edwards. **17** Moon. **18** Sony. **19** 80s. **20** Rollerblades. **21** Norway. **22** Sally Ride. **23** Desmond Tutu. **24** Mexican wave. **25** Sweden.

Quiz 89 Glitterati

Level 2

1 Which famous daughter was made chief designer at Chloe in 1997?
2 Which supermodel was married to Rod Stewart?
3 What is the occupation of Vanessa Feltz's husband?
4 Which Royal sold her autobiography for $1.3 million to Simon & Schuster?
5 Who designed Sophie Rhys-Jones' wedding dress?
6 Which French chef is famed for his Manoir aux Quat'Saisons restaurant?
7 Flamenco dancer Joaquin Cortes hit the headlines in 1996 over his relationship with which supermodel?
8 Which Italian fashion designer was murdered on the orders of his ex-wife?
9 Michael Flatley shot to fame during an interval filler on which programme?
10 Which perfume house did Helena Bonham-Carter advertise?
11 Who designed the see-through black dress Caprice wore at the 1996 National TV Awards which shot her to stardom?
12 Whose 50th birthday party did Prince Charles host at Highgrove in the summer of 1997?
13 Which pop star did model Iman marry in 1992?
14 Which crimper to the famous launched his Hairomatherapy products in the 90s?
15 What type of creature did Anthea Turner pose nude with on the front of *Tatler*?
16 Who has been the husband of Catherine Deneuve, Marie Helvin and Catherine Dyer?
17 What is the name of Terence and Shirley Conran's dress designer son?
18 Who did Princess Diana's make-up before her wedding in 1981?
19 In which country was Ivana Trump born and brought up?
20 Which drink did The Spice Girls promote?
21 Which Royal did The Beatles mention in Penny Lane?
22 Which soap star launched a perfume called Scoundrel?
23 Which blonde model appeared in *Batman*?
24 Which TV soap did Russell Grant appear in as himself?
25 The 11th Duke of Devonshire married one of which famous family of sisters?

Answers

Glitterati
1 Stella McCartney. **2** Rachel Hunter. **3** Surgeon. **4** The Duchess of York. **5** Samantha Shaw. **6** Raymond Blanc. **7** Naomi Campbell. **8** Gucci. **9** Eurovision Song Contest. **10** Yardley. **11** Versace. **12** Camilla Parker-Bowles. **13** David Bowie. **14** Nicky Clarke. **15** Snake. **16** David Bailey. **17** Jasper. **18** Barbara Daly. **19** Czechoslovakia. **20** Pepsi. **21** The Queen. **22** Joan Collins. **23** Jerry Hall. **24** Brookside. **25** Mitford.

Quiz 90 TV

Level 2

1 What is the first name of Kavanagh QC?
2 What is the mascot for *The Great Antiques Hunt*?
3 Patrick Moore is famous for playing which musical instrument?
4 In which county is *Where the Heart Is* set?
5 What is Rab C. Nesbitt's wife called?
6 Henry Sandon became famous on which TV show
7 Who did *The Simpsons* replace as TV's longest-running cartoon family in 1997?
8 Who was Jennifer Paterson's cooking partner?
9 Which female doctor succeeded Beth Glover in *Peak Practice*?
10 What is the fictional village where *Heartbeat* is set?
11 Which actor is the son of Nigel Davenport and Maria Aitken?
12 Which role did Harry Enfield play in *Men Behaving Badly*?
13 Which TV chef rides around on a scooter?
14 Who won the first *Big Brother* in 2000?
15 Which television series shocked viewers with its gay sex scenes?
16 Who is the comidienne mother of actress Suzy Aitcheson?
17 Who starred in the remake of *Randall and Hopkirk (deceased)*?
18 Which ex-Brookside star played Barbara in *The Royle Family*?
19 Who left *Blue Peter* in 1996 and presented *Songs of Praise*?
20 Who was Reginald Perrin's boss?
21 Who died when he crashed Mark Fowler's motorbike in *Eastenders*?
22 Whose catchprase in *Drop the Dead Donkey* was 'I'm not here'?
23 Which children's TV character lives in Pontypandy?
24 Who presents *University Challenge*?
25 Who was the dare-devil presenter of *Don't Try This at Home*?

Answers

TV

1 James. **2** A bloodhound. **3** Xylophone. **4** Yorkshire. **5** Mary. **6** Antiques Roadshow. **7** The Flintstones. **8** Clarissa Dixon-Wright. **9** Mastermind. **10** Erica Matthews. **11** Jack Davenport. **12** Dermots. **13** Jamie Oliver. **14** Craig. **15** Queer as Folk **16** June Whitfield. **17** Vic Reeves and Bob Mortimer. **18** Sue Johnston. **19** Diane-Louise Jordan. **20** CJ. **21** Ashley Cotton. **22** Gus Hedges. **23** Fireman Sam. **24** Jeremy Paxman. **25** Divina McCall.

Quiz 91 Rugby

Level 2

1 Who is England's most capped Union player?
2 In which decade did Ireland last win the Five Nations?
3 Who led the British Lions in their all-conquering tour of S Africa in the 70s?
4 Which Erica made a clean breast of things at Twickenham in 1982?
5 Apart from Rugby, Rob Andrew captained Cambridge in which other sport?
6 In 1998 against which team did England suffer their worst ever Union defeat?
7 Who led England to their Grand Slam triumph of 1980, the first for nearly a quarter of a century?
8 What injury did Welsh captain Gwyn Jones suffer in Dec 1997 at the Arms Park?
9 Which club thought Wendall Sailor was joining them in 1998?
10 Who did Scotland beat 85-3 in a 1999 World Cup qualifier?
11 In what year was League's Regal Trophy last contested?
12 Which team played the Welsh in the first game at the Millennium Stadium?
13 Which creature name did Hunslet adopt in the 90s?
14 Who captained the Lions' New Zealand Tour of 1993?
15 At what age did Will Carling first become England skipper?
16 Which country was thrashed 96-13 by South Africa in 1998?
17 What position did Gareth Edwards play?
18 Martin Johnson was at which club when he became England skipper?
19 Jonathan Davies was League's 1994 Man of Steel when playing for which team?
20 In which pool were England drawn for the 1999 World Cup?
21 Which team did Bath beat in 97-98 European Cup?
22 Which country does Wales coach Graham Henry come from?
23 Who was man of the match as Sheffield Eagles sensationally beat Wigan in a Challenge Cup final?
24 Which club did legendary French player Phillippe Sella join?
25 In which year did Lawrence Dallaglio take over as England's captain?

Answers

Rugby

1 Rory Underwood. **2** 80s. **3** Willie John McBride. **4** Rowe. **5** Cricket. **6** Australia. **7** Bill Beaumont. **8** Broke his neck. **9** Wigan. **10** Spain. **11** 1996. **12** S Africa. **13** Hawks. **14** Gavin Hastings. **15** 22. **16** Wales. **17** Scrum half. **18** Leicester. **19** Warrington. **20** Pool B. **21** Brive. **22** New Zealand. **23** Mark Aston. **24** Saracens. **25** 1997.

Quiz 92 The Oscars

Level 2

1 Which not-so-dizzy blonde won an Oscar for *Cactus Flower*?
2 Who did Loretta Lynn choose to play her in *Coal Miner's Daughter*?
3 How tall is an Oscar in centimetres?
4 Whose 1989 Oscar for *Glory* was the first awarded to a black American for 50 years?
5 Following his *True Grit* Oscar what did John Wayne's fellow actors and his horse wear while filming a new movie?
6 In which decade of the 20th century were the Oscars born?
7 For which film was Judi Dench nominated for her first Oscar?
8 What is the name of the daughter of Oscar winner Joel Gray who starred in *Dirty Dancing*?
9 Who was up for an Oscar as Sally Field's daughter in *Steel Magnolias*?
10 Which actress was the second in history to win an Oscar (for *Roman Holiday*) and a Tony (for *Ondine*) in the same year?
11 Which French actor was Oscar nominated for *Cyrano de Bergerac*?
12 For which movie did Barbra Streisand win an Oscar for *Evergreen*?
13 Which anniversary did the Oscars celebrate in 1998?
14 Which 1996 multi-Oscar winner was based on a novel by Michael Ondaatje?
15 For which film did Robert de Niro win his first Oscar?
16 Which Fonda won an honorary award in 1980?
17 Who won an Oscar for the music of *Chariots of Fire*?
18 What was the nationality of Sophie in the Oscar-winning *Sophie's Choice*?
19 Dr Haing S Ngor was only the second non-professional actor to win an Oscar in which film?
20 Which Stevie Wonder song won an Oscar for *The Woman in Red*?
21 Which was the first family to boast three generations of Oscar winners including middle generation John?
22 Who won a Best Supporting Actor award for *Hannah and her Sisters*?
23 Which successful song from *Top Gun* was a hit for Berlin?
24 In which film did Cher win an Oscar playing Loretta Castorini?
25 1987 was a successful year for Michael Douglas, but which movie won him an Oscar?

Answers

The Movies The Oscars
1 Goldie Hawn. **2** Sissy Spacek. **3** 30cm. **4** Denzel Washington. **5** Eye patches. **6** 20s. **7** Mrs Brown. **8** Jennifer. **9** Julia Roberts. **10** Audrey Hepburn. **11** Gerard Depardieu. **12** A Star is Born. **13** 70th. **14** The English Patient. **15** The Godfather II. **16** Henry. **17** Vangelis. **18** Polish. **19** The Killing Fields. **20** I Just Called to Say I Love You. **21** Huston. **22** Michael Caine. **23** Take My Breath Away. **24** Moonstruck. **25** Wall Street.

Quiz 93 On Line

Level 2

1 What was BT called before 1991?
2 In which decade of this century were airmail letters first carried?
3 Which Defence Department first set up the messaging system which became the Internet?
4 In telephone terms, what was a party line?
5 Which telecommunications company took its name from the Roman messenger of the gods?
6 What was BT's Speaking Clock service called?
7 What is the purpose of a dataglove?
8 BarclaySquare was an early Internet site offering what?
9 What is a message sent to a newsgroup on the Internet called?
10 What was the BBC's introduction to the Internet called?
11 What was set up in 1984 to monitor the telecommunications industry?
12 What colour were special airmail post boxes which used to be seen on city streets?
13 On the Internet, what does the first B stand for in BBS?
14 Pong was an early console type game based on which sport?
15 What was the videotext service of BT called?
16 What does V stand for in VR?
17 How many bits are there in a byte?
18 From Earth, where was the destination of the longest long distance telephone call?
19 What does D stand for in ISDN?
20 Which company launched CDi in the early 1990s?
21 On the Internet, what is Spam?
22 In the WIMP system of computing, what did W stand for?
23 What does D stand for in CAD?
24 What was the name of the first satellite to relay live TV pictures between the USA and Europe?
25 On the Internet, what is a firewall?

Answers

On Line

1 British Telecom. **2** 2nd decade. **3** Pentagon. **4** Shared phone line. **5** Mercury. **6** Timeline. **7** Allows people to touch over long distances. **8** Shopping. **9** Article. **10** Webwise. **11** Oftel. **12** Blue. **13** Bulletin. **14** Tennis. **15** Prestel. **16** Virtual. **17** Eight. **18** Moon. **19** Digital. **20** Phillips. **21** Junkmail. **22** Windows. **23** Design. **24** Telstar. **25** Security barrier.

Quiz 94 90s

Level 2

1 Which country is home to Whigfield?
2 What was Loved by Shanice in 1991 and 1992?
3 Who sang about Black Betty in both 1977 and 1990?
4 Which Wimbledon champion sang with John McEnroe?
5 Which liquid product featured the hit Like A Prayer in its advertisement?
6 Danny, Joe, Sonnie, Jon and Jordan were better known as which group?
7 Who asked you to Please Come Home for Christmas in 1994?
8 Which group took a cover of More Than A Woman to No 2 in 1998?
9 What was Blur's first top ten hit?
10 Who said Let's Get Rocked in a 1992 hit?
11 Who released an album in the 90s called Bilingual?
12 Who recorded the original version of Boyzone's Father and Son?
13 Which group were a Sight For Sore Eyes?
14 Who were Ready Or Not from 1996?
15 Who released an album in 1996 called K?
16 Who had a No.1 in 1991 with his debut single The One and Only?
17 Which Sunday paper featured the audition ads for Upside Down?
18 Which song gave The Corrs their first UK Top Ten hit?
19 Which hit by the Spice Girls gave them their 8th UK No. 1?
20 Which hit gave All Saints their 3rd UK No 1 hit in September 1998?
21 What was Boyzone's first UK Top Ten hit ?
22 Who had a UK No 1 with Gym and Tonic in October 1998?
23 What nationality are the vocal and instrumental group Aqua?
24 What was Jamiroquai's first UK Top Ten hit?
25 Which label do Shamen record on?

Answers

90s

1 Denmark. **2** Your Smile. **3** Ram Jam. **4** Pat Cash. **5** Pepsi. **6** New Kids On The Block. **7** Bon Jovi. **8** 911. **9** There's No Other Way. **10** Def Leppard. **11** Pet Shop Boys. **12** Cat Stevens. **13** M People. **14** The Fugees. **15** Kula Shaker. **16** Chesney Hawkes. **17** People. **18** Dreams. **19** Goodbye. **20** Bootie Call. **21** Love Me For A Reason. **22** Spacedust. **23** Danish. **24** Too Young To Die. **25** One Little Indian.

Quiz 95 Technology & Industry

Level 2

1 Which telescope was launched into space on board a space shuttle in 1990?
2 Which UK airport became the first to be connected to a city railway system?
3 In the late 60s Owen Finlay Maclaren pioneered what useful item for parents of small children?
4 What was the OFT?
5 In which decade were windscreen wipers patented in the UK?
6 Who launched the Skytrain air service?
7 Which city was the HQ of the European Space Programme?
8 Which Bank of England chief said losses in industry in the north east was a small price to pay for low inflation?
9 What type of aircraft was the Hawker Siddeley Harrier?
10 What does the Transalaska Pipeline System transport?
11 What was the name of the world's first nuclear-powered submarine?
12 Robin Leigh-Pemberton held the top job at which organisation from 1983 to 1993?
13 Which company linked with Sky Television to form BSkyB?
14 In which decade was the Mersey Tunnel opened?
15 What did the first letter I stand for in ICI?
16 What was Britain's first king size cigarette called?
17 In which country were Daewoo cars originally produced?
18 Which country was the first in the world to introduce a driving test?
19 What did Guinness adopt as its trademark in the 60s?
20 Which Andrei built the first factory to mass-produce rubber tyres?
21 Which underground line runs to Heathrow Airport?
22 Which Trade & Industry Secretary resigned in 1998?
23 What does Volkswagen actually mean?
24 The first cheque guarantee card was produced by which British bank?
25 In which city are the headquarters of the IMF?

Answers

Technology & Industry

1 Hubble. **2** Heathrow. **3** Baby Buggy. **4** Office of Fair Trading. **5** 20s. **6** Freddie Laker. **7** Paris. **8** Eddie George. **9** Jump jet. **10** Oil. **11** Nautilus. **12** Bank of England. **13** BSB. **14** 30s. **15** Imperial. **16** Rex. **17** Korea. **18** France. **19** Harp. **20** Michelin. **21** Piccadilly. **22** Peter Mandelson. **23** People's car. **24** Midland. **25** Washington.

Quiz 96 20th C Leaders

Level 2

1 Sir Christopher Bland replaced Sir Marmaduke Hussey as Chairman of which corporation in 1996?
2 Paul Keating was a controversial Prime Minister of which country?
3 Which Tory Home Secretary refused an application for British citizenship by the Al-Fayed brothers in 1996?
4 Who fought the 1997 election on behalf of the Referendum Party?
5 Aung San Suu Kyi is a controversial leader in which country?
6 Which Russian leader was buried in 1998 in his family's vault?
7 What was the full name of the trades union which Arthur Scargill led?
8 Who in Tony Blair's Cabinet was a racing tipster for the *Glasgow Herald*?
9 Who became president of the European Commission in 1995?
10 Which spouse of a party leader deputised for Jimmy Young on Radio 2?
11 Which French Prime Minister funeral's was attended by his wife and his mistress in 1996?
12 Who was only the second heir to the throne to marry this century?
13 Which Eurovision winner became an MEP in the 1999 elections?
14 Which political party leader's aunt was a big lottery winner in 1998?
15 Which Press Secretary left Downing Street for Radio 5 Live?
16 Which world leader married Graca Machel in 1998?
17 Which royal autographed a Man Utd football on a tour of Malaysia?
18 Bill Clinton was Governor of which US state before he became President?
19 Who did William Hague beat in the final round of the contest for the Tory Party leadership after the 1997 election?
20 Earl Spencer appeared on whose US chat show?
21 Who replaced King Hussein as King of Jordan?
22 Which surname of a British leader was Ronald Reagan's middle name?
23 What was the surname of the British Roman Catholic Cardinal who died in June 1999?
24 Which daughter of a Prime Minister was a former girlfriend of convicted ex-MP Jonathan Aitken?
25 Michael Cashman became an MEP in the 1999 elections after starring for three years in which TV soap?

Answers

20th C Leaders

1 BBC. **2** Australia. **3** Michael Howard. **4** James Goldsmith. **5** Burma. **6** Tsar Nicholas II. **7** National Union Of Mineworkers. **8** Robin Cook. **9** Jacques Santer. **10** Glenys Kinnock. **11** Francois Mitterand. **12** Prince Charles. **13** Dana. **14** William Hague's. **15** Charlie Whelan. **16** Nelson Mandela. **17** The Queen. **18** Arkansas. **19** Kenneth Clarke. **20** Oprah Winfrey. **21** Abdullah. **22** Wilson. **23** Hume. **24** Carol Thatcher. **25** EastEnders.

Quiz 97 20th C TV

Level 2

1 What was the name of the live weekday programme which Vanessa Feltz fronted in her £2 million deal with the BBC?
2 In which series did Michelle Collins play holiday rep Vicki?
3 What is the first name of the builder in *Ground Force*?
4 Which broadcaster famously said during the Falklands conflict, 'I counted them all out and I counted them all back'?
5 David Wilkinson featured in the docusoap about which West End store?
6 Which song did Robson & Jerome sing on *Soldier Soldier* which launched their singing career?
7 Sharron Davies aka Gladiator Amazon was an Olympic medallist in which sport?
8 Fred Dibnah found fame on TV as a member of what profession?
9 Which Michael Palin series followed in the steps of Phileas Fogg?
10 In which decade did the BBC's film review programme with Barry Norman begin?
11 What colour was the chair in the first series of *Mastermind*?
12 Where are the Pebble Mill studios?
13 At what time of day was *Multi Coloured Swap Shop* shown?
14 What was the manageress managing in *The Manageress*?
15 Who played Wooster in the 90s version of *Jeeves & Wooster*?
16 The action of *Sharpe* took place during which war?
17 Who was the subject of *The Private Man, The Public Role*?
18 Who narrated *The Wombles*?
19 In which drama series were Miles and Egg major characters?
20 Where on a Teletubby is its TV screen?
21 In which US state was *Sweet Valley High*?
22 Which Coronation Street actress played Jimmy Nail's ex-wife in *Spender*?
23 What was the name of Robson Green's character in *Soldier Soldier*?
24 Which airline was the subject of the docusoap *Airline*?
25 In which decade did *Newsnight* start?

Answers

20th C TV

1 The Vanessa Show. **2** Sunburn. **3** Tommy. **4** Brian Hanrahan. **5** Selfridges. **6** Unchained Melody. **7** Swimming. **8** Steeplejack. **9** Around the World in 80 Days. **10** 70s. **11** Black. **12** Birmingham. **13** Morning. **14** Football club. **15** Hugh Laurie. **16** Napoleonic. **17** Prince Charles. **18** Bernard Cribbins. **19** This Life. **20** Tummy. **21** California. **22** Denise Welch – Natalie. **23** Dave Tucker. **24** Britannia Airways. **25** 80s.

Quiz 98 Sports Bag

Level 2

1 Who said in 1998, 'The ball doesn't know how old you are'?
2 Which postwar cricketer played his first England game aged 18 and his last aged 45?
3 In which sport was Richard Upton found positive in a drugs test in 1998?
4 In the 1998 play-offs, which Sunderland player missed the final penalty?
5 In which sport in 90s Britain did Leopards overcome Sharks in a final?
6 Terry Mancini played soccer for which country?
7 In which decade did Alex Higgins first become snooker world champion?
8 What has been won by Australia II and America 3?
9 In which country and in which sport has a Blackadder played in the 90s?
10 Which Arsenal player scored in the 1998 World Cup Final?
11 Which former England captain added Dylan to his name in honour of Bob Dylan?
12 Where was the Derby held during Word War I and World War II?
13 Who was known as The Manassa Mauler?
14 How many people are there in an official tug of war team?
15 In 1994 who won the US Amateur Championship for the first time?
16 In which sport did Steve Baddeley win 143 caps in the 80s?
17 Who did Damon Hill move to when he was dropped by Williams?
18 Which country does boxer Vitali Klitschko come from?
19 In the 90s, in which sport in England did Braves perform at a Craven Park?
20 Who won golf's US Open in 1994 and 1997?
21 Which English club did Daniel Amokachi join after 1994 World Cup success with Nigeria?
22 What is the surname of the first father and son cricket captains of England?
23 In 1998 which British boxer took on Shannon Briggs and Zeljko Mavrovic?
24 Golf star Vijay Singh comes from where?
25 The early days of which sport featured the Renshaw twins, the Baddeley twins and the Doherty brothers?

Answers

Sports Bag

1 Mark O'Meara. **2** Brian Close. **3** Swimming. **4** Michael Gray. **5** Basketball. **6** Republic of Ireland. **7** 70s. **8** America's Cup. **9** New Zealand – Rugby Union. **10** Petit. **11** Bob Willis. **12** Newmarket. **13** Jack Dempsey. **14** Eight. **15** Tiger Woods. **16** Badminton. **17** Arrows. **18** Ukraine. **19** Rugby League. **20** Ernie Els. **21** Everton. **22** Cowdrey. **23** Lennox Lewis. **24** Fiji. **25** Tennis.

Quiz 99 20th C Screen Legends Level 2

1 Which swashbuckling hero's autobiography was *My Wicked Wicked Ways*?
2 What is Sean Connery's profession in *The Name of the Rose*?
3 Who did Ali McGraw marry after they had made *The Getaway* together?
4 Who spoke for the first time in *Anna Christie*?
5 Whose voice did Marni Nixon dub in the classic *My Fair Lady*?
6 In which film did David Niven play *James Bond*?
7 *I Could Go on Singing* was the last film of which screen legend?
8 Who was the first actress to receivc four Oscars?
9 John Hinckley's obsession with Jodie Foster led him to attempt to kill who?
10 Who got her first big break in *Grease 2*?
11 Who played Charlie Chaplin in Richard Attenborough's 1992 film?
12 Which star of *Gypsy* and *West Side Story* married Robert Wagner twice ?
13 Which legendary dancer was Oscar nominated for *The Towering Inferno*?
14 Which British born comedian completed a record 60th year of a contract with NBC in 1996?
15 Bogart's trademark sneer was due to an injury sustained in which conflict?
16 Which Swedish actress won the Best Supporting Actress Oscar for *Murder on the Orient Express*?
17 Who uttered the famous lines 'Frankly, my dear, I don't give a damn'?
18 Who was jailed for her 'obscene' stage play *Sex*?
19 Omar Sharif is a worldwide expert in which game?
20 Which British actor's autobiography was called '*What's It All About*?'?
21 Which screen legend's daughter shot JR in *Dallas*?
22 Which Joan's career revived in *Whatever Happened to Baby Jane?*?
23 Which much loved US actor won the Best Actor Oscar for *The Philadelphia Story*?
24 Which red-haired actress had the Margarita cocktail named after her as her real name was Margarita Cansino?
25 What colour are Elizabeth Taylor's eyes?

Answers

20th C Screen Legends
1 Errol Flynn. **2** Friar. **3** Steve McQueen. **4** Greta Garbo. **5** Audrey Hepburn. **6** Casino Royale. **7** Judy Garland. **8** Katharine Hepburn. **9** Ronald Reagan. **10** Michelle Pfeiffer. **11** Robert Downey Junior. **12** Natalie Wood. **13** Fred Astaire. **14** Bob Hope. **15** WWI. **16** Ingrid Bergman. **17** Clark Gable. **18** Mae West. **19** Bridge. **20** Michael Caine. **21** Bing Crosby. **22** Crawford. **23** James Stewart. **24** Rita Hayworth. **25** Violet.

Quiz 100 Entertainment

Level 2

1 Whose work for orchestra and chorus, Standing Stone, was premiered at the Albert Hall in 1997?
2 In which decade of the 20th century did the Gang Show cease to be staged annually in London?
3 Who was made principal conductor of the Birmingham Symphony orchestra in 1980?
4 In which part of London is The Round House?
5 The Sealed Knot Society re -enacts battles of which war?
6 Followers of raga music call themselves what?
7 Marie Rambert founded a company in what branch of entertainment?
8 Which J A owned over half of British cinemas by the mid 1940s?
9 Which ethnic group popularised salsa dancing in New York in the 1980s?
10 Which home town of Robin Hood has an 'experience' centre in his honour?
11 What and where is the Mathser?
12 How many piers does Blackpool have?
13 What type of tennis is usually played by children on a smaller court?
14 What was the first Web browser called?
15 Which dancer founded the company Dash?
16 Which seaside resort has Britain's largest theatre – and largest stage?
17 Which Russian city was famous for its State Circus?
18 The company whose full name was Radio Keith Orpheum produced what?
19 Who were Michael 'Rage' Hardy and James 'Smarty' Cools' female partner in Virtual Cop 2?
20 In which English county is the longest pleasure pier?
21 In which Austrian city, home of Mozart, has an annual music festival been held since 1920?
22 Who is the Princess in the Super Mario Gang?
23 Where in Japan is the Nintendo company based?
24 In which country did rap music begin?
25 What is BT's online gaming service called?

Answers

Entertainment

1 Paul McCartney. **2** 70s. **3** Simon Rattle. **4** Camden Town. **5** English Civil War. **6** Ragamuffins. **7** Ballet. **8** Rank. **9** Puerto Ricans. **10** Nottingham. **11** Beer selling establishment, Munich. **12** Three. **13** Short tennis. **14** Mosaic. **15** Wayne Sleep. **16** Blackpool. **17** Moscow. **18** Films – RKO. **19** Janet. **20** Essex. **21** Salzburg. **22** Daisy. **23** Kyoto. **24** USA. **25** Wireplay.

The Hard Questions

If you thought that this section of this book would prove to be little or no problem, or that the majority of the questions could be answered and a scant few would test you, then you are sorely mistaken. These questions are the *hardest* questions *ever*! So difficult are they that any attempt to answer them all in one sitting will addle your mind and mess with your senses. You'll end up leaving the pub via the window while ordering a pint from the horse brasses on the wall. Don't do it! For a kick off, there are 3,000 of them, so at 20 seconds a question it will take you over 16 hours, and that's just the time it takes to read them. What you should do instead is set them for others – befuddle your friends' minds.

Note the dangerous nature of these questions though. These are your secret weapons; use them accordingly unless, of course, someone or some team is getting your back up. In which case you should hit them hard and only let up when you have them cowering under the bench whimpering 'uncle'.

These questions work best against league teams. They are genuinely tough and should be used against those people who take their pub quizzes seriously. NEVER use these questions against your in-laws.

Quiz 1 80s Music

Level 3

1 Somewhere In My Heart was the only Top Ten hit for which group?
2 Who asked you to Kiss Me in 1985?
3 What was Amazulu's only UK Top Ten hit?
4 Whose Harbour was taken to No 10 in 1988 by All About Eve?
5 Who were on the Road to Nowhere in 1985?
6 Whose first UK Top Ten hit was The Look?
7 Who had a No 4 hit with (Something Inside) So Strong?
8 What was the first Top Ten UK hit for Heart?
9 What was the Pretenders first Top Ten hit of the 80s?
10 Which Soft Cell No 1 from 1981 got to No. 5 in 1991?
11 Who did some Wishful Thinking in their only UK Top Ten hit?
12 Which successful 80s band was fronted by Graham McPherson?
13 Which duo had a Top 20 hit from 1983 with First Picture Of You?
14 Who was Right Here Waiting on their first UK Top Ten hit from 1989?
15 Who was the only US act to achieve three successive UK No 1s in the 80s?
16 Which vocalist had a No 8 hit in 1987 with the Moonlighting theme?
17 Who had a US No 1 and a UK No 2 with Funkytown in 1980?
18 Which group had a No 5 in 1987 with It Doesn't Have To Be This Way?
19 Which female vocalist expressed Self Control in 1984?
20 Which artist spent the most number of weeks in the UK chart in 1989?
21 Which Pet Shop Boys video featured Sir Ian McKellen as Dracula?
22 Which song gave Steve Winwood his highest UK chart position?
23 What was the Oscar-winning song from Working Girl?
24 Who had a hit with Captain Beaky and Wilfred the Weasel in 1980?
25 Who requested 'If you'll be my bodyguard' in his No. 4 from 1986?

Answers

80s Music

1 Aztec Camera. **2** Stephen Tin Tin Duffy. **3** Too Good To Be Forgotten. **4** Martha's. **5** Talking Heads. **6** Roxette. **7** Labi Siffre. **8** Alone. **9** Talk of The Town. **10** Tainted Love. **11** China Crisis. **12** Madness. **13** Lotus Eaters. **14** Richard Marx. **15** Blondie. **16** Al Jarreau. **17** Lipps Inc. **18** Blow Monkeys. **19** Laura Branigan. **20** Bobby Brown. **21** Heart. **22** Higher Love. **23** Let The River Run. **24** Keith Michell. **25** Paul Simon

The Barlows – Round 3

1 What cause did Ken march for with his girlfriend Susan Cunningham in 1960?
2 Who was Ken and Valerie's bridesmaid in 1962?
3 Who did Frank Barlow become engaged to in 1963 after Ida died?
4 What ended David Barlow's football career?
5 Why did Ken go to prison for a week in 1967?
6 Who held Val Barlow hostage in 1968?
7 What was David and Irma's baby son (not seen on screen) called?
8 In which year did Uncle Albert die?
9 What did Albert's daughter Beattie give to Ken as a keepsake?
10 What was the name of Valerie Tatlock's mother?
11 Where were Valerie and Ken going to emigrate to before her death?
12 Who did Ken have an affair with in 1966 while still married to Val?
13 Who did Ken date in 1973 after being dumped by Elaine Perkins?
14 And who did he eventually dump that lady for?
15 What did Deirdre wear for her marriage to Ray Langton?
16 Why did Deirdre have a breakdown in 1977?
17 Why was the lorry crash of 1979 so traumatic for Deirdre?
18 Name the Dutchman that Deirdre dated briefly in 1981
19 What did Deirdre wear for her marriage to Ken?
20 Who were their bridesmaids?
21 Who was their best man?
22 Who once stood against Deirdre in the local elections?
23 Name the crooked businessman and amusement arcade owner that Deirdre dated in 1990
24 Name the plumber that Deirdre dated in 1990
25 How old was Ken when he became father to Daniel?

Answers

The Barlows – Round 3

1 Ban the Bomb. **2** Lucille Hewitt. **3** Christine Appleby. **4** A knee injury. **5** For taking part in a banned Anti Vietman demo. **6** Escaped prisoner Frank Riley. **7** Darren. **8** 1984. **9** His war medal. **10** Edith. **11** Jamaica. **12** Jackie Marsh. **13** Norma Ford. **14** Rita Littlewood. **15** A fawn suit. **16** She was molested. **17** She thought Tracy was trapped under the rubble. **18** Dirk Van Der Sterk. **19** A blue dress. **20** Tracy Langton and Susan Barlow. **21** Len Fairclough. **22** Alf Roberts. **23** Phil Jennings. **24** Dave Barton. **25** 55.

Quiz 3 The Royals

Level 3

1 Which monarch said, 'The thing that impresses me most about America is the way parents obey their children'?
2 Who said that pregnancy was, 'an occupational hazard of being a wife'?
3 Who wrote the words to 'I Vow to Thee My Country' which was sung at Princess Diana's wedding and at her funeral?
4 Who had the Queen for tea in her Glasgow council house in July 1999?
5 What is Princess Margaret's eldest grandson called?
6 Who was the first fund-raising manager of the Diana Memorial Fund?
7 How old was Elizabeth Taylor when she first danced in front of George V?
8 In which year was the TV film Royal Family made?
9 Who was George V's doctor who announced in 1936, 'The King's life is moving peacefully to its close'?
10 Which Earl owned a restaurant called Deals with Viscount Linley?
11 What was the name of the intruder found in the Queen's bedroom in 1982?
12 Where did the Queen, as Princess Elizabeth, spend her 21st birthday?
13 Which monarch asked a party leader to form the first Labour government?
14 Which Royal said 'I should like to be a horse' when asked her ambition?
15 Where was Princess Anne when she famous told journalists to 'Naff off!'?
16 What did Queen Mary reputedly describe to Stanley Baldwin as 'a pretty kettle of fish'?
17 Which Olympic athlete was born on the same day as Princess Diana?
18 What was Princess Michael of Kent's maiden name?
19 Which hospital was Princess Diana taken to after her tragic car accident?
20 In which city did the Queen say, 'I sometimes sense that the world is changing almost too fast for its inhabitants'?
21 Which lawyer presided over the divorce of Charles and Diana?
22 How old will the Queen be if she becomes the longest reigning monarch in British history?
23 Who was described by the Queen as, 'more royal than the rest of us'?
24 Who said, 'I don't feel relaxed at Buckingham Palace.... I don't expect anyone does when they visit their mother in law'?
25 For how long were Charles and Diana divorced?

Answers

The Royals

1 Edward VIII. **2** Princess Anne. **3** Cecil Spring-Rice. **4** Susan McCarron. **5** Samuel. **6** Paul Burrel. **7** Three. **8** 1969. **9** Viscount Dawson. **10** Lichfield. **11** Michael Fagin. **12** South Africa. **13** George V. **14** The Queen. **15** Badminton. **16** The abdication. **17** Carl Lewis. **18** Von Reibnitz. **19** La Pitie Salpetriere. **20** Islamabad. **21** Anthony Julius. **22** 89. **23** Princess Michael of Kent. **24** Mark Phillips. **25** One year.

Quiz 4 Pot Luck

Level 3

1 Which character opened the New York Stock Exchange on 8th June 1999?
2 What is the population of Austria to the nearest million?
3 What star sign is shared by Steve Bruce and Alex Ferguson?
4 Who had a UK No 3 hit with 7 Seconds in 1994?
5 Where are the 2004 Summer Olympic Games being held?
6 In which country was Yul Brynner born?
7 Which British character actor made his film debut in *The Maltese Falcon*?
8 According to the modern Olympics founder Baron de Coubertin, 'The essential thing is not conquering but...' what?
9 Who were England playing when David Gower did his Biggles impression?
10 In which decade was the Sydney Harbour bridge opened?
11 Which comedian has four initials, J P M S?
12 Vehicles from which country use the international registration letter RI?
13 In which movie did Garbo say, 'I want to be alone'?
14 Truax Field international airport is in which US state?
15 In the cartoon characters Pip, Squeak and Wilfred, what kind of creature was Pip?
16 What was ORAC?
17 When she died, how old was Karen Carpenter?
18 Which TV personality married hairdresser Stephen Way in 1998?
19 Who wrote, 'What is this life if full of care, We have no time to stand and stare?'?
20 Which paper's 17 June 1977 headline was (Prince) 'Charles To Marry Astrid – Official!'?
21 Which writer said, 'An atheist is a man who has no invisible means of support'?
22 Which country does the airline Ansett come from?
23 How many goals did Gary Lineker score for his country?
24 Which singer/actress began her career in the film *Here Come the Huggetts*?
25 What is Alexander McQueen's real first name?

Answers

Pot Luck

1 Noddy. **2** 8 million. **3** Capricorn. **4** Youssou N'Dour. **5** Athens. **6** Siberia. **7** Sydney Greenstreet. **8** Fighting well. **9** Queensland. **10** 1930s. **11** Julian Clary. **12** Indonesia. **13** Grand Hotel. **14** Wisconsin. **15** Dog. **16** A computer (in the Sci-Fi Tv show Blake's Seven). **17** 32. **18** Gloria Hunniford. **19** W H Davies. **20** Daily Express. **21** John Buchan. **22** Australia. **23** 48. **24** Petula Clark. **25** Lee.

Quiz 5 20th C Who's Who

Level 3

1 Who was Jeremy Thorpe talking about when he said, 'Greater love hath no man than this, that he lay down his friends for his life'?
2 Which major event was covered by war correspondent, Martha Gellhorn?
3 Who said, 'When you marry your mistress you create a job vacancy'?
4 Who was Tony Blair's first President of the Board of Trade?
5 Which title did Tony Benn relinquish to sit in the House of Commons?
6 What did Jorge Luis Borges refer to as 'a fight between two bald men over a comb'?
7 Who said, 'How can you rule a country which produces 246 different kinds of cheese?'?
8 To whom was Nancy Astor speaking when she said, 'You'll never get on in politics, my dear, with that hair'?
9 Who wrote a book on disarmament called *In Place of Fear*?
10 Who planned to be the Gromyko of the Labour Party for the next 30 years?
11 Whose last words were, 'Now it's on to Chicago and let's win there'?
12 Which woman was President of the Oxford Union in 1977?
13 Who put forward the industrial relations legislation *In Place of Strife*?
14 Who was the last emperor of Vietnam?
15 Who did Neil Kinnock say was 'a ditherer, a dodger, a ducker and a weaver'?
16 Who was the first freely elected Marxist president in Latin America?
17 Paddy Ashdown was in which military unit before entering politics?
18 Who was the official British observer of the atomic bomb at Nagasaki?
19 Who said, 'History is littered with wars which everybody 'knew' would never happen'?
20 Which US committee won the Nobel Peace Prize in 1997?
21 Who was First Secretary of State in John Major's last government?
22 Whose help in an election 'was like being measured by an undertaker'?
23 Who held the post of Minister of Technology from 1966–1970?
24 Who was runner up to John Major in the Personality of the Year award for 1996 organised by the Today programme?
25 Who said, 'There cannot be a crisis next week, my schedule is already full'?

Answers

20th C Who's Who

1 Harold Macmillan. **2** D Day landings. **3** James Goldsmith. **4** Margaret Beckett. **5** Viscount Stansgate. **6** Falklands conflict. **7** Charles de Gaulle. **8** Shirley Williams. **9** Aneurin Bevan. **10** Denis Healey. **11** Bobby Kennedy. **12** Benazir Bhutto. **13** Barbara Castle. **14** Bao Dai. **15** John Major. **16** Allende. **17** Royal Marines **18** Sir Leonard Cheshire. **19** Enoch Powell. **20** Land Mines. **21** Michael Heseltine. **22** Edward Heath. **23** Tony Benn. **24** Lisa Potts. **25** Henry Kissinger.

Quiz 6 Pot Luck

1 What was Elsie Tanner's favourite tipple?
2 Who killed Theresa the Turkey?
3 What was Spider's eco warrior girlfriend called?
4 Who said 'Tell me, where is the real Coronation Street.'?
5 Who shot himself after confessing to killing Steve Tanner?
6 Where did Angie Freeman go to after leaving Weatherfield?
7 What is Liz McDonald's maiden name?
8 Hilda won a trolley dash at the local delicatessan in 1976 – who helped her?
9 Who was delivery boy for Brendan Scott, who ran the Corner Shop in 1993?
10 What does 'dropped off t'hooks' mean?
11 Who sang 'We're a couple of Swells' in the 1984 Street talent contest?
12 Who took an exotic dancer for a housekeeper in 1989?
13 Who secretly kept a greyhound in Annie Walker's cellar?
14 Who fostered Vernon and Lucy Foyle in 1974?
15 How many lines of washing do we see in the last frame of the opening credits of Coronation Street?
16 In 1970 who told the Coronation Street women to withdraw all sexual favours over a football bus protest?
17 In 1968 Dot Greenhalgh had an American soldier as a boyfriend – name him.
18 What was Jackie Ingrams' middle name?
19 Which famous poem did Minnie Caldwell recite at the 1969 Rovers Christmas Party?
20 What did Stan and Hilda buy for their daughter Irma in 1965?
21 Who got into trouble with the Inland Revenue in 1989?
22 Who was caught shoplifting from Bettabuys?
23 In 1985 which schoolgirl fell under the spell of Terry Duckworth?
24 How did Hilda Ogden celebrate her 49th birthday?
25 Ken Barlow had to sell something off in March 1990 to help pay his mortgage – what was it?

Answers

Pot Luck
1 Gin and Tonic. **2** Les Battersby. **3** Log Thwaite. **4** The Queen. **5** Joe Donelli. **6** Mexico. **7** Greenwood. **8** Deirdre Langton. **9** Nicky Platt. **10** Died. **11** Vera and Ivy. **12** Alec Gilroy. **13** Fred Gee. **14** The Bishops. **15** Two. **16** Annie Walker. **17** Greg Flint. **18** Rachel. **19** The Owl and the Pussycat. **20** A partnership in the Corner Shop. **21** The Gilroys. **22** Vera Duckworth. **23** Andrea Clayton. **24** With a Barbara Cartland style party. **25** The Weatherfield Recorder.

Quiz 7 Soccer

Level 3

1 Denis Irwin joined Man Utd from which club?
2 What was the first London club that David Seaman played for?
3 Who was the first England player born after the World Cup triumph to become a full international?
4 In how many games did Mick Channon captain England?
5 Which country was the first to lose in two World Cup finals?
6 When did Scotland make their first appearance in the World Cup?
7 Who said, 'You're not a real manager until you've been sacked'?
8 In Germany in which decade was the Bundesliga formed?
9 Against which country was England's Ray Wilkins sent off?
10 What would Ryan Giggs' surname have been if he had used his father's name instead of his mother's?
11 Which club did Peter Beardsley join when he left Liverpool in 1991?
12 Steve Davis became a director of which soccer club in 1997?
13 Emmanuel Petit joined Arsenal from which soccer club?
14 When did Arsenal move to Highbury?
15 How many minutes of extra time were played in the Euro 96 final before Germany's Golden Goal winner?
16 Which team did Aberdeen beat in the 1983 European Cup Winners' Cup final?
17 Who did Billie Hampson play for in an FA Cup Final when aged nearly 42?
18 How many goals did Brian Kidd score for England?
19 In what decade was Scotland's first abandoned international match?
20 Who was the first Englishman to play for A C Milan?
21 How many of Gordon Banks's 73 England games ended in clean sheets?
22 Which Arsenal manager signed Dennis Bergkamp?
23 In which year did Wales make it to the World Cup final stages for the only time in the century?
24 Which team has played at home at Pound Park, Selhurst Park and Upton Park during the century?
25 Turek played in goal for which World Cup winning country?

Answers

Soccer

1 Oldham. **2** QPR. **3** Tony Adams. **4** Two. **5** Hungary. **6** 1954. **7** Malcolm Allison. **8** 60s. **9** Morocco. **10** Wilson. **11** Everton. **12** Leyton Orient. **13** Monaco. **14** 1913. **15** Five. **16** Real Madrid. **17** Aston Villa. **18** One. **19** 60s. **20** Jimmy Greaves. **21** 35. **22** Bruce Rioch. **23** 1958. **24** Charlton. **25** W Germany.

Quiz 8 Pot Luck

Level 3

1 In which country was Cyril Cusack born?
2 What star sign is shared by Maureen Lipman and Glenda Jackson?
3 Who or what are Pharos, Kelpe, Swift and Emma?
4 In which decade was the London Philharmonic Orchestra founded?
5 TV's *Yes Minister* took its title from the real-life writings of which Labour politician?
6 What is the population of Belgium to the nearest million?
7 Who had a UK No 1 hit with Hey Girl Don't Bother Me?
8 Who wrote the first theme music used in *The Sky at Night*?
9 Susan Ballion is better known by which name?
10 In which country is the Gladesville bridge?
11 Who directed *The Big Sleep* and *Gentlemen Prefer Blondes*?
12 Vehicles from which country use the international registration letter WG?
13 Who sang the theme song for *Trainer*?
14 What's the link between a certain Peter Scott and Lauren Bacall, Liz Taylor and Sophia Loren?
15 In which year was the talkie *The Jazz Singer* released?
16 In which city is the Burrows Toy Museum?
17 Who said, 'The great thing about the Spice Girls is that you can listen to them with the sound off'?
18 What was CBS TV news broadcaster Walter Cronkite's stock closing phrase?
19 Alborg Roedslet International airport is in which country?
20 What was Oliver Reed's real first name?
21 Tacoma international airport is in which US state?
22 Which country does the airline Sansa come from?
23 Who was England skipper in Terry Venables' first game in charge?
24 Who is the first composer to appear on a British banknote?
25 Which *Dad's Army* actor said he had conked out in *The Times* in 1983?

Answers

Pot Luck
1 South Africa. **2** Taurus. **3** Queen's corgis. **4** 40s. **5** Richard Crossman – in his diaries. **6** 10 million. **7** Tams. **8** Sibelius. **9** Siouxsie Sioux. **10** Australia. **11** Howard Hawks. **12** Grenada. **13** Cliff Richard. **14** He robbed them. **15** 1927. **16** Bath. **17** George Harrison. **18** And that's the way it is. **19** Denmark. **20** Robert. **21** Seattle. **22** Costa Rica. **23** David Platt. **24** Edward Elgar. **25** John Le Mesurier.

Quiz 9 Film Classics

Level 3

1 Which film classic took its name from Ernest Dowson's *Cynara*?
2 In *Casablanca,* who played Sam, who was asked to 'play it again'?
3 What was the first word in *Citizen Kane*?
4 Which 60s film told of the exploits of Robert Gold and Diana Scott?
5 In which film did Groucho Marx say, 'Either this man is dead or my watch has stopped'?
6 What was the motto of MGM?
7 What was Melissa Mathison's contribution to *E.T.*?
8 What are the final words of *The Face of Fu Manchu*?
9 The title of the movie *In Which We Serve* comes from which book?
10 'It was beauty killed the beast' was the last line of which film?
11 In which film did Bacall say to Bogart, 'If you want me, just whistle'?
12 'Mean, moody, magnificent.' was the slogan used to advertise which film?
13 In which film does the heroine say, 'I am big. It's the pictures that got small'?
14 Which character said, 'Love means never having to say you're sorry'?
15 What was the name of the very first sci fi movie made in 1902?
16 Who directed *The Day of the Jackal* in 1973?
17 About which film did Victor Fleming say, 'This picture is going to be one of the biggest white elephants of all time'?
18 In which film did Mae West say, 'Why don't you come up some time and see me.'?
19 In *Bringing Up Baby*, what is Baby?
20 Whose recording of a Bond theme reached highest in the UK's charts?
21 Which film finishes with Joe E. Brown saying 'Nobody's perfect' to Jack Lemmon?
22 What is the name of Katharine Hepburn's character in *The African Queen*?
23 About which film did Bob Hope say, 'I thought it was about a giraffe'?
24 Which company used the slogan A Diamond is Forever which Ian Fleming used for the book turned film *Diamonds Are Forever*?
25 In which film did Bette Davis say, 'fasten your seatbelts it's going to be a bumpy night'?

Answers

Film Classics

1 Gone With the Wind. **2** Dooley Wilson. **3** Rosebud. **4** Darling. **5** A Day at the Races. **6** Ars Gratia Artis. **7** Scriptwriter. **8** The world shall hear from me again. **9** Book of Common Prayer. **10** King Kong. **11** To Have and Have Not. **12** The Outlaw. **13** Sunset Boulevard. **14** Oliver. **15** Voyage to the Moon. **16** Fred Zimmerman. **17** Gone With the Wind. **18** She Done Him Wrong. **19** Leopard. **20** Duran Duran. **21** Some Like It Hot. **22** Rose Sayer. **23** Deep Throat. **24** De Beers. **25** All About Eve.

Quiz 10 CORONATION ST. Level 3

Early Days – 1962

1 Which actor played Dennis Tanner?
2 What was Harry and Concepta Hewitt's baby called?
3 What happened on the Hewitts' 1st wedding anniversary?
4 What was the name of Len Fairclough's first wife?
5 Who was Len's first apprentice when he started his own business?
6 What was the name of the raincoat factory where Christine Hardman worked?
7 How did Christine's husband Colin Appleby die?
8 Who played quiet Esther Hayes?
9 Who was Minnie Caldwell's lodger in 1962?
10 What was Swindley's Emporium named after Mr Papagopolus took over?
11 Which young girl became Leonard and Emily's assistant?
12 Who did she share a flat with?
13 What was the name of Jerry Booth's uncle, who was suspected of murdering his wife?
14 Who played Jerry Booth?
15 Why did Elsie Tanner split up with Bill Gregory?
16 Which wedding anniversary did Jack and Annie Walker celebrate this year?
17 What was the name of Len Fairclough's son?
18 Who was the bookie that Len fought with over Elsie Tanner's affections?
19 What outdoor job did Albert Tatlock take in 1962?
20 What was the name of the girl he befriended and later defended against her violent father?
21 What was the name of the short lived political party founded by Leonard Swindley?
22 What was the name of the play Leonard Swindley produced for the Mission Hall Players?
23 And who played the Duchess of Bannock in this play?
24 How did Ken Barlow offend the residents of Coronation Street in 1962?
25 What pet did Harry Hewitt swap his whippets for and call Lucky Lolita?

Answers

Early Days – 1962
1 Phillip Lowrie. **2** Christopher. **3** Christopher was snatched. **4** Nellie. **5** Jerry Booth. **6** Ellistons. **7** In a car accident. **8** Daphne Oxenford. **9** Jed Stone. **10** Gamma Garments. **11** Doreen Lostock. **12** Sheila Birtles. **13** Sam Leach. **14** Graham Haberfield. **15** He was married. **16** Silver. **17** Stanley. **18** Dave Smith. **19** Lollipop man. **20** Susan Schofield. **21** Progressive Property Owners Party. **22** Lady Lawson Loses. **23** Annie Walker. **24** He criticised the working classes in an article. **25** Greyhound.

Quiz 11 TV Soaps

Level 3

1 Which 60s pop star played a hairdresser in *Albion Market*?
2 Which ex-soap star used to host *The Saturday Banana*?
3 Which EastEnders actress recorded the song Little Donkey?
4 Who was the head of the sect which Zoe joined in *Coronation Street*?
5 Which soap actress switched on the Oxford Street Christmas lights in 1983?
6 Who played Mrs Eckersley in *Emmerdale* before becoming more famous in *EastEnders*?
7 As well as Liz McDonald, which other character has Beverley Callard played in *Coronation Street*?
8 Who played Malcolm Nuttall in *Coronation Street*?
9 Rosa di Marco in *EastEnders* was which assistant of *Dr Who* in a previous life?
10 Who did Angie leave Albert Square with as she headed for Majorca?
11 In which soap did Chris Lowe of The Pet Shop Boys appear as himself?
12 Which *EastEnders* character was played by David Scarboro until the actor's early death?
13 Which soap actress played Marsha Stubbs in *Soldier Soldier*?
14 What were the second surname Valene had in *Knot's Landing*?
15 Which actor who found fame as a soap star played DI Monk in the first series of *Birds of a Feather*?
16 Who left *EastEnders* and appeared in the drama Real Women?
17 What did Bill Roache alias Ken Barlow study at university?
18 The scorer Charles of *Telly Addicts* has been a regular in which soap for many years?
19 What was the name of the *EastEnders* video about the Mitchell brothers released in 1998?
20 In *EastEnders* what football team did Simon Wicks support?
21 What was Kylie Minogue's character's profession in *Neighbours*?
22 In what type of vehicle did Fallon leave at the end of *The Colbys*?
23 Which *Coronation Street* actor conducted the Halle Orchestra in 1989?
24 What is Sinbad's real name in *Brookside*?
25 In which soap was soap's first test tube baby born?

Answers

TV Soaps

1 Helen Shapiro. **2** Susan Tully. **3** June Brown. **4** Nirab. **5** Pat Phoenix. **6** Pam St Clement. **7** June Dewhurst. **8** Michael Ball. **9** Leela. **10** Sonny. **11** Neighbours. **12** Mark Fowler. **13** Denise Welch. **14** Gibson. **15** Ross Kemp. **16** Michelle Collins. **17** Medicine. **18** The Archers. **19** Naked Truths. **20** West Ham. **21** Car mechanic. **22** Flying saucer. **23** William Tarmey. **24** Thomas. **25** Crossroads.

Quiz 12 Pot Luck

Level 3

1 What is Ben Hollioake's middle name?
2 What is the name of the Westminster building near Big Ben designed to provide extra accommodation for MPS?
3 In which film did Mae West say, 'Beulah, peel me a grape'?
4 Sky Harbour international airport is in which US state?
5 Under what name did Karol Wojtyla become known to millions?
6 Who said, 'People who meet me for the first time leave thinking 'What a miserable git''?
7 What's the first word of Stand By Your Man?
8 What name did Amy Johnson's De Havilland Gipsy Moth have?
9 *Star Trek* actor DeForest Kelley wanted to train as what?
10 Actress Lucy Davis is the daughter of which comedian?
11 Michael Lubowitz is better known by which name?
12 Vehicles from which country use the international registration letter YV?
13 What star sign is shared by Dennis Taylor and Brendan Foster?
14 Amborovy International airport is in which country?
15 What is the most popular creation of Terry Nation?
16 What is the population of Brazil to the nearest million?
17 Who co-presented *Nice Time* with Kenny Everett and Jonathan Routh?
18 What was Harold Wilson's real first name?
19 Who had a UK No 1 hit with Seasons In The Sun?
20 Which element symbol Bk was discovered in 1950?
21 Sky Harbour international airport is in which US state?
22 In which city did Rudolf Nureyev seek asylum and defect to the West?
23 How many years were between Sir Harold Macmillan's maiden speeches in the Houses of Lords and Commons?
24 Who wrote the story *The Country Of The Blind*?
25 When did the Queen present her first Christmas Day TV broadcast?

Answers

Pot Luck

1 Caine. **2** Portcullis House. **3** I'm No Angel. **4** Arizona. **5** Pope John Paul II. **6** Rowan Atkinson. **7** Sometimes. **8** Jason 1. **9** Doctor. **10** Jasper Carrott. **11** Manfred Mann. **12** Venezuela. **13** Capricorn. **14** Madagascar. **15** The Daleks. **16** 158 million. **17** Germaine Greer. **18** James. **19** Terry Jacks. **20** Berkelium. **21** Arizona. **22** Paris. **23** 60. **24** H G Wells. **25** 1957.

Quiz 13 Around The UK

Level 3

1 Which UK holiday resort had the motto 'It's so bracing' from 1909?
2 Who created the Angel of the North?
3 What did the National Trust ban on its land in 1997?
4 Who designed Liverpool's Roman Catholic Cathedral?
5 Which London building designed by Alfred Waterhouse in the 19th century remains one of the most visited today?
6 In which city is the Bate Collection of Historical Instruments?
7 In which year was the first Mersey tunnel completed?
8 Where is the English end of the English Channel where it reaches its widest point?
9 Lots of people visit Alton Towers, but which county is it in?
10 Which architect was responsible for London's National Theatre?
11 In which county is the longest cave system in the UK?
12 Which London borough has the most blue plaques?
13 Who designed the eastern facade of Buckingham Palace early this century?
14 Edward Maddrell was the last Briton this century to have which language as his native tongue?
15 In which city is the world's oldest surviving passenger station?
16 In which Park are the Yorkshire based gardens of Tropical World?
17 Which city are you in if you visit the East Midlands Gas Museum?
18 To the nearest quarter of a million, how many people visited London Zoo in 1990?
19 In which city was the International Garden Festival held in 1984?
20 Which was the first of the UK cathedrals to charge admission?
21 How often does the Leeds International Pianoforte Competition take place?
22 Ben Nevis is the highest mountain in the UK, but which mountain comes next in height?
23 In which English county did Sir Robert Baden-Powell hold his first Scout camp in 1907?
24 Which city has the oldest public library in England?
25 In which country was Coventry Cathedral architect Basil Spence born?

Answers

Around the UK

1 Skegness. **2** Antony Gormley. **3** Deer Hunting. **4** Edwin Lutyens. **5** Natural History Museum. **6** Oxford. **7** 1934. **8** Lyme Bay. **9** Staffordshire. **10** Denys Lasdun. **11** West Yorkshire. **12** Westminster. **13** Aston Webb. **14** Manx. **15** Manchester. **16** Roundhay Park. **17** Leicester. **18** 1,250,000. **19** Liverpool. **20** St Paul's. **21** Every three years. **22** Ben Macdhui. **23** Dorset. **24** Manchester. **25** India.

Quiz 14 CORONATION ST. Level 3

Early Days – 1963

1 Who played singer Walter Potts – aka Brett Falcon?
2 What was the name of the song he performed in the show which also reached No. 17 in the UK charts.
3 Which *Coronation Street* character did a midnight flit to Liverpool, leaving his landlady broken-hearted?
4 Which rogue did Sheila Birtles fall in love with?
5 Who was the long-standing boyfriend that she dumped him for?
6 Who rescued Sheila when she attempted suicide?
7 What sort of shop did Frank Barlow open after resigning from the GPO?
8 Who did Jerry Booth marry after a whirlwind courtship?
9 Which actress played her?
10 Which house did they move into?
11 Who played Florrie Lindley?
12 Who was discovered to have played Lady Godiva in the 1933 Co-Op Pageant of the Ages?
13 Where was Concepta Hewitt from?
14 What was Harry Hewitt's job?
15 Who got drunk and assaulted a policeman on a trip to New Brighton?
16 Who played Lucille Hewitt?
17 Who almost had her furniture repossessed by bailiffs?
18 And who said at the time 'They can't take her bed or the tools of her trade and as far as (she's) concerned, that's the same thing'?
19 Who lived at No 3 in 1963?
20 Who played Jack Walker?
21 Who lived in the Corner Shop flat?
22 Who did Brett Falcon lodge with during his stay in Coronation Street?
23 Who played Sheila Birtles?
24 Who was Jerry Booth's best man?
25 Which actor – who later had a long role in *Coronation Street* in the 1990s – played Jerry's friend Vincent?

Answers

Early Days – 1963

1 Christopher Sandford. **2** Not too little, Not too much. **3** Jed Stone. **4** Neil Crossley. **5** Jerry Booth. **6** Dennis Tanner. **7** DIY. **8** Myra Dickenson. **9** Susan Jameson. **10** Thirteen. **11** Betty Alberge. **12** Annie Walker. **13** Ireland. **14** Bus Driver. **15** Albert Tatlock. **16** Jennifer Moss. **17** Elsie Tanner. **18** Ena Sharples. **19** Frank Barlow. **20** Arthur Leslie. **21** Doreen Lostock and Sheila Birtles. **22** The Tanners. **23** Eileen Mayers. **24** Dennis Tanner. **25** Geoff Hinsliffe (Don Brennan).

Quiz 15 90s

Level 3

1 What finally knocked (Everything I Do) I Do It For You off the No 1 position?
2 How many singles had the Manic Street Preachers put out before releasing a single that made the top three?
3 Before B*Witched, who last made the top twenty with a song called Rollercoaster?
4 Which UK male vocalist had a Peacock Suit at No 5 in 1996?
5 What was the first UK No 1 in the 1990s by Wet Wet Wet?
6 The theme from *Friends* was a No 3 hit for which group in 1995?
7 Who partnered Whitney Houston on When You Believe?
8 Which hit for D:Ream gave them their first Top Ten hit?
9 Which country was Rozalla from?
10 What was Snaps' first UK Top Ten hit?
11 What was the first record of the 90s to enter the charts at No 1?
12 Who was featured on Puff Daddy's Come with Me?
13 What was the second successive No 1 for Aqua?
14 Who covered You Might Need Somebody to No 4 in 1997?.
15 Who had a UK No 1 hit with Please Don't Go in 1992?
16 Who joined Cher, Chrissie Hynde and Neneh Cherry on Love Can Build A Bridge?
17 What was the follow-up to Saturday Night for Whigfield?
18 What nationality is Tina Arena?
19 Which Ace of Base hit was first to get into the Top Ten after All That She Wants?
20 Who sang with Elton John on his only Top Ten of 1996?
21 Who was the featured vocalist on the No 1 Killer by Adamski?
22 Whose first UK No 1 was Ice Ice Baby?
23 Who joined Debbie Gibson on You're The One That I Want?
24 What was Gina G's follow up to her Eurovision entry?
25 Which airline banned Liam Gallagher for life?

Answers

90s

1 The Fly. **2** 14. **3** Grid. **4** Paul Weller. **5** Goodnight Girl. **6** Rembrandts. **7** Mariah Carey. **8** Things Can Only Get Better. **9** Zimbabwe. **10** The Power. **11** Bring Your Daughter To The Slaughter. **12** Jimmy Page. **13** Doctor Jones. **14** Shola Ama. **15** KWS. **16** Eric Clapton. **17** Another Day. **18** Australian. **19** The Sign. **20** Luciano Pavarotti. **21** Seal. **22** Vanilla Ice. **23** Craig McLachlan. **24** I Belong To You. **25** Cathay Pacific.

Quiz 16 CORONATION ST. Level 3

Early Days – 1964

1 Where did the Hewitt family move to in 1964?
2 What did they do there?
3 Which member of the family opted to stay behind?
4 Who did she move in with?
5 What was the cause of the Booths' marital problems?
6 When they moved out, who bought their house?
7 What did Frank Barlow have to celebrate in May?
8 Who played Martha Longhurst?
9 What was the last thing Martha did in her last scene, just before she died?
10 Who opened a gambling club in the basement of Elliston's factory?
11 And who led the campaign against this?
12 Who did the Booths go to live with when they left Coronation Street?
13 Who was Minnie Caldwell's new lodger?
14 What was his job?
15 Who did Emily Nugent propose marriage to?
16 What happened on their wedding day?
17 What did Stan Ogden dig up in Albert Tatlock's back yard, causing the street to be evacuated?
18 What was the dramatic outcome of Elsie Tanner's affair with art teacher David Graham?
19 Which female character had a nervous breakdown?
20 Who played Cinderella in the Mission Hall Players' pantomime?
21 Who played the Prince in the same production?
22 What was Stan and Hilda Odgen's son called?
23 What was the name of the exotic dancer that Ken Barlow unsuccessfully tried to seduce in 1964?
24 In 1964 Valerie Barlow left Ken for his schoolteacher friend – what was his name?
25 What was the outcome of this?

Answers

Early Days – 1964

1 Ireland. **2** Run a garage. **3** Lucille. **4** The Walkers. **5** Money trouble. **6** The Ogdens. **7** A premium bonds win. **8** Lynne Carol. **9** Took off her glasses. **10** Laurie Frazer. **11** Ena Sharples and Leonard Swindley. **12** Myra's dad. **13** Charlie Moffitt. **14** Comic at the Viaduct Sporting club. **15** Leonard Swindley. **16** She stood him up. **17** An unexploded bomb. **18** He tried to kill her. **19** Florrie Lindley. **20** Lucille Hewitt. **21** Elise Tanner. **22** Trevor. **23** Pip Mistral. **24** Dave Robbins. **25** He sent her home to Ken.

Quiz 17 Famous Names

Level 3

1 Who said, 'An alcoholic is someone you don't like who drinks as much as you do'?
2 Who created the Mars bar?
3 What would Diane Keaton's surname have been if she had used her father's name instead of her mother's?
4 Who had the catchphrase 'nicky nokky, noo!'?
5 Who is the wife of Brian Blosil and father of their seven children?
6 Arnold Bax said one should try everything once except incest and what?
7 Who was dubbed the Brazilian Bombshell?
8 In 1998 who did *Vanity Fair* describe as 'simply the world's biggest heart throb'?
9 Whose business motto was 'Pile it high, sell it cheap'?
10 Who said 'I became one of the stately homos of England'?
11 Journalist Dawn Alford was responsible for 'trapping' which famous name in the late 90s?
12 How many days after Princess Diana's death was the death of Mother Teresa announced?
13 Which fellow politician was Kenneth Clarke's best man?
14 Which actor owned the restaurant Langan's Brasserie?
15 In which High Street store did Glenda Jackson work?
16 Which ex MP and broadcaster has a daughter called Aphra Kendal?
17 Which playwright went to the same school as Adrian Edmondson?
18 Michael Grade became a director of which soccer club in 1997?
19 Which American said, 'Boy George is all England needs; another Queen who can't dress'?
20 What do kd lang's initials stand for?
21 Whose portrait was removed from an exhibition called Sensation at the Royal Academy in 1997?
22 Which singer wrote the novel *Amy The Dancing Bear*?
23 Jeffrey Archer became Lord Archer of where on elevation to the peerage?
24 Who was John Major's last Heritage Secretary?
25 What part of his body did Keith Richards insure for £1 million?

Answers

Famous Names
1 Dylan Thomas. **2** Forrest Mars. **3** Hall. **4** Ken Dodd. **5** Marie Osmond. **6** Folk dancing. **7** Carmen Miranda. **8** Leonardo DiCaprio. **9** Jack Cohen. **10** Quentin Crisp. **11** William Straw. **12** Five. **13** John Selwyn Gummer. **14** Michael Caine. **15** Boots. **16** Gyles Brandreth. **17** Tom Stoppard. **18** Charlton Athletic. **19** Joan Rivers. **20** Kathryn Dawn. **21** Myra Hindley. **22** Carly Simon. **23** Weston Super Mare. **24** Virginia Bottomley. **25** Third finger, left hand.

Quiz 18 Pot Luck

Level 3

1 Which US First Lady said, 'No one can make you feel inferior unless you consent'?
2 Who brought to an end Jahangir Khan's long unbeaten run of success in squash in the 80s?
3 Which luxury did Esther Rantzen choose on *Desert Island Discs*?
4 According to Rudyard Kipling what were the 'two impostors' to meet and treat the same?
5 Peninsula international airport is in which US state?
6 What plant is tequila made from?
7 When was the Scrabble world championshiop first held?
8 Who wrote the novel *The Information*?
9 What did Abraham Saperstein start in January 1927?
10 What is Geoffrey Howe's real first name?
11 Who duetted with Barbra Streisand on Till I Loved You in 1988?
12 What are the international registration letters of a vehicle from Barbados?
13 What was David Bowie's last UK No. 1 of the 80s?
14 Where in England was Tom Courtenay born?
15 Jomo Kenyatta was born into which tribe?
16 What star sign is Prince Andrew?
17 Which European country was the first to allow women the vote?
18 Who was the defending champion when Bjorn Borg first won Wimbledon singles?
19 Arlanda International airport is in which country?
20 In which year was Grace Kelly born?
21 Which group recorded the first record played on Radio 1?
22 Which country does the airline TAAG come from?
23 What was first published on 21st December 1913 in the *New York World*?
24 Who directed *The Silence of the Lambs*?
25 What is Bob Wilson's middle name?

Answers

Pot Luck

1 Eleanor Roosevelt. **2** Ross Norman. **3** Bath salts. **4** Triumph and Disaster. **5** California. **6** Agave. **7** 1991. **8** Martin Amis. **9** Harlem Globetrotters. **10** Richard. **11** Don Johnson. **12** BDS. **13** Dancing In The Street. **14** Hull. **15** Kikuyu. **16** Pisces. **17** Finland. **18** Arthur Ashe. **19** Sweden. **20** 1929. **21** The Move. **22** Angola. **23** A crossword. **24** Jonathan Demme. **25** Primrose.

Quiz 19 US Presidents

Level 3

1 Which US President did Guiseppe Zangara attempt to assassinate?
2 Who was vice-president directly before Spiro Agnew?
3 Who used the line 'Randy, where's the rest of me?' as the title of an early autobiography?
4 Which US President had the middle name Wilson?
5 What day of the week was Kennedy assassinated?
6 Dean Acheson was US Secretary of State under which President?
7 Which US President was the heaviest?
8 Which President is credited with the quote, 'If you can't stand the heat get out of the kitchen'?
9 Who was the first assassin of a US President this century?
10 Who was the first US President to have been born in a hospital?
11 Which President conferred honorary US citizenship on Winston Churchill?
12 What did Ronald Reagan describe as a shining city on a hill?
13 Who said, 'A radical is a man with both feet planted firmly in the air'?
14 In 1996 who was Bob Dole's Vice-Presidential candidate?
15 Which US President was described as looking like 'the guy in a science fiction movie who is first to see the Creature'?
16 Who described Ronald Reagan's policies as 'Voodoo economics"?
17 What type of car was Kennedy travelling in when he was shot?
18 Which aristocratic title is one of Jimmy Carter's Christian names?
19 Al Gore was Senator of which state before becoming Bill Clinton's Vice-President in 1992?
20 How old was John F Kennedy's assassin?
21 Who was the Democrat before Clinton to be elected for a second term?
22 Who was Richard Nixon named after?
23 What was the name of the report into J F Kennedy's assassination?
24 What was the name of Kitty Kelley's biography of Jackie Kennedy Onassis?
25 Which president's campaign slogan was 'Why not the best'?

Answers

US Presidents

1 Roosevelt. **2** Hubert Humphrey. **3** Ronald Reagan. **4** Reagan. **5** Friday. **6** Truman. **7** William Taft. **8** Harry S Truman. **9** Leon Czolgosz. **10** Jimmy Carter. **11** Kennedy. **12** USA. **13** Roosevelt. **14** Jack Kemp. **15** Gerald Ford. **16** George Bush. **17** Lincoln. **18** Earl. **19** Tennessee. **20** 24. **21** FD Roosevelt. **22** Richard the Lionheart. **23** Warren Report. **24** Jackie Oh!. **25** Jimmy Carter.

Quiz 20 CORONATION ST. Level 3

Early Days – 1965

1 Who left Coronation Street to emigrate with her long-lost husband?
2 Who did she sell her business to?
3 Who told Elsie Tanner she was 'Nothing but paint and mush'?
4 Who played Lionel Petty?
5 What was the name of Lionel's daughter?
6 Who played her?
7 And which character was she in love with?
8 Which house collapsed in 1965?
9 And what did the council put in the gap for the next 17 years?
10 Which couple eloped in December?
11 Which popular *Coronation Street* actress was awarded an OBE in 1965?
12 Which babies were born this year?
13 Who inherited No. 11 from a member of the Mission Congregation?
14 And who was the tenant she tried to evict?
15 Who answered an ad to become Len Fairclough's housekeeper, but later became a partner in his business?
16 Who brewed beer in Minnie Caldwell's front room?
17 Who bought a 1959 Morris Minor called Annie and started driving lessons?
18 Who left school this year?
19 What was the name of Florrie Lindley's estranged husband?
20 Whose treasured coin collection was stolen by a vandal?
21 What was the name of Lucille Hewitt's first boyfriend?
22 Who took over as manager of Gamma Garments?
23 Who admitted 'I'm common as muck, me, and bloody proud of it'?
24 Who became chairperson of the Licensed Victuallers Association?
25 Who smashed Elsie Tanner's window with her handbag?

Answers

Early Days – 1965

1 Florrie Lindley. **2** Lionel Petty. **3** Len Fairclough. **4** Edward Evans. **5** Sandra. **6** Heather Moore. **7** Dennis Tanner. **8** Number 7. **9** A park bench. **10** David Barlow and Irma Ogden. **11** Violet Carson. **12** Peter and Susan Barlow. **13** Ena Sharples. **14** Elsie Tanner. **15** Jerry Booth. **16** Stan Ogden and Charlie Moffitt. **17** Emily Nugent. **18** Lucille Hewitt. **19** Norman. **20** Albert Tatlock. **21** Roger Wain. **22** Emily Nugent. **23** Irma Ogden. **24** Annie Walker. **25** Ena Sharples.

Quiz 21 Sport 90s Action Replay

Level 3

1 Who was the first driver in the 90s to win the first F1 race and not end the season as champion?
2 How many century breaks did John Higgins make in the 1998 World Championship?
3 At which ground did Brian Lara make his record innings of 375?
4 What was the score when England met Uruguay at Wembley in 1990?
5 Who won the first all-American French Open Men's Singles final for almost 40 years?
6 How many points did Damon Hill score in his season for Arrows?
7 In which sport did Eric Navet of France become a 1990 world champion?
8 Where did Jonathan Edwards set his 1995 triple jump world record?
9 Which jockey went flat out on the flat and set a record with 1068 rides in the 1992 season?
10 Who was Jeremy Bates' partner in winning the Australian mixed doubles?
11 After six consecutive finals, how many frames did Stephen Hendry win in the 1998 World Championship?
12 Up to his departure in Nov 98, how many years had Roy Evans been with Liverpool?
13 Who finally beat Bob Beaman's 20-plus-year long jump record?
14 Who hit a century in some 22 minutes in a county game in July, 1993?
15 Jim Leighton retired after winning how many Scottish soccer caps?
16 Which horse was Henry Cecil's first Oaks winner of the 90s?
17 Alec Stewart was captain for how many Tests?
18 Which horse finished second when Oath won the 1999 Derby?
19 Against which country did Ryan Giggs make his international debut?
20 Who were the first team in the 90s to bat first in a Nat West Final and win?
21 What is Linford Christie's best time for 100m?
22 In which sport have Uhlenhorst Mullheim dominated 90s Europe?
23 Which snooker star made a witnessed practice break of 149 in 1995?
24 Which American state renewed Mike Tyson's boxing licence in 1998?
25 Sanath Jayasuriyaset belted a limited overs century v Pakistan in 1996 off how many balls?

Answers

Sport 90s Action Replay

1 David Coulthard – in 1997. **2** 14. **3** Recreation Ground. **4** 2-1 to Uruguay. **5** Jim Courier. **6** 7. **7** Show jumping. **8** Sweden. **9** Michael Roberts. **10** Jo Durie. **11** 4. **12** 35. **13** Mike Powell. **14** Glen Chapple – of Lancashire. **15** 91. **16** Lady Carla. **17** 11. **18** Daliapour. **19** Germany. **20** Lancashire. **21** 9.87. **22** Hockey. **23** Tony Drago. **24** Nevada. **25** 48.

Quiz 22 Pot Luck

Level 3

1 Who was the next British Prime Minister after Arthur Balfour?
2 Who narrated *Stoppit and Tidyup*?
3 What was Brotherhood Of Man's last UK No 1 of the 70s?
4 What is Russ Abbot's real name?
5 From which country did Angola achieve independence in 1975?
6 Which novel written in 1813 was adapted into one of TV's hits of the 90s?
7 What first appeared in Ohio in 1914 to affect transport?
8 Who said, 'Anybody wishing to banish theft from the world must cut off the thief's hands'?
9 What star sign is Michael Caine?
10 Who wrote the novel *Evening Class*?
11 Which TV presenter was once in a group called Jet Bronx and the Forbidden?
12 What are the international registration letters of a vehicle from Belize?
13 Banting and Best pioneered the use of what?
14 What did Emma Forbes present on *Going Live!*?
15 Where in England was Dame Judi Dench born?
16 In which decade did *Billboard* magazine first publish an American hit chart?
17 Asmara International airport is in which country?
18 In which year did Andy Capp first appear in the *Daily Mirror*?
19 Which was the first European country to abolish capital punishmnent?
20 How many soccer World Cup campaigns was Walter Winterbottom involved with for England?
21 What was Enoch Powell's real first name?
22 Which country does the airline Air Pacific come from?
23 Which Irish TV celebrity received a Papal knighthood for charitable works?
24 On which lake was Donald Campbell killed?
25 Who directed the movie *La Dolce Vita*?

Answers

Pot Luck

1 Campbell-Bannerman. **2** Terry Wogan. **3** Figaro. **4** Russell Roberts. **5** Portugal. **6** Pride and Prejudice. **7** First traffic lights. **8** Ayatollah Khomeini. **9** Pisces. **10** Maeve Binchy. **11** Loyd Grossman. **12** BH. **13** Insulin. **14** Cooking. **15** York. **16** 30s. **17** Eritrea. **18** 1957. **19** Norway. **20** Four. **21** John. **22** Fiji. **23** Eamonn Andrews. **24** Coniston. **25** Federico Fellini.

Quiz 23 Who's Who?

Level 3

1 Who described his acting range as 'left eyebrow raised, right eyebrow raised'?
2 Which actor became playwright Arthur Miller's son-in-law in 1997?
3 Who played the King of Messina in the 90s *Much Ado About Nothing*?
4 Who said, 'I squint because I can't take too much light'?
5 Who was Geena Davis's husband when they made the loss maker *Cutthroat Island*?
6 In 1993 who tried to buy the rights of his first movie *Sizzle Beach USA*?
7 Which star of *The Krays* wrote a prose and poetry book called *America*?
8 Who owned the LA nightclub The Viper Room at the time of River Phoenix's death there in 1993?
9 Which future First Lady had walk-on parts in *Becky Sharp* and *Small Town Girl* in the 30s?
10 Who was described by co-star Nick Nolte as, '... a ball buster. Protect me from her'?
11 Which sportsman appeared as himself in the 1964 film *The Beauty Jungle*?
12 Which actress was Roger Moore's first Bond girl?
13 Who was the star of the film based on the record Harper Valley PTA by Jeannie C Riley?
14 Which actress is ex-beauty queen Miss Orange County 1976?
15 Which actress perished in the shower in the remake of *Psycho*?
16 Which film director was Anthony Quinn's father-in-law?
17 Who wrote the screenplay for *The Crying Game*?
18 Which novelist appeared in the film *Day For Night*?
19 What is Barbra Streisand's middle name?
20 How many films had Christopher Reeve made before *Superman* in 1978?
21 Who starred in Roger Vadim's remake of *And God Created Woman*?
22 Which actress wrote the novel *The Last of the Really Great Whangdoodles*?
23 Which film maker's first film was Pather *Panchali*?
24 Who did Winona Ryder replace on the set of *Mermaids*?
25 How is Paul Reubens also known in the film and TV world?

Answers

Who's Who?

1 Roger Moore. **2** Daniel Day-Lewis. **3** Richard Briers. **4** Clint Eastwood. **5** Renny Harlin. **6** Kevin Costner. **7** Steven Berkoff. **8** Johnny Depp. **9** Patricia Nixon. **10** Barbra Streisand. **11** Stirling Moss. **12** Jane Seymour. **13** Barbara Eden. **14** Michelle Pfeiffer. **15** Anne Heche. **16** Cecil B de Mille. **17** Neil Jordan. **18** Graham Greene. **19** Joan. **20** One. **21** Rebecca de Mornay. **22** Julie Andrews. **23** Satyajit Ray. **24** Emily Lloyd. **25** Pee Wee Herman.

Quiz 24 CORONATION ST. Level 3

Early Days – 1966

1 Which Coronation Street business re-opened as a PVC welding factory?
2 Who bought the Corner Shop after Lionel Petty sold up?
3 Which popular character returned to Coronation Street and announced his arrival by pushing his cap through his old landlady's letterbox?
4 What was the name of the Ogdens' lodger this year?
5 Which two longstanding *Coronation Street* characters went head to head in the local elections?
6 On finding they had equal votes, how was the outcome decided?
7 Which pair of rogues launched business schemes including luxury dog kennels, an auction room and the remodelling of old waxworks?
8 Who made her *Coronation Street* debut this year at the PVC factory and later re-appeared as a barmaid?
9 How did Ken Barlow meet Jackie Marsh?
10 Which respected character was in trouble for shoplifting tinned salmon?
11 What was the Mission Hall converted to this year?
12 What was the name of the lady who came to run the revamped hall?
13 Which local tradesman did she date before leaving for a life in Rome?
14 Who temporarily left her husband and returned to Coronation Street to stay with her mother?
15 What trauma happened to her 6-year-old son?
16 Who returned to Coronation Street and Jerry Booth's life?
17 What was her secret?
18 Who was behind the abusive phone calls to Elsie Tanner?
19 What was the dramatic denoument of these calls?
20 Why was Elsie menaced by some thugs from a casino?
21 Who bailed her out on both occasions?
22 Who played Ivan Cheveski?
23 Which three *Coronation Street* actors represented the show on a tour of Australia?
24 Who was diagnosed with a brain tumour?
25 Who went to a Boxing Day party as Queen Elizabeth I?

Answers

Early Days – 1966

1 Ellistons Factory. **2** David and Irma Barlow. **3** Jed Stone. **4** Jim Mount. **5** Annie Walker and Len Fairclough. **6** Tossing a coin. **7** Jed Stone and Dennis Tanner. **8** Bet Lynch. **9** She to interview David about football. **10** Ena Sharples. **11** Community Centre. **12** Ruth Winter. **13** Len Fairclough. **14** Linda Cheveski. **15** He fell in the canal. **16** Sheila Birtles. **17** She had a love child. **18** Moira Maxwell. **19** Moira threatened Elsie with a knife. **20** Dennis owed them money. **21** Len Fairclough. **22** Ernst Walder. **23** Arthur Leslie, Doris Speed and Pat Phoenix. **24** Vera Lomax. **25** Annie Walker.

Quiz 25 Famous Faces

Level 3

1 Which former Gladiator presented *Finders Keepers*?
2 What is Rowan Atkinson's middle name?
3 Which part of Dave Allen's body is partly missing?
4 Which TV interviewer was South of England show jumping champion in 1964?
5 Who designed the original *Blue Peter* badge?
6 Which Brit won the American Sportscasters' Association International Award in 1989?
7 Who played Pte Mick Hopper in *Lipstick on Your Collar* before shooting to film superstardom?
8 How old was Twiggy when she appeared on *This Is Your Life*?
9 Who was the first sports presenter on *Newsnight*?
10 What luxury did Bob Monkhouse choose on *Desert Island Discs*?
11 Whose TV debut was presenting Hippo on Sky's *Superchannel*?
12 Where does Roseanne have a tattoo of a pink rose?
13 Which star of *EastEnders* appeared on a Sammy Davis Jr Special along with Mandy Rice-Davies?
14 What was the Earl of Wessex's TV programme about his great-uncle called?
15 What was Jo Brand's profession before being a successful comic?
16 For which series did Emma Thompson win her second successive best actress BAFTA?
17 Which TV detective had received the George Cross?
18 Des O'Connor had a football trial with which club?
19 What was Zoe Ball's first children's show on terrestrial TV?
20 What relation is Jon to Peter Snow?
21 Which famous TV face was part of the girl band Faith, Hope and Charity?
22 Jim Davidson became a director of which soccer club in 1981?
23 Who presented the first edition of *News At Ten*?
24 Which character did Anthony Andrews play in *The Pallisers* before finding fame in *Brideshead Revisited*?
25 What was Trevor McDonald's codename for *This Is Your Life*?

Answers

Famous Faces

1 Diane Youdale. **2** Sebastian. **3** Finger. **4** Jonathan Dimbleby. **5** Tony Hart. **6** Harry Carpenter. **7** Ewan McGregor. **8** 20. **9** David Davies. **10** Picture of Marilyn Monroe. **11** Gaby Roslin. **12** Foot. **13** Wendy Richard. **14** Edward on Edward. **15** Psychiatric nurse. **16** The Fortunes of War. **17** Frost. **18** Northampton Town. **19** The O Zone. **20** Cousin. **21** Dani Behr. **22** Bournemouth. **23** Alastair Burnet. **24** Lord Stockbridge. **25** Burger.

Quiz 26 Pot Luck

Level 3

1 What was Bette Davis' real first name?
2 In which decade was Alzheimer's disease first clinically described?
3 What star sign is Glenda Jackson?
4 Who was the first British Prime Minister to be born overseas?
5 Robert Mueller Municipal Airport is in which US state?
6 Which sitcom star was married to script writer Jeremy Lloyd for only four months?
7 What was the first name of the original food manufacturer Mr Heinz?
8 How old was Ronald Reagan when he became US President?
9 Which country does the airline Garuda come from?
10 Which Brit broke the land speed record in 1990 in Thrust 2?
11 Who wrote *The Ghost Road*?
12 What are the international registration letters of a vehicle from Bahrain?
13 In which sport did Hollywood star Sonja Henie win Olympic Gold?
14 Which soccer side does Tim Vincent support?
15 In which brothers pop group was Craig Logan not a brother?
16 What was David Cassidy's last UK No 1 of the 70s?
17 Where in England was Albert Finney born?
18 In soccer, who holds Liverpool's league appearance record?
19 Balice International airport is in which country?
20 Panama proclaimed independence in 1903 from which country?
21 How old was Jimi Hendrix when he died?
22 Which sculptor died in a fire in a studio in the 70s?
23 Who directed *How The West Was Won*?
24 What is Christian Slater's real name?
25 Which song by a solo singer stopped Penny Lane from getting to No 1?

Answers

Pot Luck

1 Ruth. **2** First decade. **3** Taurus. **4** Bonar Law. **5** Texas. **6** Joanna Lumley. **7** Henry. **8** 69. **9** Indonesia. **10** Richard Noble. **11** Pat Barker. **12** BRN. **13** Ice skating. **14** Wrexham. **15** Bros. **16** Daydreamer. **17** Salford. **18** Ian Callaghan. **19** Poland. **20** Colombia. **21** 27. **22** Barbara Hepworth. **23** John Ford. **24** Christian Hawkins. **25** Release Me.

Quiz 27 Euro Tour

Level 3

1 In which city is the Glynn Vivian Art Gallery and Museum?
2 Which city did Truman Capote describe as 'eating an entire box of chocolate liqueurs in one go'?
3 Where in Europe is the Sikkens Museum of Signs?
4 Which monarch popularised the Homburg which came from the German town of the same name?
5 What is Switzerland's largest city?
6 Which city was the cultural capital of Europe in 1990?
7 Which architect designed the Pompidou Centre in Paris?
8 In which European city would you go to the Bardini Museum and the Bargello Museum?
9 What is the name of the lake which remained when the Zuider Zee was closed and reclaimed in 1932?
10 Which country was the first to break away from Yugoslavia after Tito's death?
11 Where is the Optimisticeskaja cave, the second longest in the world?
12 How many countries does the Danube pass through?
13 Which European country saw one of the major avalanches of the 20th century in December 1916?
14 What is the second largest of the Ionian Islands?
15 Where is Tingwall airport?
16 Where would you be if the Parliament was called The Althing?
17 Down which valley does the Mistral blow?
18 Inishmor is part of which island group?
19 Syracuse is part of New York, but where does it exist in Europe?
20 Which European country was first this century to give women the vote?
21 What is Europe's second largest city in terms of population?
22 Where would you spend stotinki?
23 Which French phrase described an innovative movement in the cinema?
24 Which was the first European city this century to open an underground railway system?
25 What is the longest river in Portugal, and the fifth longest in Europe?

Answers

Euro Tour

1 Swansea. **2** Venice. **3** The Hague. **4** Edward VII. **5** Zurich. **6** Glasgow. **7** Richard Rodgers. **8** Florence. **9** Ijsselmeer. **10** Slovenia. **11** Ukraine. **12** Seven. **13** Italy. **14** Corfu. **15** Lerwick. **16** Iceland. **17** Rhone. **18** Aran. **19** Sicily. **20** Finland. **21** London. **22** Bulgaria. **23** Nouvelle vague. **24** Paris. **25** Tagus.

Quiz 28 CORONATION ST. Level 3

Early Days – 1967

1 Who died when a train crashed off the viaduct?
2 Who rescued Ena Sharples when she was trapped under the debris?
3 Which couple fostered 11-year-old Jill Morris?
4 Who fell in love with Swedish sisters Inga and Karen Olsen?
5 Name Elsie Tanner's friend who accompanied her on dates with US servicemen.
6 What was the name of her American boyfriend?
7 And which actress played her?
8 Who opened a boarding house in his mum's home, taking in a family of acrobats and a girls' pipe band?
9 Who joined a marriage bureau?
10 Who played Elsie's wartime sweetheart and 2nd husband, Steve Tanner?
11 Who gave Elsie away at her wedding?
12 In which month did she get married?
13 Who died on the way to the wedding reception?
14 How did the tragedy happen?
15 Who was with him at the time?
16 Where did the Tanners emigrate to on Christmas Day?
17 Who had a nervous breakdown and was found in Liverpool in her slippers?
18 Who started a fire in Len's builders' yard?
19 Which street won the Best Kept Street this year – Rosamund or Inkerman?
20 Who was discovered squatting in No. 3?
21 Why were the Barlows divided over this family?
22 In which month did Vera Lomax die?
23 Who celebrated her 18th birthday this year?
24 Which character had a miscarriage?
25 Which building was condemned to demolition, making one of the residents homeless?

Answers

Early Days – 1967
1 Sonia Peters. **2** David Barlow. **3** David and Irma Barlow. **4** Dennis Tanner. **5** Dot Greenhalgh. **6** Gregg Flint. **7** Joan Francis. **8** Dennis Tanner. **9** Emily Nugent. **10** Paul Maxwell. **11** Dennis Tanner. **12** September. **13** Harry Hewitt. **14** He was crushed by a car. **15** Len Fairclough. **16** America. **17** Hilda Ogden. **18** His son Stanley. **19** Inkerman. **20** Betty Lawson and her children. **21** Ken wanted them evicted, Val didn't. **22** January. **23** Lucille Hewitt. **24** Irma Ogden. **25** The Mission Hall.

Quiz 29 Charts

Level 3

1 Who was the first female with two UK million-selling singles?
2 Which was the first Spice Girls hit which did not reach No 1?
3 Whose debut album Ten Good Reasons was the UK's top seller in '89?
4 Which female artist was the first to achieve 32 consecutive UK Top 10 hits?
5 Who was the first act to put his first eleven hits into the UK Top Ten?
6 Who topped the US chart in 1976 with the triple-platinum album Breezin'?
7 Who sang on at least one hit every year for 33 years?
8 Which band released the chart topping album Steeltown in 1984?
9 Which hit reached No 1 in the UK and US for Phil Collins?
10 Who was the first UK male to score two US Top Ten hits?
11 Whose debut single was How Do I Live?
12 Who had a UK No 1 in 1998 with You Make Me Wanna?
13 Who was the first act to release eight singles which entered at No 1?
14 Which group achieved the UK's biggest selling album of 1994?
15 What was on the original double A side of Prince's No 1 hit 1999?
16 What was the title of U2's third UK No 1?
17 Who was the first UK group to top the US chart after The Beatles?
18 Who was the first female to score twelve hits in the American Top Five?
19 Who, after Gerry and the Pacemakers, were first to reach No 1 with their first three releases?
20 Who had a UK No 10 hit in 1987 with Walk The Dinosaur?
21 What was the Monkees' first Top Ten UK hit after their first No 1?
22 What was the top selling single of 1998?
23 What was the Manic Street Preachers' second UK Top Ten hit?
24 Whose first UK Top Ten hit was You're Still The One?
25 What was the first Top Ten hit of the 90s for Michael Jackson?

Answers

Charts

1 Celine Dion. **2** Stop. **3** Jason Donovan. **4** Madonna. **5** Gary Glitter. **6** George Benson. **7** Diana Ross. **8** Big Country. **9** A Groovy Kind of Love. **10** Lonnie Donegan. **11** LeAnn Rimes. **12** Usher. **13** Take That. **14** Bon Jovi. **15** Little Red Corvette. **16** Discotheque. **17** Animals. **18** Olivia Newton-John. **19** Frankie Goes to Hollywood. **20** Was (Not Was). **21** A Little Bit of Me A Little Bit of You. **22** Never Ever. **23** A Design For Life. **24** Shania Twain. **25** Black or White.

Quiz 30 Pot Luck

Level 3

1 What was Phil Collins' last UK No 1 of the 80s?
2 What are Paul Ince's middle names?
3 Who discovered the layer of electrically charged particles in the upper atmosphere which now bears his name?
4 Since the first to 18 frames began in snooker's World Championship, who recorded the lowest losing score in a final?
5 What was replaced by Teletext Ltd in 1993?
6 In which year did Alcock and Brown make their Atlantic crossing?
7 Which singer wrote the musical *Someone Like You*?
8 In *Coronation Street,* how did Ken Barlow's first wife die?
9 Who created the St Trinians schoolgirls?
10 In which country is the Howrah bridge?
11 Who was the first person to fly at over 100 miles an hour?
12 What are the international registration letters of a vehicle from Brunei?
13 What was Oliver Hardy's real first name?
14 Who wrote *Babel Tower*?
15 Benito Juarez International airport is in which country?
16 Otis Barton was a pioneer in exploring where?
17 Where in England was Nigel Hawthorne born?
18 What would the Kelvin Scale have been called if it had adopted the originator's first name?
19 What is Sigourney Weaver's real name?
20 In which principal language did TV station S4C begin transmitting in 1982?
21 In which year were the first Winter Olympics?
22 Which country does the airline Gronlandsfly come from?
23 What star sign is Bob Carolgees?
24 Who directed *The Exorcist*?
25 What was Jeremy Beadle's profession when he worked in the circus?

Answers

Pot Luck

1 A Groovy Kind of Love. **2** Emerson Carlyle. **3** Edward Appleton. **4** John Parrot. **5** Oracle. **6** 1919. **7** Petula Clark. **8** Electrocuted with a hair dryer. **9** Ronald Searle. **10** India. **11** Lionel Twiss. **12** BRU. **13** Norvell. **14** A.S. Byatt. **15** Mexico. **16** Underwater. **17** Coventry. **18** William Scale. **19** Susan Weaver. **20** Welsh. **21** 1924. **22** Greenland. **23** Taurus. **24** William Friedkin. **25** Ringmaster.

Quiz 31 20th C Celebs

Level 3

1 Who said, 'Some women get excited about nothing – and then they marry him'?
2 What was the occupation of Roger Moore's father?
3 Which newspaper did Lord Linley sue in 1990?
4 What breed of dog was Barry Manilow's Bagel?
5 Who was fashion designer of the year in 1990?
6 Which White House resident's book was a bestseller in the late 80s?
7 Who was the fourth successive PM this century to go to a state school?
8 Who became Paul Mowatt's mother-in-law when he joined the Royal Family in the 90s?
9 Pamela Stephenson stood for Parliament for which party?
10 Which TV presenter owned a restaurant called Midsummer House?
11 Who was Jeremy Irons' best man?
12 What is the name of Dave Stewart and Siobhan Fahey's son?
13 Who said, 'I'd rather have a cup of tea than go to bed with someone – any day'?
14 Who is the famous mother of Elijah Blue?
15 Who designed Victoria Adams' wedding dress?
16 Which rock star did Cindy Crawford name her first son after?
17 What did Michael Jackson say instead of 'I do' when he married Lisa Marie Presley?
18 Who said, 'The only place a man wants depth in a woman is in her decolletage'?
19 In which Sydney cathedral did Michael Hutchence's funeral take place?
20 Who became chief designer at Givenchy in 1996?
21 Whose first West End club was the Hanover Grand?
22 Who was Axl Rose's famous singer father-in-law?
23 Who was Joaquim Cortes' girlfriend, who was rushed to hospital after a suspected overdose in 1997?
24 Who designed the dress which made the most at Diana's dress auction?
25 Richard Gere won a scholarship to the University of Massachusetts in which sport?

Answers

20th C Celebs

1 Cher. **2** Policeman. **3** Today. **4** Beagle. **5** Vivienne Westwood. **6** Millie the dog. **7** Thatcher. **8** Princess Alexandra. **9** Blancmange Thrower. **10** Chris Kelly. **11** Christopher Biggins. **12** Django. **13** Boy George. **14** Cher. **15** Vera Wang. **16** Presley. **17** Why not?. **18** Zsa Zsa Gabor. **19** St Andrew's. **20** Alexander McQueen. **21** Piers Adam. **22** Don Everly. **23** Naomi Campbell. **24** Victor Edelstein. **25** Gymnastics.

Quiz 32 CORONATION ST. Level 3

Early Days – 1968

1. What was put up in place of the demolished Mission Hall and warehouse?
2. Which family made their debut in the Corner Shop?
3. Which longstanding character married Jenny Sutton and moved to Bristol?
4. Who lost her cat and adopted a stray moggie called Sunny Jim?
5. Which character was played by Arthur Pentilow, who later became Mr Wilkes in *Emmerdale Farm*?
6. Which character was an alcoholic who left *Coronation Street* to move to a drying-out hospital?
7. Prim Emily Nugent fell in love with a Hungarian – what was his name?
8. Who did Len Fairclough take in as a lodger?
9. Whose wife tried to force a reconciliation with him days before the divorce was finalised?
10. Who temporarily took in Tommy Deakin's donkey, Dolores?
11. Which couple emigrated to Australia?
12. Which couple eloped to Gretna Green but didn't get married?
13. Which ex-girlfriend of Jack Walker moved in next door to Ena Sharples?
14. Who played Dickie Flemming?
15. What was his job?
16. Name the schoolgirl that he married
17. Which character was killed, sparking a police enquiry?
18. Which regular character was a suspect?
19. Who played Aladdin in a local production?
20. Who played Widow Twankey in the same play?
21. Who played Wishee Washee?
22. Who played Abanazer?
23. And who produced the play?
24. Who did Len Fairclough propose marriage to – only to be aghast when she accepted?
25. Who bought a window cleaning round from I-Spy Dwyer?

Answers

Early Days – 1968

1 Maisonettes. **2** The Cleggs. **3** Dennis Tanner. **4** Minnie Caldwell. **5** George Greenwood. **6** Les Clegg. **7** Miklos Zadic. **8** Ray Langton. **9** Jerry Booth. **10** Emily Bishop. **11** David and Irma Barlow. **12** Lucille Hewitt and Gordon Clegg. **13** Effie Spicer. **14** Nigel Humphries. **15** Engineering apprentice. **16** Audrey Bright. **17** Steve Tanner. **18** Len Fairclough. **19** Lucille Hewitt. **20** Stan Ogden. **21** Hilda Ogden. **22** Len Fairclough. **23** Emily Nugent. **24** Marj Griffin. **25** Stan Ogden.

Quiz 33 First 50 Years

Level 3

1 The British police adopted fingerprinting after it had been used where?
2 In what month was the attack on Pearl Harbor?
3 Which magazine ran the 'Your country needs you!' ad which was then used widely for recruitment?
4 What did the Labour Party change its name from after the 1906 Election?
5 Who was British PM when independence was granted to India and Pakistan?
6 In 1939 who described the actions of Russia as 'a riddle wrapped in a mystery inside an enigma'?
7 Whose epitaph reads 'Hereabouts died a very gallant gentleman'?
8 In which month did the 1951 election take place?
9 Who became mayor of Cologne in 1945?
10 At which Embassy did Kim Philby work with Guy Burgess after WWII?
11 In 1910 Paul Ehrlich developed a cure for which disease?
12 Who was Churchill referring to when he said 'never was so much owed by so many to so few'?
13 In Nazi Germany what was Endl slung?
14 Who founded the American Institution of Public Opinion in 1935?
15 Who was the first President of the National Union of Women's Suffrage Societies?
16 Who did L S Amery say 'In the name of God go!' to in 1940?
17 Which writer and politician became Lord Tweedsmuir?
18 At which British airport did Neville Chamberlain wave the Munich agreement in 1938 believing he had averted war?
19 'A bridge too far' referred to airborne landings in which country?
20 Which future MP was president of the Oxford Union in 1947?
21 On whose tomb are the words 'They buried him among Kings because he had done good toward God and toward his house'?
22 'Tora tora tora' was the signal to attack Pearl Harbor, but what does it mean?
23 Who said Chamberlain was 'a good mayor of Birmingham in an off year'?
24 The Rotary Club was founded in 1905 in which American city?
25 Who was Hitler's Prime Minister in Prussia?

Answers

First 50 Years

1 India. **2** December. **3** London Opinion. **4** Labour Representative Committee. **5** Attlee. **6** Churchill. **7** Captain Oates. **8** October. **9** Konrad Adenauer. **10** Washington. **11** Syphilis. **12** RAF pilots in the Battle of Britain. **13** The Final Solution. **14** Gallup. **15** Millicent Fawcett. **16** Neville Chamberlain. **17** John Buchan. **18** Heston. **19** Netherlands. **20** Tony Benn. **21** Unknown Soldier. **22** Tiger. **23** Lloyd George. **24** Chicago. **25** Goering.

Quiz 34 Pot Luck

Level 3

1 Who said, 'It is better to die on your feet than live on your knees'?
2 In which decade did motor car pioneer Henry Ford die?
3 What is Viv Richard's real first name?
4 On what date in 1969 did Neil Armstrong first set foot on the moon?
5 What star sign is Barry Norman?
6 What was the day job that Boris Yeltsin started out with?
7 Where did Tessa Sanderson finish in the 1992 Olympics?
8 Which supermodel said, 'I look very scary in the mornings'?
9 What position did Alfred Austin hold from 1896 to 1913?
10 Which Spice Girl appeared in *Emmerdale* as an extra?
11 What nationality were Mother Teresa's parents?
12 What are the international registration letters of a vehicle from The Bahamas?
13 What was Jason Donovan's last UK No 1 of the 80s?
14 In which year did Tanganyika and Zanzibar merge to form Tanzania?
15 Who wrote the novel *Love Solves The Problem*?
16 Bandar Seri Begawan International airport is in which country?
17 Who presented sport on *Saturday Superstore*?
18 Where in England was Bob Hoskins born?
19 What was special about Fred Balasare's 1962 Channel swim?
20 What is Diane Keaton's real name?
21 Lincoln international airport is in which US state?
22 Which country hosted the very first Eurovision Song Contest?
23 How many teams contested the first World Cup held in 1930?
24 Who was Richard Nixon's Vice-President from 1973 to 1974?
25 Who directed *The Sting*?

Answers

Pot Luck

1 Emiliano Zapata. **2** 40s. **3** Isaac. **4** July 20th. **5** Leo. **6** Builder. **7** 4th. **8** Linda Evangelista. **9** Poet Laureate. **10** Mel B. **11** Albanian. **12** BS. **13** Sealed With A Kiss. **14** 1964. **15** Barbara Cartland. **16** Brunei. **17** David Icke. **18** Bury St Edmunds. **19** Swam underwater. **20** Diane Hall. **21** Nebraska. **22** Switzerland. **23** 13. **24** Gerald Ford. **25** George Roy Hill.

Quiz 35 Sport Who's Who

Level 3

1 Who was the last person to score for both teams in an FA Cup Final?
2 Which England cricket captain has played hockey for London University?
3 Who was the oldest British Open winner of the century?
4 Which sportswoman wrote the novel *Total Zone*?
5 Who was the first winner of the first to 18 frames format in snooker's World Championship?
6 Who was the only American Wimbledon men's singles champion of the 60s?
7 Who said, 'The atmosphere is so tense you could cut it with a cricket stump'?
8 Who was the first National Hunt jockey to reach 1000 wins?
9 Who was the winner of the last Open at Carnoustie before Paul Lawrie?
10 Bill Beaumont established the then record for captaining England – how many times?
11 Who is the youngest ever Wightman Cup player?
12 Who was hacked down when Scholes got his second England booking v Sweden?
13 Roberto Rempi was the doctor of which sportsperson in a 90s drugs row?
14 Who won the Oaks on Dunfermline, Sun Princess and Unite?
15 Which record breaker became Master of Pembroke College, Oxford in the 80s?
16 Arnaud Massey is the only Frenchman to have won what?
17 Which snooker champion was a torch-bearer at the 1956 Melbourne Olympics?
18 John Potter has been England's most capped player in which sport?
19 Who was the British soccer manager sacked by Real Madrid in 1990?
20 Who was champion jockey on the flat five times in the 50s?
21 Who was Ole Gunnar Solskjaer playing for before he joined Man Utd?
22 Who scored England's winner in Italia 90 v Egypt?
23 Who was runner-up when Niki Lauda won his last F1 championship?
24 What is Brian Lara's middle name?
25 Who rode Arkle to a hat trick of Cheltenham Gold Cup triumphs?

Answers

Sport Who's Who

1 Gary Mabbutt. **2** David Gower. **3** Robert de Vincenzo - 44 years 93 days. **4** Martina Navratilova. **5** Cliff Thorburn. **6** Chuck McKinley. **7** Murray Walker. **8** Stan Mellor. **9** Tom Watson. **10** 21. **11** Jennifer Capriati. **12** Schwarz. **13** Marco Pantani. **14** Willie Carson. **15** Roger Bannister. **16** Golf's British Open. **17** Eddie Charlton. **18** Hockey. **19** John Toshack. **20** Doug Smith. **21** Molde. **22** Mark Wright. **23** Alain Prost. **24** Charles. **25** Pat Taffe.

Quiz 36 Pot Luck

Level 3

1 What star sign is shared by John Major and Sir David Frost?
2 Which character was on the first cover of the *Beano*?
3 What is the population of India to the nearest million?
4 What is Fidel Castro's real first name?
5 At which hospital did the first heart transplant take place?
6 Who had a UK No 1 hit with Free?
7 Which British news reader interviewed Saddam Hussein just before the Gulf War?
8 What did Anne Robinson report on on *Breakfast Time*?
9 Who was the next British Prime Minister after Ramsay Macdonald?
10 In which country is the Humen bridge?
11 Who has been Pope longest in the 20th C?
12 Vehicles from which country use the international registration letter RCB?
13 What did the M stand for in J M Barrie's name?
14 Who was in charge at Blackburn after Roy Hodgson's sacking and before Brian Kidd's arrival?
15 Whose autobiography was called *Addicted*?
16 Bill Skate and Julius Chan had been 90s Prime Ministers of which country?
17 Which veteran rock musician said, 'If I had my time again I would like to take up archaeology'?
18 Which future film star played Angela Reid in *Emmerdale*?
19 Bole International airport is in which country?
20 How many caps did Bobby Robson gain as an England player?
21 Which British fashion designer received her OBE on 15th December 1992?
22 Hubert Humphrey was Vice-President to which US President?
23 What is Robson Green's middle name?
24 Which country does the airline Kiwi International Airlines come from?
25 In which year was the State Opening of Parliament televised for the first time?

Answers

Pot Luck

1 Aries. **2** Big Eggo – an ostrich. **3** 953 million. **4** Ruz. **5** Groote Schuur. **6** Deniece Williams. **7** Trevor McDonald. **8** TV. **9** Baldwin. **10** China. **11** John Paul II. **12** Congo. **13** Matthew. **14** Tony Parkes. **15** Tony Adams. **16** Papua New Guinea. **17** Bill Wyman. **18** Joanne Whalley. **19** Ethiopia. **20** 20. **21** Vivienne Westwood. **22** Lyndon Johnson. **23** Golightly. **24** USA. **25** 1958.

Quiz 37 Musical Movies

Level 3

1 Who directed *Finian's Rainbow,* his first film for a major studio?
2 Who directed the 2001 musical *Moulin Rouge*?
3 Where in Europe was much of *Evita* filmed?
4 Who directed the film version of *Hair*?
5 Which musical was Victor Fleming making the same time as he was making *Gone With the Wind*?
6 What was Xanadu in the title of the film?
7 Who was the voice of O'Malley in The *Aristocats*?
8 In which 70s musical did Paul Michael Glaser star?
9 How many different hats does Madonna wear in *Evita*?
10 Who played the title role in the film version of *Jesus Christ Superstar*?
11 In *Cabaret,* what was the profession of Sally Bowles' father?
12 In which film was chorus girl Peggy Sawyer told to 'come back a star!'?
13 What are the last lines of *My Fair Lady*?
14 What was the name of the brothel in *The Best Little Whorehouse in Texas*?
15 Which musical includes the lines 'Got no cheque books, got no banks. Still I'd like to express my thanks'?
16 What was the name of the butler in *The Rocky Horror Picture Show*?
17 Which Club featured in *Cabaret*?
18 'The corn is as high as an elephant's eye' is in which musical?
19 Who was the male star of the movie *The Man of La Mancha*?
20 What was the name of Bob Fosse's character in *All That Jazz*?
21 In *Saturday Night Fever* where does Tony work by day?
22 *A Little Night Music* was based on which non-musical film?
23 What was the name of the sax player in New York New York who fell for Francine?
24 Who was the father-in-law of the male star of *Grease 2*?
25 In *The Muppet Movie* what was the name of the restaurant Doc Hopper wanted to open?

Answers

20th C Musical Movies

1 Francis Ford Coppola. **2** Baz Luhrmann. **3** Hungary. **4** Milos Forman. **5** The Wizard of Oz. **6** Roller disco. **7** Phil Harris. **8** Fiddler on the Roof. **9** 39. **10** Ted Neeley. **11** US diplomat. **12** 42nd Street. **13** Where the devil are my slippers. **14** Chicken Ranch. **15** Annie Get Your Gun. **16** Riff Raff. **17** Kit Kat. **18** Oklahoma. **19** Peter O'Toole. **20** Joe Gideon. **21** DIY store. **22** Smiles of a Summer Night. **23** Jimmy. **24** John Mills – star was Maxwell Caulfield. **25** Frogs' Legs.

Quiz 38 CORONATION ST. Level 3

Early Days – 1969

1 What sort of shop did Ernie Bishop own on Rosamund Street?
2 Who was exposed as a bigot when her son got engaged to Chinese Jasmine Choong?
3 What was the result of her outburst?
4 Which bride was jilted as she tried on her wedding dress?
5 What happened to the cowardly groom?
6 Which long term character made her debut in the Rovers this year?
7 Who was forced into proposing to Alice Pickens?
8 Who played Alice?
9 Why was the marriage called off?
10 What disaster happened during a coach trip to the Lakes?
11 Who suffered a spinal injury in the coach crash and ended up in a wheelchair?
12 Who did Elsie work for and fall in love with this year?
13 Who played the lucky man?
14 What was his profession?
15 Who called off his unwanted engagement by pretending to have two sons?
16 Whose sister arrived in Coronation Street on the run from her probation officer and stole a car?
17 What was her name?
18 Who ran away after Dave Smith harangued her for a gambling debt?
19 Who – besides Lucille – was lodging at the Rovers this year?
20 Whose get rich quick schemes included antique dealing and street photography with a monkey called Marlon?
21 Who did Audrey Flemming cheat on her husband with?
22 Sandra and Bernard Butler were the niece and nephew of who?
23 Whose estranged wife arrived and asked for a divorce?
24 Who did she cite as co-respondent?
25 Who appeared as Hylda Baker and Cynthia in the Christmas Eve concert?

Answers

Early Days – 1969
1 Camera shop. **2** Annie Walker. **3** Jasmine called off the engagement. **4** Lucille Hewitt. **5** He moved to London. **6** Betty Turpin. **7** Albert Tatlock. **8** Doris Hare. **9** The vicar was late and they changed their minds. **10** It Crashed. **11** Ray Langton. **12** Alan Howard. **13** Alan Browing. **14** Hairdresser. **15** Len Fairclough. **16** Ray Langton's. **17** Janice. **18** Minnie Caldwell. **19** Emily Nugent. **20** Stan Ogden. **21** Ray Langton. **22** Elsie. **23** Dave Smith. **24** Elsie Tanner. **25** Irma Barlow and Bernard Butler.

Quiz 39 Quiz & Game Shows

Level 3

1 What were Neil and Christine Hamilton presented with when they appeared on *Have I Got News For You*?
2 What was the name of the quiz show on *Crackerjack*?
3 Which record was broken on the first *Record Breakers*?
4 Who presented the first edition of *The Golden Shot*?
5 *Mastermind* champion Christopher Hughes followed which profession?
6 Which quiz of the 80s was hosted by *Angela Rippon*?
7 Which US show was *University Challenge* based on?
8 Which show was based on a Dutch programme called *One From Eight*?
9 In the very first *University Challenge* Reading played who?
10 Which Radio 5 Live presenter was the first UK host of *Wheel of Fortune*?
11 Who is acknowledged as the creator of *Countdown*?
12 For how many years were there female winners of *Mastermind* before the programme had its first male winner?
13 On which part of *Double Your Money* could you win the £1,000?
14 Who hosted ITV's early rival to *Telly Addicts, We Love TV*?
15 Which female joined Jeremy Beadle on *Game For A Laugh* after Sarah Kennedy?
16 Which show offered losers a Dusty Bin?
17 What was the junior version of *Big Break* called?
18 Who presented *Ice Warriors*?
19 What surname did Malandra Burrows, later of *Emmerdale*, use when she appeared on *New Faces* aged nine?
20 Who replaced Terry Wogan on *Blankety Blank*?
21 Who first presented *The Price is Right* in the UK?
22 Which celebrity chef produced the first recipe book spin-off from *Ready Steady Cook* with Brian Turner?
23 Who was the very first woman to be a *Call My Bluff* team captain, albeit for a one-off special?
24 Who hosted *What's My Line*? when it was revived yet again in 1994?
25 Who did Carol Smillie replace on *Wheel of Fortune*?

Answers

Quiz and Game Shows
1 Brown envelopes. **2** Double or Drop. **3** Biggest one man band. **4** Jackie Rae. **5** Train driver. **6** Masterteam. **7** College Bowl. **8** The Generation Game. **9** Leeds. **10** Nicky Campbell. **11** Armand Jammot. **12** Three. **13** Treasure Trail. **14** Gloria Hunniford. **15** Rustie Lee. **16** 3-2-1. **17** Big Break - Stars of the Future. **18** Dani Behr. **19** Newman. **20** Les Dawson. **21** Leslie Crowther. **22** Anthony Worrall Thompson. **23** Joanna Lumley. **24** Emma Forbes. **25** Angela Ekaette.

Quiz 40 Pot Luck

Level 3

1 What was John Major's father's profession in the circus?
2 How old was George Gershwin when he died?
3 Who won the 90s European Cup Final staged at Wembley?
4 In which country did Paris-born Paul Gaugin spend his childhood?
5 Who was US President at the start of the 20th C?
6 Here we ask what was the year, when Rupert Bear did first appear?
7 Which actress's real name is Ilynea Lydia Mironoff?
8 Which ex-Prime Minister became the first Earl of Bewdley?
9 Eugene Wiedmann was the last person to meet his death how in 1939?
10 Which country does the airline Linjeflyg come from?
11 Which knight has appeared on *Baywatch*?
12 Vehicles from which country use the international registration letter RCH?
13 What is John Humphry's real first name?
14 Who had a UK No 1 hit with Ring My Bell?
15 Whose alter ego was Gayle Tuesday?
16 What star sign is shared by William Shatner and Marlon Brando?
17 What is the population of Iran to the nearest million?
18 Which game show did Annabel Croft star in after *Treasure Hunt*?
19 Bromma International airport is in which country?
20 On 26th October in which year did the Beatles receive their MBEs?
21 In the classic sitcom *Mr Ed*, what did Mr Ed call Wilbur?
22 In which decade was the Tay road bridge opened?
23 What was patented in 1903 by Italian merchant Italio Marcione?
24 In which country was Audrey Hepburn born?
25 What is Keanu Reeves' real name?

Answers

Pot Luck 20

1 Trapeze artist. **2** 38. **3** Barcelona - in 1992. **4** Peru. **5** William McKinley. **6** 1920. **7** Helen Mirren. **8** Stanley Baldwin. **9** Guillotined. **10** Sweden. **11** Sir Paul McCartney. **12** Chile. **13** Desmond. **14** Anita Ward. **15** Brenda Gilhooly. **16** Aries. **17** 62 million. **18** Interceptor. **19** Sweden. **20** 1965. **21** Buddy Boy. **22** 1960s. **23** Ice Cream Cone. **24** Belgium. **25** Keanu Reeves.

Quiz 41 On the Road

Level 3

1 Which tree features most frequently in London street names?
2 In which year was the National Parks and Access to the Countryside Act passed?
3 In 1983 which car company ran an April Fool's day ad for an open top car that kept out the rain?
4 The fastest man on land at the beginning of this century came from which country?
5 Which town did Britain's first motorway bypass?
6 Which was the last country in mainland Europe to switch to driving on the left?
7 In what year did the millionth Volkswagen roll off the assembly line?
8 In which country were motorised ambulances first used?
9 By the end of the 80s, what percentage of British households had two cars?
10 When did the first Morris car appear?
11 Which work designed by Aston Webb do people drive under in London?
12 Which Asian country has the longest road network?
13 Where was the world's first production line producing Model T Fords?
14 According to a 50s ad, what was the loudest noise in the new Rolls Royce?
15 Where was Stenson Cooke's signature seen by motorists in the early years of the century?
16 What was the starting price for a Morris Cowley when it came off the production line in 1920?
17 Who was the President of the AA at the beginning of the 1990s?
18 When were yellow lines used as parking restrictions on Britain's roads?
19 How old must you be to accompany a learner driver?
20 In which city was the first Model T produced outside the USA?
21 Which celebrity chose a motorway service station as a luxury when he appeared on *Desert Island Discs*?
22 In which city is the Blackfriars Museum of Antiquities?
23 What animal appears on a road sign to show there are wild animals?
24 Where were London's first traffic lights installed in 1926?
25 Which company manufactured the first car to run on diesel?

Answers

On the Road

1 Elm. **2** 1949. **3** BMW. **4** Belgium. **5** Preston. **6** Sweden. **7** 1955. **8** France. **9** 20%. **10** 1913. **11** Admiralty Arch. **12** India. **13** Detroit. **14** Electric clock. **15** First AA badge – he was its secretary. **16** £165. **17** Duke of Kent. **18** 1958. **19** 21. **20** Manchester. **21** Noel Edmonds. **22** Newcastle. **23** Stag. **24** Piccadilly Circus. **25** Mercedes Benz.

Quiz 42 CORONATION ST. Level 3

Early Days – 1970

1 Who died abroad this year?
2 Who died (off screen) in Derby?
3 Which popular character returned to *Coronation Street* after a one-off appearance in 1966?
4 Who did Ray Langton become engaged to?
5 Why was the wedding cancelled?
6 Who asked Elsie to move to Portugal with him?
7 Who kidnapped baby Anthony Lock?
8 Who looked after Tommy Deakin's greyhound, and overfed it until it couldn't race?
9 Where did Elsie and Alan Howard go for their honeymoon?
10 What was the name of Alan's teenage son who came to live with them?
11 Who returned from London and bought the Canal Garage?
12 Who resigned from his job after attacking a man who stalked his wife?
13 Who did Handel Gartside fall for when he returned to Weatherfield?
14 Who stood by 12-year-old Tony Parsons and talked the local school into giving him a music scholarship?
15 Who had a passionate affair with jailbird Frank Bradley?
16 Which actor played club entertainer Mickey Malone?
17 Who was arrested after throwing a brick through a police car window?
18 Who gave Val Barlow driving lessons?
19 Which character had to undergo emergency surgery for appendicitis?
20 What was the name of the troublesome pensioner Lucille Hewitt tried to help?
21 Which US army deserter dated Irma Barlow?
22 What unsolved crime did he later confess to?
23 Who did he hold at gunpoint?
24 How did he die?
25 Who took a sabbatical in New York to study education techniques?

Answers

Early Days – 1970

1 David and Darren Barlow. **2** Jack Walker. **3** Bet Lynch. **4** Sandra Butler. **5** She found out about his fling with Audrey Flemming. **6** Bill Gregory. **7** Irma Barlow. **8** The Ogdens. **9** Paris. **10** Mark. **11** Billy Walker. **12** Cyril Turpin. **13** Minnie Caldwell. **14** Ena Sharples. **15** Bet Lynch. **16** Bill Maynard. **17** Lucille Hewitt. **18** Ray Langton. **19** Susan Barlow. **20** Arthur Noblett. **21** Joe Donelli. **22** Steve Tanner's murder. **23** Minnie Caldwell and Stan Ogden. **24** He shot himself. **25** Ken Barlow.

Quiz 43 Legends

Level 3

1 Who has accumulated the most UK and US Top 10 albums and grossed most income from foreign touring?
2 Who was Elton John's early idol?
3 Which superstar fronted The Nomads and Blackjack before going solo?
4 Who was posthumously awarded a Lifetime Achievement Grammy in 1996?
5 Who compered Buddy Holly's only UK tour?
6 Which artist has spent most weeks in the UK Top Ten?
7 Who married Julianne Phillips in May 1985 in Oregon?
8 Who issued bonds in his name for people to invest in in 1997?
9 Who was the first group to hold the top two US and UK album places on the week of release?
10 Which duo were joined by Tammy Wynette on their No 2 in 1991?
11 Who won the BRIT award for Outstanding Contribution to British Music in 1996?
12 Who had a record eight albums simultaneously in the UK chart three months after his death?
13 Which name links Whitney Houston's childhood nickname with her TV production company?
14 Who made his stage debut in a 1960 production of *The Pyjama Game*?
15 What honour was awarded to Eric Clapton in January 1995?
16 Who duetted on the 1992 version of Crying with Roy Orbison?
17 How many UK Top Ten hits has Marvin Gaye had since his death?
18 Who jumped off the top of a moving bus during a Swedish tour and broke a foot?
19 Who was awarded a Lifetime Achievement Award at the 1993 Brit Awards?
20 Who collaborated with Michael Bolton on Bolton's Steel Bars hit?
21 Who did Celine Dion support in his Canadian tour in 1991?
22 Who is the sister of the drummer of the Dakotas during their 60s heyday?
23 Whose autobiography was titled *Laughter in the Rain*?
24 Which group sponsored Clydebank Football Club in 1993?
25 Who had a rabies jab after biting a rat on stage?

Answers

Legends

1 Rolling Stones. **2** Winifred Atwell. **3** Michael Bolton. **4** Marvin Gaye. **5** Des O'Connor. **6** Elvis Presley. **7** Bruce Springsteen. **8** David Bowie. **9** Guns 'N'Roses. **10** KLF. **11** David Bowie. **12** Jim Reeves. **13** Nippy. **14** David Cassidy. **15** OBE. **16** k.d.lang. **17** One. **18** Liam Gallagher. **19** Rod Stewart. **20** Bob Dylan. **21** Michael Bolton. **22** Elkie Brooks. **23** Neil Sedaka. **24** Wet Wet Wet. **25** Ozzy Osbourne.

Quiz 44 Pot Luck

Level 3

1 Which TV series intro said, 'Return with us now to those thrilling days of yesteryear...'?
2 What star sign is shared by Peter Gabriel and Stevie Wonder?
3 Who had a UK No 1 hit with Together We Are Beautiful?
4 What is the population of Italy to the nearest million?
5 What is Marie Osmond's real first name?
6 Which boxer is quoted as saying, 'He can run, but he can't hide'?
7 Who was Prime Minister at the beginning of the century?
8 Albert Giacometti found fame as what?
9 Which actress's autobiography was called *Hold on to the Messy Times*?
10 Who first flew in Friendship 7?
11 Who or what was Dale Winton named after?
12 Vehicles from which country use the international registration letter RB?
13 Who wrote the novel *Gentlemen Prefer Blondes*?
14 Whose barrel organ played the music for *The Magic Roundabout*?
15 Where did Brad Pitt, Darcey Bussell and William Hague appear together?
16 In which German city was the original Volkswagen factory?
17 What were mortgage rates in Feb 1990 – an all time high?
18 Who sang a solo at Prince Charles and Lady Di's wedding?
19 Calabar International airport is in which country?
20 Who wrote the Channel 4 sitcom *Blue Heaven*?
21 McCarran international airport is in which US state?
22 Which country does the airline LOT come from?
23 What was W.G. Grace's profession other than a cricketer?
24 Which British gold medallist had the middle name Wipper?
25 In which year did Wimbledon's famous commentator Dan Maskell die?

Answers

Pot Luck

1 The Lone Ranger. **2** Taurus. **3** Fern Kinney. **4** 58 million. **5** Olive. **6** Joe Louis. **7** Marquis of Salisbury. **8** Sculptor. **9** Sue Johnston. **10** John Glenn. **11** Dale Robertson the actor. **12** Botswana. **13** Anita Loos. **14** Mr Rusty. **15** Madame Tussaud's. **16** Wolfsburg. **17** 15.4%. **18** Kiri Te Kanawa. **19** Nigeria. **20** Frank Skinner. **21** Nevada. **22** Poland. **23** Doctor. **24** Allan Wells. **25** 1992.

Quiz 45 Heroes & Villains

Level 3

1. Which prison did Jonathan Aitken go to after he was convicted in 1999?
2. What was the official occupation of Sir Anthony Blunt who was unmasked as a Soviet spy in 1979?
3. Which fictional character was based on Scottish soldier William Ironside?
4. Who said, 'Being a thief is a terrific life, but the trouble is they do put you in the nick for it'?
5. Under who did Joseph McCarthy carry out his 'witch hunts'?
6. Where did Ferdinand Marcos live in exile?
7. Which MP wrote *The Young Meteors*?
8. Which medal did Robert Maxwell win in WWII?
9. Which terrorist group murdered Italian PM Aldo Moro?
10. Which was the first party Oswald Mosley was in Parliament with?
11. Which American was nicknamed Old Blood and Guts?
12. Who was Jeremy Thorpe accused of attempting to murder in 1976?
13. Which Conservative MP was killed by an IRA bomb in 1990?
14. Which organisation handed over Brian Keenan in Beirut after 1600 days?
15. Which stockbroker was given an 18 month prison sentence for his role in the Guinness scandal?
16. According to Neil Kinnock, whose principles 'produce martyrdom for the followers and never sacrifice the leaders'?
17. Which company headed by Asil Nadir collapsed in 1990?
18. In 1985 Terry Waite returned to Beirut after securing the release of four British hostages where?
19. Which little boy appeared on TV screens with Saddam Hussein as one of his 'guests' during the Gulf crisis?
20. Where did the Pope land on his arrival in Britain in 1982?
21. General Boris Gromov was the last Soviet soldier to leave where in 1989?
22. In the Profumo scandal, which Russian had an affair with Christine Keeler?
23. Who referred to drawing 'a line in the sand' about the Gulf War?
24. What was Ronald Biggs' official occupation when he was convicted of the Great Train Robbery?
25. What was Mother Teresa's real first name?

Answers

20th C Heroes & Villains

1 Standford Hill. **2** Art historian. **3** Richard Hannay. **4** John McVicar. **5** Truman. **6** Hawaii. **7** Jonathan Aitken. **8** Military Cross. **9** Red Brigades. **10** Conservative. **11** Patton. **12** Norman Scott. **13** Ian Gow. **14** Islamic Dawn. **15** Tony Parnes. **16** Arthur Scargill. **17** Polly Peck. **18** Libya. **19** Stuart Lockwood. **20** Cardiff. **21** Afghanistan. **22** Ivanov. **23** George Bush. **24** Carpenter. **25** Agnes.

Quiz 46 CORONATION ST. Level 3

Early Days – 1971

1 Which two longstanding female characters left this year?
2 Which couple borrowed a Rolls Royce and pretended to be mayor and mayoress?
3 What replaced the demolished maisonettes?
4 Which actress made her debut in 1971 but proved such a hit she returned in 1973 and stayed till the late 90s?
5 Lynne Perrie (Ivy) made her debut this year, fresh from success in which film?
6 Name the busty blonde who Ray and Len employed as housekeeper.
7 Who had an affair with Alan Howard?
8 Who was supervisor at the new warehouse?
9 Who did she refuse to employ?
10 What was that character's revenge?
11 How did drayman Arthur Burrows cause trouble for Annie Walker?
12 Who joined a band but was asked to leave by the other members?
13 Which company owned the warehouse?
14 Who was appointed caretaker of the new community centre?
15 Who won the first Coronation Street flower show?
16 Which unlikely character was charged with offending public morals for taking topless photos on a beach?
17 Who formed his own union SODU – and what did it stand for?
18 Which couple won £500 on the Premium Bonds?
19 Who mugged Lucille Hewitt?
20 Who became engaged to snobby Jennifer Swann?
21 Which two ladies dated footballer Eddie Duncan?
22 Who got a job as a go-go dancer?
23 Who returned to Coronation Street after a 3-year absence to work for Len?
24 Whose job did he take?
25 Which famous Northern comedian made a guest appearance as himself?

Answers

Early Days – 1971
1 Irma and Val Barlow. **2** Elsie and Alan Howard. **3** A warehouse and community centre. **4**. Thelma Barlow. **5** Kes. **6** Gina Fletcher. **7** Janet Reid. **8** Elsie Howard. **9** Hilda Ogden. **10** She told Elsie's boss that she was a shoplifter. **11** By watering the gin. **12** Ken Barlow. **13** Mark Brittain. **14** Ena Sharples. **15** Albert Tatlock. **16** Ernie Bishop. **17** Stan Ogden District Union. **18** The Ogdens. **19** Frank Bradley. **20** Gordon Clegg. **21** Irma Barlow and Bet Lynch. **22** Lucille Hewitt. **23** Jerry Booth. **24** Stan Ogden's. **25** Bernard Manning.

Quiz 47 90s News

Level 3

1 Which David headed the Cult which staged a 1993 mass suicide in Waco?
2 How many Northern Ireland MPs were there at the 1997 General Election?
3 Who won Miss World the first time it was held in India?
4 Who won Taiwan's first democratic Presidential election?
5 Where was the UN Earth summit held in 1992?
6 What number TWA flight exploded shortly after take-off in July 1996?
7 What was the name of the mother of the Iowa septuplets born in 1997?
8 Who did Grant Ferrie marry in prison in 1997?
9 Where in the USA was there a total eclipse in 1991?
10 What was O J Simpson driving in the famous police chase?
11 Britain's worst rail disaster in recent times occurred at which station?
12 Who went on trial for the Oklahoma bombing after Timothy McVeigh was sentenced to death for the crime?
13 Who was the brother of the nurse Deborah Parry was accused of murdering in Saudi Arabia?
14 What was the name of the judge in the Louise Woodward trial?
15 Who was investigated with Neil Hamilton in the cash for questions affair?
16 Which prominent Nigerian writer was executed in 1996?
17 Name the car in which Andy Green broke the land speed record in 1997?
18 Whose sacking caused an attack on Michael Howard by Ann Widdecombe?
19 Which company won a libel action against Dave Morris and Helen Street?
20 Where did Princess Diana have her last meeting with Mother Teresa?
21 Which charity along with the Aids Crisis Trust chiefly benefited from the sale of Diana's dresses at Christie's in 1997 ?
22 Which Kennedy was due to marry when John F Kennedy's plane crashed on its way to the wedding?
23 In September 1996 who pledged a £1 million, making it the then largest donation to the Labour Party by any individual?
24 The advertising of which products was banned on Guernsey in 1996?
25 On what did the Queen sign her autograph on a tour of Kuala Lumpur in September 1998?

Answers

90s News
1 Koresh. **2** 17. **3** Irene Skliva. **4** Lee Teng-Hui. **5** Rio. **6** 800. **7** Bobbi McCaughey. **8** Lucille McLauchlan. **9** Hawaii. **10** Ford Bronco. **11** Clapham Junction. **12** Terry Nichols. **13** Frank Gilford. **14** Hiller Zobel. **15** Tim Smith. **16** Ken Saro Wiwa. **17** Thrust. **18** Derek Lewis. **19** McDonalds. **20** New York. **21** Royal Marsden Cancer Fund. **22** Rory. **23** Matthew Harding. **24** Cigarettes. **25** Man Utd football.

Quiz 48 Pot Luck

Level 3

1 In which US state was Tennessee Williams born?
2 Which Hi De Hi star was a member of a group called Midnight News?
3 Who won soccer's World Cup with his last international goal?
4 What is Robert Redford's real first name?
5 Which country does the airline LTU International Airways come from?
6 In music, in which decade was the Academy of St Martin-in-the-Fields founded?
7 Who was the son of Jor-El and Lara Lor-Van?
8 What star sign is shared by Sir David Attenborough and Paula Yates?
9 Where in Canada is the Lion's Gate bridge?
10 Who had a UK No. 1 hit with Use It Up and Wear It Out?
11 What is the population of Japan to the nearest million?
12 Vehicles from which country use the international registration letter RA?
13 Who was pictured for the first time on new £10 notes isssued in 1975?
14 What is Julian Clary's real name?
15 Which writer was married to actor Clive Swift aka Richard Bucket?
16 In which American state is the Harrah's Auto Collection situated?
17 Who did Eamonn Holmes nickname Miss Tippy Toes?
18 Which musical star played Caroline Winthrop in *Crossroads*?
19 Carrasco International airport is in which country?
20 What did Richard Branson once pour over Clive Anderson?
21 What was the first single to sell over 2 million copies in the UK?
22 In which country was Anjelica Huston born?
23 What was the name of Rigsby's cat in TV's *Rising Damp*?
24 Who was Israeli Prime Minister from 1969 to 1974?
25 What are Lawrence Dallaglio's middle names?

Answers

Pot Luck

1 Mississippi. **2** Su Pollard. **3** Gerd Muller. **4** Charles. **5** Germany. **6** 50s. **7** Superman. **8** Taurus. **9** Vancouver. **10** Odyssey. **11** 126 million. **12** Argentina. **13** Florence Nightingale. **14** Julian Clary. **15** Margaret Drabble. **16** Nevada. **17** Anthea Turner. **18** Elaine Paige. **19** Uruguay. **20** Glass of water. **21** Mull Of Kintyre. **22** Ireland. **23** Vienna. **24** Golda Meir. **25** Bruno Nero.

Quiz 49 20th C Summer Sports Level 3

1 How many times was Wes Hall named as Wisden Cricketer of the Year?
2 At which venue did Tony Jacklin win the US Open?
3 Who was the defending champion when Stefan Edberg first won the Wimbledon singles?
4 Who ended Graham Gooch's mammoth 333 England innings at Lord's?
5 Which horse landed the Derby and the Irish Derby in 1993?
6 Who was the last man out in England's 1999 World Cup campiagn?
7 What were the initials of W G Grace's brother who played for England?
8 What was the total prize money for the British Open in 1945?
9 Which country does sprinter David Ezinwa come from?
10 By the end of the 20th century which country has had the most Men's Singles winners at Wimbledon?
11 How many members joined the original International Amateur Athletic Federation?
12 Which assistant manager of England's cricket team sadly died of a heart attack on the 1981 tour of W Indies?
13 At which venue did Greg Norman first win the British Open?
14 In the summer of 98 Jap Stam joined Man Utd from which club?
15 Which golden girl athlete married comedian Bobby Knut?
16 Which Brit won the doubles at Wimbledon in 1987 and in Australia in 1991?
17 Who was the first lady golfer to land the British and US Open in the same year?
18 Which country did 70s French Open women's singles winner Virginia Rusici come from?
19 What is the nickname of cycling's Marco Pantani?
20 What was Sue Barker's highest world ranking?
21 Why was Kieran Fallon fined £1000 at the 1999 Derby?
22 Gary Sobers' then record Test score of 365 was made against which team?
23 Who was Britian's first Singles winner at Wimbledon in the second half of the 20th century?
24 What is the lowest total for the British Open in the century?
25 In which country was Ted Dexter born?

Answers

20th C Summer Sports

1 Never. **2** Hazeltine. **3** Pat Cash. **4** Prabhakar. **5** Commander In Chief. **6** Alan Mullally. **7** E C. **8** £1,000. **9** Nigeria. **10** UK. **11** 17. **12** Ken Barrington. **13** Turnberry. **14** PSV. **15** Donna Hartley. **16** Jeremy Bates. **17** Patty Sheehan. **18** Romania. **19** The Pirate. **20** 6th. **21** Breaking early from the parade. **22** Pakistan. **23** Angela Mortimer. **24** 267. **25** Italy.

Quiz 50 CORONATION ST. Level 3

Early Days – 1972

1 What was the name of Hilda's brother?
2 Who did Billy Walker sell his interest in the Canal Garage to?
3 Who did Ken Barlow move in with this year?
4 Who said of Elsie Tanner's pink bath 'That's not a flippin' bath, it's phonographic (sic)'?
5 Which popular and longstanding character returned to *Coronation Street* after an eight-year absence?
6 Who opened a betting shop and nightclub?
7 What was the name of the nightclub?
8 Who thought of the name?
9 Who did Maggie Clegg employ at the Corner Shop?
10 Who was Terry Bates' stepmother?
11 Which couple got married this year?
12 Which house did they buy?
13 Who dismantled the Ogdens' porch?
14 Who was injured in a motoring accident?
15 What was the name of Norma Ford's dad?
16 Why did he find it hard to integrate into the community?
17 Who kissed Concepta's new man Sean Regan at his engagement party?
18 Which 18-year-old Oldham Rep actress made her *Coronation Street* debut this year?
19 Who was released from prison in Spain?
20 Which lady had liaisons with Benny Lewis, Ken Barlow and Len Fairclough?
21 Who dated alcoholic Ron Cooke?
22 Who paid Ken for English lessons?
23 Who built a boat called *Shangri-La*?
24 Who appeared as Carmen Miranda in the Christmas Day 1940s show?
25 And who was Marlene Dietrich?

Answers

Early Days – 1972

1 Archie Crabtree. **2** Alan Howard. **3** Albert Tatlock. **4** Hilda Ogden. **5** Rita. **6** Benny Lewis. **7** The Capricorn. **8** Hilda Ogden. **9** Norma Ford. **10** Rita. **11** The Bishops. **12** Number 3. **13** Ray Langton. **14** Stan Ogden. **15** Jacko. **16** He'd been in prison. **17** Bet Lynch. **18** Anne Kirkbride. **19** Ernie Bishop. **20** Rita. **21** Maggie Clegg. **22** Norma Ford. **23** Jerry Booth. **24** Emily Bishop. **25** Rita.

Quiz 51 20th C 90s Movies

Level 3

1 On whose life was the film *Reversal of Fortune* based?
2 Which sitcom did the director of *Sliding Doors* appear in in the 80s?
3 In which US state is *The Horse Whisperer* with Redford & Scott Thomas largely set?
4 Which writer directed *Sleepless in Seattle*?
5 What was the name of the Miss Haversham figure played by Anne Bancroft in the 90s *Great Expectations*?
6 Which 90s film was a remake of the 1987 German film *Wings of Desire*?
7 Who had a No 1 hit with the theme from *Buddy's Song*?
8 What was the name of Bruce Willis's character in *Armageddon*?
9 Where in Florida was *Wild Things* set?
10 What year was it in *The Fifth Element*?
11 Which 1997 film held the record at the time for the biggest opening for a British film, taking £2.5 million in three days?
12 In which film is Elliot Carver the villain?
13 *Ten Things I Hate About You* is based on which Shakespeare play?
14 Which original Picasso picture was used in *Titanic*, as one of Rose's possessions?
15 In the 'human' version of *101 Dalmatians* what is Roger's occupation?
16 Who played the delicate daughter in *Little Women*?
17 What is the name of the Sikh bomb disposal expert in *The English Patient*?
18 What was the eighth *Star Trek* film called?
19 What is the name of the President in *Independence Day*?
20 In which film did Morgan Freeman play cop William Somerset?
21 Which studio worked with Disney on *Toy Story*?
22 What was the first film to have a budget of over $100 million?
23 Which Derek Jarman film was based on a Christopher Marlowe play?
24 What was the name of the weather girl played by Nicole Kidman in *To Die For*?
25 Which Pennsylvania town is the setting for *Groundhog Day*?

Answers

20th C 90's Movies

1 Claus Von Bulow. **2** Bread. **3** Montana. **4** Nora Ephron. **5** Ms Dinsmoor. **6** City of Angels. **7** Chesney Hawkes. **8** Harry Stamper. **9** Blue Bay. **10** 2259. **11** Bean: The Ultimate Disaster Movie. **12** Tomorrow Never Dies. **13** The Taming of the Shrew. **14** The Guitar Player. **15** Computer games programmer. **16** Claire Danes. **17** Kip. **18** The First Contact. **19** Whitmore. **20** Se7en. **21** Pixar. **22** True Lies. **23** Edward II. **24** Suzanne Stone. **25** Punxsutawney.

Quiz 52 CORONATION ST. Level 3

Early Days – 1973

1 Who took on an assignment photographing a group of strippers?
2 Who was arrested for the kidnap of baby Jason Lomax?
3 What was the name of the Kabin before Len and Rita took it over?
4 Who was romantically linked with Mavis Riley this year, although the relationship never really got off the ground?
5 Who went for counselling for a drink problem?
6 Who moved in to lodge with the Howards at No. 11?
7 Which couple tracked down their long lost son and found he was married with a child?
8 What was the name of their estranged grandson?
9 Where did the Howards go this year when they left Coronation Street?
10 Who discovered a letter showing that her husband had been in love with her old friend?
11 And who was that friend?
12 Who had to be placed in an oxygen tent after a disaster with a badly fitted gas pipe in his home?
13 Who installed the pipe?
14 And who threatened to sue him?
15 Who suffered two heart attacks this year before moving to the Lake District?
16 Who won £75 on the pools?
17 Whose real life son played his screen son this year?
18 Who gambled away more than £200 of the Rovers' takings?
19 Who proposed to Minnie Caldwell?
20 Who was caught underage drinking in the Rovers?
21 Whose wife wrongly accused him of having an affair with Clara Regan?
22 Who tried to walk the Pennine Way but gave up after their pal died of a heart attack?
23 Whose house had to be fumigated after a mouse was found in the kitchen?
24 Who was the singer at the Capricorn club?
25 Who was found in Elsie's bed after a party?

Answers

Early Days – 1973

1 Emily Bishop. **2** Christine Peters. **3** Biddulphs. **4** Jerry Booth. **5** Alan Howard. **6** Lucille Hewitt. **7** The Ogdens. **8** Damien. **9** Newcastle. **10** Minnie Caldwell. **11** Ena Sharples. **12** Albert Tatlock. **13** Jerry Booth. **14** Beattie Tatlock, Albert's daughter. **15** Ena Sharples. **16** Bet Lynch. **17** Bill Roache's son Linus played Peter Barlow. **18** Billy Walker. **18** Albert Tatlock. **20** Tricia Hopkins. **21** Stan Ogden. **22** Jerry Booth and Albert Tatlock. **23** The Ogdens'. **24** Rita. **25** Deirdre Hunt.

Quiz 53 20th C TV Classics

Level 3

1 In what year was the famous Spaghetti Harvest April Fool's Day prank shown on BBC TV?
2 What was the first name of the person *The Fugitive* was accused of killing?
3 Whose song provided the music for *In Sickness and In Health*?
4 Who famously announced 'Heeeere's Johnny' on the *Johnny Carson Show* from the early 60s?
5 From whose diaries did Jonathan Lynn and Anthony Jay come up with the title *Yes Minister*?
6 Who presented the first edition of *Come Dancing*?
7 Which series produced the catchphrase, 'Excuse me sir, do you think that's wise?'?
8 Which classic TV series had the catchphrase 'Kookie, Kookie lend me your comb'?
9 Who wrote the original scripts of *Dr Who*?
10 *Stuebenville* was a US pilot based on which UK classic?
11 In *Friday Night Live* what football team did Stavros support?
12 Which of Kenny Everett's characters said, 'It's all done in the best possible taste'?
13 Which comedy programme won The Golden Rose of Montreux in 1967?
14 On which show was the catchphrase 'I'm in charge' first used?
15 Which show had the Flying Fickle Finger of Fate?
16 Who created the drama series *Minder*?
17 On which TV show did Janice Nicholls regularly appear?
18 Which show had the slogan 'The weekend starts here'?
19 What is the longest running children's programme?
20 Who played The Siren in the original *Batman* TV series?
21 In *Upstairs Downstairs* where did Lady Marjorie die?
22 What name did Reginald Perrin use when he went his own funeral?
23 Who was the sixth Dr Who?
24 Which role did Colin Welland play in *Z Cars* for many years?
25 Who played Dixon's daughter in the early years of *Dixon of Dock Green*?

Answers

20th C TV Classics

1 1957. **2** Helen. **3** Chas & Dave. **4** Ed McMahon. **5** Richard Crossman. **6** Sylvia Peters. **7** Dad's Army. **8** 77 Sunset Strip. **9** Terry Nation. **10** The Likely Lads. **11** Arsenal. **12** Cupid Stunt. **13** The Frost Report. **14** Sunday Night at the London Palladium. **15** Rowan & Martin's Laugh In. **16** Leon Griffiths. **17** Thank Your Lucky Stars. **18** Ready Steady Go. **19** Sooty. **20** Joan Collins. **21** On the Titanic. **22** Martin Wellbourne. **23** Peter Davison. **24** David Graham. **25** Billie Whitelaw.

Quiz 54 Pot Luck

Level 3

1 Who directed the movie *The Blues Brothers*?
2 How many years after the end of the Great War was the first 'Poppy Day' held?
3 What is Don Johnson's real name?
4 Where in England was Michael Palin born?
5 Which US soap actress's real name is Patsy McClenny?
6 Kent County international airport is in which US state?
7 Which long time star of *The Bill* is a qualified scuba diving instructor?
8 What is Brad Pitt's real first name?
9 *You Bet!* was based on a game show from which country?
10 Which two countries are joined by the Rainbow bridge?
11 Who is the most famous creation of Mary Tourtel?
12 What are the international registration letters of a vehicle from Tanzania?
13 Who became the first European Player Of The Year?
14 In which city was the peace treaty ending the Vietnam war signed?
15 Who hosted *Trick or Treat* with Julian Clary?
16 What was the name of the island off Iceland which appeared in 1963 as a result of an underwater volcano?
17 Who is dad to Betty Kitten and Honey Kinny?
18 Why was Al Capone sent to prison in 1931?
19 Costa Smeralda International airport is in which country?
20 Which playwright said, 'I think age is a very high price to pay for maturity'?
21 What star sign is Chris Tarrant?
22 Which country does the airline Norontair come from?
23 What was Michael Jackson's last UK No 1 of the 80s?
24 What is Jeremy Paxman's middle name?
25 Who wrote the novel *Tycoon* in 1996?

Answers

Pot Luck

1 John Landis. **2** Three. **3** Donald Wayne. **4** Sheffield. **5** Morgan Fairchild. **6** Michigan. **7** Mark Wingett. **8** William. **9** Holland. **10** Canada/USA. **11** Rupert Bear. **12** EAT. **13** Stanley Matthews. **14** Paris. **15** Mike Smith. **16** Surtsey. **17** Jonathan Ross. **18** Tax evasion. **19** Sardinia. **20** Tom Stoppard. **21** Libra. **22** Canada. **23** I Just Can't Stop Loving You. **24** Dickson. **25** Harold Robbins.

Quiz 55 20th C World Tour

Level 3

1 In what year did the first McDonald's open in Moscow?
2 In which city was the Olympic stadium designed by Pier Luigi Nervi?
3 What was the name by which Lesotho used to be known?
4 Who designed New York's Guggenheim Museum?
5 Which US mountains gave their name to a fever discovered in that area in the early 20th century?
6 Where was Ian Botham talking about when he said everyone should send his mother-in-law there, all expenses paid?
7 In which American state is the Rockefeller Folk Art Collection?
8 In which US state is the only major military academy founded this century?
9 Who designed the Mile High Centre, Boston, and The Glass Pyramid at the Louvre?
10 What would an American be talking about if he mentioned a scallion?
11 Lassa fever is so called as it was first reported in 1970 in Lassa in which country?
12 In which American city would you go to see the Frick Collection?
13 Who designed the Hiroshima Peace Centre?
14 Who said, 'Concorde is great. It gives you three extra hours to find your luggage'?
15 In the 50s, who designed The Museum of Modern Art in Tokyo?
16 Where did the Pope consecrate the world's biggest church in 1990?
17 In which city was the Olympic stadium designed by Felix Candela?
18 How is Tenochtitlan now known?
19 During which marathon do runners cross the Verrazano Bridge?
20 Whose tomb was opened to the public in Egypt for the first time in 1996?
21 The architect who designed the Sydney Opera House came from which country?
22 In *California Suite,* which city is described as 'not Mecca. It just smells like it'?
23 Which airport was opened in 1994 on a specially made island?
24 What is the English title of the new South African National Anthem?
25 Where did the largest rollercoaster in the world open in 1994?

Answers

20th C World Tour

1 1990. **2** Rome. **3** Basutoland. **4** Frank Lloyd Wright. **5** Rocky Mountains. **6** Pakistan. **7** Virginia. **8** Colorado USAF. **9** Leah Meng Pei. **10** Spring onion. **11** Nigeria. **12** New York. **13** Kenzo Tange. **14** Bob Hope. **15** Le Corbusier. **16** Ivory Coast. **17** Mexico. **18** Mexico City. **19** New York. **20** Queen Nefertiti. **21** Denmark – It was Jorn Utzon. **22** New York. **23** Kansai. **24** God Bless Africa. **25** Blackpool.

Quiz 56 CORONATION ST. Level 3

Early Days – 1974

1 Which character was played by two different actresses this year?
2 Which character left to marry an old flame?
3 Who took over from Ena at the Community Centre?
4 Name her nephew, who gave up a footballing career to become a chef.
5 Who set up an action group to stop the council demolishing the street to make high rise flats?
6 Who did Nellie Harvey's husband Arthur declare himself in love with?
7 Soldier Martin Downes appeared in Coronation Street looking for his real mother. Who was she?
8 Who threw a brick through Len Fairclough's window?
9 Why did Stuart Draper drive his car through the doors of the Rovers?
10 Who got a 6 week job as a cleaner on a cruise ship?
11 Which couple broke off their engagement?
12 Who took in lodgers Tommy Deakin, Michael Ryan and Dolores the Donkey?
13 Jed Stone's prison cell mate arrived and ended up at Minnie Caldwell's. Who was he?
14 What did Ernie Bishop's society RADA stand for?
15 What was the first play they produced?
16 And what part did Annie Walker take in the play?
17 Why did Lucille split up with Danny Burrows?
18 Who won a holiday for 8 in Majorca in a Spot the Ball competition?
19 Which couple became foster parents this year?
20 Whose husband died from a heart attack?
21 Who fell for a Spanish electrician called Pedro?
22 Which actor – currently in *Coronation Street* playing a different character - played a character called Carlos who was romantically linked to Mavis?
23 Who proposed to Maggie Clegg and was turned down?
24 Who defiantly said 'I never fitted in in Coronation Street because I never wanted to. I despised it round 'ere'.
25 Who left Coronation Street to live in Ireland?

Answers

Early Days – 1974

1 Blanche Hunt. **2** Maggie Clegg. **3** Gertie Robson. **4** Gary Turner. **5** The Bishops. **6** Annie Walker. **7** Bet Lynch. **8** Emily. **9** Billy Walker had sold it to him for £600 profit. **10** Hilda. **11** Minnie Caldwell and Albert Tatlock. **12** Stan Ogden. **13** Eddie Yeats. **14** Rovers Amateur Dramatics Association. **15** The Importance of Being Earnest. **16** Lady Bracknell. **17** He was married with a baby. **18** Bet Lynch. **19** The Bishops. **20** Betty's husband Cyril. **21** Mavis. **22** Malcolm Hebden (Norris Cole). **23** Alf Roberts. **24** Janet Barlow. **25** Lucille Hewitt.

Quiz 57 Sounds of the 60s & 70s Level 3

1 Who said I was Made For Dancing in a 70s No 4 hit?
2 Who released an album in 1961 called 21 Today?
3 What was the follow-up to Fleetwood Mac's first No 1?
4 What was the first UK No 1 by KC and The Sunshine Band?
5 What was the first Top Ten Hit for The Kinks in the 70s?
6 Where was yodeller Frank Ifield born?
7 What was the second 70s No 1 by Mud?
8 Who was the UK's biggest-selling artist in 1967?
9 What UK chart position was achieved by the original release of Je t'aime?
10 Which group did Steve Marriott form after leaving the Small Faces?
11 Which No 1 group from 1974 were recognised by their white berets?
12 Who was On The Rebound in 1961?
13 Which group were fronted by Dennis Locorriere and Ray Sawyer?
14 Which female vocalist said Yes My Darling Daughter in '62 ?
15 How many Top Ten hits had Lindisfarne had before Run For Home?
16 What was the only UK No 1 for the Dave Clark Five?
17 Which group achieved their 4th successive Top Ten hit with Belfast?
18 Which rock group was voted World's Top Band in 1972?
19 Which band consisted of the Cluskeys and John Stokes?
20 What was Brotherhood of Man's first Top Ten hit after Save Your Kisses?
21 Who got to No 10 with Sunshine After The Rain in Jubilee Year?
22 Which Top Ten hit followed Mr Tambourine Man for the Byrds?
23 Who released an album in the 60s called Please Get My Name Right?
24 Who had most weeks in the charts in 1974?
25 Who danced a Morning Dance in 1979?

Answers

Sounds of the 60s and 70s

1 Leif Garrett. **2** Cliff Richard. **3** Man Of The World. **4** Give It Up. **5** Lola. **6** Coventry. **7** Lonely This Christmas. **8** Engelbert Humperdinck. **9** 2. **10** Humble Pie. **11** The Rubettes. **12** Floyd Cramer. **13** Dr Hook. **14** Eydie Gorme. **15** Two. **16** Glad All Over. **17** Boney M. **18** Alice Cooper. **19** Bachelors. **20** Oh Boy - The Mood I'm In. **21** Elkie Brooks. **22** All I Really Want To Do. **23** Twiggy. **24** The Wombles. **25** Spyro Gyra.

Quiz 58 Pot Luck

Level 3

1 Who wrote the novel *Delta Connection*?
2 What is Sid Owen's real name?
3 Who preceeded Hosni Mubarak as President of Egypt?
4 What was the Jam's last UK No. 1 of the 80s?
5 'Even your best friends won't tell you' was part of an ad to promote what?
6 Where in England was Emma Thompson born?
7 Who was the defending champion when Martina Navratilova first won Wimbledon singles?
8 In *The Rockford Files* what was Jim Rockford's daily fee?
9 How is Lady Nicholas Lloyd better known?
10 What name was given to followers of cartoon characters Pip, Squeak and Wilfred?
11 Who first sang the *Neighbours* theme song?
12 What are the international registration letters of a vehicle from Uganda?
13 What was the first organisation to have its charter mark withdrawn?
14 In the 70s George Lee was a world champion in which sport?
15 Which river is spanned by the world's longest cantilever bridge?
16 Toothpaste was the first ever TV ad in the UK, but what was the first TV ad in colour for?
17 What type of aid was developed by Miller Hutchinson in the early years of the 20th century?
18 In the cartoon characters Pip, Squeak and Wilfred what kind of creature was Squeak?
19 Cuscatlan International airport is in which country?
20 Who was Pope for the shortest length of time in the 20th C?
21 General Mitchell international airport is in which US state?
22 Which country does the airline Pluna come from?
23 Who directed *A Passage to India*?
24 What star sign is Pauline Quirke?
25 What is Gregory Peck's real first name?

Answers

Pot Luck

1 Hammond Innes. **2** David Sutton. **3** Anwar El-Sadat. **4** Beat Surrender. **5** Listerine mouthwash. **6** Cambridge. **7** Virginia Wade. **8** $200 plus expenses. **9** Eve Pollard. **10** Gugnuncs. **11** Barry Crocker. **12** EAU. **13** Passport Agency. **14** Gliding. **15** St Lawrence. **16** Frozen peas. **17** Hearing aid. **18** Penguin. **19** El Salvador. **20** John Paul I. **21** Wisconsin. **22** Uruguay. **23** David Lean. **24** Cancer. **25** Eldred.

Quiz 59 Headline Makers

Level 3

1 How much did Vivian Nicholson win on the pools in 1961?
2 Which boat capsized in the 1997 Vendee Globe round the world race?
3 Who was Mandy Rice-Davies referring to when she said, 'Well he would, wouldn't he?'?
4 How old was the man who was granted the first divorce in Irish history?
5 How old was Ruth Lawrence when she passed A level maths?
6 Who investigated the cash for questions affair involving Neil Hamilton?
7 In the painting by Michael Browne featuring Eric Cantona, who was Alex Ferguson depicted as?
8 What description did Dr Desmond Morris give of a city as opposed to a concrete jungle?
9 Princess Diana made a public apology after underage William and Harry saw which 15 certificate film?
10 Sue Ryder became Baroness Ryder of where along with Cavendish?
11 Which university did Andrew Morton represent on *University Challenge*?
12 Who founded Gordonstoun school in 1934?
13 What were Bomber Harris's real first names?
14 How many years elapsed between DH Lawrence's writing of *Lady Chatterley's Lover* and the book's publication?
15 In which city were the 'Chariots Of Fire' Olympic Games?
16 Lindbergh wrote about his New York to Paris flight in which book?
17 Maria Montessori was the first woman in Italy to be awarded a degree in which subject?
18 Rudolf Nureyev took citizenship of which country in 1982?
19 In which country was Pasternak's *Dr Zhivago* first published?
20 Which Peter co-founded the Aldeburgh Festival?
21 Which seat did Cherie Booth unsuccessfully contend in 1983?
22 Child expert Dr Spock won an Olympic gold medal in what event?
23 In 1990 a cinema owner was fined for refusing to remove what from the roof of his house?
24 Which British nurse was imprisoned in Iraq in 1990 for spying?
25 Which athlete sued Mirror Newspapers for libel?

Answers

Headline Makers

1 £152,000. **2** Exide Challenger. **3** Lord Astor. **4** 68. **5** Nine. **6** Gordon Downey. **7** Julius Caesar. **8** Human zoo. **9** The Devil's Own. **10** Warsaw. **11** Sussex. **12** Kurt Hahn. **13** Arthur Travers. **14** 32. **15** Paris. **16** Spirit of St Louis. **17** Medicine. **18** Austria. **19** Italy. **20** Pears. **21** Thanet East. **22** Rowing. **23** A fibreglass shark. **24** Daphne Parish. **25** Tessa Sanderson.

Quiz 60 CORONATION ST. Level 3

Early Days – 1975

1 Who died in a warehouse fire?
2 Which much loved actor died this year, aged 34?
3 What did his character die of in the programme?
4 Who bought a German Shepherd called Fury?
5 Who was murdered by her husband?
6 Who was wrongly suspected of the murder?
7 Whose son died in a car crash in Ireland?
8 Who became manageress of the Corner Shop after the Hopkins left?
9 Who joined a dating agency and ended up being matched with Ken Barlow?
10 What was the name of Ralph Lancaster's club where Rita was a singer?
11 Which temptress tricked Alf Roberts out of £500?
12 Who formed WARP – the Weatherfield Association of Rate Payers?
13 Who dated stripper Michelle Turnbull?
14 Who thumped Tricia Hopkins and why?
15 Which old flame of Bet's turned up again?
16 Who fell downstairs and ended up in hospital?
17 Who won Personality of the Pub in 1975?
18 Who did she nominate as Best Customer?
19 Name the fishmonger who took a fancy to Betty.
20 Who adopted a stray pigeon called Gilbert?
21 Who ate Gilbert?
22 Who produced *Cinderella* at the Community Centre?
23 Who played Prince Charming but mimed the songs?
24 Who celebrated an 80th birthday?
25 Who became engaged to one man but ended up marrying another?

Answers

Early Days – 1975

1 Edna Gee. **2** Graham Haberfield. **3** Pneumonia. **4** Eddie Yeats. **5** Lynne Johnson. **6** Len Fairclough. **7** Bet's. **8** Blanche Hunt. **9** Mavis. **10** The Gatsby. **11** Donna Parker. **12** Ernie Bishop. **13** Eddie Yeats. **14** Deirdre, because she said Ray was having an affair. **15** Frank Bradley. **16** Annie Walker. **17** Betty Turpin. **18** Stan Odgen. **19** Bert Gosling. **20** Albert Tatlock. **21** Minnie's cat, Bobby. **22** Rita. **23** Bet. **24** Albert Tatlock. **25** Deirdre.

Quiz 61 World Leaders

Level 3

1 Who was described by his foreign minister as having 'a nice smile, but he has got iron teeth'?
2 Who became president of Zambia in 1991?
3 Who succeeded Brezhnev as President of the USSR?
4 Who was Nigeria's first president and has been described as the father of modern Nigeria?
5 Who was born Karl Herbert Frahm?
6 Who was chairman of the Organisation of African Unity from 1975–76?
7 Errol Flynn's last film was a documentary tribute to which world leader?
8 Gorbachev introduced the expression perestroika, but what does it mean?
9 Who was the first PM of South Africa?
10 Who said of Margaret Thatcher, 'She adds the diplomacy of Alf Garnett to the economics of Arthur Daley'?
11 In what year did Hussein become King of Jordan?
12 How was Papa Doc also known?
13 Which leader did Churchill say was like a 'female llama surprised in her bath'?
14 Who was the last leader of Communist East Germany?
15 Who did Lionel Jospin replace as French PM?
16 What name was given to the period of rule of Emperor Hirohito?
17 Which part of Lenin was preserved after his death?
18 Who said, 'We are not at war with Egypt. We are in armed conflict'?
19 In what year was the world's first woman Prime Minister elected?
20 Who was the leader of ZAPU?
21 Which British Prime Minister was Rudyard Kipling's cousin?
22 Who said, 'We have the happiest Africans in the world'?
23 What did Mao Tse Tung call the 'great leap forward'?
24 Which newspaper originally coined the term Iron Lady about Margaret Thatcher?
25 Which role did Harold Macmillan say was, 'forever poised between a cliche and an indiscretion'?

Answers

World Leaders

1 Mikhail Gorbachev. **2** Chiluba. **3** Andropov. **4** Nnamdi Azikiwe. **5** Willy Brandt. **6** Idi Amin. **7** Castro. **8** Reconstruction. **9** Louis Botha. **10** Denis Healey. **11** 1952. **12** Francois Duvalier. **13** Charles de Gaulle. **14** Egon Krenz. **15** Alain Juppe. **16** Showa. **17** Brain. **18** Anthony Eden. **19** 1960. **20** Joshua Nkomo. **21** Stanley Baldwin. **22** Ian Smith. **23** Enforced industrialisation. **24** Red Star. **25** Foreign Secretary.

Quiz 62 Pot Luck

Level 3

1 According to hippy guru Dr Timothy Leary, what did you do before you 'drop out'?
2 Who was the first Welshman to become angling's World Freshwater Champion?
3 Who wrote the novel *The Rector's Wife*?
4 In which year were breathalyser tests introduced in Britain?
5 What is Angus Deayton's real first name?
6 Hancock Field international airport is in which US state?
7 What did Franz Kafka do for a day job?
8 What was the name of the TV profile of Elton John made by his partner David Furnish?
9 Where in England was Julie Walters born?
10 What star sign is Harrison Ford?
11 Which profession did Janet Street-Porter study for before her media career?
12 What are the international registration letters of a vehicle from Ethiopia?
13 Which entertainer said, 'He was into animal husbandry – until they caught him at it'?
14 How many policewomen went on duty when women first went on the beat?
15 What was Jive Bunny and the Mastermixers' last UK No 1 of the 80s?
16 How did Guenter Parche leave his mark on sport in the 90s?
17 What is Iggy Pop's real name?
18 Dorval International airport is in which country?
19 Which soap star recorded When I Need You in 1998?
20 What could be bought at the Post Office in late 1966 which had not been available before?
21 In which year were both sides of the Channel Tunnel linked by the service tunnel?
22 Harry Weinstein became a world champion under which name?
23 Whose face appeared for the first time on a bank note in June 1999?
24 Who directed *Good Morning Vietnam*?
25 Where did the Shining Path terrorists operate?

Answers

Pot Luck

1 Turn on, tune in. **2** Clive Branson. **3** Joanna Trollope. **4** 1967. **5** Gordon. **6** New York. **7** Worked in insurance. **8** Tantrums and Tiaras. **9** Birmingham. **10** Cancer. **11** Architect. **12** ETH. **13** Tom Lehrer. **14** Two. **15** Let's Party. **16** Stabbed Monica Seles. **17** James Osterberg. **18** Canada. **19** Will Mellor. **20** Special Christmas stamps. **21** 1990. **22** Gary Kasparov. **23** Edward Elgar. **24** Barry Levinson. **25** Peru.

Quiz 63 20th C Olympics

Level 3

1 Which country broke the India/Pakistan 50 year monopoly of men's hockey tournaments?
2 Who won Great Britain's first medal of the Atlanta Games?
3 Who last won the 100m gold for Canada before Donovan Bailey?
4 In which sport did Mike Agassi, father of Andre, compete in the 1948 and 1952 Olympics?
5 In which event did Great Britain's Henry Taylor land eight Golds?
6 Ralph Craig ran the 100 metres for the US in 1912; when did he next compete in the Olympics?
7 Who won Silver when Tessa Sanderson won Gold in the javelin?
8 Which was the first city to host the Summer Olympics twice?
9 In which event did Michelle Smith win bronze in 1996?
10 What did Paavo Nurmi always carry with him during his gold medal winning races?
11 Who won the 400m hurdles in the games sandwiched between Ed Moses' two triumphs?
12 Which country did 70s star Lassie Virren come from?
13 Who wore a T shirt saying 'Thank You America For A Wonderful Games'?
14 Why was Finn Volmari Iso-Hollo's 1932 steeplechase win exceptional?
15 In 1956 Australia hosted the Games except for equestrian events, which were held in which country?
16 Charles Bennett and Arnold Jackson have both taken gold for Britain in which athletic event?
17 Who came second when Donovan Bailey won 100m Gold?
18 How many Gold medals did Great Britain win in 1996?
19 In which event did an individual first won four successive Golds?
20 At which venue did Steve Redgrave first win Gold?
21 Britain and which other country have won Gold in every Summer Games?
22 In what year did baseball become a medal sport?
23 In which sporting event did John Huish claim 1996 Olympic Gold?
24 Tessa Sanderson first competed in the Olympics in which country?
25 Which country had its only Gold in men's basketball in 1980?

Answers

20th C Olympics

1 Germany. **2** Paul Palmer. **3** Percy Williams. **4** Boxing. **5** Swimming. **6** 1948 – yachting team. **7** Tiina Lillak. **8** Paris. **9** 200m butterfly. **10** Stopwatch. **11** Volker Beck. **12** Finland. **13** Daley Thompson. **14** He ran an extra lap by mistake. **15** Sweden. **16** 1500m. **17** Frankie Fredericks. **18** One. **19** Discus. **20** Los Angeles. **21** France. **22** 1992. **23** Archery. **24** Canada. **25** Yugoslavia.

Early Days – 1976

1 Name the married woman that Ken Barlow dated this year.
2 What was her husband's name?
3 Who had his electricity cut off because he couldn't pay the bills?
4 Who took over the Corner Shop and fought Annie Walker to obtain an alcohol licence?
5 Who became the resident pianist at the Gatsby Club?
6 Which young girl was drawn into a messy divorce case after an affair?
7 Who took Mavis away for a romantic weekend?
8 Why did he then cool off their romance?
9 Who put up Hilda's 'panoramic contrast wall' or 'muriel'?
10 Name the shop where Gail and Elsie worked.
11 Who left Coronation Street and moved to Whaley Bridge?
12 Who made himself unpopular by sticking up in court for the Marsh Brothers who started the warehouse fire?
13 Who was falsely accused of embezzling the mission funds when he lost a £5 postal order?
14 Which massively popular female character returned after a 3-year absence?
15 Who had a romantic liaison with pensioner Bertha Lumley?
16 Who set fire to his TV?
17 Who was terrorised by obscene phone calls?
18 Who wrote a steamy novel called *Song of a Scarlet Summer*?
19 Which two characters got locked in the Rovers' cellar?
20 Who passed her driving test after 83 lessons?
21 Which cockney character made his *Coronation Street* debut this year?
22 Which number Coronation Street did he buy?
23 Who was debagged at the denim factory Christmas party?
24 Who was employed as a potman at the Rovers?
25 Who had an allotment?

Answers

Early Days – 1976
1 Wendy Nightingale. **2** Roger. **3** Albert Tatlock. **4** Renee Bradshaw. **5** Ernie Bishop. **6** Gail Potter (with Roy Thornley). **7** Derek Wilton. **8** His mother told him they weren't suited. **9** Eddie Yeats. **10** Sylvia's Seperates. **11** Minnie Caldwell. **12** Ken Barlow. **13** Ernie Bishop. **14** Elsie Tanner. **15** Albert Tatlock. **16** Stan Ogden. **17** Gail Potter. **18** Mavis Riley. **19** Stan Ogden and Albert Tatlock. **20** Annie Walker. **21** Mike Baldwin. **22** Number 5. **23** Ernie Bishop. **24** Fred Gee. **25** Albert Tatlock.

Quiz 65 20th C Hollywood

Level 3

1 In how many countries did *A Few Good Men* open simultaneously, making it the largest premiere on record?
2 In which film is Vince LaRocca the gangster boyfriend of Deloris?
3 What was the third sequel to *Child's Play*?
4 The documentary *Hearts of Darkness* told of the making of which film?
5 Who said, 'I knew that with a mouth like mine I just had to be a star or something'?
6 How many years after *Terminator* was *Terminator* 2 released?
7 Which director of Madonna's Vogue video directed *Alien 3*?
8 Which Clint Eastwood film had the highest stuntman ratio?
9 In *Reversal of Fortune* what is the name of Claus's wife whom he is found guilty of attempting to murder?
10 Which Hollywood couple called one of their children Dakota Mayi?
11 Whose slogan was 'More stars than there are in heaven'?
12 In which 1990 Robert de Niro film did the director's parents both appear?
13 Who played Judy, Doralee and Violet's boss in *9 to 5*?
14 What was the name of the first sci fi movie to cost more than $1 million?
15 During the making of which film did Grace Kelly meet Prince Rainier of Monaco, thus ending her Hollywood career?
16 Which actor said of Hollywood, 'If you say what you mean in this town, you're an outlaw'?
17 What was included inside the wooden horse for *Helen of Troy*, to make the actors more comfortable?
18 Which 50s film held the record for the most number of animals in a film?
19 Who said, 'I'm old. I'm young. I'm intelligent. I'm stupid'?
20 What was John Cazale's last film?
21 Who was Tatum O'Neal's equestrian coach in *International Velvet*?
22 Who directed *Eyes Wide Shut*?
23 Who won the Best Actress Oscar the year Princess Diana died?
24 How old was Richard Gere when he starred in *An Officer and a Gentleman*?
25 Although Anthony Hopkins starred in the film of *Shadowlands*, who had played it on Broadway and the West End?

Answers

20th C Hollywood

1 51. **2** Sister Act. **3** Bride of Chucky. **4** Apocalypse Now. **5** Barbra Streisand. **6** Seven. **7** David Fincher. **8** The Rookie. **9** Sunny. **10** Don Johnson & Melanie Griffith. **11** MGM. **12** Goodfellas. **13** Dabney Coleman. **14** Forbidden Planet. **15** To Catch a Thief. **16** Kevin Costner. **17** Air conditioning. **18** Around the World in 80 Days. **19** Warren Beatty. **20** The Deer Hunter. **21** Marcia Williams. **22** Stanley Kubrick. **23** Helen Hunt. **24** 30. **25** Nigel Hawthorne.

Quiz 66 Pot Luck

Level 3

1 Lake Echternach was the first venue for which world championship?
2 In which decade did Dennis the Menace start his menacing?
3 What are Hugh Grant's middle names?
4 Which senior post did Nigel Havers' father hold in Margaret Thatcher's government?
5 How many games did England lose in soccer's 1982 World Cup in Spain?
6 Who wrote the best seller *Shogun*?
7 How old was Stacey Hillyard when she first became snooker's World Amateur Champion?
8 Hartsfield international airport is in which US state?
9 What star sign is George Best?
10 Where in England was Sir Richard Attenborough born?
11 What was John Lennon's last UK No 1 of the 80s?
12 What are the international registration letters of a vehicle from Fiji?
13 Who was the first Wimbledon men's singles champion after World War II?
14 In 1957 an air service was set up between London and which city?
15 What is Brigitte Bardot's real name?
16 In what year was the ambulance service introduced in London?
17 In all, how many England managers did Kevin Keegan play for?
18 In which country is the Salazar bridge?
19 'Dull it isn't' was part of an ad to promote which profession?
20 In which year was the then tallest building the Post Office Tower opened?
21 Greg Lake's I Believe in Father Christmas was based on a suite by which composer?
22 Which country does the airline Varig come from?
23 What was Anthony Newley's real first name?
24 Who directed *American Graffiti*?
25 Who played Monsieur Alfonse in the TV comedy *'Allo 'Allo*?

Answers

Pot Luck

1 Fly fishing. **2** 50s. **3** John Mungo. **4** Attorney General. **5** None. **6** James Clavell. **7** 15. **8** Georgia. **9** Gemini. **10** Cambridge. **11** Woman. **12** FJI. **13** Yvon Petra. **14** Moscow. **15** Camille Javal. **16** 1905. **17** Four. **18** Portugal. **19** Police. **20** 1965. **21** Prokofiev. **22** Brazil. **23** George. **24** George Lucas. **25** Kenneth Connor.

Quiz 67 20th C Sit Coms

Level 3

1 Which Deputy Party leader appeared in an episode of *Chef!*?
2 What was the provisional title of *Last of the Summer Wine*?
3 *Empty Nest* was a spin off from which sitcom?
4 Which Seinfeld star was the voice of Hugo in *The Hunchback of Notre Dame*?
5 Whose song provided the music for *Girls On Top*?
6 In *Man About the House* what football team did Robin Tripp support?
7 What was the business owned by Ted Simcock called in *A Bit of a Do*?
8 What was Jean Boht's codename for *This Is Your Life*?
9 What was the name of the singles club in *Dear John* by John Sullivan?
10 In *May to December* Miss Flood became Mrs Who?
11 What was Polly's surname in *Fawlty Towers*?
12 On which UK sitcom special did Fergie make a guest appearance?
13 In what type of hospital was *Get Well Soon* set?
14 In 1979, which sitcom netted the highest audience of the year of 24 million viewers?
15 What was the surname of Rhoda in the sitcom spin-off from the *Mary Tyler Moore Show*?
16 When *Fawlty Towers* was shown in Spain, Manuel became what nationality in order to avoid offence to the Spaniards?
17 Which star of a popular sitcom made a fitness video called *Let's Dance*?
18 In which state was *Roseanne* set?
19 Which sitcom star released a solo album called What Is Going to Become of Us All in 1976?
20 Which star of *Barbara* was mayoress of her home town, Blackburn?
21 Which show was originally called *These Friends of Mine*?
22 What was the name of the house Hester and William rented in *French Fields*?
23 What was the name of the housekeeper in *Father Ted*?
24 Who sang the theme music for *You Rang M'Lord*, along with one its stars, Paul Shane?
25 Alf Garnett was originally to have had what name?

Answers

20th C Sit Coms

1 Roy Hattersley. **2** Last of the Summer Wine. **3** The Golden Girls. **4** Jason Alexander. **5** Squeeze. **6** Southampton. **7** Jupiter Foundry. **8** Yeast. **9** 1-2-1. **10** Tipple. **11** Sherman. **12** The Vicar of Dibley. **13** TB sanatorium. **14** To The Manor Born. **15** Morgenstern. **16** Italian. **17** Richard Wilson. **18** Illinois. **19** John LeMesurier. **20** Madge Hindle - Doreen. **21** Ellen. **22** Les Hirondelles. **23** Mrs Doyle. **24** Bob Monkhouse. **25** Alf Ramsey.

Quiz 68 CORONATION ST. Level 3

Early Days – 1977

1 Which redhead joined *Coronation Street* this year?
2 Which *Coronation Street* baby was born this year?
3 Which female character comitted suicide?
4 On which holiday island was Rita offered a singing contract before turning it down to marry Len?
5 Who was best man at her wedding to Len?
6 And who was the bridesmaid?
7 Which house did the newly wed Faircloughs move into?
8 How did Hilda try to counteract the 'bad luck' from her house number, 13?
9 What was the name of Mavis Riley's aunt?
10 Why did she sabotage Mavis' relationship with Derek Wilton?
11 Who sold Annie Walker an initialled carpet – from the Alhambra Weatherfield?
12 Which couple won a romantic night in the Midland Hotel?
13 Who moved into the Kabin flat this year?
14 Annie Walker had an anniversary party at the Rovers – to celebrate how many years in charge of the pub?
15 Who did Elsie date after meeting him at the Faircloughs' wedding reception?
16 Who had to be winched to safety by the mountain rescue after a fall in the Peak District?
17 Who was Bet Lynch's rival for Mike Baldwin's affections?
18 What was the name of Annie Walker's conman cousin?
19 Where did Dawn Perks work?
20 Who was Emily's rival for Ernest's affections?
21 Who moved into the Corner Shop flat this year?
22 Who contemplated suicide by jumping off a railway bridge?
23 Who took in washing at £1 a load, but struggled when his wife refused to do it?
24 Who played Queen Elizabeth I in the Jubilee Pageant?
25 Who was Queen Victoria?

Answers

Early Days – 1977

1 Suzie Birchall. **2** Tracy Langton. **3** Janet Reid (Barlow). **4** Tenerife. **5** Alf Roberts. **6** Mavis Riley. **7** Number 9. **8** She renamed it 12A. **9** Edie. **10** She lived with Mavis and didn't want her to move out. **11** Eddie Yeats. **12** Stan and Hilda Ogden. **13**. Mavis Riley. **14** Forty. **15** Ted Brownlow. **16** Ken Barlow. **17** Marie Stanton. **18** Charles Beaumont. **19** The Rovers Return. **20** Thelma James. **21** Bet Lynch. **22** Deirdre Langton. **23** Stan Ogden. **24** Annie Walker. **25** Ena Sharples.

Quiz 69 Books

Level 3

1 In which Ian Fleming novel did the dog Edison appear?
2 Which MP wrote *The Smile on the Face of the Tiger*?
3 Which country's national anthem was used by John Steinbeck for his book *The Grapes of Wrath*?
4 Which British novelist said, 'Fame is a powerful aphrodisiac'?
5 Which writer did Sean O'Casey describe as English Literature's performing flea?
6 Which novelist was the cousin of actor Christopher Lee?
7 *Ten Days That Shook the World* is about what?
8 How was H H Munro better known?
9 Who completed his novel *Omerta* shortly before his death?
10 What was DH Lawrence's *Lady Chatterley's Lover* originally to have been called?
11 In *Peter Pan*, what are Hook's last words?
12 Which novelist wrote *The ABC of French Food*?
13 What was Ian Fleming's first novel?
14 Which sit com actress was a judge for the Booker Prize in 1985?
15 What was Robert Graves' autobiography called?
16 Which opera singer's memoirs were called *Full Circle*?
17 John Betjeman's book *Ghastly Good Taste* was on the subject of what?
18 Which country banned *Black Beauty* for its supposed to racist title?
19 Which novelist is the mother of actress Rudi Davies?
20 What was the first volume of Dirk Bogarde's autobiography called?
21 Which actress wrote the children's book *Nibbles & Me*?
22 Which children's author's autobiography was called *Boy*?
23 What was William Golding's follow-up to *Lord of the Flies*?
24 What is the first name of P G Wodehouse's character Cheesewright?
25 Which French novelist played in goal for Algeria?

Answers

Books
1 Chitty Chitty Bang Bang. **2** Douglas Hurd. **3** USA. **4** Graham Greene. **5** P.G.Wodehouse. **6** Ian Fleming. **7** Russian Revolution. **8** Saki. **9** Mario Puzo. **10** Tenderness. **11** Floreat Etona. **12** Len Deighton. **13** Casino Royale. **14** Joanna Lumley. **15** Goodbye to All That. **16** Janet Baker. **17** Architecture. **18** Namibia. **19** Beryl Bainbridge. **20** A Postilion Struck By Lightning. **21** Elizabeth Taylor. **22** Roald Dahl. **23** The Inheritors. **24** Stilton. **25** Albert Camus.

Quiz 70 Pot Luck

Level 3

1 What is Michael Crawford's real name?
2 Which company sponsored snooker's British Gold Cup from 1981–1984?
3 Who directed the three-hour silent movie epic *The Birth Of A Nation*?
4 Who designed the Westminster building to provided MPs with more office space from 2000 onwards?
5 What did Dennis Connor win three times in the 80s?
6 In which European city is the Goulandis Natural History Museum?
7 Who wrote the book *The Hammer of God*?
8 Wayne Gretzky first played league ice hockey with which team?
9 What was the date of the October 1987 gales that hit Britain?
10 What was launched on Tuesday 30 July, 1938 and kept going to the end of the century?
11 Where in England was actor Tom Baker born?
12 What are the international registration letters of a vehicle from Liechtenstein?
13 Ex-PM James Callaghan became Baron Callaghan of where?
14 Esenboga International airport is in which country?
15 Which female was in the coffee shop in *Saturday Superstore*?
16 What star sign is Mikhail Gorbachev?
17 Who made her TV debut in Dennis Potter's *Christabel*?
18 What was the last UK No 1 of the 80s featuring Paul McCartney?
19 Who was runner up when James Hunt was F1 champion?
20 What did Che Guevara train to be?
21 What single word did boxer Joe Louis want on his tombstone?
22 Which country does the airline Sahsa come from?
23 In which year was TV personality Ernie Wise born?
24 Who directed the movie *Tess*?
25 Which TV presenter wrote the novel *A Time To Dance*?

Answers

Pot Luck

1 Michael Dumble-Smith. **2** Yamaha. **3** D W Griffith. **4** Sir Michael Hopkins. **5** America's Cup. **6** Athens. **7** Arthur C Clarke. **8** Edmonton Oilers. **9** 15th. **10** The Beano Comic. **11** Liverpool. **12** FL. **13** Cardiff. **14** Turkey. **15** Vicky Licorish. **16** Pisces. **17** Liz Hurley. **18** Ferry 'Cross The Mersey. **19** Niki Lauda. **20** Doctor. **21** Even. **22** Honduras. **23** 1925. **24** Roman Polanski. **25** Melvyn Bragg.

Quiz 71 Who's Who

Level 3

1 Who partnered Patti Austin on Baby Come To Me?
2 Which artist was the biggest-selling singles artist in the UK in 1991?
3 Which male singer fronted the group Change before his solo career took off?
4 Which London based group featured two Davies brothers?
5 What nationality is Peter Andre?
6 Who sang with R Kelly on I'm Your Angel?
7 Who featured on You Got The Love, with Source?
8 How many members were in the Mancunian band The Smiths?
9 Who partnered Michael McDonald with On My Own?
10 Which act were voted Best British Dance Act at the 1994 BRIT awards?
11 Who was born Gloria Fajarda?
12 Which member of Def Leppard died in 1991?
13 Vince Clarke and Andy Bell achieved chart success as who?
14 Who won a record four BRIT awards in 1995?
15 Who was the lead vocalist for The Go-Gos?
16 How is Douglas Trendle better known?
17 Who was the first British female to win a Grammy award?
18 Who featured on If You Ever by East 17?
19 Who was the oldest solo female singer to have a No 1 by the final year of the century?
20 Which artist has had the most UK Top Ten hits in the 1990s?
21 What relationship was Brian Connolly of Sweet to Mark McManus aka Taggart?
22 Who played the heavy metal guitar on Michael Jackson's Beat It?
23 Which Manic Street Preacher has been missing, presumed dead since, '95?
24 Which artist has achieved the most consecutive UK Top Ten hits?
25 What nationality were Rednex?

Answers

Who's Who

1 James Ingram. **2** Bryan Adams. **3** Luther Vandross. **4** Kinks. **5** English. **6** Celine Dion. **7** Candi Staton. **8** 4. **9** Patti Labelle. **10** M People. **11** Gloria Estefan. **12** Steve Clark. **13** Erasure. **14** Blur. **15** Belinda Carlisle. **16** Buster Bloodvessel. **17** Petula Clark. **18** Gabrielle. **19** Cher. **20** Madonna. **21** Brother. **22** Eddie Van Halen. **23** Richey Edwards. **24** Madonna. **25** Swedish.

Quiz 72 CORONATION ST. Level 3

Early Days – 1978

1 Who was murdered this year?
2 Which factory workers' son appeared this year and began dating Gail?
3 Who befriended battered wife Brenda Summers?
4 Who received a visit from an old flame, GI Ralph Curtis?
5 Who sought Mavis' help in freeing him from fiancee Beryl Challis?
6 Who became Annie Walker's chauffeur?
7 Who put her foot through the Ogdens' ceiling?
8 Which couple married this year and honeymooned in Capri?
9 Who caused a fight at their wedding by telling the groom he was only marrying her for her business interests?
10 Who lost his place on the council following a drunk and disorderly charge?
11 Which charity event paired Mavis Riley with Eddie Yeats, Suzie Birchall with Steve Fisher and Gail Potter with Fred Gee?
12 Who was furious when she discovered the hospital 'consultant' treating her back was actually a porter?
13 Who won the brewery competition to prove they were the Rovers' oldest customer?
14 What car did Annie Walker own?
15 Fred Gee was offered tenancy of his own pub – on what condition?
16 Who was sacked after a row concerning a broom?
17 Who fixed Ken up with chiropodist Sally Robson?
18 Who was mistaken for a prostitute during a night out following the arrival of her decree absolute?
19 Which married man did Dawson's waitress Janice Stubbs fall for?
20 Who turned up to visit his dad after failing his O levels
21 Who dated taxi driver Ron Mather?
22 Name Baldwin's factory's driver who was a big favourite with Gail and Suzie
23 Who played Ida Clough?
24 Who camped out all night to buy a cheap colour TV?
25 Who stored a one-armed bandit at number 13?

Answers

Early Days – 1978

1 Ernie Bishop. **2** Brian Tilsley, Ivy's son. **3** Emily Bishop. **4** Hilda Ogden. **5** Derek Wilton. **6** Fred Gee. **7** Suzie Birchall. **8** Renee Bradshaw and Alf Roberts. **9** Renee's stepfather Joe Hibbert. **10** Len Fairclough. **11** A charity pram race. **12** Annie Walker. **13** Ena Sharples. **14** A Rover 2000. **15** That he was married. **16** Hilda Ogden. **17** Albert Tatlock. **18** Elsie Tanner. **19** Ray Langton. **20** Peter Barlow. **21** Elsie Tanner. **22** Steve Fisher. **23** Helene Palmer. **24** Hilda Ogden. **25** Eddie Yeats.

Quiz 73 20th C Rich & Famous

Level 3

1 Whose marriage was headlined in *Variety* as 'Egghead weds Hourglass'?
2 At whose castle did Elizabeth Taylor spend her 60th birthday?
3 Who launched her own perfume called White Diamonds?
4 Josie Borain was the partner of which rich and famous person during his difficult divorce settlement?
5 What is Jose Carreras' middle name?
6 Marion and Tito were two members of which famous family group?
7 What breed of dog was Madonna's Chiquita?
8 Whose funeral caused Sam Goldwyn say, 'The only reason people showed up was to make sure he was dead'?
9 From which year did Martina Navratilova compete officially as an American rather than a Czech player?
10 Lady Elizabeth Anson is the sister of which Lord?
11 Chevy Chase was a professional in which sport?
12 Which woman was head of Sock Shop?
13 What was the name of John Gummer's daughter photographed burger- munching in the early days of the BSE scare?
14 Who was the first British royal to visit the Soviet Union after 1917?
15 Who said, 'I'd rather go mad than see a psychiatrist'?
16 Where was the wedding of David Beckham and Victoria Adams held?
17 Prince Charles said, 'Diana only married me so that she could . . .' what?
18 Who said, 'I never really hated a man enough to give him his diamonds back'?
19 What did Elvis's widow Priscilla call her child by a different partner?
20 Which disease did Lord Snowdon suffer from as a child?
21 Which ex-MP had the car registration plate ANY 1 on his Rolls Royce?
22 Which name is shared by the daughters of Tony Curtis and Vanessa Feltz?
23 What type of car was Isadora Duncan test driving when her scarf caught in the wheel spokes and strangled her?
24 Who said, 'I'm into pop because I want to get rich, famous and laid'?
25 Which sportsman said of his autobiography, 'I can honestly say I have written one more book than I have read'?

Answers

20th C Rich & Famous

1 Arthur Miller & Marilyn Monroe. **2** Sleeping Beauty's. **3** Elizabeth Taylor. **4** Earl Spencer. **5** Maria. **6** Jackson Five. **7** Chihuahua. **8** Louis B Mayer. **9** 1981. **10** Lichfield. **11** Tennis. **12** Sophie Mirman. **13** Cordelia. **14** Princess Anne. **15** Michael Caine. **16** Luttrellstown Castle. **17** Go through red lights. **18** Zsa Zsa Gabor. **19** Navarone. **20** Polio. **21** Jeffrey Archer. **22** Allegra. **23** Bugatti. **24** Bob Geldof. **25** Merv Hughes.

Quiz 74 Pot Luck

Level 3

1 What was Madonna's last UK No 1 of the 80s?
2 Who was the famous wife of pilot Jim Mollison?
3 What was Dame Barbara Cartland's real first name?
4 In which year did *Carry On* star Hattie Jacques die?
5 Who was the first US President to be re-elected for a fourth term of office?
6 What does the P stand for in BUPA?
7 Who did John Spencer defeat in snooker's first knockout World Championship final?
8 Who wrote *The Lady Who Liked Clean Rest Rooms*?
9 Who was the first woman weather presenter on BBC TV?
10 Which university did Michael Jordan play basketball for?
11 Which was the first country to win soccer's World Cup on foreign soil?
12 What are the international registration letters of a vehicle from Guatemala?
13 Where was Kenneth Branagh born?
14 In what year did the first woman qualify as a barrister in the UK?
15 How many years after her death were Garbo's ashes returned to her Swedish homeland?
16 What is Cheryl Baker's real name?
17 In what year was Australia reached by air from England?
18 Cricketer Anil Humble has qualified as what?
19 Fornebu International airport is in which country?
20 Which company first advertised 'Is it true blondes have more fun?'?
21 Which writer described newspaper reports of his own death as being 'greatly exaggerated'?
22 What star sign is Omar Sharif?
23 In which year did the world's longest-running stage play, *The Mousetrap* open?
24 Who directed *Out Of Africa*?
25 Which country does the airline LAM come from?

Answers

Pot Luck

1 Like A Prayer. **2** Amy Johnson. **3** Mary. **4** 1980. **5** Franklin D Roosevelt. **6** Provident. **7** Gary Owen. **8** J P Donleavy. **9** Barbara Edwards. **10** North Carolina. **11** Italy. **12** GCA. **13** Belfast. **14** 1921. **15** Nine. **16** Rita Crudgington. **17** 1919. **18** Engineer. **19** Norway. **20** Clairol. **21** Mark Twain. **22** Aries. **23** 1952. **24** Sydney Pollack. **25** Mozambique.

Quiz 75 Murder Most Foul

Level 3

1 Who was murdered along with O J Simpson's estranged wife Nicole?
2 Who was nicknamed the Vampire of Dusseldorf?
3 Who was the first woman to be executed for murder in Texas after 1863?
4 *The Sicilian Specialist* by Norman Lewis is a thinly disguised fictional account of which assassination plot?
5 Where was Martin Luther King assassinated?
6 What was the real name of Butch Cassidy?
7 Who was convicted with Jon Venables of the murder of Jamie Bulger?
8 Which famous name was killed by Kenneth Halliwell?
9 Under what name did Dr Crippen leave the country after the murder of his wife?
10 In which Lake did Peter Hogg dump the body of his wife in 1976 although it was 11 years before he was jailed?
11 Keith Blakelock was killed in riots where?
12 Where did Michael Ryan carry out an horrific massacre?
13 How many men did Dennis Nilsen admit to killing between 1978 and 1983?
14 Where did John Christie live?
15 Who did Gaetano Bresci assassinate?
16 What was gangster Lucky Luciano's real first name?
17 What was the name of Ruth Ellis's lover whom she murdered?
18 How was murderer Pedro Alonzo Lopez nicknamed?
19 How old was the Yorkshire Ripper when he was captured?
20 What was the name of the Captain who sent the first wireless telegraphy message which brought about the capture of Dr Crippen?
21 Who was convicted of the murder of aviator Charles Lindbergh's son?
22 On which island did Martin Bryant massacre 34 people in 1996?
23 What was the name of the rally which Yitzhak Rabin had attended just before his assassination?
24 What was the name of the man killed in the A6 Murder, for which James Hanratty was hanged?
25 Who did the Boston Strangler say he worked for in order to gain his victims' confidence?

Answers

Murder Most Foul

1 Ronald Goldman. **2** Peter Kurten. **3** Karla Faye Tucker. **4** JF Kennedy. **5** Memphis. **6** Robert LeRoy Parker. **7** Robert Thompson. **8** Joe Orton. **9** Robinson. **10** Wast Water. **11** Tottenham. **12** Hungerford. **13** 15. **14** 10 Rillington Place. **15** King Umberto I of Italy. **16** Salvatore. **17** David Blakely. **18** The Monster of the Andes. **19** 34. **20** Kendall. **21** Bruno Hauptmann. **22** Tasmania. **23** Peace Yes Violence No. **24** Michael Gregsten. **25** Model agency.

Quiz 76 CORONATION ST. Level 3

Early Days – 1979

1 Which factory worker moved into Coronation Street with her family?
2 Name her friend, who also introduced her husband this year.
3 Sue Nicholls made her debut as Audrey Potter this year, but who did she play in *Crossroads*?
4 Which actress accepted a lifetime achievement award from John Betjeman?
5 Why did Dave Barnes attack Ken Barlow?
6 Which baby did Sally Norton kidnap, unwittingly saving her from a potentially fatal accident?
7 Who suffered a personality change after being injured when a lorry crashed into the Rovers?
8 What reason did Ivy Tisley give for objecting to Gail and Brian's marriage?
9 Who ran a betting scam from behind the Rovers bar?
10 Who took a weekend job on an ice cream van as a cover for selling beer?
11 Who gave Gail Potter away at her wedding?
12 Who retired from the post office this year?
13 Who organised a jogging class at the community centre?
14 And who was the only person to turn up?
15 Who said of Elsie 'there've 'bin times when Elsie Tanner's life's kept mine going. I've a lot to thank her for.'
16 Who was kidnapped by students during Rag Week?
17 Who discovered a talent for copying abstract art?
18 And who did Eddie Yeats sell one of her paintings to?
19 Who moved to Torquay with her boyfriend, then moved back to Coronation Street when they fell out?
20 Who accompanied Rita Fairclough on her caravanning holiday?
21 Who found a budgie trapped in her chimney, and named it Harry?
22 Who returned from London calling herself a model, but could only get work demonstrating sausages in a supermarket?
23 Who played Bert Tilsley?
24 Who kept hens in their back yard?
25 What was their favourite hen called?

Answers

Early Days – 1979

1 Ivy Tilsley, with Bert and Brian. **2** Vera Duckworth and Jack. **3** Marilyn Gates. **4** Doris Speed. **5** Because Ken was teaching his wife to read. **6** Tracy Langton. **7** Alf Roberts. **8** Gail was not a Catholic. **9** Fred Gee. **10** Eddie Yeats. **11** Mike Baldwin. **12** Alf Roberts. **13** Ken Barlow. **14** Mavis Riley. **15** Ena Shaples. **16** Bet Lynch. **17** Hilda Ogden. **18** Annie Walker. **19** Elsie Tanner. **20** Bet Lynch. **21** Mavis Riley. **22** Suzie Birchall. **23** Peter Dudley. **24** The Ogdens and Eddie Yeats. **25** Little Hilda.

Quiz 77 Sporting Chance

Level 3

1 Why does the leader of the Tour de France wear a yellow jersey?
2 Where did golfer Mark Calcavecchia win his only British Open?
3 In the season Damon Hill was F1 champion, how many races did he win?
4 Who was Czechoslovakia's only Wimbledon Men's Singles winner of the 20th century, playing as a Czech?
5 As well as Red Rum, which other Red did Brian Fletcher ride to a Grand National victory?
6 How many games had Steve Davis won before Dennis Taylor opened his account in the classic 1985 World Snooker final?
7 How many times did Terry Venables play for England?
8 In which country did Lynn Davies set the British long jump record that has stood for 30 years?
9 What was the first sport shown on ITV?
10 What was Jack Dempsey's nickname?
11 Brian Barnes played golf for Scotland in the 70s but where was he born?
12 What do JPR Williams' initials stand for?
13 Who went airborne during a cricket match with David Gower in the Gooch-led Australia tour?
14 How old was Stephen Hendry when he appeared on *This Is Your Life*?
15 Who has won the Badminton Horse Trials on Priceless and Master Craftsman?
16 Which boxer appeared in the film *Spirit of Youth*?
17 In which year did none of the four golf majors go to an American?
18 Who was team leader of Williams when Damon Hill was promoted to No 2?
19 What was the name of the horse on which Pat Eddery first won the Derby?
20 Who were the first winners of hockey's English National Cup?
21 What breed of dog was Steffi Graf's Ben?
22 In what year was snooker's World Championship first contested?
23 What is the middle name of golfer Mark James?
24 In how many games did Ray Wilkins captain England?
25 At which race circuit did Ayrton Senna lose his life?

Answers

Sporting Chance

1 Its sponsor printed its newspaper on yellow paper. **2** Troon. **3** 8. **4** Jan Kodes. **5** Red Alligator. **6** 8. **7** Twice. **8** Switzerland. **9** Boxing. **10** Manassa Mauler. **11** London. **12** John Peter Rhys. **13** John Morris. **14** 21. **15** Virginia Leng – nee Holgate. **16** Joe Louis. **17** 1993. **18** Alain Prost. **19** Grundy. **20** Hounslow. **21** Boxer. **22** 1927. **23** Hugh. **24** Ten. **25** Imola.

Quiz 78 CORONATION ST. Level 3

Who Said What?

1 Drinking is a serious business. You've got to keep at it, like a football match.
2 He gets very absorbed in his food does Alf. Not to say covered in it.
3 If my wife put her mind to it, she could find a reason why Mary and Joseph were unfit parents.
4 Just because I'm in a wheelchair, they think they can push me around.
5 Us buy a telly? I've got more chance of a proposal off Michael Heseltine.
6 I have been the hub of the community. You might even say that I have had my own little kingdom.
7 Come to think of it, I don't think I even said I love me own mother.
8 Love me or loathe me. You've got to admit I've got style.
9 I'm not the callow youth of yesteryear. I'm a man of steel, honed on the handle of life.
10 Three milk stouts – and make sure there's no lipstick on the glasses.
11 In darkest Africa they use a set of drums. Here we've got Hilda.
12 When you've made gravy under gunfire you can do anything.
13 Not many people have been disappointed in life as much as I have.
14 Me behind a bar, I'm in me element. Like Santa Claus in his grotto.
15 My mother-in-law ... she's like Boris Karloff after a busy night at the graveyard.
16 Reg Holdsworth'd admire an orang-utan if it wore a short skirt.
17 They've bin talkin' about me ever since I put me first pair of nylons on.
18 Annie Walker'd attend her own funeral if God let 'er.
19 Life turns out to be just a bloody cheat, and I can't even whimper.
20 Them Duckworths are like stray cats. Invite 'em in for a saucer of milk and they're asleep in front of the fire before you can blink.
21 Decent women have white baths.
22 We've all had our nightmares. We're the walking wounded. It's just that some of us get more wounded than others.
23 I'm not pulled as easy as a pint of Newton and Ridleys.
24 You could meet Alf Roberts riding on a horse in the middle of the Sahara Desert and still know he's a grocer.
25 You know what your trouble is, Stan Ogden? You're lax – lax from the neck up and relax from the neck down.

Answers

Who Said What?
1 Stan Ogden. **2** Audrey Roberts. **3** Don Brennan. **4** Maud Grimes. **5** Hilda Ogden. **6** Annie Walker. **7** Alec Gilroy. **8** Mike Baldwin. **9** Reg Holdsworth. **10** Ena Sharples. **11** Renee Roberts. **12** Percy Sugden. **13** Mavis Wilton. **14** Bet Lynch. **15** Jack Duckworth. **16** Rita Sullivan. **17** Elsie Tanner. **18** Albert Tatlock. **19** Ken Barlow. **20** Hilda Ogden. **21** Betty Turpin. **22** Rita Sullivan. **23** Natalie Barnes. **24** Audrey Roberts. **25** Hilda Ogden.

Quiz 79 20th C Comedies

Level 3

1 Who wrote the lyrics for the song from *Notting Hill* sung by Elvis Costello?
2 What was Michael Palin's occupation in *A Private Function*?
3 Which boxer appeared in the film *Carry On Constable*?
4 Which film tells of the exploits of singer Deco Duffe?
5 What was the name of the orphanage where The Blues brothers were brought up?
6 *Airplane!* was triggered off by which movie?
7 How old was Macaulay Culkin when he was cast for his role in *Home Alone*?
8 In *Private Benjamin* what is the name of Benjamin's captain?
9 What was the name of the High School in *Porky's*?
10 What was Tootsie's name before he turned into Tootsie?
11 Who was the leader of the band that appeared in *The Brady Bunch Movie*?
12 Who directed *The Cable Guy*?
13 What type of drug is Sherman Klump trying to perfect in *The Nutty Professor*?
14 In what year does *Demolition Man* take place?
15 Which comedy contained the song A Wink and a Smile?
16 What was Steve Martin's first film?
17 In which category was *Mrs Doubtfire* Oscar-nominated?
18 On which film was *Three Men and a Baby* based?
19 Which canine caper had the song The Day I Fall in Love?
20 Whose poems returned to the best sellers list after *Four Weddings and a Funeral*?
21 Who was both Oscar and BAFTA nominated for *When Harry Met Sally*?
22 What was the third *Road* movie?
23 What was the signal for an angel getting its wings in *It's A Wonderful Life*?
24 Who was Louise Lasser's husband when she starred with him in *What's Up, Tiger Lily*?
25 What was the first sequel to *The Pink Panther* called?

Answers

20th C Comedies

1 Herbert Kretzmer. **2** Chiropodist. **3** Freddie Mills. **4** The Commitments. **5** Saint Helen of the Blessed Shroud. **6** Zero Hour!. **7** Nine. **8** Lewis. **9** Angel Beach. **10** Michael Dorsey. **11** Davy Jones. **12** Ben Stiller. **13** Weight loss. **14** 2032. **15** Sleepless in Seattle. **16** The Jerk. **17** Best Make up. **18** Trois Hommes et un Couffin. **19** Beethoven's 2nd. **20** W H Auden. **21** Nora Ephron – writer. **22** Road to Morocco. **23** Bell ringing. **24** Woody Allen. **25** A Shot in the Dark.

Quiz 80 Pot Luck

Level 3

1 What was the name of the REAL mother of Ashley Peacock?
2 Who played Maxine's mum Doreen?
3 Who ran the Lenny Phillips Theatrical Agency?
4 Who gave Curly money to pay off his debts when his telescope was stolen?
5 In 1967 a famous novelist sent a letter to a television magazine about Elsie Tanner's love life. Who was she?
6 Who was left behind on the 1961 coach trip to Blackpool?
7 What course did Jenny Bradley study at the Polytechnic?
8 Which Coronation Street actor appeared in *The High Game*?
9 Who had a premium bond win in 1961?
10 Who introduced a fruit machine into the Rovers for the first time in 1973?
11 What was Jack Walker's brother called?
12 What was Annie Walker's maiden name?
13 Who played Detective Sergeant Russell in *No Hiding Place* and appeared in the film Cosh Boy before joining *Coronation Street*?
14 Which *Coronation Street* actress played Polly Barraclough in *Sam*?
15 Who played Jonathan Broughton?
16 Which *Coronation Street* scriptwriter also wrote *Nearest and Dearest*?
17 What did Joe Makinson do for a living?
18 What is Maxine's dad called?
19 What crime had Eddie Ramsden done time for?
20 Who took Ken Barlow's virginity?
21 Which *Coronation Street* actor appeared briefly in *Behind the Mask* with Michael Redgrave?
22 Who played Wanda Pickles in *Up The Elephant And Round The Castle*?
23 Who travelled to London with Mavis to watch the Royal Wedding?
24 What colour was Mavis' wedding outfit when she married Derek?
25 Who had a friend called Monkey Gibbon?

Answers

Pot Luck

1 Kathleen Gutteridge. **2** Prunella Gee. **3** Dennis Tanner. **4** Emily Bishop. **5** Barbara Cartland. **6** Ena Sharples. **7** Biology. **8** Bryan Mosley. **9** Florrie Lindley. **10** Glyn Thomas. **11** Arthur. **12** Beaumont. **13** Johnny Briggs. **14** Maggie Jones. **15** Tom Lewis. **16** John Stephenson. **17** Plumber. **18** Derek Heavey. **19** GBH. **20** Marion Lund. **21** Bill Roache. **22** Sue Nicholls. **23** Betty Turpin. **24** Lilac. **25** Eddie Yeats.

Quiz 81 20th C TV Ads

Level 3

1 Which actor famous for a series of TV ads writes poetry under the pseudonym Robert Williams?
2 Toothpaste was famously the first ad on ITV. What was the second?
3 'Nice one Cyril' was the slogan to advertise what?
4 What did the Hoddles advertise when they performed in a TV ad?
5 Which drink suitable for children was advertised by Sharron Davies?
6 Who famously threw away her ring and fur coat but kept her VW Golf?
7 Which *Dynasty* character is 'worth it' in the hair ads?
8 Who played Prunella Scales' daughter in the Tesco ads?
9 Who wrote Adiemus, which was used by BA to advertise their services?
10 Characters from which soap were used to advertise BT?
11 Which company said, 'Never forget you have a choice'?
12 Which supermarket chain sacked John Cleese because customers found his ads very unfunny?
13 Which personality famous for voiceovers described this way of earning money as the late 20th century equivalent of taking in washing?
14 Which wine store used Pachelbel's Canon as an advertising theme?
15 Which lager was advertised to the accompaniment of Verdi's La forza del destino?
16 Which female writer is credited with coming up with the slogan 'Go to work on an egg'?
17 Which theme music did BT use to promote their Internet services?
18 When did Guinness first say their drink was 'good for you'?
19 'Does she or doesn't she..?' was a slogan used to advertise what?
20 Which make of car had the slogan Vorsprung durch Technik?
21 When did the word pinta enter the English language via an ad for milk?
22 What was advertised as the chocolate bar you could eat 'without ruining your appetite'?
23 Who made over 50 ads for Schh you know who in nine years?
24 According to the ad, what put the T in Britain?
25 When did the first anti-drink driving campaign start?

Answers

20th C TV Ads

1 Bob Hoskins. **2** Drinking chocolate. **3** Wonderloaf bread. **4** Breakfast cereal. **5** Ribena Toothkind. **6** Paula Hamilton. **7** Sammy Jo. **8** Jane Horrocks. **9** Carl Jenkins. **10** EastEnders. **11** British Caledonian Airways. **12** Sainsbury's. **13** John Peel. **14** Thresher. **15** Stella Artois. **16** Fay Weldon. **17** E.T. **18** 1930. **19** Hair colour. **20** Audi. **21** 1958. **22** Milky Way. **23** William Franklin. **24** Typhoo. **25** 1964.

Quiz 82 Pot Luck

Level 3

1 In which American state is the Merril Collection and the Burke Museum of Fine Arts?
2 From 1903 to 1958 all the Popes bar one had which name?
3 What star sign is Pauline Collins?
4 What is Whoopi Goldberg's real name?
5 What was Mud's last UK No 1 of the 70s?
6 Which political party had the Golden Lion in Ashburton, Devon, as its meeting place?
7 Who hosted the quiz show *Home Truths*?
8 What was the first oldies pop song used in a Levi's TV ad?
9 Which actress played a hotel manager in *The Duchess of Duke Street*?
10 What was the name of William Shatner's Doberman Pinscher dog?
11 Which nation was the first to ratify the United Nations charter in 1945?
12 What are the international registration letters of a vehicle from Jordan?
13 Who wrote the novel *Time and Tide*?
14 What is the Alaskan terminus of the Alaskan Highway?
15 'Put a tiger in your tank' was originally an advertising slogan for what?
16 In which year did David Bedford set a new 10,000m record?
17 What is Mel Gibson's middle name?
18 In which country was Julie Christie born?
19 In the 60s the last London trolleybus journey started where?
20 What does Mark Lester, child star of *Oliver!*, do now?
21 Cannon international airport is in which US state?
22 Which country does the airline VIASA come from?
23 To the nearest 30 minutes, how long was the longest speech ever made at the United Nations?
24 Who directed *Back To The Future*?
25 Richard Daley was mayor of which city for 21 years?

Answers

Pot Luck

1 Texas. **2** Pius. **3** Virgo. **4** Caryn Johnson. **5** Oh Boy. **6** Monster Raving Loony Party. **7** Steve Wright. **8** I Heard It Through The Grapevine. **9** Gemma Jones. **10** Kirk. **11** Nicaragua. **12** HKJ. **13** Edna O'Brien. **14** Fairbanks. **15** Esso petrol. **16** 1973. **17** Columcille. **18** India. **19** Wimbledon. **20** Osteopath. **21** Nevada. **22** Venezuela. **23** 4.5 hours. **24** Robert Zemeckis. **25** Chicago.

Quiz 83 Media

Level 3

1 'All human life is there' was a slogan used to advertise which newspaper?
2 Which newspaper published detailed photographs of Diana's car crash?
3 In 1980 which radio station ran an April Fool's day prank saying Big Ben's clockface would be replaced by a digital one?
4 Who founded the Pergamon Press?
5 Who drew Felix the Cat?
6 In what profession did Bruce Bairnsfather find fame?
7 In radio's *Beyond Our Ken* which Kenneth Williams character's catchphrase was, 'The answer lies in the soil'?
8 Which newspaper was launched in January 1990?
9 When he was on *Desert Island Discs*, which newspaper did Des O'Connor ask to have delivered regularly as his luxury?
10 Tessa Sanderson won libel damages in 1990 against which newspapers?
11 Who was DC Thomson's first cartoonist allowed to sign his name?
12 Who found fame on radio as Lady Beatrice Counterblast?
13 Who created the line from a cartoon, 'Happiness is a warm puppy'?
14 Whose poem For the Fallen was printed in *The Times* in 1914?
15 When did the Popeye cartoon begin?
16 For which magazine did a pregnant Cindy Crawford pose naked?
17 Which group of people did radio producer D G Bridson describe as 'The wriggling ponces of the spoken word'?
18 Who said, 'When a journalist enters the room, your privacy ends and his begins'?
19 Which radio DJ said, 'And don't forget on Sunday you can hear the two minute silence on Radio One'?
20 Who played Little Jim in The Goons?
21 'Good girls go to heaven, bad girls go everywhere' was the slogan used to launch which magazine?
22 Which journalist took the name Cassandra?
23 Who scripted *The Navy Lark*?
24 Who launched the news magazine *Now!* around 1980?
25 Which classic radio show had the line, 'Can I do you now sir'?

Answers

Media

1 The News of the World. **2** Bild. **3** BBC World Service. **4** Robert Maxwell. **5** Otto Messmer. **6** Cartoonist. **7** Arthur Fallowfield. **8** The Independent on Sunday. **9** The Sporting Life. **10** Sunday Mirror/People. **11** Dudley Watkins. **12** Betty Marsden. **13** Charles Schulz. **14** Laurence Binyon. **15** 1933. **16** W. **17** Disc jockeys. **18** Warren Beatty. **19** Steve Wright. **20** Spike Milligan. **21** Cosmopolitan. **22** William Connor. **23** Lawrie Wyman. **24** James Goldsmith. **25** ITMA.

Quiz 84 CORONATION ST. Level 3

Pot Luck, Early Days

1 What did the council threaten to change the name of Coronation Street to in 1962?
2 And who led the campaign against this proposal?
3 Who was the beauty queen briefly engaged to Billy Walker?
4 Name the actress who played Doreen Lostock
5 What creatures did Dennis Tanner keep in Annie Walker's bathtub?
6 What was Myra's job when she met Jerry?
7 Why did Granada have to change a story line concerning Sheila Birtles?
8 Whose car did Jed Stone 'borrow' when he left Coronation Street?
9 Who played Concepta Hewitt?
10 Who played Harry Hewitt?
11 Which famous character – still in Coronation Street today – made a single appearance in the programme in 1964 as an exotic dancer?
12 Which character pronounced Martha Longhurst dead?
13 Who won the talent contest at the Viaduct Sporting Club with her version of the song 'My Guy'?
14 In 1964, who enrolled in a hairdressing academy ?
15 Who was the Irishman that Florrie Lindley fell in love with?
16 What was Lionel Petty's occupation before moving to Coronation Street?
17 What nationality was Lionel Petty?
18 Where did Ken and Valerie Barlow live in 1965?
19 Who flew to Boston for three months after a surprise visit from her American nephew in 1965?
20 In 1965, who had a fling with a married man and was questioned by police when he subsequently died?
21 Where did the Cheveski family go to start a new life?
22 Who proposed to Albert Tatlock on holiday in Cleveleys?
23 Who fell for Minnie Caldwell in 1966?
24 In this year, who thought he had won the pools, only to find his wife had filled the coupon in after the results?
25 Who made his debut in 1966 as a plumber that Lucille Hewitt fell for?

Answers

Pot Luck, Early Days

1 Florida Street. **2** Ena Sharples. **3** Philippa Scopes. **4** Angela Crow. **5** Sealions. **6** Typist. **7** There were complaints following a press leak that she was to kill herself. **8** Harry Hewitt. **9** Doreen Keogh. **10** Ivan Beavis. **11** Rita Littlewood (now Sullivan). **12** Len Fairclough. **13** Lucille Hewitt. **14** Dennis Tanner. **15** 'Tickler' Murphy. **16** Army Sergeant Major. **17** Welsh. **18** Number 9. **19** Ena Sharples. **20** Elsie Tanner. **20** Birmingham. **22** Clara Midgely. **23** Wally Tanner. **24** Stan Ogden. **25**. Ray Langton.

Quiz 85 Words & Music

Level 3

1 Who was the first female to top the singles chart with a self-composed song?
2 Whose album Fat of the Land debuted at No 1 in more than 20 countries?
3 What was the first UK No 1 written by Shakin' Stevens himself?
4 What was the first TV theme to top the UK charts?
5 Who used, and wrote under, the pseudonym Bernard Webb?
6 Whose book of poems was called *Songs for While I'm Away*?
7 Who won Grammys for Best Album, Male Vocalist and Producer in 1986?
8 Lennon and McCartney wrote Goodbye for which vocalist?
9 Who was described as 'a woman who pulled herself up by her bra straps'?
10 How many times was 'Walk On By' sung by Gabrielle in the first chorus?
11 What type of vehicle were Reo Speedwagon named after?
12 What was Barry Manilow's Mandy originally titled in the US?
13 What was Sir Cliff Richard's first self-produced UK No 1?
14 What was the first UK No 1 with 'rock and roll' in the title?
15 Which song by Paul Simon begins 'Wish I Was a Kellogg's Corn Flake'?
16 In the film *Grease*, who sang Beauty School Dropout?
17 On what date did Elton John first sing his biggest selling single in public?
18 What was the average age of a soldier in World War II in the UK No 1 hit, 19?
19 Which artist was the subject of a 1991 biography by Randy Taraborelli?
20 Which Kenny Rogers song was written by Lionel Richie?
21 Which song by Lisa Stansfield featured in *Indecent Proposal*?
22 Who co-wrote Fame with David Bowie?
23 Who was Michael Jackson's massive hit Ben originally intended for?
24 Whose 1991 autobiography was called *And The Beat Goes On*?
25 Who was Willy Russell's co-writer on the musical *Tallulah Who*?

Answers

Words & Music

1 Kate Bush. **2** Prodigy. **3** Oh Julie!. **4** Eye Level. **5** Paul McCartney. **6** Phil Lynott. **7** Phil Collins. **8** Mary Hopkin. **9** Madonna. **10** 3. **11** A fire engine. **12** Brandy. **13** Mistletoe and Wine. **14** Rock and Roll Waltz. **15** Punky's Dilemma. **13** Frankie Avalon. **17** 6th Sept 1997. **18** 26. **19** Michael Jackson. **20** Lady. **21** In All The Right Places. **22** John Lennon. **23** Donny Osmond. **24** Sonny Bono. **25** Suzy Quatro.

Quiz 86 CORONATION ST. Level 3

Early Days

1 In 1967, which two young people did Emily employ as sales assistants in the newly revamped Gamma Garments?
2 Name the female football team coached by David Barlow in this year.
3 What happened when a jealous Irma joined the team?
4 In 1967, what happened when Lucille persuaded a friend to chat Emily up?
5 In the same year, who was conned out of £72?
6 Which actor – later to become famous for another *Coronation Street* role – played I-Spy Dwyer in 1968?
7 Who entered a beauty contest and became Miss Petrol Pump 1968?
8 Who played Maggie Clegg?
9 What did Stan buy Hilda for their Silver Wedding?
10 Who temporarily left Coronation Street to become caretaker at a museum in Bury?
11 In 1969, who asked Jack Walker for £300?
12 Who lent Jack the money to fund the loan?
13 Name the fashion shop where Elsie and Dot Greenhalgh worked at this time.
14 Why were they sacked?
15 Name the actor who played Cyril Turpin
16 Who bought Alan Howard's hair salon?
17 Which teenage couple split up in June 1970?
18 Who played Dave Smith?
19 Who shared the Corner Shop flat with Bet Lynch?
20 In 1970, who called Elsie Tanner 'A sparrow in a dirty street'?
21 Who fell for Annie Walker and took her on a cruise?
22 In 1971, who walked out on his wife on New Year's Eve?
23 Which couple got engaged in 1970?
24 Who put an industrial sized serving hatch in their house?
25 Who played Ernie Bishop?

Answers

Early Days
1 Dennis Tanner and Lucille Hewitt. **2** Weatherfield Hotspurs. **3** She strained a ligament. **4** He fell in love with her. **5** Minnie Caldwell. **6** Roy Barraclough. **7** Audrey Bright. **8** Irene Sutcliffe. **9** Fun Fur. **10** Albert Tatlock. **11** Len Fairclough. **12** Elsie Tanner. **13** Miami Modes. **14** Dot was stealing dresses and framed Elsie. **15** Willliam Moore. **16** Dave Smith. **17** Dickie and Audrey Fleming. **18** Reginald Marsh. **19** Irma Ogden. **20** Len Fairclough. **21** Harold Dewhurst. **22** Alan Howard. **23** Ernie Bishop and Emily Nugent. **24** The Ogdens. **25** Stephen Hancock.

Quiz 87 Unforgettables

Level 3

1 What would Pablo Picasso's surname have been if he had used his father's name instead of his mother's?
2 In what country was British choreographer Sir Frederick Ashton born?
3 Who made the film *Renaldo and Clara* with Bob Dylan?
4 Who said, 'The hardest thing to understand in the world is income tax'?
5 Four minute miler Dr Roger Bannister has published papers on what?
6 Which orchestral conductor was married to one of the subjects of the film *Hilary and Jackie*?
7 Groucho Marx resigned from where as he didn't care to belong to any club that would have him as a member?
8 Which of the Barrymores wrote the memoir *We Barrymores*?
9 Which British composer wrote the theme music for the film *Murder on the Orient Express*?
10 Who said, 'Middle age is when your age starts to show around your middle'?
11 What was Humphrey Bogart's middle name?
12 Which director's autobiography was called *The Name Above the Title*?
13 About whom did Kenneth Tynan say, 'What one sees in other women drunk, one sees in... sober'?
14 Who designed the WRAC uniform?
15 The expression Great White Hope was used to describe which black boxer's opponents?
16 Where did Anne Frank die?
17 Who created Bugs Bunny?
18 What was Buster Keaton's real first name?
19 Whose famous teacher was Anne Sullivan?
20 In which craft did Bernard Leach find fame?
21 Where was blues singer Leadbelly when he was 'discovered' musically?
22 In which film did Harold Lloyd hang from a clockface?
23 Which Marx brother was not in *Duck Soup*?
24 How many England caps did Stanley Matthews win in 22 years?
25 Which political party did Emmeline Pankhurst join in 1926?

Answers

Unforgettables

1 Ruiz. **2** Ecuador. **3** Joan Baez. **4** Albert Einstein. **5** Neurology. **6** Daniel Barenboim. **7** Friars Club. **8** Lionel. **9** Richard Rodney Bennett. **10** Bob Hope. **11** De Forrest. **12** Frank Capra. **13** Greta Garbo. **14** Norman Hartnell. **15** Jack Johnson. **16** Belsen. **17** Chuck Jones. **18** Joseph. **19** Helen Keller. **20** Pottery. **21** Prison. **22** Safety Last. **23** Gummo. **24** 54. **25** Conservative.

Quiz 88 CORONATION ST. Level 3

Early Days

1. What was Stan Ogden falsely accused of in 1972?
2. Who proposed marriage to Rita but was dumped for Len Fairclough?
3. Which on-screen couple also married in real life in 1972?
4. In 1972, which character's wife died of cancer?
5. Who played Norma Ford?
6. Name the manager who the brewery installed when Annie decided to retire.
7. In the Rovers Drag Show in 1973, who played Ken Dodd?
8. Who dressed up as Danny La Rue?
9. Who performed a Laurel and Hardy routine?
10. Who won the men versus women bowls match?
11. In 1974, who was wrongly accused of fathering Alison Wright's baby?
12. Who left Coronation Street to live in St Annes?
13. Who got a job as a warehouse manager?
14. Which blonde made her *Coronation Street* debut in 1974 as shop steward for the warehouse?
15. Who played ferocious Granny Hopkins?
16. Who did local businessman Harold Digby send a see-through nightie to in 1975?
17. Why did Mavis refuse to marry Carlos in this year?
18. Who was Frank Bradley's rival for Bet at this time?
19. Who rented the shop flat this year?
20. Who had an operation to remove shrapnel from his body?
21. In 1976, who was locked in chains in a sack by his pal Wally Fisher?
22. Who bought a greyhound called Fred's Folly?
23. Whose brother had a crush on Gail in 1976?
24. What was the name of Derek Wilton's mother?
25. Who played Renee Bradshaw?

Answers

Early Days

1 Being a peeping Tom. **2** Benny Lewis. **3** Alan Browning and Pat Phoenix. **4** Alf Robert's wife Phyllis. **5** Diana Davis. **6** Glyn Thomas. **7** Norma Ford. **8** Rita. **9** Bet and Betty. **10** The men. **11** Ray Langton. **12** Ena Sharples. **13** Ken Barlow. **14** Vera Duckworth. **15** Jesse Evans. **16** Rita. **17** He only wanted a work permit. **18** Sean Regan. **19** Gail Potter and Tricia Hopkins. **20** Albert Tatlock. **21** Stan Ogden. **22** Fred Gee. **23** Renee's brother, Terry. **24** Amy. **25** Madge Hindle.

Quiz 89 Famous Firsts

Level 3

1 Who was the first person to make a solo trek to the South Pole on foot?
2 In what year was the first external heart pacemaker fitted?
3 Who was the first woman to sail around the world?
4 SRN1 was the first what?
5 The first Miss World came from which country?
6 What did Carlton Magee devise in the US for motorists?
7 What was first revealed at Lord's in 1975?
8 What was the name of the first long lasting perfume, launched in Japan in 1993?
9 Which two national teams made the first flight over Everest in a hot air balloon?
10 In which country was the first kidney transplant carried out?
11 What was Lester Piggott's first Derby winner back in 1954?
12 Which British bank was the first to issue cash dispenser cards?
13 Which orchestra was the first in London to be conducted by a woman?
14 Which support group was founded in Ohio in 1935?
15 Who founded the Cubism movement with Picasso?
16 Joseph Mornier patented which building material?
17 Who was the first black American to win the Nobel Peace Prize?
18 In what year did Plaid Cymru win its first seat in the House of Commons?
19 Jacqui Mofokeng was the first black woman to win what?
20 At what mph did Malcolm Campbell set the land speed record in 1931?
21 In which category did Marie Curie win her second Nobel Prize, becoming the first person to win a Nobel Prize twice?
22 Where was the first nuclear reactor built, by Enrico Fermi?
23 Who led the team that made the first successful overland crossing of Antarctica?
24 Who was the first Governor General of Pakistan?
25 After record breaking flights to Australia and Cape Town, where was Amy Johnson's plane lost?

Answers

Famous Firsts

1 Erling Kagge. **2** 1952. **3** Naomi James. **4** Cross channel Hovercraft. **5** Sweden. **6** Parking meter. **7** A streaker. **8** Shiseido. **9** Australia/UK. **10** USA. **11** Never Say Die. **12** Barclays. **13** Royal Philharmonic. **14** Alcoholics Anonymous. **15** Braque. **16** Reinforced concrete. **17** Ralph Bunche. **18** 1966. **19** Miss South Africa. **20** 246. **21** Chemistry. **22** Chicago. **23** Fuchs. **24** Jinnah. **25** Thames Estuary.

Quiz 90 Pot Luck

Level 3

1 What colour was Sally's wedding outfit when she married Kevin?
2 What department did Elsie Tanner and Dot Greenhalgh work in at Miami Modes?
3 Which prison did Dennis Tanner serve time in?
4 Which *Coronation Street* actor also appeared in the film *International Velvet*?
5 John G Temple once produced Coronation Street – name the Scottish soap he also produced.
6 Which two men did Deirdre Langton have to choose between in 1979?
7 Who came third in the Confectionery Salesman of the Year contest?
8 And who helped him out by ordering 2 gross of chocolate bunnies?
9 Who conned the Ogdens into turning over their allotment?
10 Why was *Coronation Street* taken off air from August to October 1979?
11 Who said, 'I've always wanted to be stormy, passionate and tempestuous. But you can't be. Not when you're born with a tidy mind'?
12 Who said, 'Natalie Barnes is that hard faced, if she fell on the pavement she'd crack a flag'?
13 Who said, 'Steve (McDonald) wasn't even innocent in the womb'?
14 Who said, 'There's some very peculiar people in this Street'?
15 Who said, 'They once named a trifle after me at one Labour Club I played'?
16 In 1977, who did Ken Barlow dress up as?
17 And who went as Brittania?
18 Who tried to introduce a 3-day week, to the disgust of his workforce?
19 Who bought number 5 this year?
20 Who did Annie Walker falsely accuse of theft?
21 In 1978, who tried to clean Elsie's chimney with a brick?
22 Where did Ray Langton move to?
23 Who moved onto the street after 18 years as a non-resident regular?
24 Who was Annie Walker's lodger?
25 Which country did Billy Walker live in?

Answers

Pot Luck

1 Peach. **2** The Slightly Better Dress Department. **3**. Pentonville. **4** Chris Quinten. **5** Take The High Road. **6** Billy Walker and Ken Barlow. **7** Derek Wilton. **8** Mavis Riley. **9** Albert Tatlock. **10** There was a strike at ITV. **11** Emily Bishop. **12** Vera Duckworth. **13** Andy McDonald. **14** Ena Sharples. **15** Rita Littlewood. **16** Sir Edmund Hillary. **17** Bet Lynch. **18** Mike Baldwin. **19** The Langtons. **20** Betty Turpin. **21** Suzie Birchall. **22** Holland. **23** Alf Roberts. **24** Fred Gee. **25** Jersey.

Quiz 91 Horse Racing

Level 3

1 Which horse gave Lester Piggott his 30th victory in an English Classic?
2 On the flat, what is the most number of winners achieved by a jockey in a season in the 20th century?
3 Which horse finished first in the abandoned 1993 Grand National?
4 The Coronation Cup celebrates which coronation?
5 In the 1989 Oaks, which 'winning' horse was later disqualified after a post-race test?
6 Who rode Red Rum for the third Grand National triumph?
7 Who was the first National Hunt jockey to employ an agent?
8 How many winners did Frankie Dettori ride in his 1994 super season?
9 Which of the English Classics has Lester Piggott won least times?
10 At the beginning of the century, what did Sceptre achieve in 1902?
11 Which horse gave Richard Dunwoody his first Grand National success?
12 What's the only Derby winner of the century to have a date as its name?
13 In which year did the Grand National witness Devon Loch's sensational fall 50 yards from home?
14 Which was the first English Classic to be raced in Scotland?
15 Which horse was the first on which Lester Piggott won two Classics?
16 Who sponsored the 1000 Guineas from 1984 to 1992?
17 What was the last Grand National winner ridden by an amateur before Mr Fisk?
18 Who trained the prolific winner Brigadier Gerard?
19 What was the name of the horse on which Geoff Lewis won his only Derby?
20 To the nearest 1,000, how many rides did the legendary Willie Shoemaker have?
21 Which horse gave Mick Kinane his first 2000 Guineas success?
22 Who was the youngest jockey to win the Grand National in the 20th century?
23 What did Golden Miller win five years in a row back in the 30s?
24 Who won the Oaks on Oh So Sharp and on Diminuendo?
25 How many times has Lester Piggott ridden over 200 winners in a season?

Answers

Horse Racing

1 Rodrigo de Triano. **2** 269. **3** Esha Ness. **4** Edward VII. **5** Aliyssa. **6** Tommy Stack. **7** Jonjo O'Neill. **8** 233. **9** 1000 Guineas. **10** Won four Classics. **11** West Tip. **12** April the Fifth. **13** 1956. **14** St Leger - in 1989. **15** Crepello. **16** General Accident. **17** Grittar. **18** John Hislop. **19** Mill Reef. **20** 40,000. **21** Tirol. **22** Bruce Hobbs. **23** Cheltenham Gold Cup. **24** Steve Cauthen. **25** Never.

Quiz 92 The Oscars

Level 3

1 Who was the only British actor to win the Best Actor Oscar in the 80s?
2 Whose Oscar was sold in 1994 for over half a million dollars?
3 Which film won the Best Film Oscar on the 60th anniversary of the awards?
4 For which film did Katharine Hepburn win the first of her four 20th century Oscars?
5 Robert de Niro was Oscar nominated for his portrayal of which ex-con in *Cape Fear*?
6 Who eventually played the part Kate Winslet went for in *Sense & Sensibility*?
7 For which film did Barbra Streisand win her second Oscar?
8 Who was the first actress to win an Oscar for playing the role of an Oscar nominee?
9 Who was the first woman to receive an Oscar for acting and scripting?
10 Who was the oldest winner of the Best Actress Oscar in the 20th century?
11 Which 1994 film won the Oscar for best costume design?
12 Who failed to win an Oscar after six nominations but received an honorary award in 1993?
13 How many times was Richard Burton nominated for an Oscar, though he never won?
14 For which 1990 film did Bruce Joel Rubin win Best Screenplay Oscar?
15 In 1982 who won a special award for 50 years of film making?
16 What was the first film to have its whole cast Oscar-nominated?
17 In 1990 which short cartoon won Nick Park an Oscar?
18 Which movie won Best Film the year Charles and Diana were married?
19 Who was Oscar-nominated in the same year as her daughter?
20 What was Best Picture the year of the Los Angeles Olympics?
21 Who was the first British actor in the 90s to win the Best Actor Oscar?
22 In 1986 which film had 11 nominations and won nothing?
23 Who were the first father and son to win acting Oscars for the same film?
24 In 1990 who won an achievement Oscar with Myrna Loy?
25 For which film did Callie Khouri win an Oscar in 1991 for screenplay?

Answers

The Oscars

1 Ben Kingsley. **2** Vivienne Leigh. **3** Rain Man. **4** Morning Glory. **5** Max Cady. **6** Imogen Stubbs. **7** A Star is Born - the song. **8** Maggie Smith. **9** Emma Thompson. **10** Jessica Tandy. **11** The Adventures of Priscilla Queen of the Desert. **12** Deborah Kerr. **13** Seven. **14** Ghost. **15** Mickey Rooney. **16** Who's Afraid of Virginia Woolf?. **17** Creature Comforts. **18** Chariots of Fire. **19** Diane Ladd. **20** Amadeus. **21** Daniel Day Lewis. **22** The Color Purple. **23** Walter & John Huston. **24** Sophia Loren. **25** Thelma and Louise.

Quiz 93 TV Times

Level 3

1 Which celebrity couple had the number plate 8 DEB?
2 Which TV cook went to the same school as Jeffrey Archer?
3 What was William Shatner's codename for *This Is Your Life*?
4 Which TV detective wrote *A Cook For All Seasons* under his own name?
5 Which British programme won The Golden Rose of Montreux in 1995?
6 Who wrote the song which launched Channel 5?
7 Which former *Breakfast Time* presenter is a former Miss Great Britain?
8 Who was the first woman on *This is Your Life* when it transferred to ITV in 1969?
9 Who was the first BBC Sports Personality of the Year of the 1990s?
10 Which actor wrote the show *Mac and Beth*?
11 Who was described by an interviewee as 'the thinking woman's crumpet gone stale'?
12 Who hosted the BBC version of *You've Been Framed, Caught In the Act*?
13 Which 80s medical drama had the same production company as *Hill Street Blues*?
14 Which West End show starring ex-EastEnder Anita Dobson closed after just three weeks in 1993?
15 Which TV writer was born Romana Barrack?
16 Eileen Downey shot to fame in a docu soap about what?
17 Whose song provided the music for In *The Seven Faces of Woman*?
18 What is the name of the cafe owned by Hayley's husband in *Coronation Street*?
19 How much was Seinfeld offered for each episode of his comedy show when he announced in 1998 he wanted to quit?
20 What was Michael Barrymore's occupation before becoming a TV star?
21 Who was the third soccer player to win BBC Sports Personality of the year?
22 Which Gilbert & Sullivan opera was playing on Derek Wilton's car radio as he suffered his fatal heart attack in *Coronation Street*?
23 Which character opened the first ever episode of *Crossroads* ?
24 What was Tosh Lines' real first name in *The Bill*?
25 Wilma's vacuum cleaner in *The Flintstones* was what animal?

Answers

TV Times

1 Paul Daniels & Debbie McGee. **2** Keith Floyd. **3** Beam. **4** George Baker. **5** Don't Forget Your Toothbrush. **6** The Spice Girls. **7** Debbie Greenwood. **8** Twiggy. **9** Paul Gascoigne. **10** Michael Praed. **11** Melvyn Bragg. **12** Shane Richie. **13** St Elsewhere. **14** Eurovision. **15** Carla Lane. **16** Hotel. **17** Charles Aznavour. **18** Roy's Rolls. **19** $5 million. **20** Hairdresser. **21** Michael Owen. **22** The Mikado. **23** Jill. **24** Alfred. **25** Elephant.

Quiz 94 Invention and Technology Level 3

1 What was the name of the first home computer to be manufactured?
2 What was France's on-line telecom service called?
3 Who developed the Gaia Theory?
4 How was Trevor Baylis's revolutionary radio powered?
5 Alan Roberts' special super glue was used to join what?
6 What does O stand for in the equipment NOSE, which imitates the human nose?
7 What was the occupation of Bruce Rushin, who designed the £2 coin to symbolise the progress of technology in British history?
8 Sir Jagadis Chandra Bose's invention, the crescograph, measures what?
9 Which play by Capek introduced the word robot?
10 What type of camera did Edwin Land develop?
11 Edward Salk developed a vaccine against what?
12 Which hospital performed the first heart surgery on a baby in its mother's womb?
13 Adolf Loos was a designer of what?
14 In which islands is Bikini Atoll where the first atomic bombs were tested?
15 Who was the first Nobel Prize winner to come from Pakistan?
16 What was the first shopping mall on the Internet called?
17 Leslie Rogge was the first person to be arrested due to what?
18 Who led the team which invented transistors in the 1940s?
19 What was the codename of the first atomic bomb dropped on Hiroshima?
20 In 1908 Wilbur Wright travelled what record breaking number of miles in 2 hours 20 minutes?
21 William Henry Hoover started making vacuum cleaners because his original trade was dying out; what was it?
22 Which company manufactured the first electric razor?
23 How long did Bleriot's first cross-channel flight last?
24 What nationality of plane first broke the 100mph sound barrier?
25 The first air collision took place over which country?

Answers

Invention and Technology

1 Altair. **2** Minitel. **3** Sanford. **4** Clockwork. **5** Wounds. **6** Olfactory. **7** Art teacher. **8** Plant movements. **9** R.U.R.. **10** Polaroid. **11** Polio. **12** Guy's. **13** Buildings. **14** Marshall Islands. **15** Abdus Salam. **16** The Branch Mall. **17** The Internet. **18** Shockley. **19** Little Boy. **20** 77. **21** Harness maker. **22** Schick. **23** 43 minutes. **24** French. **25** Austria.

Quiz 95 20th C Leaders

Level 3

1 Paddy Ashdown is fluent in which oriental language?
2 How is Tenzin Gyatso better known?
3 Roy Jenkins became Lord Jenkins of where?
4 Which politician was a judge for the Booker Prize in 1988?
5 Neil Kinnock became MP for which constituency when he entered Parliament in 1970?
6 Who was the first leader of the Belgian Congo?
7 Who replaced Geoffrey Howe as Foreign Secretary in Thatcher's government?
8 Who was Greece's first socialist Prime Minister?
9 Canadian leader Lester Pearson won the Nobel Peace Prize for his mediation role in which conflict?
10 Who was Pope during WWII?
11 Which former Tory Party Chairman wrote *I Have No Gun But I Can Spit*?
12 What was Ronald Reagan's last film?
13 Who formulated his Sinatra Doctrine – foreign policy to be constructed on a My Way basis?
14 Vaclav Havel and George VI both lost what part of their bodies?
15 Which former leader wrote the novel *The Cardinal's Hat*?
16 Which 'stalking horse' stood for the Tory leadership against Margaret Thatcher in 1989?
17 Where was Nelson Mandela's first foreign trip to after his release from prison?
18 Who did Jonathan Sacks replace as Chief Rabbi in 1990?
19 In 1990 Transport Minister Cecil Parkinson called for a new inquiry into the sinking of what ship?
20 Which leader has played in goal for Polish soccer side Wotsyla?
21 Who became first President of Israel?
22 In 1990 who faced banners saying Goodbye Pineapple Face?
23 Who took over as President of Romania after Ceaucescu was executed?
24 Who did Lord McNally describe as the Kevin Keegan of politics?
25 Who did Thatcher describe as 'a man we can do business with'?

Answers

20th C Leaders

1 Mandarin. **2** The Dalai Lama. **3** Hillhead. **4** Michael Foot. **5** Bedwelty. **6** Lumumba. **7** John Major. **8** Papandreou. **9** Suez. **10** Pius XII. **11** Kenneth Baker. **12** The Killers. **13** Eduard Shevardnadze . **14** Lung. **15** Mussolini. **16** Sir Anthony Meyer. **17** Zambia. **18** Lord Jakobovits. **19** Titanic. **20** The Pope. **21** Chaim Weizmann. **22** Manuel Noriega. **23** Ion Iliescu. **24** Paddy Ashdown. **25** Gorbachev.

Quiz 96 Space - The Final Frontier Level 3

1 What was the name of the first chimpanzee the Americans sent in space?
2 How long did the record-breaking space walk from space shuttle *Endeavour* last in 1993?
3 Where did the European space probe *Ulysses* set off for in 1991?
4 What did Neil Armstrong say immediately before 'the eagle has landed'?
5 Which space first was achieved by Toyohiro Akiyama in 1991?
6 On what date in 1997 did *Pathfinder* land on Mars right on schedule?
7 Who was the next American in space after Shephard?
8 In which year were all three astronauts on the first moon landing expedition born?
9 Which probe sent back the first major pictures of Jupiter in 1995?
10 Who made the first untethered space walk of the 1990s?
11 On which ship did President Nixon welcome the astronauts back from the Moon?
12 On which island is the Kennedy Space Centre?
13 Which scientist located Pluto?
14 In what year was Hale Bopp first seen?
15 Which astronaut said, 'Houston, we have a problem'?
16 What is Neil Armstrong's middle name?
17 What was the name of the Japanese Moon Orbiter launched in 1990?
18 Which cosmonaut returned to Earth in 1996 after spending a record-breaking 438 days in space?
19 Who was the second Soviet cosmonaut?
20 What was the nationality of the journalist who accompanied a docking mission to *Mir* in 1990?
21 What was the name of the first probe to send back pictures from Mars?
22 How long did Sergei Krikalyev spend on *Mir* in the early 90s?
23 What was the role of Rocco Petrone in the *Apollo XI* project?
24 Who was the first woman to captain a space shuttle crew?
25 How many orbits of the moon were there on the first manned orbit?

Answers

Space – The Final Frontier
1 Ham. **2** Five hours. **3** The Sun. **4** Tranquillity base here. **5** First fare-paying passenger. **6** 4th July. **7** Virgil Grissom. **8** 1930. **9** Galileo. **10** Mark Lee. **11** Hornet. **12** Merritt. **13** Clyde Tombaugh. **14** 1995. **15** James Lovell. **16** Alden. **17** Muses-A. **18** Polyakov. **19** Titov. **20** Japanese. **21** Viking. **22** Ten months. **23** Launch director. **24** Eileen Collins. **25** 10.

Quiz 97 Sports Bag

Level 3

1 At which venue did Sandy Lyle win the British Open?
2 In women's hockey, which country has won the World Cup most times?
3 In which sport did actor Noel Harrison compete in the 1952 Olympics?
4 In which year did Graham Hill win the Le Mans 24 hour race?
5 Who did Terry Griffiths beat in the final in his only snooker World Championship triumph?
6 Great Britain's Rugby League side toured where for the first time in 1984?
7 The Stoke Poges golf club was used for location shots for which film?
8 In Red Rum's first Grand National triumph, which 9 -1 favourite had led the field until the final dash?
9 In how many games did Bobby Charlton captain England?
10 Anton Geesink was the first person not from Japan to win a judo world championship, but which country did he come from?
11 Who played Harlequins in the first Rugby Union game at Twickenham?
12 How many of his 45 races did Mike Hawthorn, F1 world champion, win?
13 In which decade were the Badminton Horse Trials first held?
14 In how many of his 39 Tests was Mike Brearley not the captain?
15 Name France's last Wimbledon Men's Singles winner of this century.
16 Who did Spurs meet in the first all-British European final?
17 In which soap did Fred Trueman appear as himself?
18 Which was the last horse before Nijinsky to win the triple of Derby, 2000 Guineas and St Leger?
19 In which UK event did Tony Jacklin make the first live TV hole in one?
20 When Wimbledon became Open in 1968, what was the men's singles prize money?
21 Britain's William Lane became a world champion in which sport?
22 In which events did Gert Frederiksson win six Olympic Golds?
23 Who was the defending champion when Chris Evert first won Wimbledon singles?
24 Which first is held by the New Zealander E J 'Murt' O'Donoghue?
25 Which British Open winner's dad was a professional at Hawkstone Park, Shropshire?

Answers

Sports Bag

1 Sandwich. **2** Netherlands. **3** Alpine skiing. **4** 1972. **5** Dennis Taylor. **6** Papua New Guinea. **7** Goldfinger. **8** Crisp. **9** Three. **10** Holland. **11** Richmond. **12** 3. **13** 40s. **14** 8. **15** Yvon Petra. **16** Wolves. **17** Emmerdale. **18** Bahram. **19** Dunlop Masters. **20** £2,000. **21** Angling. **22** Canoeing. **23** Billie Jean King. **24** 147 snooker break. **25** Sandy Lyle.

Quiz 98 20th C Film Legends Level 3

1 What was Katharine Hepburn and Spencer Tracy's first film together?
2 Which actress said, 'I'm as pure as driven slush'?
3 In which film did James Cagney say 'You dirty double crossing rat', which led to his catchphrase?
4 In which sport did John Kelly compete in the 1920 Olympics?
5 Who said, 'All I need to make a comedy is a park, a policeman and a pretty girl'?
6 Which actor was Tony Hancock impersonating with his 'Ha harr Jim lad' routine?
7 Who was 'the man you love to hate'?
8 Which famous character was played by Butterfly McQueen in *Gone With the Wind*?
9 Why was Buddy Ebsen forced to quit his role as the Tin Man in *The Wizard of Oz*?
10 In what year did David Lean die?
11 In which country did Steve McQueen die?
12 Whose autobiography was called *The Ragman's Son*?
13 In which state did Robert Redford found the Sundance Institute?
14 How old was Shirley Temple when she received an honorary Oscar?
15 What would Rita Hayworth's surname have been if she had used her father's name instead of her mother's?
16 On which 30s screen legend was Catwoman in *Batman* based?
17 Which Marilyn Monroe co-star said, 'Kissing her is like kissing Hitler'?
18 About who or what did Elizabeth Taylor say, 'It was like an illness one had a very difficult time recuperating from'?
19 Which musical star was a cousin of Rita Hayworth?
20 For which film did Elizabeth Taylor win her second Oscar?
21 Which character did Frank Sinatra play in *From Here to Eternity*?
22 How old was Mae West when she starred in the film *Sextet*?
23 Which lingerie company did Jane Russell work for in the 1970s?
24 Who had the nickname 'The Stick' as a child?
25 Who said, 'I never forget a face, but in your case I'll make an exception'?

Answers

20th C Film Legends

1 Woman of the Year. **2** Tallulah Bankhead. **3** Blonde Crazy. **4** Rowing. **5** Charlie Chaplin. **6** Robert Newton – in Treasure Island. **7** Erich Von Stroheim. **8** Prissy. **9** He was allergic to the make up. **10** 1991. **11** Mexico. **12** Kirk Douglas. **13** Utah. **14** Six. **15** Cansino. **16** Jean Harlow. **17** Tony Curtis. **18** Making Cleopatra. **19** Ginger Rogers. **20** Who's Afraid of Virginia Woolf?. **21** Angelo Maggio. **22** 85. **23** Playtex. **24** Sophia Loren. **25** Groucho Marx.

Quiz 99 20th C TV Trivia

Level 3

1 Who was the first sportsman to appear on *This Is Your Life*?
2 What was the first feature film shown on BBC2?
3 In *Tutti Frutti*, who was bass player with The Majestics?
4 Which TV presenter once held the title Miss Parallel Bars?
5 Which newsreader was a judge for the Booker Prize in 1987?
6 Margo Turner's life was researched for *This Is Your Life* and then became the basis for which drama series?
7 Which *Coronation Street* star played Christine Keeler's mother in *Scandal*?
8 Which TV presenter produced a fitness video called *Fit For Life*?
9 In which real life store did Wendy Richard used to work?
10 What was Winston Churchill referring to when he said, 'Why do we need this peep show?'?
11 In which event did Bill Nankeville, father of Bobby Davro, compete in the 1948 Olympics?
12 What was the first *Dr Who* series called in which The Daleks appeared?
13 In *Minder* what football team did Terry McCann support?
14 Which show of the 50s used the catchphrase 'Goody goody gumdrops'?
15 Where was Brian Hanrahan when he 'counted them all out, and counted them all back'?
16 Which TV presenter wrote *The Hired Man* with Howard Goodall?
17 Which building designed by Norman Shaw in the 19th C appeared on TV screens throughout the 20th C?
18 What was Nigel Kennedy's codename for *This Is Your Life*?
19 What did Harry Enfield study at university?
20 Which music was used for the BBC's last World Cup coverage of the century?
21 Who was the only woman in the 1980s to win the BBC Sports Personality of the Year single-handed?
22 Which newsreader advertised Cow & Gate baby food as a child?
23 What was the occupation of Noel Edmonds' father?
24 Who was the first soap star to receive an honour from the Queen?
25 Who presented Channel 4's religious series *Canterbury Tales*?

Answers

20th C TV Trivia

1 Stanley Matthews. **2** Kiss Me Kate. **3** Fud O'Donnell. **4** Carol Smillie. **5** Trevor McDonald. **6** Tenko. **7** Jean Alexander. **8** Gloria Hunniford. **9** Fortnum & Mason. **10** Commercial TV. **11** 1500 metres. **12** The Dead Planet. **13** Fulham. **14** Whirligig. **15** Port Stanley. **16** Melvyn Bragg. **17** New Scotland Yard. **18** Bow. **19** Politics. **20** Faure's Pavane. **21** Fatima Whitbread. **22** Martyn Lewis. **23** Headmaster. **24** Violet Carson. **25** Ian Hislop.

Quiz 100 Entertainment

Level 3

1. Which London theatre saw the premiere of *Look Back in Anger*?
2. Which show made dancer Robert Helpmann say, 'The trouble with nude dancing is that not everything stops when the music does'?
3. According to bishop Mervyn Stockwood, who would 'go to the Folies Bergere and look at the audience'?
4. Who wrote the music for the show *Betjeman* with words by the poet himself?
5. What is the name of the theatre in Scarborough linked with Alan Ayckbourn?
6. The slogan 'The Big One' was originally used to advertise what?
7. Which brothers bought Shepperton studios in 1994?
8. Who founded the New York City ballet in 1928?
9. To which conductor did Vaughan Williams dedicate his 8th Symphony?
10. Who was known as Big Hearted Arthur?
11. What food has sexual overtones in Bertolucci's *Last Tango in Paris*?
12. Which stage play was the last to be banned by the Lord Chamberlain in the UK?
13. What did critic John Mason Brown describe as 'chewing gum for the eyes'?
14. In what year did Elstree studios open?
15. Where is the location of the Glastonbury Festival?
16. On whose life was the short lived musical *Winnie* based?
17. Which singer had the first names Harry Lillis?
18. Which studios did the Rank Organisation open in 1936?
19. How many Gilbert & Sullivan operas are there?
20. Which show made critic Clive Barnes say, 'It gives pornography a bad name'?
21. Who wrote the book on which the musical *Whistle Down the Wind* was based?
22. The first great rock charity show was in aid of the people of which country?
23. What was the name of Hylda Baker's silent friend?
24. In what year did the first Edinburgh Festival take place?
25. Which London theatre is home to the ENO?

Answers

Entertainment

1 Royal Court. **2** Oh Calcutta. **3** A psychiatrist. **4** Mike Read. **5** Stephen Joseph Theatre. **6** Circus. **7** Scott. **8** Balanchine. **9** Barbirolli. **10** Arthur Askey. **11** Butter. **12** Early Morning. **13** TV. **14** 1926. **15** Pilton. **16** Winston Churchill. **17** Bing Crosby. **18** Pinewood. **19** 13. **20** Oh Calcutta. **21** Mary Hayley Bell. **22** Bangladesh. **23** Cynthia. **24** 1947. **25** Coliseum.

ROVERS RETURN

HOW TO SET UP YOUR OWN
PUB QUIZ

It isn't easy, get that right from the start. This isn't going to be easy. Think instead of words like 'difficult', 'taxing', 'infuriating'. Consider yourself with damp palms and a dry throat and then, when you have concentrated on that, put it out of your mind and think of the recognition you will receive down the local. Imagine all the regulars lifting you high upon their shoulders, dancing and weaving their way around the pub. It won't help, but it's good to dream every once in a while.

ROVERS RETURN

What you will need:

- A good selection of Biros (never be tempted to give your own pen up, not even to family members)
- A copy of *The Rovers Return Pub Quiz Book*
- A set of answer sheets photocopied from the back of the book
- A good speaking voice and possibly a microphone and an amp
- A pub
- A table
- At least one pint inside you
- At least one more on your table

What to do:

Choose your local to start with. Not all Pubs are as friendly as the Rovers Return and you don't want to get halfway through your first quiz and decide you weren't cut out for all this and then find yourself in the roughest pub in Christendom, 30 miles and a long run from home.

Chat it through with the landlord and agree on whether you will be charging or not. If you don't then there is little chance of a prize for the winners other than a free pint each, and this is obviously at the landlord's discretion – if you pack his pub to bursting then five free pints won't worry him, but if it's only you and two others then he may be less than willing, as publicans tend to be.

If you decide on a payment entry, keep it reasonable; you don't want to take the fun out of the quiz. Some people will be well aware that they have very little hope of winning and will be reluctant to celebrate the fact by mortgaging their house.

Once location and prize are all sorted, then advertising the event is paramount. Get people's attention, sell, sell, sell, or, alternatively, stick up a gaudy looking poster on the door of the bogs. Be sure to specify all the details – time, prize and so on. Remember you are selling to people whose tiny attention span is being whittled down to nothing by alcohol.

After this it is time for the big night. If you are holding the event in a 'snug' which seats ten or so you can rely on your voice; if not you should get hold of a good microphone and an amplifier so that you can boom out your questions and enunciate the length and breadth of the pub (once again, clear this with the landlord and don't let liquid anywhere near the electrical equipment). Make sure to practise, and get comfortable with the sound of your own voice and relax as much as possible. Try not to rely on alcohol too much or "round one" will be followed by "rown' too" which will eventually give way to "runfree". Relax with your voice so that you can handle any queries from the teams, and any venomous abuse from the 'lively' bar area.

When you enter the pub make sure you take everything listed above. Also, make sure you have a set of tie-break questions and that you instruct everybody who is taking part of the rules – and be firm. It will only upset people if you start handing out impromptu solutions and, let's face it, the wisdom of Solomon is not needed when you are talking pub quiz rules; 'no cheating' is a perfectly healthy stance to start with.

Finally, keep the teams to a maximum of five members. Hand out your answer papers and pens and, when everybody is good and settled, start the quiz. It might not be easy and it might not propel you to international stardom or pay for a life of luxury, but you will enjoy yourself. No, really.

ANSWERS Part One

1 ______________________

2 ______________________

3 ______________________

4 ______________________

5 ______________________

6 ______________________

7 ______________________

8 ______________________

9 ______________________

10 ______________________

11 ______________________

12 ______________________

13 ______________________

14 ______________________

15 ______________________

16 ______________________

17 ______________________

18 ______________________

19 ______________________

20 ______________________

21 ______________________

22 ______________________

23 ______________________

24 ______________________

25 ______________________

ROVERS RETURN

ANSWERS Part One

1 ______________________

2 ______________________

3 ______________________

4 ______________________

5 ______________________

6 ______________________

7 ______________________

8 ______________________

9 ______________________

10 ______________________

11 ______________________

12 ______________________

13 ______________________

14 ______________________

15 ______________________

16 ______________________

17 ______________________

18 ______________________

19 ______________________

20 ______________________

21 ______________________

22 ______________________

23 ______________________

24 ______________________

25 ______________________

ROVERS RETURN

ANSWERS Part One

1 __________

2 __________

3 __________

4 __________

5 __________

6 __________

7 __________

8 __________

9 __________

10 __________

11 __________

12 __________

13 __________

14 __________

15 __________

16 __________

17 __________

18 __________

19 __________

20 __________

21 __________

22 __________

23 __________

24 __________

25 __________

ROVERS RETURN